Buddhist Masculinities

BUDDHIST MASCULINITIES

EDITED BY MEGAN BRYSON
AND KEVIN BUCKELEW

COLUMBIA UNIVERSITY PRESS *NEW YORK*

Columbia University Press
Publishers Since 1893
New York Chichester, West Sussex
cup.columbia.edu

Library of Congress Cataloging-in-Publication Data
Names: Bryson, Megan, editor. | Buckelew, Kevin, editor.
Title: Buddhist masculinities / edited by Megan Bryson and Kevin Buckelew.
Description: New York : Columbia University Press, 2023. | Includes bibliographical references and index.
Identifiers: LCCN 2022054036 (print) | LCCN 2022054037 (ebook) | ISBN 9780231210461 (hardback) | ISBN 9780231210478 (trade paperback) | ISBN 9780231558433 (ebook)
Subjects: LCSH: Masculinity—Religious aspects—Buddhism.
Classification: LCC BQ4570.M365 B83 2023 (print) | LCC BQ4570.M365 (ebook) | DDC 294.3/422—dc23/eng/20230130
LC record available at https://lccn.loc.gov/2022054036
LC ebook record available at https://lccn.loc.gov/2022054037

Buddhist vestment (Kesa), made from a Noh costume (Karaori), with autumn grasses and butterflies, Japan, 18th–19th century. Public domain, Metropolitan Museum of Art.

We dedicate this volume to Miriam Levering, whose work on the "great man" of Chan Buddhism inspired this project.

Contents

Acknowledgments xi

Abbreviations xiii

Introduction: Masculinities Beyond the Buddha 1
Megan Bryson

PART ONE: Masculine Models

ONE Middle Way Masculinity: The Bodhisattva Siddhārtha as a Renunciant in Early Buddhist Texts and Art 21
Dessislava Vendova

TWO How Chan Masters Became "Great Men": Masculinity in Chinese Chan Buddhism 51
Kevin Buckelew

THREE Men of Virtue: Reexamining the Bodhisattva King in Sri Lanka 78
Stephen C. Berkwitz

PART TWO: Mighty Masters

FOUR The Siddha Who Tamed Tibet: Padmasambhava's Tantric Masculinity 103
Joshua Brallier Shelton

FIVE Building a Nation on the Dharma Battlefield: Lay Zen Masculinities in Modern Japan 129
Rebecca Mendelson

SIX Macho Buddhism (Redux): Gender and Sexualities in the Diamond Way 154
Bee Scherer

PART THREE: Making Men

SEVEN Being a Man vs. Being a Monk: Alternative Versions of Burmese Buddhist Masculinity 183
Ward Keeler

EIGHT Hanuman, Heroes, and Buddhist Masculinity in Contemporary Thailand 206
Natawan Wongchalard

NINE Buddhism and Afro-Asian Masculinities in *The Man with the Iron Fists* 233
Marcus Evans

PART FOUR: Breaking Boundaries

TEN The Afterlife of the Tang Monk: Buddhist Masculinity and the Image of Xuanzang in East Asia 259
Geng Song

ELEVEN Real Monks Don't Have *Gṛhastha* Sex:
Revisiting Male Celibacy in Classical South Asian Buddhism 288
Amy Paris Langenberg

Appendix: Character Glossary 313

Contributors 319

Index 321

Acknowledgments

The editors would like to thank everyone who has been a part of this project, especially all of the contributors who worked through the uncertainty of the COVID-19 pandemic. We greatly appreciate the patience of those who have been with the project since its inception, and the alacrity of those who joined later. Special thanks go to Miriam Levering and Bernard Faure for their pioneering work on gender in East Asian Buddhism, which inspired us both in our scholarly pursuits; and to Gina Cogan for spearheading the 2013 panel on Buddhist Masculinities at the annual meeting of the American Academy of Religion, which inspired this volume years later. We are also grateful to the following individuals who have supported us and this project in various ways throughout the process: Dan Magilow; Michelle Yu; Tina Shepardson; Sarah Jacoby; the University of Tennessee Humanities Center's Faculty Research Seminar on Gender and Sexuality in Historical Perspective, organized by Helene Sinnreich and Margaret Anderson; and Lowell Frye at Columbia University Press, whose guidance has been invaluable.

Abbreviations

Languages

Ch.	Chinese (Mandarin)
J.	Japanese
K.	Korean
P.	Pāli
Si.	Sinhala
Sk.	Sanskrit
T.	Tibetan (Wylie transliteration)
Th.	Thai

Collections

T.	*Taishō shinshū daizōkyō* 大正新脩大蔵経, 85 vols. (Tokyo: Taishō issaikyō kankōkai, 1924–1932)
X.	*Xuzangjing* 續藏經, 150 vols. (Taipei: Xinwenfeng, 1968)

Buddhist Masculinities

Introduction

Masculinities Beyond the Buddha

MEGAN BRYSON

WOMEN FOUND THE Buddha irresistible: they lusted after his perfect body and concocted all kinds of schemes to get close to him. In the palace, "some of the young women pretended to be intoxicated and touched [Prince Siddhārtha] with their firm, rounded, close-set, alluring breasts. One made a false stumble and clasped him strongly with her tender arm-creepers, which hung down loosely from her drooping shoulders."[1] While the Buddha's physical beauty drew admirers, his appeal went beyond conventional good looks. Buddhas' bodies differ from those of ordinary people: they display the thirty-two marks of a "great man" (Sk. *mahāpuruṣa*), which include a long, broad tongue; a tuft of hair between the eyebrows; webbed hands and feet; and a sheathed penis, like that of a horse or elephant, which defines Buddha bodies as both masculine and exceptional.[2] Buddhist monarchs (Sk. *cakravartins*, or "wheel-turners") also sport these thirty-two marks, offering a masculine counterpart to buddhas. According to his hagiography, the Buddha's fate was to become either a great religious leader or a great ruler, and these twin possibilities hint at the contours of hegemonic Buddhist masculinities.[3] It is, in fact, the Buddha's simultaneous embodiment of religious and political perfection that makes him such a superman.

Understandably, the Buddha's masculine example holds considerable sway in the religion he founded. However, as people continuously inscribed, portrayed, and enacted his teachings, they developed other models and concepts of Buddhist masculinity. This volume explores the variety of masculinities in Buddhism across place and time, from early India to medieval China to modern Europe, considering rulership in Sri Lanka and Tibet, machismo in Japan and Europe, and laymen in Burma and Thailand. The Buddha still looms large as the Buddhist man par excellence, but he is joined by other masculine figures and ideals that make up the Buddhist world, such as Tibet's demon-tamer Padmasambhava, the bodhisattva-kings of medieval Sri Lanka, and macho Zen practitioners in twentieth-century Japan.

Exploring Buddhist masculinities over a wide historical and geographical range reveals the diversities in Buddhist conceptions of masculinity as well as highlights recurring concerns: How should Buddhist rulers behave as paragons of lay masculinity? How should monks deal with their own and others' sexual desires? How should people adapt Buddhist norms for masculinity to new regions, which have their own norms? How should Buddhists respond to gendered behaviors that diverge from perceived canonical or cultural norms for men? Each of these questions centers on norms for men's behavior, even if those norms differ according to context. As such, this volume as a whole considers how Buddhists in different times and places have engaged with hegemonic masculinities.

Adopting Antonio Gramsci's notion of hegemony, Raewyn Connell defines hegemonic masculinity as "the configuration of gender practice which embodies the currently accepted answer to the problem of the legitimacy of patriarchy, which guarantees (or is taken to guarantee) the dominant position of men and the subordination of women."[4] As a configuration of gender practice, hegemonic masculinity does not just mean one kind of ideal man or male role: in the United States in the twenty-first-century, professional athletes may embody hegemonic masculinity, and so can CEOs, manual laborers, and certain actors, together forming a matrix of masculinity that undergirds the patriarchy's legitimacy. As a key part of patriarchal power, hegemonic masculinity not only perpetuates men's domination of women, nonbinary, and third gender people but also subordinates other masculinities, and the people who embody those subordinated masculinities.

Specific forms of hegemonic and subordinated masculinities are historical. As Tim Carrigan, Raewyn Connell, and John Lee explain, " 'Hegemony,' then, always refers to a historical situation, a set of circumstances in which power is won and held. The construction of hegemony is not a matter of pushing and pulling between ready-formed groupings, but is partly a matter of the *formation* of those groupings. To understand the different kinds of masculinity demands, above all, an examination of the practices in which hegemony is constituted and contested—in short, the political techniques of the patriarchal social order."[5] In the Buddhist contexts under consideration here, we encounter both hegemonic masculinity in the figures of virile bodhisattvas, Buddhist rulers, and macho monks, as well as subordinated masculinities in the form of figures like the effeminate monk Xuanzang (a.k.a. Trepiṭaka) from the East Asian epic *Journey to the West* (Ch. *Xiyou ji*; J. *Saiyūki*).

Hegemonic masculinity necessarily encompasses contradictory conceptions of what it means to be an ideal man, similar to the virgin-whore dichotomy for women in the modern West. For example, an ideal man might show self-control in abstaining from sexual activity, or he might show virility (and possibly control over others) in having many sexual partners. These apparent contradictions in what it means to be a "real man" also manifest in Buddhist discourses and practices, where the Buddha stands out as encompassing the paradox of hegemonic masculinity: he is a virile ascetic, a martial meditator, and a royal monk detached from his own remarkable beauty.

Connell's term uses the singular *masculinity* to underscore the patriarchal system in which masculinity holds sway over femininity. The different Buddhist contexts under consideration here entail plural hegemonic masculinities. Despite their differences, these Buddhist contexts could generally be understood as patriarchal, but patriarchy is not only about men's domination of women; it also concerns senior generations' domination of their juniors. Moreover, the configuration of gender practices that are central to hegemonic masculinity operate together with other historically contingent categories of difference, including race or ethnicity, social class, age, and ability. Any informed study of Buddhism and gender, including Buddhist masculinities, must take into account how gender norms intersect with these other kinds of norms. For example, in the contemporary globalized world, hegemonic masculinity works together with hegemonic whiteness to legitimate and naturalize white supremacist patriarchy.[6] This means that images of Buddhist men in the modern West often traffic in Orientalist stereotypes of wise, peaceful sages or kung-fu monks, or cast Buddhist men as effeminate.[7]

Though not all of these categories of difference translate to the various regions and time periods covered in this volume, many do: although

Buddhist kingship engages hegemonic masculinity, it also connects directly with political power and socioeconomic status. Similarly, representations of the monk Xuanzang in contemporary East Asian retellings of *Journey to the West* engage concepts of queer identity and gender fluidity. Focusing on gender alone, without attending to other categories of difference, risks conflating the masculinities embodied by medieval Sri Lankan bodhisattva kings and the queer and genderfluid masculinities represented through the figure of Xuanzang in contemporary East Asia.

What Do We Mean by *Buddhist Masculinities*?

One of this volume's foundational claims is that the concept of masculinities helps us make sense of Buddhist thought, practice, and embodiment in different times and places. This does not mean, however, that we see masculinity as an ahistorical, unchanging concept, or even a concept that our sources would use to describe their own practices. As Connell notes, the concept of masculinity "presupposes a belief in individual difference and personal agency. In that sense it is built on the conception of individuality that developed in early-modern Europe with the growth of colonial empires and capitalist economic relations."[8] Like the terms *sexuality* and *gender*, *masculinity* emerges from a particular historical moment and belongs to notions of selfhood that support, and are supported by, imperialism and capitalism.[9] By the early twenty-first century, masculinity had become part of the increasingly fractured and cataloged selfhood engendered through the rise of transnational corporations and personal brands. It is in this context that we find masculinities that can be modified by categories of race, sexuality, gender identity, ability, class, and religion.

Foregrounding masculinities may in some respects naturalize and reinforce this late capitalist web of power, encompassing the imbricated realms of religion, politics, economics, and personhood. This applies equally to other concepts undergirding this project, such as Buddhism, gender, and religion. We continue to use (and translate) this vocabulary to participate in ongoing conversations about these topics and to create new conversations. For example, Jarrod Whitaker's study of Vedic masculinities connects the Sanskrit terms *śūra* and *vīrá* (among others) to the concept of masculinity, because both describe standards for men's behavior.[10] Whitaker criticizes the common translation of *vīrá* as "hero" because of the confusion with Greek heroism and contemporary hero inflation (e.g., ubiquitous superheroes), preferring "brave man" instead.[11] However, some terms defy translation because their many meanings overwhelm any single English term. For example, Indian Buddhist texts use the Sanskrit term *paṇḍaka* to indicate people with nonnormative bodies, sexual proclivities, or sexual capacities, which can include ambiguous genitalia, voyeurism, or impotence.[12] Bee Scherer has compellingly argued that the term *paṇḍaka* should remain untranslated—or, if necessary, be rendered as "gender-deficient"—because translations such as "queer" or "sexual deviant" introduce anachronism and flatten the Sanskrit term's polyvalence.[13] Such conversations can also occur around the Chinese term *da zhangfu* (great man), whose meaning was reshaped by Buddhist scriptures in Chinese translation that used it to render the Sanskrit *mahāpuruṣa*, which Kevin Buckelew examines in his chapter. By acknowledging multiple Buddhist masculinities and multiple ways of translating these masculinities, we resist the notion that Buddhists throughout history have identified only one way to be an ideal man or to embody traits associated with men or male beings.

Of course, defining masculinities as qualities associated with men risks devolving into recursion, if men are defined as men by virtue of their masculinity. Attempts to define masculinity or male identity through specific social roles or notions of biological sex will also fail due to the vast temporal and geographical range under consideration here. One virtue of our broad coverage is that there is no universal consensus on a singular kind of masculine body or identity. Our sources generally ascribe to human men or anthropomorphic masculine beings (implicitly or explicitly) a body with a penis and testicles, a relatively flat chest, and, possibly, facial hair, but Buddhist texts also describe exceptional bodies lacking any genitalia, fluid bodies capable of manifesting different kinds and combinations of primary or secondary sex characteristics, or bodies with ambiguous or otherwise nonnormative genitalia. For example, the Nara-period (710–784) Japanese nun Sari was said to lack a vagina, and this physical distinction was tied to her Buddhist prowess.[14]

Scholars such as Thomas Laqueur, Michel Foucault, and Judith Butler have shown how different historical and cultural contexts give rise to different understandings of, and categories for, norms surrounding bodies and genders.[15] For example, in South Asia the Brahmanical *Laws of Nārada*

(Sk. *Nāradasmṛti*) describes the ideal man as follows: "His vertebrae, knees, bones, shoulders, and neck should be well built. The nape of his neck should be tough, as should his torso, thighs, and skin. He should have a smooth gait and voice. His feces should sink in water, his urine should be noisy and foamy. If he has these characteristics he is virile; if not, he is [a *paṇḍaka*]."[16] Later Chinese medical thought defined male bodies as those capable of penetrating others, and female bodies as those capable of being penetrated.[17] Contemporary biomedical discourse defines sex based on chromosomes as well as primary and secondary sex characteristics, which then renders "unnatural" gender identities and sexual orientations that do not conform to these biological features.[18] These examples show that understandings of what make people male, female, both, or neither, and related understandings of how people might diverge from those norms, vary according to context. In arguing for the relevance of masculinities across a wide temporal span and geographical range, this volume does not take for granted that there is an obviously male or masculine body or identity that transcends time and place. Furthermore, in juxtaposing our sources' many sex/gender binaries (some of which mark the two ends of a spectrum rather than marking only two possibilities), this volume creates a sex/gender matrix that undermines any single binary.

The first word in *Buddhist masculinities* also requires reflection: What exactly makes these masculinities *Buddhist*? As José Cabezón and John Powers have shown, early Indian Buddhism belonged to a broader context with hegemonic masculinities that crossed religious boundaries, such that even unambiguously Buddhist figures like buddhas, bodhisattvas, and arhats show continuities with Vedic and Brahmanical masculinities.[19] Later, as monks and merchants took Buddhism to other parts of Asia, people from Thailand to Tibet to Tokyo brought the religion into conversation with existing traditions, which involved adapting to new understandings of masculinity. As Marcus Evans demonstrates in his chapter, RZA, the "Abbot" of hip-hop's Wu-Tang Clan, draws on Chan (J. Zen) Buddhism to foreground Afro-Asian brotherhood and challenge the hegemony of white American masculinities in his *The Man with the Iron Fists* films. Buddhist masculinities thus include those forms of masculinity with strong connections to Buddhism, but that might not be solely or uniquely Buddhist. We adopt a broad, flexible understanding of Buddhism that allows for the forms of masculinity under consideration here to simultaneously belong to other religions. If it were grammatically possible, this volume's title would highlight the multiplicity of Buddhisms in addition to multiple masculinities.[20]

Why Buddhist Masculinities?

It is an understatement to say that Buddhist men have already received considerable scholarly attention, but the study of Buddhist men is not the same as the study of Buddhist masculinities. The difference is that scholarship on Buddhist men rarely addresses gender as an object of analysis, allowing masculinity to go unnoticed and unmarked, which perpetuates its normative status. Only when the masculinity in question diverges from the normative does it become marked, as in male same-sex encounters or relationships, or in gender identities such as *paṇḍaka* or *chigo*.[21] This volume does address nonnormative masculinities, but focuses on normative or hegemonic masculinities. In calling attention to how Buddhists have developed various forms of masculinity in different historical and geographical contexts, our goal is to reveal how masculinities are constructed and contingent, rather than natural and inevitable.

When gender is an object of investigation in Buddhist studies, it is usually women and femininity that take center stage. Such projects do valuable work in redressing our sources' disproportionate attention to men, an imbalance that modern scholarship reproduces. However, if the phrase *Buddhism and gender* only conjures images of nuns, exceptional female rulers, laywomen, and goddesses, we reproduce the imbalance in which only femininity is marked, and masculinity (at least its hegemonic versions) gets to be normal. Studies of Buddhist women usually treat gender as a key facet of their experience, but studies of Buddhist men rarely do the same. By foregrounding hegemonic Buddhist masculinities, this volume demonstrates how scholars can recognize and analyze masculinity even—or especially—when it is unmarked in our sources, thus opening up additional possibilities for understanding Buddhism and gender. Expanding the scope of Buddhism and gender involves not only incorporating studies of men and masculinity but also allowing for feminine men, masculine women, and those who defy binary categorization. Nuns, female rulers, and goddesses like Marīcī combine masculine and feminine qualities in ways that go unnoticed if we limit our inquiries to masculine men and feminine women.

While the study of Buddhism benefits from incorporating questions of masculinity, Buddhism contributes to the study of masculinities as well. First, studying Buddhist masculinities in different places and times highlights several counterexamples to Orientalist stereotypes of Buddhist men and offers a more thorough and nuanced account of hegemonic and subordinated masculinities across the Buddhist world. Second, as Cabezón notes, Buddhists have had their own theories of gender, including masculinity, that both underscore the contextually contingent nature of contemporary gender discourse and offer a repertoire of concepts for rethinking gender in our own places and times. Finally, Buddhism's global spread allows us to better consider how religion and gender interrelate: by observing which questions persist in different forms of Buddhism, we gain a clearer view of what makes particular forms of masculinity "Buddhist," and we better understand the process of mutual transformation as people bring Buddhist teachings and practices to new regions.

By the time Connell published *Masculinities* in 1995, there were already a plethora of ways to study men and masculinity, from sociological investigations of different groups of men to psychoanalytical explorations of masculine archetypes. Many early studies focused on subordinated masculinities, but by the 1990s more scholars were turning their attention to normative masculinities. This new focus paralleled developments in studies of race and ethnicity, where whiteness began to receive more scholarly notice as well.[22] More recently, studies of both gender and race/ethnicity, along with other categories of difference, have shifted to models that treat systems of oppression as intersectional, meaning that patriarchy and racism (along with, e.g., classism, cisheterosexism, ableism) work together to form webs of inequalities that require similarly intersectional responses to disentangle and dismantle.[23]

While the field of Buddhist studies as a whole has been slower than others to treat masculinity as an object of scholarly inquiry, several notable early works have inspired and shaped this volume. One of the first scholars to address masculinity in Buddhism was Charles Keyes, an anthropologist who examined the transformation of maleness in Thai monastic ordination rituals, which, he argued, create the third category of monastic gender.[24] He proposed that even temporary ordination (the type most common in Thailand) mediated the competing masculinities of monastic detachment and worldly machismo so that neither could overwhelm the other.[25] Keyes's work stands out in the 1980s for its attention to masculinity; it was not until the 1990s that we see an increase in studies of Buddhism and gender, including a handful of works that engaged seriously with masculinity.

The foremost among these is José Cabezón's edited volume *Buddhism, Sexuality, and Gender* (1992), which made significant inroads to the study of Buddhist masculinities, and gender more broadly, by bringing together scholars working on a range of regions and time periods.[26] In addition to the chapters by Leonard Zwilling and Paul Gordon Schalow on male homosexuality in Indian and Japanese Buddhism, respectively, Cabezón's and Miriam Levering's contributions concern other aspects of Buddhist masculinities: Cabezón explores gendered symbolism in Mahāyāna Buddhism, including the description of love as paternal, while Levering shows how Chan (J. Zen) discourse labeled advanced female practitioners as masculine "great men" (Ch. *da zhangfu*). These chapters made important contributions to the study of symbolic and normative masculinity, a topic that has often been overshadowed by equally important studies of women and the feminine (as in Diana Paul's *Women in Buddhism: Images of the Feminine in Mahāyāna Tradition*), as well as studies of transgressive masculine sexuality. Another example of the latter appeared with Bernard Faure's *The Red Thread: Buddhist Approaches to Sexuality* (1998), which focuses on male monastic sexuality—especially its transgressive manifestations—in Japanese texts.[27]

The late 1990s and 2000s saw the publication of works that engaged with Buddhist masculinity (especially in South Asian contexts), even if masculinity was not their primary focus. Liz Wilson's *Charming Cadavers* (1996) explores the South Asian Buddhist practice of monks meditating on decomposing female bodies to cut off sexual desire. As Wilson demonstrated, this practice constituted subjectivity as masculine and turned female bodies into abject signs of impermanence. Gender emerges as a key theme in Susanne Mrozik's *Virtuous Bodies* (2007), which takes up South Asian constructions of bodhisattva bodies. Mrozik distinguishes between conventional and ascetic discourses about bodies: the former treats them as materializations of virtue (or lack thereof), while the latter treats them as abject. However, buddha bodies combine the virtuous with the abject and, in so doing, constitute alterior gender rather than normative masculinity.[28]

It was not until 2009, with John Powers's *Bull of a Man: Images of Masculinity, Sex, and the Body in Indian Buddhism*, that a book-length project focused largely on normative masculinity, in this case centered on the Buddha as a paradigm for later Buddhist monks. Powers takes up gendered descriptions of the Buddha and further considers how the monastic code reflects and shapes South Asian Buddhists' understandings of masculine sexuality. He, too, draws on Connell's concept of hegemonic masculinity, Foucault's notion of historically contingent discourses, and Butler's theory of performativity to explain norms for Buddhist masculine behavior, especially sexual behavior, in South Asia during the first millennium CE.[29] In 2017 Cabezón published a longer monograph, *Sexualities in Classical South Asian Buddhism*, which devotes most of its attention to masculine sexualities, as well as to concepts of sex and gender in South Asian Buddhism. Cabezón points out that South Asian Buddhists had their own theories of gender—that is, of what made people male, female, both, or neither—and that vocabularies of gender were polysemic, depending in large part on their genre.[30]

These works have many methodological differences, but they share a textual focus. To come full circle with Charles Keyes's earlier contribution, anthropologists have begun paying more attention to Buddhist masculinities. Charlene Makley's *The Violence of Liberation: Gender and Tibetan Buddhist Revival in Post-Mao China* considers how the masculine authority of Buddhist ritual masters is maṇḍalized in the concept of the Tibetan fatherland (T. *pha yul*), which exists in tension with the paternal Chinese state. Alexander Soucy's *The Buddha Side: Gender, Power, and Buddhist Practice in Vietnam* devotes a chapter to the masculine discourse of rationality and skepticism that genders state-approved Buddhism as masculine, and devotional Buddhism as feminine. Ward Keeler's *Traffic in Hierarchy: Masculinity and Its Others in Buddhist Burma* argues that the association of self-reliance with masculinity and social dependence with femininity undergirds respect for monks in Burmese society. These monographs mark an important shift in taking masculinity seriously as an object of analysis within the larger topic of gender in lived Buddhism.

Masculinities Beyond the Buddha

This volume builds on existing scholarship on Buddhist masculinities by devoting more attention to normative masculinities, covering Buddhist masculinities across a wide range of regions and time periods, and exploring Buddhist masculinities beyond the Buddha. Our chapters connect to each other thematically to reveal continuities and discontinuities in Buddhist conceptions of masculinities—for example, by putting the Indo-Tibetan demon tamer Padmasambhava next to Sinhalese bodhisattva-kings, or rules about seminal emissions in the monastic code (Sk. *vinaya*, or more specifically here, *pratimokṣa*) beside contemporary East Asian media about the effeminate monk Xuanzang. This thematic organization—rather than regional or chronological organizations—aims to generate new conversations about Buddhism and gender across temporal and geographical specializations.

We begin with male figures who embody normative masculinities and end with male figures who diverge from or violate those norms. Part 1, "Masculine Models," explores idealized masculine types in different premodern Buddhist media and contexts. Dessislava Vendova examines two kinds of visual and textual depictions of the historical buddha Siddhārtha Gautama prior to his awakening. Images of the robust "Recluse Gautama" and skeletal "Ascetic Gautama" from early South Asia reveal that the Middle Way refers not only to the spiritual path between the extremes of luxury and asceticism but also to an embodied, masculine ideal. Kevin Buckelew turns to Song-dynasty (960–1279) China to study the paradigm of the "great man" (Ch. *da zhangfu*; Sk. *mahāpuruṣa*). The Chinese great man hybridized South and East Asian understandings of ideal masculinity to create a new sense of Buddhist masculinity. The ideal masculinity of the bodhisattva-king in medieval Sri Lanka (eleventh to fifteenth centuries) is the focus of Stephen C. Berkwitz's chapter, which demonstrates how texts invoke the bodhisattva ideal to enhance Sinhalese kings' image as paragons of masculine beauty, virtue, and power.

Part 2, "Mighty Masters," continues our focus on normative masculinities, but shifts to consider masculine power, or machismo, as embodied by figures in premodern Tibet, modern Japan, and contemporary Europe. Joshua Brallier Shelton analyzes legends about the eighth-century Indo-Tibetan Buddhist master Padmasambhava, whose hagiography emphasizes his ability to humiliate kings, along with his powers to violently subjugate demons in the name of spreading Buddhism. As Shelton argues, Padmasambhava's legend defines Tibetan Buddhist masculinity in terms of the power of tantric masters rather than kingly power. Rebecca Mendelson focuses on another aspect of macho power in considering Rinzai Zen ideals for laymen in twentieth-century Japan. Mendelson shows how these ideals converged with the hegemonic martial masculinity of the "way of the warrior" (J. *bushidō*) to attract male lay practitioners to the Rinzai school. Bee Scherer rounds out this section of the book with an examination of the macho masculinity of the Danish Lama Ole Nydahl, founder and leader of the Diamond Way, a Western Tibetan Buddhist movement in the Karma Kagyu tradition. Scherer demonstrates how the heteromachismo of Nydahl and the Diamond Way both conforms to and diverges from Indian and Tibetan Buddhist sexual ethics and traditional Tibetan cultural attitudes on sexualities.

"Making Men," part 3, addresses how Buddhism plays a role—along with other cultural and religious factors—in developing understandings of what it means to be a good man. Ward Keeler's contribution considers the monastic masculine ideal in contemporary Burmese Buddhism. Drawing on years of fieldwork, Keeler argues that in Burma monastic masculinity remains hegemonic because monks embody an idealized form of masculine autonomy and detachment that is unavailable to laymen, who are enmeshed in familial and social relationships. However, Natawan Wongchalard highlights the community-oriented and selfless dimensions of Buddhist masculinity in the 2018 Tham Luang cave rescue in Thailand. Wongchalard shows how three of the heroes from the cave rescue embody a form of hegemonic Buddhist masculinity associated with Hanuman, the loyal soldier and selfless devotee of Rama in the Thai *Ramakien* (a Buddhist retelling of the Hindu *Rāmāyaṇa*). In his chapter, Marcus Evans turns to RZA's films *The Man with the Iron Fists* (2012) and *The Man with the Iron Fists 2* (2015). Evans shows how these films present Buddhism as a locus for Afro-Asian brotherhood by telling the story of how a formerly enslaved Black man, Thaddeus Smith (played by RZA), winds up in a Chan Buddhist monastery in nineteenth-century China. Chan Buddhism facilitates the main character's journey to becoming a free and empowered man.

Finally, part 4, "Breaking Boundaries," shifts away from normative masculinities to focus instead on departures from those norms. Geng Song's chapter on representations of the effeminate scripture-seeking Buddhist monk Xuanzang in contemporary East Asia addresses the figure's feminization. By examining televisual series and films in China, Japan, and South Korea, Song shows how Buddhist approaches to gender inform depictions of male effeminacy and gender fluidity in East Asian popular culture. Amy Paris Langenberg's chapter concludes this volume with an exploration of the monastic rule that expels monks for engaging in penetrative sex.

Langenberg uses literary sources to argue that early South Asian Buddhists were primarily concerned with defining monastic celibacy in opposition to the procreative, sacred sex of the Vedic householder, rather than in opposition to sexual hedonism.

These chapters address a wide range of Buddhist masculinities, but they are not (nor could they be) completely comprehensive. There remain opportunities for scholars to engage more with visual, material, and lived Buddhist masculinities. There is also ample room for the study of masculinity and women in Buddhism, whether centered on women engaging with masculine ideals or figures, women who themselves embody stereotypically masculine roles (such as ruler, ascetic, or even monastic), or women's perspectives on masculinities. We look forward to continuing the conversation.

NOTES

1. John Powers, *Bull of a Man: Images of Masculinity, Sex, and the Body in Indian Buddhism* (Cambridge, Mass.: Harvard University Press, 2009), 35–36; the translation of this passage from Aśvaghoṣa's *Deeds of the Buddha* (Sk. *Buddhacarita*) comes from E. H. Johnston, *Aśvaghoṣa's Buddhacarita, or Acts of the Buddha* (New Delhi: Oriental, 1972 [1885–1942]), 33–35.
2. Powers lists all thirty-two major and eighty minor marks of a great man (*mahāpuruṣa-lakṣaṇa*) in *Bull of a Man*, appendix 1, 235–39.
3. See, for example, the *Buddhacarita*, which reads, "The signs on the body of this illustrious one, with the brilliance of gold, the radiance of a lamp, foretell that he'll be either an Awakened Seer, or a World Conqueror on the earth among men." Aśvaghoṣa, *Life of the Buddha*, trans. Patrick Olivelle (New York: New York University Press / JJC Foundation, 2008), 13. This section of the text is only preserved in Chinese and Tibetan versions—for example, Aśvaghoṣa [Ch. Maming], *Fo suoxing zan* [Sk. *Buddhacarita*], trans. Dharmakṣema [Ch. Tan Wuchen], *T.*192.4:2a11–12. For a longer account, see *Fo benxingji jing* (*Scripture of the Buddha's Past Actions*; Sk. *Buddha-carita-saṃgrāha*), trans. Jñānagupta [Ch. Shenajueduo], *T.*190.3:692c10–18.
4. Raewyn Connell, *Masculinities* (Cambridge: Polity, 1995), 77. "Hegemonic masculinity" was first introduced in a coauthored article as "a particular variety of masculinity to which others—among them young and effeminate as well as homosexual men—are subordinated. It is particular groups of men, not men in general, who are oppressed within patriarchal sexual relations, and whose situations are related in different ways to the overall logic of the subordination of women to men." Tim Carrigan, Raewyn Connell, and John Lee, "Toward a New Sociology of Masculinity," *Theory and Society* 14, no. 5 (September 1985): 551–604, 587.

5. Carrigan, Connell, and Lee, "Toward a New Sociology of Masculinity," 594 (original emphasis).
6. See Matthew W. Hughey, "Hegemonic Whiteness: From Structure and Agency to Identity Allegiance," in *The Construction of Whiteness: An Interdisciplinary Analysis of Race Formation and the Meaning of a White Identity*, ed. Stephen Middleton, David R. Roediger, and Donald M. Shaffer (Jackson: University Press of Mississippi, 2016), 213–14.
7. Jane Naomi Iwamura, *Virtual Orientalism: Asian Religions and American Popular Culture* (New York: Oxford University Press, 2011), chapter 4; Sharon A. Suh, *Silver Screen Buddha: Buddhism in Asian and Western Film* (New York: Bloomsbury Academic, 2015), 34.
8. Connell, *Masculinities*, 68.
9. Michel Foucault, *The History of Sexuality*, vol. 1: *An Introduction*, trans. Robert Hurley (New York: Vintage, 1980), 54–55.
10. Jarrod Whitaker, *Strong Arms and Drinking Strength: Masculinity, Violence, and the Body in Ancient India* (New York: Oxford University Press, 2011), 15–17.
11. Whitaker, *Strong Arms and Drinking Strength*, 60–62.
12. Janet Gyatso, "One Plus One Makes Three: Buddhist Gender, Monasticism, and the Law of the Non-Excluded Middle," *History of Religions* 43, no. 2 (November 2003): 89–115, 94ff.
13. Bee Scherer, "Queering Buddhist Traditions," *Oxford Research Encyclopedia of Religion*, June 28, 2021, https://doi.org/10.1093/acrefore/9780199340378.013.765.
14. Bernard Faure, *The Red Thread: Buddhist Approaches to Sexuality* (Princeton, N.J.: Princeton University Press, 1998), 140.
15. Thomas Laqueur, *Making Sex: Body and Gender from the Greeks to Freud* (Cambridge, Mass.: Harvard University Press, 1992); Foucault, *History of Sexuality*; Judith Butler, *Gender Trouble: Feminism and the Subversion of Identity* (New York: Routledge, 1990).
16. Cabezón, *Sexuality in Classical South Asian Buddhism*, 306.
17. Charlotte Furth, *A Flourishing Yin: Gender in China's Medical History, 960–1665* (Berkeley: University of California Press, 1999), 55.
18. Primary sex characteristics refer to the sexual organs (penis, testicles, vagina, uterus, ovaries), while secondary sex characteristics refer to, for instance, body shape and size (including size of breasts) and distribution of hair. For a discussion of how cultural attitudes toward gender have informed modern understandings of biological (or "natural") bodies, see Laqueur, *Making Sex*, especially chapters 5–6; and Foucault, *History of Sexuality*, vol. 1.
19. Powers, *Bull of a Man*, 17–19; Cabezón, *Sexuality in Classical South Asian Buddhism*.
20. Faure, *Red Thread*, 11.
21. *Chigo* is a Japanese term for adolescent male acolytes who were seen as embodying masculine and feminine qualities (as well as both human and divine qualities), and who served as idealized sexual partners for older monks. For recent scholarship on *chigo*, see Or Porath, "The Flower of Dharma Nature: Sexual Consecration and Amalgamation in Medieval Japanese Buddhism," PhD diss., University of California, Santa Barbara, 2019; and Sachi Schmidt-Hori, *Tales of*

Idolized Boys: Male-Male Love in Medieval Japanese Buddhist Narratives (Honolulu: University of Hawai'i Press, 2021).

22. On whiteness studies, see Theodore Allen, *The Invention of the White Race* (New York: Verso, 1994).
23. While other scholars had attended to the interrelationships of various systems of oppression, including classism, racism, and sexism, Kimberlé Crenshaw pioneered intersectionality as a theoretical concept to explain the multiplicatory effect of racist and sexist systems of oppression on Black women. See Kimberlé Crenshaw, "Mapping the Margins: Intersectionality, Identity Politics, and Violence Against Women of Color," *Stanford Law Review* 43, no. 6 (July 1991): 1241–99.
24. Charles F. Keyes, "Ambiguous Gender: Male Initiation in a Northern Thai Buddhist Society," in *Gender and Religion: On the Complexity of Symbols*, ed. Caroline Walker Bynum, Stevan Harrell, and Paula Richman (Boston: Beacon, 1986), 85–86. In Thailand it is common for young men to ordain as novice monks temporarily as a kind of coming-of-age rite.
25. Keyes, "Ambiguous Gender," 88.
26. Here I focus on book-length projects; there are several articles and book chapters on Buddhist masculinities as well, but spatial limitations prevent me from including them all.
27. Other examples can be found in Peter Jackson's work from the 1980s and 1990s, which concerned male homosexuality in Thai Buddhism, but also understandings of sexuality in modern Thailand more broadly. See Peter A. Jackson and Nerida M. Cook, *Genders and Sexuality in Modern Thailand* (Chiang Mai: Silkworm, 1999).
28. See Susanne Mrozik, *Virtuous Bodies: The Physical Dimensions of Morality in Buddhist Ethics* (New York: Oxford University Press, 2007), especially 56–59 and chapters 4–5. For specific discussions of abjection and alterior gender, see Susanne Mrozik, "Materializations of Virtue: Buddhist Discourses on Bodies," in *Bodily Citations: Religion and Judith Butler*, ed. Ellen T. Armour and Susan M. St. Ville (New York: Columbia University Press, 2006), 25–26, 31.
29. Powers, *Bull of a Man*, 8–9, 19–20.
30. Cabezón, *Sexuality in Classical South Asian Buddhism*, 299, 305.

Bibliography

Allen, Theodore. *The Invention of the White Race*. New York: Verso, 1994.

Aśvaghoṣa [Ch. Maming 馬鳴]. *Fo suoxing zan* 佛所行讚 [Sk. *Buddhacarita*]. Translated by Dharmakṣema (385–433; Ch. Tan Wuchen 曇無讖). *T.* vol. 4, no. 192.

——. *Life of the Buddha*. Translated by Patrick Olivelle. New York: New York University Press / JJC Foundation, 2008.

Butler, Judith. *Gender Trouble: Feminism and the Subversion of Identity*. New York: Routledge, 1990.

Cabezón, José Ignacio. *Sexuality in Classical South Asian Buddhism*. Boston: Wisdom, 2017.

Carrigan, Tim, Raewyn Connell, and John Lee. "Toward a New Sociology of Masculinity." *Theory and Society* 14, no. 5 (September 1985): 551–604.
Connell, Raewyn. *Masculinities*. Cambridge: Polity, 1995.
Crenshaw, Kimberlé. "Mapping the Margins: Intersectionality, Identity Politics, and Violence Against Women of Color." *Stanford Law Review* 43, no. 6 (July 1991): 1241–99.
Faure, Bernard. *The Red Thread: Buddhist Approaches to Sexuality*. Princeton, N.J.: Princeton University Press, 1998.
Fo benxingji jing 佛本行集經 [Sk. *Buddha-carita-saṃgrāha*]. Translated by Jñānagupta [528–605; Ch. Shenajueduo 闍那崛多]. *T.* vol. 3, no. 190.
Foucault, Michel. *The History of Sexuality*, vol. 1: *An Introduction*. Translated by Robert Hurley. New York: Vintage, 1980.
Furth, Charlotte. *A Flourishing Yin: Gender in China's Medical History, 960-1665*. Berkeley: University of California Press, 1999.
Gyatso, Janet. "One Plus One Makes Three: Buddhist Gender, Monasticism, and the Law of the Non-Excluded Middle." *History of Religions* 43, no. 2 (November 2003): 89–115.
Hughey, Matthew W. "Hegemonic Whiteness: From Structure and Agency to Identity Allegiance." In *The Construction of Whiteness: An Interdisciplinary Analysis of Race Formation and the Meaning of a White Identity*, edited by Stephen Middleton, David R. Roediger, and Donald M. Shaffer, 212–33. Jackson: University Press of Mississippi, 2016.
Iwamura, Jane Naomi. *Virtual Orientalism: Asian Religions and American Popular Culture*. New York: Oxford University Press, 2011.
Jackson, Peter A., and Nerida M. Cook. *Genders and Sexuality in Modern Thailand*. Chiang Mai: Silkworm, 1999.
Johnston, E. H. [Edward Hamilton], ed. and trans. *Aśvaghoṣa's Buddhacarita, or Acts of the Buddha*. New Delhi: Oriental, [1885–1942] 1972.
Keyes, Charles F. "Ambiguous Gender: Male Initiation in a Northern Thai Buddhist Society." In *Gender and Religion: On the Complexity of Symbols*, edited by Caroline Walker Bynum, Stevan Harrell, and Paula Richman, 66–96. Boston: Beacon, 1986.
Laqueur, Thomas. *Making Sex: Body and Gender from the Greeks to Freud*. Cambridge, Mass.: Harvard University Press, 1992.
Makley, Charlene E. *The Violence of Liberation: Gender and Tibetan Buddhist Revival in Post-Mao China*. Berkeley: University of California Press, 2007.
Mrozik, Susanne. "Materializations of Virtue: Buddhist Discourses on Bodies." In *Bodily Citations: Religion and Judith Butler*, edited by Ellen T. Armour and Susan M. St. Ville, 15–47. New York: Columbia University Press, 2006.
——. *Virtuous Bodies: The Physical Dimensions of Morality in Buddhist Ethics*. New York: Oxford University Press, 2007.
Porath, Or. "The Flower of Dharma Nature: Sexual Consecration and Amalgamation in Medieval Japanese Buddhism." PhD diss., University of California, Santa Barbara, 2019.
Powers, John. *Bull of a Man: Images of Masculinity, Sex, and the Body in Indian Buddhism*. Cambridge, Mass.: Harvard University Press, 2009.

Scherer, Bee. “Queering Buddhist Traditions.” *Oxford Research Encyclopedia of Religion*, June 28, 2021. https://doi.org/10.1093/acrefore/9780199340378.013.765.
Schmidt-Hori, Sachi. *Tales of Idolized Boys: Male-Male Love in Medieval Japanese Buddhist Narratives*. Honolulu: University of Hawaiʻi Press, 2021.
Suh, Sharon A. *Silver Screen Buddha: Buddhism in Asian and Western Film*. New York: Bloomsbury Academic, 2015.
Whitaker, Jarrod. *Strong Arms and Drinking Strength: Masculinity, Violence, and the Body in Ancient India*. New York: Oxford University Press, 2011.

PART ONE
Masculine Models

HEGEMONIC MODELS OF masculinity rarely conform directly to people's social realities, but they still support men's domination of women and other men who stray too far from the hegemonic ideal. This section explores different models of Buddhist masculinities in premodern Asia, starting with the paradigmatic "great man," the historical Buddha, Siddhārtha Gautama (a.k.a. Śākyamuni). Dessislava Vendova demonstrates how early Buddhist visual and textual depictions of Siddhārtha's body prior to buddhahood (i.e., when he was the Bodhisattva) critique the masculine extremes of rulership and asceticism and instead champion Middle Way masculinity. Kevin Buckelew continues this focus on the great man ideal by examining how Chan Buddhists in Song-dynasty China (960–1279) merged the Indian great man (Sk. *mahāpuruṣa*) figure with Chinese ideals of martial (Ch. *wu*) and civil (Ch. *wen*) masculinity to construct the ideal Chan master as a great man (Ch. *da zhangfu*). Finally, Stephen C. Berkwitz considers literary representations of the bodhisattva-king, a paragon of masculinity in medieval Sri Lanka. As Berkwitz demonstrates, this ideal type combined the ruler, who represented the apex of lay masculinity, with the bodhisattva, who represented the apex of religious masculinity. These three masculine models—Siddhārtha himself, the Chan great man, and the Sri Lankan bodhisattva-king—are hegemonic ideals characterized by paradox. In other words, while achieving the Buddha's synthesis and transcendence of royalty and renunciation, the Chan master's martial literary posture, or the bodhisattva-king's mastery of both religious and lay manhood, lie beyond the reach of most men, it is precisely this inaccessibility that makes them masculine models.

ONE

Middle Way Masculinity

The Bodhisattva Siddhārtha as a Renunciant in Early Buddhist Texts and Art

DESSISLAVA VENDOVA

> Oh! Sweet is the fruit of acts that are pure in their intention. By karma was this body made, not by power or by accident.

BUDDHIST TEXTS DESCRIBE the Buddha as "the ultimate man" and extoll his extraordinary, manly body as the Bhagavat.[1] During his previous lives, the Bodhisattva—the historical Buddha Śākyamuni (a.k.a. Siddhārtha Gautama) prior to his awakening—practiced various perfections working toward his buddhahood. In doing so, he karmically built the body he had as Siddhārtha Gautama, endowed with the thirty-two major marks of a "great man" (P. *mahāpurisa-lakkhaṇa*; Sk. *mahāpuruṣa-lakṣaṇa*), which is by definition male.[2]

Early Buddhist tradition held that women could attain awakening as *arahants* (Sk. *arhat*), but that buddhahood could be reached only in a male body, so a woman must first be reborn as a man to achieve that state. This attitude clearly reflects the patriarchal society in which a female birth was deemed undesirable. Even aspiring to future buddhahood was possible only in a male body.[3] Furthermore, the male body necessary for achieving buddhahood had to be the epitome of masculine perfection, which aligns with the notion of hegemonic masculinity wherein male bodies are preferred to female bodies, and perfect male bodies (such as that of the Bodhisattva/Buddha) physically and spiritually dominate other less spiritually advanced male ones.[4] As explained in the introduction to this volume, the Buddha thus stands out as encompassing the paradox of hegemonic masculinity: the epitome of the heroic prince who willingly abandons all comfort and supreme rulership, but who nevertheless retains his virile masculinity as an ascetic and an indomitable meditator.

Some of the most notable marks of the Bodhisattva/Buddha's body were smooth golden skin, flat feet, auspicious wheel patterns on the soles of his feet and the palms of his hands, webbed fingers and toes, a straight torso, rounded shoulders with no indentation, a curled tuft of hair between the eyebrows (Sk. *ūrṇā*), blue eyes, a protuberance at the top of his cranium (Sk. *uṣṇīṣa*), light emanating from the body, and a sheathed penis.[5] Some of these marks, such as the golden skin, emanated light, auspicious wheel patterns, curled tuft of hair, and cranial protuberance, became distinguishing characteristics in iconographical representations of the Bodhisattva/Buddha's body.

This chapter draws on early textual and visual sources from South and East Asia to demonstrate that the Bhagavat's body was not a singular, unchanging form, but underwent many transformations prior to his attainment of buddhahood. In focusing on two forms of Gautama as a recluse and an ascetic, I show how the Buddha's paradigmatic masculinity encompasses and supersedes the masculine extremes of the ruler, who epitomizes power over others, and the ascetic, who epitomizes power over oneself. My analysis of this topic anticipates the way Ward Keeler, in his chapter in this volume, juxtaposes lay and monastic masculinities in contemporary Burma. But the Buddha is distinctive for embodying what we might call *Middle Way masculinity* between and beyond the universal ruler (Sk. *cakravartin*) and the emaciated ascetic. As the Bodhisattva, his renunciant and ascetic forms also underscore Buddhist ambivalence toward the supreme masculine body as both a sign of virtue and a karmic burden. Accounts emphasizing the impermanence and inevitable demise of the Buddha's body show the limitations of even the most perfect physical forms.

The Bodhisattva/Buddha's unique physiognomy is presented as the epitome of male bodily perfection and beauty. While buddhas and universal monarchs share these thirty-two marks, buddhas' bodies are superior.[6] Nonbuddhas gain these marks by accumulating merit—that is, through a karmalogical process. [7] Buddhas gain them through consciously acting with the selfless aspiration to attain perfect enlightenment (in their many lifetimes as bodhisattvas)—that is, through a dharmalogical process. While the bodies might look outwardly similar, they differ on a fundamental level.[8] The difference lies not in *possessing* the bodily marks, but rather in *how* they were obtained.[9] Even though Siddhārtha is born with all of the major and minor marks, he continues to perfect his body until he becomes the Buddha under the bodhi tree. Only when he obtains the perfect knowledge of supreme buddhahood does his outwardly perfect body become the body of a buddha.[10]

Negative attitudes toward the body that are commonly found in Buddhist texts are markedly different than those expressed about the body of the Bodhisattva/Buddha.[11] The emphasis on the somatic dimensions of moral behavior, pervasive in Buddhist texts, reveals the Indian Buddhist understanding that one's physical attributes and outward appearance reflect one's spiritual and moral attainment.[12] Susanne Mrozik has noted that there is "a common misperception that Indian Buddhist[s], especially 'early Buddhists,' ascribed little value to bodies because these are impermanent and without enduring essence."[13] She points out that "Buddhist ethical discourse in fact displays great interest in bodies, because bodies are closely associated with virtues" and "are portrayed as the material effects of past virtues and vices."[14] Mrozik writes:

> Buddhist traditions admit no easy or absolute separation between the physical and moral dimensions of living beings. Body and morality are inextricably linked. Thus Buddhist literature is replete with descriptions of living beings who literally stink with sin, are disfigured by vices, and, conversely, are perfumed or adorned with merit and virtues. The close relationship Buddhists posit between body and morality means that the formation of ethical persons is conceived of as a process of both physical and moral transformation, affecting the entire complex of body, feelings, and thoughts.[15]

As John Powers has pointed out, Indian Buddhist texts "posit a close linkage between a person's physical endowments, social status, and wealth and both past and present ethical behavior."[16] The body is a particularly important marker of morality, and physical beauty indicates past or present virtue.[17] "Somatic consequences of actions," Powers writes, "are construed as both testimony to one's attainments and powerful tools that are used to promote virtue in the world."[18]

Physical attributes are often associated with specific virtues or vices, and karma determines one's realm of rebirth. Virtuous beings who are reborn as humans experience physical beauty, good health, and longevity, and they lack physical deformities or mental disabilities. Thus, while bodies are a result of past virtue, they are also the material conditions for practicing virtue in the present. Certain kinds of bodies make the practice of virtues difficult, if not impossible.[19] Bad actions have negative somatic consequences that usually manifest in later rebirths, but occasionally unfortunate karma yields immediate bodily transformations. When the Bodhisattva performed extreme ascetic practices, his body's drastic change resulted from following an incorrect practice in his efforts to reach enlightenment.

The Buddha's physical "features are the material effects of many eons spent practicing diverse virtues, particularly the perfections ([Sk.] *pāramitā*)."[20] According to Powers, "Two aspects of his [the Buddha's] psychophysical persona operate in tandem: his physical endowments are the natural result of his practice of virtue, and others recognize him as outstandingly virtuous because of his external appearance."[21] Daniel Boucher calls the Buddha's bodily marks a "physiognomy of virtue," "the sine qua non of [the Buddha's] attainment, the visible signs of his spiritual transformation, and the symbols of maximal greatness for a human being."[22] Vidya Dehejia has also made this point by noting that the Buddha's well-formed body "is both a *sign* of moral perfection and a *result* of moral perfection."[23]

By casting the Buddha's body as the pinnacle of physical perfection, Buddhist tradition attaches his spiritual achievements of wisdom, compassion, and morality to a particular vision of embodied masculinity. His physique is so magnificent that those who see him are overwhelmed and transfixed and gaze at him in wonder.[24] And, while the Buddha's teachings were powerful and authoritative, it was the extraordinary qualities of his physical body that had a more immediate effect upon those in his presence.[25]

The idea that people are transformed merely by gazing upon the Buddha's body has shaped the creation and worship of Bodhisattva/Buddha images. Just as textual narratives emphasize the transformative effects of looking at the Buddha's body, so, too, do images of the Bodhisattva/Buddha aim to reproduce his physical presence in his absence. One of the most memorable and dramatic examples of the urge to glimpse the Buddha's physical body is from the *Story of Aśoka* (Sk. *Aśokāvadāna*), where Gautama's archenemy, the god Māra, adopts the perfect form of the Buddha at the monk Upagupta's request.[26] Upagupta, living one hundred years after the Buddha's death, could only see the Buddha's perfect form through Māra's magical power. So perfect was the illusion, Upagupta forgets that it is really Māra and spontaneously pays reverence to it, exclaiming:

> Ah! The splendid form of the Blessed One! What more can be said?
> For his face surpasses the red lotus
> [in beauty], his eyes the blue lotus,
> his splendor a forest of flowers
> . . .
> Oh! Sweet is the fruit of acts
> that are pure in their intention.
> By karma was this body made,
> not by power or by accident.
> By giving, patience, meditation,
> wisdom, and restraint,
> this *arhat* has purified that which was produced
> by [the acts of] body, speech, and mind,
> during innumerable *koṭis*
> of thousands of eons.
> In this way he produced this pure form
> that is pleasing to the eyes of men.[27]

Through his unlikely alliance with Māra, Upagupta sees (or visualizes) the Buddha's perfect form—including its floral beauty—and remembers the Buddha's qualities that are intrinsically connected with it. In essence, Upagupta is "recollecting the Buddha" (Sk. *buddhānusmṛti*), a practice for developing concentration by focusing on the Buddha's spiritual and bodily virtues.[28]

The Image of the Bodhisattva as a Renunciant

Visual narratives of the Buddha's previous lives and final existence were ubiquitous at early Buddhist sites such as *stūpas* and rock-cut cave temples by at least the second century BCE. However, the Buddha's anthropomorphic form is missing entirely in the earliest visual narratives of his final life as Siddhārtha. This absence has long puzzled art historians and Buddhologists and still lacks a satisfactory explanation. Given the great prominence of Śākyamuni's body within his biography (in its many versions), it is not surprising that Buddhists felt the need for visual representations of it. Finally, sometime in the early years of the first century CE, artists created the first anthropomorphic depictions of Siddhārtha Gautama.[29] The emergence of these images dramatically changed Buddhism and Buddhist ritual practice.[30] Bodily representations became part of the already well-established cult around Śākyamuni's biography, and they soon became a focal point of Buddhist devotion and worship.

While Siddhārtha was born with the full set of a great man's bodily marks, his body changed up to his enlightenment. His different appearances each have their own distinct iconographies that vary stylistically by region. Through a close reading of textual and visual depictions of the Buddha and his body, I identify four distinct bodily identities associated with pivotal episodes in the Buddha's life story: the Bodhisattva Deva in Tuṣita Heaven, the Crown Prince Siddhārtha, the Renunciant Gautama, and the Fully Enlightened Buddha.[31] These identities are distinguished both iconographically and in textual narratives of the Buddha's final life.[32]

Images of the Renunciant Gautama actually encompass two different iconographical types. The first one, which I call *Recluse Gautama*, depicts his body after his renunciation but prior to his extreme ascetic practices. This representation is of a robust, well-built figure, the epitome of male bodily perfection. If it were not for the humble robes and lack of adornments, this image would hardly align with usual notions of a world renouncer or ascetic's appearance. The second type, *Ascetic Gautama*, is an iconographic representation of the Bodhisattva's body during, and as a result of, his extreme ascetic practices. This is the gaunt and startling figure of an emaciated ascetic—the exact opposite of the hearty figure of Recluse Gautama. These two different visual representations of the Renunciant Gautama express multiple and contradictory attitudes toward the masculine body as conveyed in the Buddha's biography.

The Unequaled Manly Appearance of the Recluse Gautama

After Prince Siddhārtha leaves the palace (the Great Departure), he sheds his royal identity by drastically changing his appearance to become Gautama the Renunciant (fig. 1.1). Having removed his princely clothes, turban, and jewelry, cut off his long hair, and sent back his servant and royal steed,

FIGURE 1.1 Siddhārtha becomes a renunciant. Nagarjunakonda *stūpa* slab (detail), Limestone, third–fourth century CE. Archaeological Survey of India Nagarjunakonda Museum (A.C.C. -50).

he becomes a wandering seeker determined to resolve the suffering of existence.

Though Siddhārtha has given up all the outward characteristics of royalty, his body is still that of the robust prince. He became a renunciant "while still young, a black-haired young man endowed with the blessing of youth, in the prime of life."[33] One of the Buddha's earliest extant biographies, the poet Aśvaghoṣa's *Deeds of the Buddha* (Sk. *Buddhacarita*), notes this contradiction:

> Then being detached through his longing
> for the forest
> and dismissing [the horse groom] Chanda, teary-eyed and weeping,
> Sarvārthasiddha went into that hermitage,
> like a *siddha*, engulfing it with his beauty.[34]
>
> The king's son, walking like the king of beasts,
> like a deer, entered that abode of deer;
> though stripped of royal majesty,
> the majesty of his body
> gripped the eyes of all in that hermitage.[35]
> . . .
> And they looked in wonder at him,
> who looked like [the god] Indra.[36]

Even though Siddhārtha's body is here stripped of its royal adornments, it still embodies royal masculinity by virtue of its likeness to majestic animals. *Deeds of the Buddha* further compares Siddhārtha to another symbol of masculine royal power, Indra, the king of the gods.[37]

A few verses later in *Deeds of the Buddha*, when the people of Rājagṛha encounter the Recluse Gautama, they, too, stop to gaze upon the former prince, whose "chest was broad and stout," with "his effulgent body surpassing the human."[38] Gautama's beauty transfixed them: "When the people of the land saw that the virtues in the Crown Prince's appearance were profound and bright, that the figure of the youth was bright, with an unequaled manly appearance, they all thought it was wonderful. . . . As they saw the primary and secondary marks of his four limbs, their eyes did not move."[39] The Bodhisattva's arrival in Rājagṛha soon attracts the attention of its ruler, King Bimbisāra. The king is also struck by the majestic body of the young Recluse Gautama, who blazed like the sun and looked worthy of ruling the world, even though he was wearing the garb of a renunciant.[40] King Bimbisāra, amazed and impressed, ends up offering Siddhārtha half his kingdom. Bimbisāra brings up various arguments for why a young man like Siddhārtha, with his radiant, beautiful body, ought to be a ruler rather than

FIGURE 1.2 Detail from a *stūpa* railpost, ca. first century BCE–first century CE, red sandstone, from Kankālī Tīlā, Mathura. Lucknow Museum (S.M.L. No. J. 531).

a renunciant. He emphasizes the Bodhisattva's youth, virility and strength: "It's not right that you should let / these two stout arms / fit for drawing a bow remain unproductive."[41]

I believe a relief carving from Kankālī Tīlā, Mathura (fig. 1.2), represents this meeting between King Bimbisāra and the Recluse Gautama. Scholars usually identify this image as depicting the Buddha's postenlightenment meeting with his father, but the form represented is that of the Bodhisattva as a renunciant (i.e., pre-enlightenment).[42] This is also considered to be one of the earliest anthropomorphic representations of the Bodhisattva/Buddha. In fact, several of these early anthropomorphic images probably represent the young, robust figure of the Bodhisattva as a renunciant. For example, colossal figures sponsored by the monk Bala (a.k.a. "Bhikṣu Bala"), including the famous statue from Sārnāth and an example from Śrāvastī (fig. 1.3), are inscribed not as "the Buddha," but as "the Bodhisattva."[43] I suggest that these figures portray pre-enlightenment Śākyamuni as the Recluse Gautama.[44]

These colossal Bodhisattva images are very much alike. Most of them were erected at places famously associated with Śākyamuni, but they depict his pre-enlightenment body as the Bodhisattva. These visual representations

FIGURE 1.3 Colossal Bodhisattva. Found in Śrāvastī, Uttar Pradesh, India, ca. first century CE, red sandstone, 238 cm x 91 cm x 47 cm. Indian Museum, Kolkata (S.1B/ A25028).

FIGURE 1.4 Standing Bodhisattva Siddhārtha, ca. second–third century, Mathura. Government Museum Mathura (Photo: Biswarup Ganguly, CC BY-3.0).

of the Bodhisattva's body evoke many of the characteristics of the great man's body and constitute the epitome of male bodily perfection (fig. 1.4). They show Gautama's body clothed in a simple diaphanous robe, his right shoulder bared.[45] With a broad chest and rounded shoulders, tightly clenched fist held at his left hip, and well-articulated male genitalia, these figures project the healthy, robust, and virile body of a young man in his prime.

The *Great Story* (Sk. *Mahāvastu*) provides a textual description of the newly renounced Gautama's appearance that is a remarkably close match to the colossal Bodhisattva visual representations of the Recluse Gautama:

> Glorious of form, dazzling more than the lightning's flash, all golden, gleaming like a smokeless, blazing fire.
> Broadchested was he, with mighty arms, and admirable hands and fingers; compact was his belly, slender his figure; his carriage that of an antelope, and his hips were prominent.
> He was like a pillar of gold, and his eyes flashed like a bull's. His bust was like that of a tiger, his feet and hands like the lotus.
> His body was bright with the marks won by the virtues of a hundred lives, as the moon is bright among the stars.
> There were no befitting bright ornaments on his limbs; these characteristics alone adorned the body of the great-souled one.[46]

These physical characteristics, whether rendered in images or text, signal Gautama's first move away from one masculine extreme, that of the ruler who enjoys worldly power and adornments.

The Ascetic Gautama and His Emaciated Body

Even when Siddhārtha became a renunciant and wore only a humble robe, his body remained as vigorous, beautiful, and strong as it was before he left the palace. However, the next stage of his life story entailed more dramatic physical transformations. Iconographically, the Ascetic Gautama's emaciated appearance inverts the great man's features and starkly contrasts with images of Siddhārtha's body as Crown Prince and Recluse Gautama. The Crown Prince and Recluse Gautama's limbs are youthful, unmarred, unimpaired, and well shaped. They have a rounded belly, concealed and unknotted veins covered by smooth skin, with no indentation between the shoulders. Conversely, the emaciated Ascetic Gautama has knotted, bulging veins and angular, protruding shoulders. His body is haggard and bony, his cheeks and stomach hollow.[47] The Bodhisattva no longer looks like a young man in his prime, but appears far older, worn, and cadaverous (fig 1.5).

The Ascetic Gautama looks entirely unlike the beautiful, youthful Prince Siddhārtha and Recluse Gautama. The *Account of Origins* (P. *Nidānakathā*) describes his striking transformation: "By this fasting, however, he became as thin as a skeleton; the color of his body, once fair as gold, became dark; and the thirty-two signs of a great [man] disappeared."[48] The loss of the great man's distinguishing marks meant that Gautama's hard-earned spiritual superiority could no longer be outwardly recognized. While textual sources state that the Bodhisattva lost all his bodily marks, images of the Ascetic Gautama still retained a few distinguishing characteristics, such as the tuft of hair between the eyebrows (Sk. *ūrṇā*), the cranial protuberance (Sk. *uṣṇīṣa*), and sometimes a halo, though the body had supposedly lost its luminosity. These features were probably retained to make the image more easily recognizable as the Bodhisattva.

Early texts, such as the *Great Story*, not only describe the Ascetic Gautama's body but also recount the reactions of those who saw him: "All this became known in the provinces and hamlets, and women and men talked about it, now saying that the recluse [Gautama] was black, now that he was dark brown, and now that he had the sallow color of a *madgura* [fish]. So ruined by my austere abstinence was the wonted [i.e., usual] bright and pure complexion of my body."[49] Losing the bodily marks is a crucial element of the narrative, as it denotes how wrong practices can bring about a negative, regressive bodily transformation.[50] This is in contrast to how correct practices elicit positive, progressive change. According to the *Collection of Stories of the Six Perfections* (Ch. *Liudujijing*), Siddhārtha's six years of extreme asceticism were a karmic result of an unwholesome deed during a past existence. In that previous life, the Bodhisattva was a king who accidentally left an ascetic to wait without food or drink for six days. Thus, in the Bodhisattva's last existence, he had to endure excruciating asceticism for six years.[51]

On the pedestal of the image from the Metropolitan Museum of Art (fig. 1.6) we find a narrative scene that at first glance may not seem at all connected with the main figure of the emaciated Ascetic Gautama. This postenlightenment episode depicts the First Sermon and features the seated

FIGURE 1.5 The Ascetic Gautama. Kushana period, grey stone. Government Museum Mathura (18.1550).

FIGURE 1.6 Fasting Gautama, Pakistan (the ancient region of Gandhāra), ca. third–fifth century CE, schist sculpture. Metropolitan Museum of Art, New York (1987.218.5).

Buddha and five seated monks. These five monks are Gautama's former companions, who abandoned him as soon as he abandoned his extreme asceticism.[52] They are the first to whom the Buddha preaches the Dharma after reaching enlightenment under the Bodhi tree. After the Bodhisattva realizes that extreme asceticism is not the correct path to enlightenment and disavows it, the five ascetics accuse him of slacking off and living "luxuriously." They decide to leave him and continue their ascetic practices without him. While the main figure of Ascetic Gautama and the scene of the First Sermon depicted on its pedestal are not immediately connected as biographical episodes, they connect around the theme of asceticism. This connection is also illustrated by the contents of the First Sermon, which features a discussion of the Middle Way between the sensual indulgences of the body and the extreme mortifications of the body.[53]

A similar mode of visually combining the figure of Ascetic Gautama with a postenlightenment episode appears in a sculpture of the Ascetic Gautama from Takht-i-Bahi, now at the Peshawar Museum.[54] Instead of the First Sermon episode, on the pedestal of the Takht-i-Bahi figure we find a representation of the episode in which the merchants Trapuṣa and Bhallika make offerings of food to the Buddha—his first postenlightenment meal.[55] Both examples feature a postenlightenment episode, but in both cases this later episode alludes to the Middle Way of Buddhist renunciation that denounces extreme deprivation.[56] Thus framed, the emaciated figures of Gautama should not be seen as glorifying ascetic masculinity, but, rather, as warning against it while affirming the Middle Way masculinity of renunciation without extremes.[57] At the same time, these images represented a pivotal episode from the life of the Buddha and as such were worthy of veneration. The Bodhisattva's perfect meditation posture in these images projects his unyielding determination, even if extreme ascetic practice damaged his body. This representation also elevates Siddhārtha as the pinnacle of ascetic masculinity compared to all other non-Buddhist ascetics or recluses depicted in Buddhist art. Siddhārtha could have been a universal ruler, and he could have been the supreme ascetic, but he rejects those forms of masculinity in favor of the Middle Way.

After collapsing from exhaustion caused by his severe practices, the Ascetic Gautama suddenly remembers the meditation experience he had as a prince, an episode known as the First Meditation, during which he reached the first stage of meditative absorption (Sk. *dhyāna*). Having recalled his meditative experience under the Jambu (i.e., rose apple) tree, Gautama decides to renounce his austerities and give that same type of meditation another try. Before he does so, however, he realizes that he must first restore his body to its former appearance: "He perceived that penance was not the way to wisdom; and begging through the villages and towns, he collected ordinary material food, and lived upon it. And the thirty-two signs of a great [man] appeared again upon him, and his body became fair in color, like unto gold."[58]

This idea is supported by a Gandhāran relief (fig. 1.7) that features three scenes of the pre-enlightenment renunciant Gautama. The images start with

FIGURE 1.7 Siddhārtha Gautama Ends His Fasting, Gandhāra, second–third century, slate. Copyright: © Staatliche Museen zu Berlin, Museum für Asiatische Kunst (Museum of Asian Art, Berlin), Inv. Nr. I 79, photo: Jürgen Liepe.

Ascetic Gautama being visited by Brahma and Indra (right). This is followed by Gautama, still weak with an emaciated body, bathing in the Nairañjāna River (middle), an episode that biographies often place after his decision to abandon asceticism. The final scene depicts local women (and/or the woman Sujātā) offering him a bowl with milk rice (left). Here Gautama's body appears restored to its appearance prior to his ascetic practice. This relief highlights Siddhārtha's physical transformations, as well as the superiority of the Middle Way masculine body over the ascetic masculine body.

The emaciated body could also signify undesirable forms of masculinity, as some Buddhist texts link extreme austerities with the evil tempter Māra and heterodox practices. For example, when the Buddha exclaims with palpable relief at reaching enlightenment after having abandoned "that useless grueling asceticism," Māra accuses him of having "deviated from the austere practice by which men purify themselves."[59] This "austere practice" alludes to non-Buddhist bodily mortification. The Bodhisattva's extreme fasting is reminiscent of the Jain ideal mode of solitary death in which one fasts to death while meditating (Sk. *sallekhanā*).[60] This practice is sometimes performed by Jain monks even at the height of their physical and mental powers.[61] It is a voluntary, planned religious death that must be undertaken with calmness of mind.

In one version of the Buddha's biography, the Bodhisattva's inner monologue reveals a concern that his extreme austerities will be misunderstood by followers of other religious paths such as the Jains:

> My body is withered and emaciated, resembling a dead tree. I have been practicing severe austerities for six full years but did not attain enlightenment, thus I know this is not the Way. I should practice the type of meditation that I once experienced under the Jambu tree, which is removed from pleasures but abiding in a tranquil state. [It is that type of meditation] that leads to the [attainment] of the Utmost True Enlightenment. Further, if I were to obtain the Way in this emaciated body, the various followers of other teachings would surely say that I obtained *nirvāṇa* by starving myself. Even though these joints of mine still have some manly power[62] left, I should not attempt to attain enlightenment's fruit [in this emaciated body]. I should receive some food and only then attain enlightenment.[63]

It seems that Gautama thinks he could still attain enlightenment in his emaciated body, but he deliberately chooses not to do so, lest others mistakenly think that he had reached enlightenment due to the practice of bodily mortification. There is an undercurrent of awareness of how others will perceive the process of his enlightenment and the body in which he attains it. This passage thus betrays awareness of the visual representations of the Ascetic Gautama. In this version, after Siddhārtha realizes that ascetic practice is not the correct way toward enlightenment, he takes a bath and eats some food, which restores his body's luminosity.[64] From this perspective, Buddhists may be claiming a superior form of masculinity to the ascetic masculinity embraced by competing religious groups (or competing Buddhist factions): after all, the Buddha was perfectly capable of extreme asceticism, but he rejected such practices upon determining that they could not lead to awakening.

Early Buddhist texts underscore the fluidity and beauty of Siddhārtha's body—and further critique his emaciated form—by comparing his physical transformations to the changes of a flower. In the *Sūtra on the Origin of the*

[Buddha's] Practice (Ch. *Xiuxing benqijing*), the god Indra encourages two village girls to offer "food for a universal monarch" to the emaciated Bodhisattva to restore his physical glory (i.e., the great man's body that buddhas and universal monarchs share).[65] Indra then uses his divine power to make the girls dream of a single lotus flower in the middle of a watery expanse. The flower initially appears bright and lustrous, but in an instant it withers and fades. Indra explains that this lotus flower represents Siddhārtha, whose form had become "gaunt and meager" from his austerities.[66]

While, in this context, flowers were an established metaphor for male beauty, specific comparisons of Siddhārtha's beauty to the rare *uḍumbara* flower further emphasize his distinctive physique. A passage from *Various Matters in the Vinaya of the Mūlasarvāstivādins* (Sk. *Mūlasarvāstivāda-vinaya-kṣudrakavastu*; Ch. *Genben shuo yiqie youbu pinaiye zashi*) correlates the *uḍumbara* flower's different phases to different biographical episodes in the Buddha's life. It starts by referencing an *uḍumbara* tree at the bank of the lotus lake Mandākini near Kuśinagara, then explains:

> In the past, at the time when the Bodhisattva was in Tuṣita heaven, and he, having made [himself appear as] a white elephant, entered his mother's womb, the flower bud of this *uḍumbara* tree formed. When [the Bodhisattva] was born, this flower bud became luminous in appearance. When the Bodhisattva was a Prince the flower bud was just about to bloom. When [the Bodhisattva] was repulsed by old age, sickness, and death and, wanting to overcome them, went into the forest [i.e., became a renunciant], that flower bloomed as big as a crow's beak. When [the Bodhisattva] was practicing extreme asceticism, the flower became wan and withered. When [the Bodhisattva] abandoned the practice of extreme asceticism, regained his normal breathing, and nourished himself with food and drink, the flower expanded and regained its previous [beautiful] shape and form. It was when [the Bodhisattva] attained to Perfect Enlightenment that the flower unfolded its bloom in full.[67]

In Buddhist legend, the mythical flowering of the *uḍumbara* tree is said to happen only once every three thousand years and thus symbolize very rare events, such as a buddha's appearance. When the Buddha dies, the *uḍumbara* flowers wither and fade away again. In fact, the Buddha's last act before his final extinction (Sk. *parinirvāṇa*) is to reveal his body to his followers one last time, saying, "Look, O monks, at the body of the Tathāgata, behold, O monks, the body of the Tathāgata. Why? Because just like the *uḍumbara*, *tathāgatas*, [who are] *arahants* [and] complete and perfect buddhas, rarely appear [in the world] to be seen."[68] The Buddha's final act is both an opportunity to see his body one last time, and a lesson that even perfect beings' bodies are subject to the laws of impermanence. Buddhist texts, in comparing the Bhagavat's bodily transformations to the flower's life cycle, highlight both Gautama's physical beauty (and its extreme rarity) and the impermanence of buddhas' unique combination of bodily and spiritual perfection. This comparison introduces another measure of ambivalence toward Siddhārtha's body in its various forms: while the emaciated Ascetic Gautama is a withered blossom in contrast to the full bloom of buddhahood, all flowers ultimately wither and die, no matter how beautiful and rare they may be. Ascetic Gautama could thus serve as a potentially positive reminder of old age, sickness, and death.

Though the negative portrayal of the Ascetic Gautama body remained dominant, it is evident that some Buddhists venerated the Bhagavat in this form. The seventh-century travel record of the Chinese monk-pilgrim Xuanzang (602–64; see also Geng Song's chapter in this volume) mentions the worship of the Ascetic Gautama image. Xuanzang identifies an enshrined statue of the emaciated Gautama as a representation of the Bodhisattva during his extreme asceticism. Moreover, he identifies the shrine as the spot of Gautama's ascetic practice. According to Xuanzang, "In the past and at present it is the custom of the local people to anoint the image with fragrant oil when they are afflicted with a disease, and in most cases they are cured of their illness. This was the place where the Bodhisattva practiced austerities."[69]

This excerpt provides important evidence about some of the practices related to visual representations of Ascetic Gautama. The gaunt, emaciated images represent the inverse of the Bodhisattva's ideal body. Therefore, Xuanzang's account of the local veneration practice he witnessed at Bodhgaya—which involved applying scented oils to the image—could be interpreted as the symbolic healing of an unhealthy body. The Ascetic Gautama image, as a representation of an important episode of the Buddha's biography, deserved veneration; at the same time, as demonstrated by textual and visual sources, the image of the emaciated body carried strongly negative connotations. Just as the Bodhisattva sought to restore his body to its former wholesomeness, health, and beauty, so, too, did the people worshiping the emaciated Ascetic Gautama statue seek to restore their own bodily health.

* * *

Many Buddhist texts strongly emphasize the connection between physical appearance and spiritual attainment. The Bodhisattva/Buddha's body was particularly important to the authors of Śākyamuni's biographies. This attitude transferred to visual representations of the Bhagavat's unique physiognomy, which was simultaneously presented as the epitome of male bodily perfection and spiritual perfection. Siddhārtha's unique body resulted from his eons-long cultivation of virtues, and his remarkable appearance had an immediate, transformative impact on those who saw him. Just as Siddhārtha's body positively affected those who saw him during his life, images of his body offered later Buddhists a posthumous substitute.

The Bodhisattva's journey to enlightenment presented an example to admire and, if possible, emulate. Images representing pivotal moments in the Bodhisattva's journey toward buddhahood, including those of Gautama as a world renouncer, became a focal point of Buddhist devotion. Images of Gautama as a renunciant projected an ideal of male bodily perfection, conveying powerful robustness, determination, and resolve. Those images presented a unique type of renouncer who fell between the body of the perfect universal monarch and the body of the ideal ascetic; he visually embodied the Middle Way between these two extremes. But, even when extreme asceticism inverted that bodily ideal, images of this pivotal episode served as visual reminders of the correct path that Śākyamuni discovered himself through trial and error. Textual and visual representations of the Ascetic Gautama strongly convey the message that extreme asceticism does not lead to awakening. Instead, the essential components of the Buddha's Middle Way are training the mind, perfecting virtue, meditating correctly, and attaining wisdom.

This Middle Way is not only a spiritual ideal. It also takes form in a particular type of masculine body. One cannot achieve Middle Way masculinity without first embodying the extremes of royal and ascetic masculinity, which could each be considered hegemonic in their respective emphases on control over others and control over the self. The Buddha's Middle Way masculinity encompasses and transcends these forms of masculinity while claiming its own hegemonic power.

NOTES

The epigraph is from John S. Strong, *The Legend of King Aśoka: A Study and Translation of the Aśokāvadāna* (Princeton, N.J.: Princeton University Press, 1983), 195.

1. "Bhagavat," or "World-Honored One," is one of the ten epithets for the Buddha. The term is useful here because it can encompass both stages of Siddhārtha Gautama's life, meaning his life as a Bodhisattva (i.e., preawakening), and his life as a Buddha (i.e., postawakening). This chapter refers to the historical Buddha by the following names: Siddhārtha, Gautama, Śākyamuni, Bodhisattva, Buddha, and Bhagavat. These names are used interchangeably, except for Bodhisattva and Buddha.
2. John Strong notes that tales of the Buddha's previous lives identify particular spiritual perfections with a Buddha's specific physical characteristics. See John S. Strong, *Relics of the Buddha* (Princeton, N.J.: Princeton University Press, 2004), 51.
3. *The Account of Origins* (P. *Nidānakathā*) of the Jātaka commentary lists eight conditions to receive the prediction of buddhahood. Among other conditions, such as being a renunciant and making an aspiration for future buddhahood in the presence of a living Buddha, one had to be a human male in order to receive a prediction of buddhahood. For a narrative example, see Karen Derris, " 'My Sister's Future Buddhahood': A Jātaka of the Buddha's Lifetime as a Woman," in *Eminent Buddhist Women*, ed. Karma Lekshe Tsomo (Albany: State University of New York Press, 2014), 13–24. Also see Ven. Anālayo, "The Buddha's Past Life as a Princess in the *Ekottarika-āgama*," *Journal of Buddhist Ethics* 22 (2015): 95–137.
4. See, for example, the explanation of hegemonic masculinity as both allowing men's dominance over women and the dominance of hegemonic masculinity over subordinated masculinities in Raewyn Connell and James W. Messerschmidt, "Hegemonic Masculinity: Rethinking the Concept," *Gender & Society* 19, no. 6 (December 2005): 829–59, 832.
5. As noted in this volume's introduction, in addition to the thirty-two marks there was an additional list of eighty secondary (or minor) marks (Sk. *anuvyañjana*). See John Powers, *A Bull of a Man: Images of Masculinity, Sex, and the Body in Indian Buddhism* (Cambridge, Mass.: Harvard University Press, 2009), 235–39.
6. The "*Sutta* on the Marks" of the *Dīgha-nikāya* (DN 30 *Lakkhaṇa-sutta*) explains the karmic reasons for the thirty-two marks of a great man possessed by both *cakravartins* and buddhas but also stresses that buddhas' bodies are superior. See *The Long Discourses of the Buddha: A Translation of the Dīgha Nikāya*, trans. Maurice Walshe (Boston: Wisdom, 1995), 441–79.
7. These physical signs of moral perfection cannot be faked. In the *Mūlasarvāstivāda vinaya*, the Buddha's evil cousin Devadatta attempts to supplant the Buddha by hiring a goldsmith to gild him so that he would have the requisite golden skin. In another version, Devadatta hired a blacksmith to brand him with wheel patterns on his hands and feet. Powers, *Bull of a Man*, 294n1. See also John Powers, "The Gendered Buddha: Neither God nor Man, but Supremely Manly," in *God's Own Gender? Masculinities in World Religions*, ed. Daniel Gerster and Michael

Krüggeler (Baden-Baden: Ergon-Verlag, 2018), 251–52. While depicted as evil on numerous occasions and serving as a foil to the Buddha, Devadatta was said to possess thirty of the thirty-two marks. Gautama's half-brother, Nanda, also possessed thirty of the marks and approached Śākyamuni's beauty. Also see *Traité de la grande vertu de sagesse de Nāgārjuna (Mahāprajñāpāramitāśāstra)*, book 1, trans. Étienne Lamotte (Louvain: Institut Orientaliste, 1944), 285–87.

8. These distinctions are a topic of discussion in the *Commentary on the Great Perfection of Wisdom* (Sk. *Mahāprajñāpāramitopadeśa*, Ch. *Dazhidu lun*), an important Mahāyāna exegetical treatise attributed to Nāgārjuna. *Dazhidu lun*, trans. Kumārajīva (344–414), *T.*1509.25:683a1–12.
9. For example, a bodily mark can be the physical result of good karmic action, such as practicing charity, but the intention and the manner in which the gift-giving was performed is the crucial distinction. A bodily mark gained through a karmalogical process is a result of ordinary karmically beneficial acts, whereas the bodily mark of a Bodhisattva/Buddha is a psychophysical result of conscious, intentional, and truly selfless efforts over multiple births. The former is obtained following the ordinary laws of karma; the latter, we would say, follows buddhological (i.e., dharmalogical) laws.
10. Even the Buddha's perfect body was bound by the laws of impermanence and succumbed to illness, old age, and ultimately death. See John S. Strong, "Explicating the Buddha's Final Illness in the Context of His Other Ailments: The Making and Unmaking of some Jātaka Tales," *Buddhist Studies Review* 29, no. 1 (2012): 17–33; and Jonathan S. Walters, "The Buddha's Bad Karma: A Problem in the History of Theravāda Buddhism," *Numen* 37, no. 1 (1990): 70–95.
11. On Buddhist ambivalence toward bodies, see Powers, *Bull of a Man*, chapter 4; and Sue Hamilton, *Identity and Experience: The Constitution of the Human Being According to Early Buddhism* (London: Luzac Oriental, 1996), 169–93. While all ordinary bodies are viewed negatively, in a textual tradition written almost exclusively for celibate monastic men, by other men, female bodies are viewed in an even more negative light. See Liz Wilson, *Charming Cadavers: Horrific Figurations of the Feminine in Indian Buddhist Hagiographic Literature* (Chicago: University of Chicago Press, 1996); and Reiko Ohnuma, "Woman, Bodhisattva, and Buddha," *Journal of Feminist Studies in Religion* 17, no. 1 (2001): 63–83.
12. John Powers, "Why Practicing Virtue Is Better than Working Out: Bodies and Ethics in Indian Buddhism," *Chung-Hwa Buddhist Journal* 22 (2009): 125–52.
13. Susanne Mrozik, "The Value of Human Differences: South Asian Buddhist Contributions Toward an Embodied Virtue Theory," *Journal of Buddhist Ethics* 9 (2002): 1–33, 5.
14. Mrozik, "Value of Human Differences," 5.
15. Susanne Mrozik, *Virtuous Bodies: The Physical Dimensions of Morality in Buddhist Ethics* (New York: Oxford University Press, 2007), 3–4.
16. Powers, "Practicing Virtue," 130.
17. With very minor exceptions virtuous beings are beautiful and a body with the thirty-two marks is a prerequisite for becoming a Buddha. A notable exception to this rule is Upagupta, the third-century BCE Indian monk who was not

beautiful, but who was predicted to become a Buddha without the marks. Strong, *Legend of King Aśoka*, 187.

18. Powers, "Practicing Virtue," 130.
19. Mrozik, *Virtuous Bodies*, 12. For example, rebirth in hell is undesirable not only because of the extreme suffering one endures there, but also because one's spiritual practice and advancement is hindered by such rebirth.
20. Mrozik, "Value of Human Differences," 6.
21. Powers, "Practicing Virtue," 139. While Powers is referring to a particular previous life as the Bodhisattva in the *Culladhanuggaha-jātaka*, this observation applies to many of the Bodhisattva's other prior existences and also to his final life as Siddhārtha Gautama.
22. Daniel Boucher, *Bodhisattvas of the Forest and the Formation of the Mahāyāna: A Study and Translation of the "Rāṣṭrapālaparipṛcchā-sūtra"* (Honolulu: University of Hawai'i Press, 2008), 10.
23. Vidya Dehejia, *The Body Adorned: Dissolving Boundaries Between Sacred and Profane in Indian Art* (New York: Columbia University Press, 2009), 65 (emphasis added).
24. Powers, "Practicing Virtue," 131.
25. There are several stories in the Pāli canon in which skeptical *brahmans*, while impressed with the Buddha's wise words, are ultimately converted to his teaching by seeing his physique, the ultimate proof of wisdom and ethical perfection.
26. For an English translation see Strong, *Legend of King Aśoka*, 189–96. Aśoka (ca. 300–232 BCE) was an emperor of the Maurya dynasty whom Buddhist tradition remembers as the paradigmatic Buddhist monarch. The evil Māra tried to prevent Siddhārtha from reaching full awakening, and his personal encounters with Śākyamuni are another reason why he was able to take on the Buddha's form.
27. Adapted from Strong, *Legend of King Aśoka*, 194–95.
28. John S. Strong, "Buddha Bhakti and the Absence of the Blessed One," in *Premier Colloque Étienne Lamotte (Bruxelles et Liège, 24-27 Septembre 1989)*, Publications de l'Institut Orientaliste de Louvain, no. 42 (Louvain: Institut Orientaliste, 1993), 131–40.
29. For an overview of art historical debates about the early absence of anthropomorphic Bodhisattva/Buddha images, see Rob Linrothe, "Inquiries Into the Origin of the Buddha Image: A Review," *East and West* 43, no. 14 (1993): 241–56. For one of the more recent hypotheses, see Robert DeCaroli, *Image Problems: The Origin and Development of the Buddha's Image in Early South Asia* (Seattle: University of Washington Press, 2015). For my own views on the subject, see Dessislava Vendova, "The Great Life Story of the Body of the Buddha: Re-examination and Re-assessment of the Images and Narratives of the Life of Buddha Shakyamuni" (PhD diss., Columbia University, 2021).
30. For an insightful discussion of early Bodhisattva/Buddha images see Ju-Hyung Rhi, "From Bodhisattva to Buddha: The Beginning of Iconic Representation in Buddhist Art," *Artibus Asiae* 54, nos. 3–4 (1994): 207–25.
31. The Bodhisattva Deva is the form that the Bodhisattva took while dwelling in Tuṣita Heaven before his final birth as Siddhārtha Gautama and is technically a previous existence.

32. For an extended discussion of these four identities, see Vendova, "Great Life Story."
33. See the *Ariyapariyesanā-sutta* of the *Majjhima-nikāya* (MN 26) in *The Middle Length Discourses of the Buddha: A Translation of the Majjhima Nikāya*, trans. Bhikkhu Ñāṇamoli and Bhikkhu Bodhi (Boston: Wisdom, 1995), 256.
34. Sarvārthasiddha (Sk.) is a variant of Śākyamuni's personal name Siddhārtha—that is, one who has accomplished all his aims. A *siddha* is a perfected being (see also Shelton in this volume).
35. This verse plays on the word adornment. A literal translation would be: "Even though stripped of adornments, the body was adorned" (Sk. *lakṣmī/viyukto 'pi śarīra/lakṣmyā*).
36. Aśvaghoṣa, *Life of the Buddha*, trans. Patrick Olivelle (New York: New York University Press / JJC Foundation, 2008), 187, verses 7.1–7.3.
37. Some iconographic depictions of Indra with a royal turban mirror the visual representations of Prince Siddhārtha.
38. Aśvaghoṣa, *Life of the Buddha*, 279.
39. Charles Willemen, *Buddhacarita: In Praise of Buddha's Acts by Aśvaghoṣa* (Berkeley, Calif.: Numata Center for Buddhist Translation and Research, 2009), 69.
40. Aśvaghoṣa, *Life of the Buddha*, 281, verse 10.9; 283, verses 10.11 and 10.15.
41. Aśvaghoṣa, 289, verse 10.31. In several versions of the Buddha's life, Prince Siddhārtha had earlier proven his martial artistry, virility, and strength in an archery competition.
42. For the theory that this image depicts the Buddha meeting his father Śuddhodana upon the Buddha's return to Kapilavastu after his enlightenment, see Johanna E. van Lohuizen-de Leeuw, *The "Scythian" Period: An Approach to the History, Art, Epigraphy, and Palaeography of North India from the 1st Century BC to the 3rd Century AD* (Leiden: E. J. Brill, 1949), 159; and Rekha Morris, "Buddha Under a Ficus Tree and Two Sculptures from Mathurā in the Sackler Museum, Harvard University," *Archives of Asian Art* 51 (1998): 80–91, 86.
43. For the inscription on the statue from Śrāvastī, see T. Bloch, "Two Inscriptions on Buddhist Images," *Epigraphia Indica* 8 (1905): 179–82, 180.
44. There are many similar representations of Siddhārtha as a renunciant from that period. The epigraphic evidence attests that monks and nuns commissioned those early images, which indicates that Buddhist monastics were involved in the image cult from its earliest stages. Gregory Schopen, "On Monks, Nuns and 'Vulgar' Practices: The Introduction of the Image Cult Into Indian Buddhism," *Artibus Asiae* 49, nos. 1–2 (1988): 153–68.
45. Some scholars interpret the cluster of lotuses found between the feet of several images as representing Siddhārtha's royal turban, which he removed in becoming a renunciant. See Ramesh C. Sharma, *Buddhist Art of Mathurā* (Delhi: Agam Kala Prakashan, 1984), 187. This would further support identifying the figures as the renunciant Gautama.
46. *The Mahāvastu*, trans. J. J. Jones (London: Luzac, 1949–1956), 2:196.
47. Perhaps the most famous is the emaciated Gautama statue in the Lahore Museum, Pakistan. Many museums and art historians refer to the emaciated

Siddhārtha image as "Fasting Buddha," which is incorrect. The distinction between Gautama as the Bodhisattva versus as the Buddha was important for the people who produced the texts and images, so it is important to maintain that distinction.

48. *Buddhist Birth-stories (Jataka Tales): The Commentarial Introduction Entitled* Nidāna-kātha, *the Story of the Lineage*, trans. Thomas William Rhys Davids (London: Trubner, 1880), 90.
49. *The Mahāvastu*, trans. J. J. Jones (London: Luzac, 1949–1956), 2:122. A similar narrative also appears in the *Mahāsaccaka-sutta* from the *Majjhima-nikāya*. See Bhikkhu Ñāṇamoli and Bhikkhu Bodhi, *The Middle Length Discourses of the Buddha*, 339–40 (*Majjhima Nikāya* 36: i 246 §29).
50. Buddhist texts mention that in his old age the Buddha suffered constant backache and upset stomach due to the austerities he practiced during these six years. Even with a buddha's perfect body, previous karma caught up with Śākyamuni in the form of bodily ailments. See Strong, "Explicating the Buddha's Final Illness."
51. *Liudujijing* (Sk. **Ṣaṭ-pāramitā-saṃgraha*), trans. Kang Senghui (251), *T.*152.3: 30a10–b27.
52. A sixth standing figure may represent the Ajivika ascetic Upaka, who meets the Buddha on his way to Sārnāth.
53. *The Connected Discourses of the Buddha: A Translation of the Saṃyutta Nikāya*, trans. Bhikkhu Bodhi (Boston: Wisdom, 2003), 2:1843–47.
54. For a photo of this figure, see Islay Lyons and Harald Ingholt, *Gandhāran Art in Pakistan* (New York: Pantheon, 1957), figure 53; and Harold Hargreaves, *Handbook to the Sculptures in the Peshawar Museum* (Calcutta: Government of India Central Publication Branch, 1930), plate 3.
55. Scholars have debated the Fasting Gautama image, particularly this example since it features a postenlightenment episode. Robert Brown speculates that at least some of the representations, especially those in Gandhāran art, may depict Śākyamuni's seven-week fast after his enlightenment. See Robert L. Brown, "The Emaciated Buddha Images: Asceticism, Health, and Body," in *Living in a Life in Accord with Dhamma: Papers in Honor of Jean Boisselier on His Eightieth Birthday*, ed. Natasha Eilenberg, M. C. Subhadradis Diskul, and Robert L. Brown (Bangkok: Silpakorn University, 1997), 105–15. However, most scholars see the fasting images as depicting the Bodhisattva's pre-enlightenment asceticism. See Juhyung Rhi, "Some Textual Parallels for Gandhāran Art: Fasting Buddhas, Lalitavistara, and Karuṇāpuṇḍarīka," *Journal of the International Association of Buddhist Studies* 29, no. 1 (2006): 125–53.
56. Most texts discussing the Bodhisattva's extreme asceticism frame it negatively, but there are several exceptions, in which texts frame the Bodhisattva's bodily mortification as a positive achievement of unwavering endurance and unshakable will. Oliver Freiberger argues that ambivalence toward asceticism may reflect tensions between two camps in the early Buddhist community. See Oliver Freiberger, "Early Buddhism, Asceticism, and the Politics of the Middle Way," in *Asceticism and Its Critics: Historical Accounts and Comparative Perspectives*, ed. Oliver Freiberger (New York: Oxford University Press, 2006), 235–58.

57. Juhyung Rhi has suggested that the Fasting Gautama images in Gandhāra may have been made in reaction to more positive views of Gautama's asceticism, such as the views in the *Lotus of Compassion* (Sk. *Karuṇāpuṇḍarīka*). Rhi tentatively suggests that texts that framed Gautama's asceticism in a positive light may have been regionally popular, which could explain the popularity of Fasting Gautama images in Gandhāra, while they are absent elsewhere in Mathura and Northern India at this time. See Rhi, "Some Textual Parallels for Gandhāran Art."
58. Adapted from Rhys Davids, *Buddhist Birth-stories*, 91.
59. *The Connected Discourses of the Buddha: A New Translation of the Saṃyutta Nikāya*, trans. Bhikkhu Bodhi (Boston: Wisdom, 2003), 1:195–96.
60. Paul Dundas, *The Jains* (London: Routledge, 1992), 179; Pabst M. Battin, *The Ethics of Suicide: Historical Sources* (New York: Oxford University Press, 2015), 46–47.
61. There are a number of Jain texts that prescribe it for people (particularly monks) who have become sick and are in poor health. See Dundas, *Jains*, 180.
62. Literally, Nārāyaṇa power (Ch. Naluoyan *li*), which as an adjective means manly and strong due to the might of the god Nārāyaṇa.
63. *Guoqu xianzai yinguo jing*, trans. Guṇabhadra (435–443), *T.*189.3:639a25–b2.
64. *Guoqu xianzai yinguo jing*, *T.*189.3:639b15–17.
65. *Xiuxing benqijing*, *T.*184.3:469c10–13.
66. *Xiuxing benqijing*, *T.*184.3:469c19–20.
67. *Genben shuo yiqie youbu pinaiye zashi*, *T.*1451.24:396a13–24.
68. Adapted from Ernst Waldschmidt, *Das Mahaparinirvanasutra, Text in Sanskrit und Tibetisch, verglichen mit dem Pali nebst einer Übersetzung der chinesischen Entsprechung im Vinaya der Mulasarvastivadins, auf Grund von Turfan-Handschriften herausgegeben und bearbeitet* (Berlin: Akademie Verlag, 1950–1951), 394 (42.10).
69. *The Great Tang Dynasty Record of the Western Regions*, Rongxi Li (Berkeley, Calif.: Numata Center for Buddhist Translation and Research, BDK America, 1996), 224. I have corrected the translation where Li has used "Buddha," whereas in the original text the word used is "Bodhisattva." Xuanzang, *Da Tang xiyuji*, *T.*2087.51:917b20–21.

Additional Primary Sources

Behrendt, Kurt A. *The Art of Gandhara in the Metropolitan Museum of Art*. New York: Metropolitan Museum of Art, 2007.
Czuma, Stanislaw J. *Kushan Sculpture: Images from Early India*. Cleveland: Cleveland Museum of Art, 1985.
Foucher, Alfred. *The Life of the Buddha: According to the Ancient Texts and Monuments of India*. Middletown, Conn.: Wesleyan University Press, 1963.
Rotman, Andy. *Divine Stories: Divyāvadāna*. 2 vols. Boston: Wisdom, 2008–2017.
Zwalf, Wladimir. *A Catalogue of the Gandhāra Sculpture in the British Museum*. London: Trustees of the British Museum by the British Museum Press, 1996.

Bibliography

Anālayo, Ven. "The Buddha's Past Life as a Princess in the *Ekottarika-āgama*." *Journal of Buddhist Ethics* 22 (2015): 95–137.

Aśvaghoṣa. *Life of the Buddha*. Translated by Patrick Olivelle. New York: New York University Press / JJC Foundation, 2008.

Battin, Pabst M. *The Ethics of Suicide: Historical Sources*. New York: Oxford University Press, 2015.

Bloch, T[heodor]. "Two Inscriptions on Buddhist Images." *Epigraphia Indica* 8 (1905): 179–82.

Boucher, Daniel. *Bodhisattvas of the Forest and the Formation of the Mahāyāna: A Study and Translation of the "Rāṣṭrapālaparipṛcchā-sūtra."* Honolulu: University of Hawai'i Press, 2008.

Brown, Robert L. "The Emaciated Buddha Images: Asceticism, Health, and Body." In *Living in a Life in Accord with Dhamma: Papers in Honor of Jean Boisselier on His Eightieth Birthday*, edited by Natasha Eilenberg, M. C. Subhadradis Diskul, and Robert L. Brown, 105–15. Bangkok: Silpakorn University, 1997.

Buddhacarita: In Praise of Buddha's Acts by Aśvaghoṣa. Translated by Charles Willemen. Berkeley, Calif.: Numata Center for Buddhist Translation and Research, 2009.

Buddhist Birth-stories (Jataka Tales): The Commentarial Introduction Entitled Nidāna-kātha, the Story of the Lineage. Translated by Thomas William Rhys Davids. London: Trubner, 1880.

The Connected Discourses of the Buddha: A Translation of the Saṃyutta Nikāya. 2 vols. Translated by Bhikkhu Bodhi. Boston: Wisdom, 2003.

Connell, Raewyn, and James W. Messerschmidt. "Hegemonic Masculinity: Rethinking the Concept." *Gender & Society* 19, no. 6 (December 2005): 829–59.

Dazhidu lun 大智度論 [Sk. **Mahāprajñāpāramitopadeśa*]. Translated by Kumārajīva (344–413). *T.* vol. 25, no. 1509.

DeCaroli, Robert. *Image Problems: The Origin and Development of the Buddha's Image in Early South Asia*. Seattle: University of Washington Press, 2015.

Dehejia, Vidya. *The Body Adorned: Dissolving Boundaries Between Sacred and Profane in Indian Art*. New York: Columbia University Press, 2009.

Derris, Karen. " 'My Sister's Future Buddhahood': A Jātaka of the Buddha's Lifetime as a Woman." In *Eminent Buddhist Women*, edited by Karma Lekshe Tsomo, 13–24. Albany: State University of New York Press, 2014.

Dundas, Paul. *The Jains*. London: Routledge, 1992.

Freiberger, Oliver. "Early Buddhism, Asceticism, and the Politics of the Middle Way." In *Asceticism and Its Critics: Historical Accounts and Comparative Perspectives*, edited by Oliver Freiberger, 235–58. New York: Oxford University Press, 2006.

Genben shuo yiqie youbu pinaiye zashi 根本說一切有部毘奈耶雜事 [Sk. *Mūlasarvāstivāda-vinaya-kṣudrakavastu*]. *T.* vol. 24, no. 1451.

The Great Tang Dynasty Record of the Western Regions. Translated by Rongxi Li. Berkeley, Calif.: Numata Center for Buddhist Translation and Research, BDK America, 1996.

Guoqu xianzai yinguo jing 過去現在因果經. Translated by Guṇabhadra (435–443). *T.* vol. 3, no. 189.
Hamilton, Sue. *Identity and Experience: The Constitution of the Human Being According to Early Buddhism*. London: Luzac Oriental, 1996.
Hargreaves, Harold. *Handbook to the Sculptures in the Peshawar Museum*. Calcutta: Government of India Central Publication Branch, 1930.
Linrothe, Rob. "Inquiries Into the Origin of the Buddha Image: A Review." *East and West* 43, no. 14 (1993): 241–256.
Liudujijing 六度集經 (Sk. **Ṣaṭ-pāramitā-saṃgraha*). Translated by Kang Senghui 康僧會 (251). *T.* vol. 3, no. 152.
The Long Discourses of the Buddha: A Translation of the Dīgha Nikāya. Translated by Maurice Walshe. Boston: Wisdom, 1995.
Lyons, Islay, and Harald Ingholt. *Gandhāran Art in Pakistan*. New York: Pantheon, 1957.
The Mahāvastu. 3 vols. Translated by J. J. Jones. London: Luzac, 1949–1956.
The Middle Length Discourses of the Buddha: A Translation of the Majjhima Nikāya. Translated by Bhikkhu Ñāṇamoli and Bhikkhu Bodhi. Boston: Wisdom, 1995.
Morris, Rekha. "Buddha Under a Ficus Tree and Two Sculptures from Mathurā in the Sackler Museum, Harvard University." *Archives of Asian Art* 51 (1998): 80–91.
Mrozik, Susanne. "The Value of Human Differences: South Asian Buddhist Contributions Toward an Embodied Virtue Theory." *Journal of Buddhist Ethics* 9 (2002): 1–33.
——. *Virtuous Bodies: The Physical Dimensions of Morality in Buddhist Ethics*. New York: Oxford University Press, 2007.
Ohnuma, Reiko. "Woman, Bodhisattva, and Buddha." *Journal of Feminist Studies in Religion* 17, no. 1 (2001): 63–83.
Powers, John. *A Bull of a Man: Images of Masculinity, Sex, and the Body in Indian Buddhism*. Cambridge, Mass.: Harvard University Press, 2009.
——. "The Gendered Buddha: Neither God nor Man, but Supremely Manly." In *God's Own Gender? Masculinities in World Religions*, edited by Daniel Gerster and Michael Krüggeler, 245–64. Baden-Baden: Ergon-Verlag, 2018.
——. "Why Practicing Virtue Is Better than Working Out: Bodies and Ethics in Indian Buddhism." *Chung-Hwa Buddhist Journal* 22 (2009): 125–52.
Rhi, Ju-Hyung [a.k.a. Juhyung]. "From Bodhisattva to Buddha: The Beginning of Iconic Representation in Buddhist Art." *Artibus Asiae* 54, nos. 3–4 (1994): 207–25.
——. "Some Textual Parallels for Gandhāran Art: Fasting Buddhas, Lalitavistara, and Karuṇāpuṇḍarīka." *Journal of the International Association of Buddhist Studies* 29, no. 1 (2006): 125–53.
Schopen, Gregory. "On Monks, Nuns and 'Vulgar' Practices: The Introduction of the Image Cult Into Indian Buddhism." *Artibus Asiae* 49, nos. 1–2 (1988): 153–68.
Sharma, Ramesh C. *Buddhist Art of Mathurā*. Delhi: Agam Kala Prakashan, 1984.
Strong, John S. "Buddha Bhakti and the Absence of the Blessed One." In *Premier Colloque Étienne Lamotte (Bruxelles et Liège, 24–27 Septembre 1989)*, 131–40. Publications de l'Institut Orientaliste de Louvain, no. 42. Louvain: Institut Orientaliste, 1993.
——. "Explicating the Buddha's Final Illness in the Context of His Other Ailments: The Making and Unmaking of Some Jātaka Tales." *Buddhist Studies Review* 29, no. 1 (2012): 17–33.

——. *The Legend of King Aśoka: A Study and Translation of the Aśokāvadāna*. Princeton, N.J.: Princeton University Press, 1983.
——. *Relics of the Buddha*. Princeton, N.J.: Princeton University Press, 2004.
Traité de la grande vertu de sagesse de Nāgārjuna (Mahāprajñāpāramitāśāstra). Book 1. Translated by Étienne Lamotte. Louvain: Institut Orientaliste, 1944.
van Lohuizen-de Leeuw, Johanna E. *The "Scythian" Period: An Approach to the History, Art, Epigraphy, and Palaeography of North India from the 1st Century BC to the 3rd Century AD*. Leiden: E. J. Brill, 1949.
Vendova, Dessislava. "The Great Life Story of the Body of the Buddha: Re-examination and Re-assessment of the Images and Narratives of the Life of Buddha Shakyamuni." PhD diss., Columbia University, 2021.
Waldschmidt, Ernst. *Das Mahaparinirvanasutra, Text in Sanskrit und Tibetisch, verglichen mit dem Pali nebst einer Übersetzung der chinesischen Entsprechung im Vinaya der Mulasarvastivadins, auf Grund von Turfan-Handschriften herausgegeben und bearbeitet*. 3 vols. Berlin: Akademie Verlag, 1950–1951.
Walters, Jonathan S. "The Buddha's Bad Karma: A Problem in the History of Theravāda Buddhism." *Numen* 37, no. 1 (1990): 70–95.
Wilson, Liz. *Charming Cadavers: Horrific Figurations of the Feminine in Indian Buddhist Hagiographic Literature*. Chicago: University of Chicago Press, 1996.
Xiuxing benqijing 修行本起經. *T.* vol. 3, no. 184.
Xuanzang 玄奘 (602–664). *Da Tang xiyuji* 大唐西域記. *T.* vol. 51, no. 2087.

TWO

How Chan Masters Became "Great Men"

Masculinity in Chinese Chan Buddhism

KEVIN BUCKELEW

DURING THE INTERREGNUM separating the Tang (618–907) and the Song (960–1279) dynasties, Chinese Buddhist monastics belonging to Chan (J. Zen) lineages obtained patronage from a powerful array of regional rulers.[1] In the Song, Chan Buddhists solidified their newfound power by securing privileged access to the abbacies of the empire's most prestigious public monasteries.[2] In addition, they composed a vast body of literature that was read and circulated with enthusiasm in Buddhist monastic communities as well as by literati and even emperors, granting the Chan tradition a profound cultural influence over elite society.[3] How did Chan Buddhists accomplish this remarkable feat?

They did so in part by reinventing norms of Chinese Buddhist excellence established in prior centuries, casting aside many inherited ideals while deploying others drawn from inside and outside the Buddhist scriptural canon in new and original ways. Whereas the Chan tradition emerged during the Tang dynasty out of an imagined genealogy of experts in meditation—the literal meaning of *chan* referred to a kind of meditation practice—by the tenth century, most Chan Buddhists had come to insist that Chan mastery entailed much more than skill in meditation. Key to the Chan tradition's reinvention of old ideals, I suggest, was the notion that Chan masters constituted an intrepid band of "great men" (Ch. *da zhangfu*).

When, during the tenth century, Chan Buddhists began deploying the trope of great manhood to articulate a normative Chan identity, the term evoked two paradigms of ideal masculinity at once. On the one hand, *great man* was used in medieval Chinese translations of Buddhist scriptures to render the Sanskrit *mahāpuruṣa*, one of the traditional epithets by which the Buddha Śākyamuni's greatness was extolled, which is also typically translated into English as "great man." As John Powers has shown, the Buddha's masculinity figured pivotally into the way he was represented and acclaimed in Indian Buddhist literature.[4] On the other hand, the term *da zhangfu* had an ancient pedigree in China extending back before the arrival of Buddhism.[5] By China's medieval period, great manhood had come to be closely associated in Chinese culture with heroic generals and ministers who risked their lives in service to the imperial state. Adopting the trope of great manhood as a normative ideal thus allowed Chan Buddhists to portray themselves and the Chan "patriarchs" that preceded them as Chinese buddhas who also embodied masculine ideals widely shared by Chinese elites.

As a number of scholars have demonstrated, the ways Chan Buddhists relied on tropes of masculinity to articulate ideals of Chan mastery demonstrably impacted how women participated in the Chan tradition. Miriam Levering has referred to Chan Buddhists' use of the term *great man* as a gendered "rhetoric of heroism," which contradicted many Song-period Chan masters' avowed commitment to the idea that men and women possess equal capacities for buddhahood.[6] Ding-hwa Hsieh notes that women students of Chan were often praised by their male Chan teachers for being "a true man among women,"[7] or in terms like the following: "Although she is a woman, she acts like a man. She is superior to any number of worthless [male] abbots."[8] Hsieh points out that praise for women Chan aspirants expressed in this manner "plays to the presumption that the distinction between men and women in the phenomenal world implies a hierarchy of superiority and inferiority. Hence it is a matter of astonishment when a woman attains the ultimate goal of the Ch'an path and a great shame when a man fails to."[9]

The same kind of formulation, in which a male Chan master praises a talented woman disciple as a great man, is found as early as the eighth century in documents from the Bao Tang school of early Chan, as Wendi Adamek has shown.[10] Such ideas cast a long shadow into the subsequent history of Chan. Building on the findings of Levering and Hsieh, Beata Grant has analyzed how the trope of great manhood continued to shape women's aspirations to Chan mastery in the Ming (1368–1644) and Qing (1644–1912) periods.[11] Most recently, several scholars have analyzed how the term *great man* continues to inform the lives of Buddhist nuns in contemporary Taiwan.[12]

In this chapter, I pursue a more comprehensive understanding of how Chan Buddhists adopted and mobilized the trope of great manhood during the Song period, as well as the sources they drew upon to do so. I also examine how the ideal of great manhood shaped male Chan masters' understandings of themselves and their spiritual goals, and how the integration of this ideal into Chan identity operated as part of an effective appeal for patronage to male Chinese elites. As the chapters by Rebecca Mendelson and Marcus Evans in this volume demonstrate, these ideals went on to reverberate well beyond Song-dynasty Chan, up to the present day, across East Asia and the globe. At the same time, I pay attention to tensions and contradictions built into Chan ideals of manhood, traces of which are evident in the writings of both Chan Buddhists and Song-period literati.

Great Manhood and Military Valor

An idiom popular among Song-dynasty Chan Buddhists exemplifies the tradition's growing emphasis on the need for Chan masters to be brave, bold, and daring: "If you don't go into the tiger cave, you won't catch the tiger cub." Finding this phrase repeated in numerous Song-period Chan discourse records, we might be forgiven for assuming it to be one of the countless aphorisms that Chan Buddhists themselves invented during the Song. In fact, this proverb is a quotation whose origins lie many hundreds of years before the rise of Chan. It is attributed to the illustrious Eastern Han-period (25–220) military general Ban Chao (32–102), who is said to have uttered the phrase while formulating a plan of battle against the nomadic Xiongnu people beyond the Han empire's northwestern frontier.[13]

Ban's biography describes him in his youth as "a man of great ambition, who did not concern himself with trifling details," but who nevertheless labored at secretarial work in order to support his parents.[14] In the course of his work, it is said, Ban came across stories of exemplary heroes from times past who had served the empire in battle and diplomacy. "After toiling a long time," we are told, "one day he abandoned his work and threw aside his brush, exclaiming: 'A great man [can] have no other ambition than to imitate Fu Jiezi (d. 65 CE) and Zhang Qian (164–114 BCE), serving meritoriously in foreign lands and being enfeoffed as a lord. How can I remain forever working amid brush and inkstone?' "[15] Although his colleagues laughed at this outburst, a physiognomist examined Ban's features and confirmed that his "swallow's chin and tiger's head" destined him for greatness, a prediction that was realized when he enlisted in the military and embarked on an extraordinary military career.[16]

In Ban's life story, imitation of inherited ideals serves as a key mechanism by which norms of heroic manhood are perpetuated from the past into the future. Only by imitating famous great men who lived before him was Ban able to conceive his own future as a martial hero, linking him into a long chain of normative exemplarity. When, a millennium later, Chan Buddhists took Ban himself as a model of great manhood that might be adapted to a Buddhist context, they connected themselves to this same chain of exemplarity. Indeed, Ban's life story appears to have been well known to Chan Buddhists in the Song. The entry for "tiger cave" (Ch. *huxue*) in an early twelfth-century Chan lexicon, for example, consists solely of a summary of Ban's biography.[17] Song-period literati also knew Ban's life story well. For example, the famous poet Su Shi (1037–1101) alluded to the "swallow's chin and tiger's head," while literati Huang Tingjian (1045–1105) and He Zhu (1052–1125) both joked about being fated to remain forever bound to literary activity rather than achieving renown for military exploits like Ban.[18]

In addition to the widely repeated phrase "If you don't go into the tiger cave, you won't catch the tiger cub," several hagiographical accounts of Chan Buddhists dating to the tenth century bear a striking resemblance to this episode in Ban's life. Chan master Yaoshan Weiyan's (746–829) entry in the 952 CE *Patriarchs' Hall Collection* (Ch. *Zutang ji*), a collection of hagiographies and discourse records attributed to Chan masters, narrates that after initially receiving the precepts from a master specializing in the study of the Buddhist monastic code (the Vinaya), Yaoshan nevertheless declined to take up his ordination master's field of expertise. He explained this decision by remarking: "A great man ought to detach from [mundane] *dharmas* (*fa*) and purify himself. How could I dedicate myself to parsing trivial behavioral matters concerning [what kind of] cloth [is appropriate for monks to wear]?"[19] Then he called upon Chan master Shitou Xiqian (701–791), from whom he went on to receive lineage transmission. Along very similar lines, the entry for Chan master Yunju Daoying (d. 902) in the same collection tells us that he received the precepts and began to specialize in study of the monastic code, but then experienced a change of heart, pronouncing: "How can a great man be confined to such a petty path and leave obscure the open-ended vastness [of the true Way]?"[20] He, too, is then said to have set out in search of a Chan master, finally receiving lineage transmission from Dongshan Liangjie (807–869).

Although the Chan masters depicted in these hagiographies lived in the eighth and ninth centuries, the appearance of these accounts for the first time in a mid-tenth-century collection suggests that—like much of Chan literature of this period—they were likely later fabrications. As such, they tell us more about emerging rhetorical strategies of tenth-century Chan Buddhists than they do about the values of those who lived in the eighth and ninth centuries.

In both cases, the rhetorical rejection of excessive concern with the Buddhist monastic code is authorized by the figure of the great man, whose lofty aspirations are understood to far exceed adherence to the inherited rules and conventions by which Buddhist monastic identity was traditionally defined in China. Just as Ban Chao's life story described him as "a man of great ambition, who did not cultivate trifling details," so Yaoshan Weiyan and Yunju Daoying are represented here as harboring ambitions that trifling matters of monastic decorum could only hold back. The idea that interest in the finer points of the Buddhist monastic code amounts to mere pedantry serves as a convenient foil against which normative Chan mastery can be defined as generous, open minded, and not bound by inherited trappings of Buddhist monasticism.

Beyond the rhetorical rejection of excessive concern with the Buddhist monastic code, these accounts might be read as rejecting the entire medieval Chinese paradigm of evaluating Buddhist monastic excellence in terms of outstanding accomplishment in a particular vocation, including not only expertise in expounding the monastic code but also other skills such as translation, thaumaturgy, or the chanting of scripture. During the Song period, Chan Buddhists repeatedly suggested that great men are expected to transcend fixed patterns of excellence.[21] But whether the stories of Yaoshan and Daoying were deliberately written to allude to Ban Chao's life story or not, like Ban these Chan Buddhists were only able to reject one set of normative ideals by appealing to another—supposedly superior—example in the trope of great manhood.

Three of a Kind: General, Minister, and Chan Master

Loyal ministers, valiant warriors: such exemplary figures filled the ranks of China's lore about great men. What about Chan masters? The idea that they were in any way comparable to these two groups was far from self-evident at the start of the Song dynasty. Rather, Chan Buddhists and their literati supporters had to invent the logic by which they could be compared to these icons of civil and martial heroism. Of course, Chan Buddhists could not manufacture such commensurability out of whole cloth. But, by chance of translation, the figure of the great man offered a shared measure of excellence.

One important example is located in a commentary on the famous *Song of Realizing the Way* (Ch. *Zhengdao ge*). The *Song* was attributed to Chan master Yongjia Xuanjue (665–713), but is first found only in the *Jingde-era Record of the Transmission of the Lamp* (Ch. *Jingde chuandeng lu*), completed in 1009, and therefore likely long postdates Yongjia's life. Four lines from the *Song of Realizing the Way* went on to be quoted again and again by Song-period Chan Buddhists:

> A great man wields the sword of wisdom,
> Its *prajñā*-edge of flaming diamond;
> Not only able to subdue heterodox minds,
> He already long ago cut off the bravery of the god Māra.[22]

At first glance, this verse seems fairly conventional for Buddhist literature. The diamond "sword of wisdom" and the subjugation of demons are common tropes in Buddhist scriptures—but here these tropes are mobilized for a new purpose.

Buddhist scriptures deploy these themes to laud the almost inconceivable achievements and capacities of the Buddha Śākyamuni and famous bodhisattvas. In the *Flower Ornament Sūtra* (Ch. *Huayan jing*), for example, the pilgrim Sudhana attributes these powers to the Bodhisattva Mañjuśrī in the context of a verse requesting that the bodhisattva bless Sudhana with divine assistance:

> O you whose body is adorned by the armor of forbearance,
> And who holds the sword of wisdom:

Against demonic dangers and evil paths,
Would that you aid me in avoiding the myriad difficulties![23]

By contrast, Yongjia's *Song of Realizing the Way* is no petition. It offers a normative definition of the great man, no longer understood to be a buddha or bodhisattva to whom one offers devotion and from whom one requests assistance, but instead standing for the buddha or bodhisattva that all students of Chan are encouraged to become.

In a commentary on Yongjia's poem, the otherwise little-known Yanqi (fl. Northern Song) gives the following remarks on the line "The great man wields the sword of wisdom, / Its *prajñā*-edge of flaming diamond":

> Among worldly fellows, those who have fervent resolution, who take up the sword of Mo Ye, whose hearts are loyal and filial, who assist and support bright gentlemen [rulers], exerting martial power over all under Heaven—these are called "men." Here [in Yongjia's *Song*, however,] the discussion of the "great man" refers to one who possesses the great wisdom that comes from having left the world to become a Buddhist monastic; who grasps the sword of wisdom, with *prajñā* as its blade, its diamond makeup a fierce flame, cutting the net of afflictions, leaving the realm of life and death. Thus is such a one called a "great man."[24]

Here not only does Yanqi connect the Buddhist "great man" to worldly martial heroes and compare the Buddhist "sword of wisdom" to the legendary "sword of Mo Ye" from Chinese antiquity; he also suggests that, between the two options, it is the Chan master and his wisdom-sword that is greater.[25] A gallant warrior is truly a "man" (Ch. *zhangfu*), Yanqi tells us, but only a Chan master warrants the loftier appellation of "*great* man."

The idea that Chan masters are equal or even superior to generals and ministers was both popular within Chan communities and effective in securing patronage from the highest levels of Chinese society during the eleventh century. Perhaps the best illustration of this rhetorical strategy's effectiveness appears in an anecdote narrated by Li Zunxu (988–1038), the brother-in-law of Song emperor Zhenzong (968–1022; r. 997–1022), about his experiences undergoing Chan training. Li's enthusiasm for Chan led him to study under and eventually receive lineage transmission (while still a layman) from Linji-lineage Chan master Guyin Yuncong (965–1032).[26]

After Yuncong's death, Li wrote a funeral epitaph commemorating his master's life and teachings in which he included the following story about his own experience of sudden awakening while studying under the master:

> The master [Yuncong] once told me of the story in which the official Fang Rufu asked [Chan master] Jingshan, "Can I study Chan?" [Jingshan] said: "This is a matter for great men; it's not something generals or ministers can do." As soon as I heard this story raised [for my consideration], it was like "a single shout left my ears deaf for three days."[27] Like being in a dark room, in a flash all was suddenly bright.[28] As though I were facing Vulture Peak [where the Buddha preached], upon hearing this I smiled [like the first Indian patriarch of the Chan lineage Mahākāśyapa].[29]

In this passage, Li describes how powerfully affected he was when Yuncong raised for his consideration a preexisting dialogue attributed to an earlier Chan master. In that earlier dialogue, Tang-period Chan master Jingshan Faqin (715–793) is said to have rebuffed a civil official requesting religious instruction by dismissively suggesting that Chan training is far too demanding for mere generals and ministers. Jingshan's reply to the official's inquiry plays upon the widespread understanding that *great manhood* was an epithet reserved precisely for heroic generals and ministers. Jingshan rhetorically overturns this assumption, suggesting instead that only Chan masters deserve to be called *great men*, and that generals and ministers ought to be excluded from this elite category.

Despite Li's close connections to the highest levels of the imperial government, he was not offended by the assertion that generals and ministers are not great men and have no business meddling in the lofty affair of Chan mastery. It is clear that he found the comparison, and the assertion that Chan masters are superior to generals and ministers, surprising—but, evidently, it was a pleasant surprise, because it triggered his enlightenment. Li's postenlightenment smile alludes to the Chan legend that when the Buddha held up a flower instead of giving a spoken sermon, everyone in his audience looked on in bewilderment except Mahākāśyapa, whose comprehension of the Buddha's meaning was demonstrated with a smile.[30]

Li's story of his own powerful reaction when Yuncong told him about the encounter between Fang Rufu and Chan master Jingshan was in turn quoted and embellished in subsequent Chan literature. A version repeated in the discourse record of Yuanwu Keqin (1063–1135), for example, adds a new element to the story. Immediately upon undergoing this awakening experience, Yuanwu tells us, Li spontaneously composed the following poem:

> To study the Way, you must be a man of iron;
> As soon as you set down your hand, your mind will be judged.
> You should directly seek unsurpassed *bodhi*;
> Don't bother with any questions of right and wrong.[31]

Here Li is credited with identifying the ideal Chan master as a "man of iron" (Ch. *tiehan*), a term closely allied with great manhood that also connotes Han Chinese ethnicity. According to the 1155 Chan miscellany *Unofficial Record of Lake Luo* (Ch. *Luohu yelu*), this poem was indeed written by Li, but not as a spontaneous response to his experience of enlightenment. Instead, Li arrived at this poem through a long series of poetic exchanges with two other literati and with the Chan master Fushan Fayuan (991–1067), during the course of which the poem went through various iterations before it reached the four-line version that Yuanwu here presents.[32]

This poem's likely origin as a collaborative effort between three literati and a Chan master exemplifies how discussing Chan mastery in terms of normative masculinity facilitated the formation of homosocial bonds between Chan masters and their elite male patrons. At the same time, Yuanwu's transposition of the finished poem into the context of Li's enlightenment is also interesting in its own right. Yuanwu reimagines Li's autobiographical anecdote to imply that hearing the story of Jingshan rebuffing a civil official prompted Li not only to suddenly comprehend the wordless truth of Chan in a flash of insight but also to grasp the normative disposition expected by Chan Buddhists of great men. In other words, even more emphatically than Li's own account, Yuanwu's narrative stages Li's experience of sudden enlightenment—a key leitmotif of Chan soteriology—as the experience of being provoked by Chan rhetoric into a new understanding of what it means to be a man.

About two centuries later, the same Jingshan story prompted the classicist and historian Li Xinchuan (1166–1243) to reflect critically on shortcomings in the class of educated men (Ch. *shidafu*) to which he belonged. As Mark Halperin notes, Li was no supporter of Buddhism, but he nonetheless agreed on several occasions to write prose commemorations of newly constructed

Buddhist buildings.[33] In one commemoration of a Buddhist temple, Li quotes the Jingshan legend alongside another (equally apocryphal) Chan anecdote, in which Chan master Yaoshan tells the famous Tang-dynasty scholar-official Li Ao (772–841) that pursuing Buddhist liberation requires one to go to the peaks of mountains and to the bottom of the sea. That dialogue concludes with Yaoshan telling Li Ao: "If your useless boudoir articles cannot be discarded, your sense of purpose will be corroded by them."[34] Although Yaoshan does not invoke here the figure of great manhood, he casts the association of Chan mastery with normative masculinity in relief by using the trope of "boudoir articles" to code attachment to domestic life as a feminine vice.[35]

On these two episodes from Chan literature, Li Xinchuan comments: "As I examine today's *shidafu*, many have [indeed] been corroded. Thus, although in name they are generals and ministers, in reality they are not great men. This is why the Buddhists look down upon and far surpass them."[36] As Halperin observes, Li's background betrays no hint of familiarity with Chan literature, so his reference to these two Chan episodes comes as a surprise.[37] It is also striking that Li goes so far as to explicitly agree with Jingshan's assertion that generals and ministers are not truly great men. In so doing, he cedes the ground of normative masculinity to Chan Buddhists, providing another example of the rhetorical power of the trope of great manhood in articulating a vision of Chan identity that would be compelling to Song-period literati.

By comparing themselves to ministers and generals, Chan Buddhists entered into a larger conversation about the relationship between civil (Ch. *wen*) and martial (Ch. *wu*) virtues in China. Because these virtues were always normatively gendered masculine, Kam Louie has proposed that elite masculinity in premodern China was mainly discussed within what he names the "*wen-wu* paradigm," rather than the better-known binary framework of yin and yang.[38] Louie's thesis suggests that civil and martial virtue together constituted the nexus of what Raewyn Connell calls "hegemonic masculinity" in premodern China. " 'Hegemonic masculinity,' " Connell writes, "is not a fixed character type, always and everywhere the same. It is, rather, the masculinity that occupies the hegemonic position in a given pattern of gender relations, a position always contestable."[39] Louie's perspective helps us see how tropes of civil and martial virtue provided essential vocabulary for the negotiation of hegemonic norms of masculinity over the course of Chinese history. In turn, such a perspective allows us to glimpse some of the ways Chan Buddhists used the language of great manhood to participate in such negotiations and partake of elite masculine hegemony.

The fact that Chan Buddhists found inspiration in the life story of Ban Chao, which offered a model of normative masculinity that privileged military service over civil work undertaken "amid brush and inkstone"—combined with countless other instances in which Chan Buddhists invoked bravery, ferocity, skill wielding a sword, and other tropes of martial heroism to characterize ideals of Chan mastery—illuminates something important about exactly how those Chan Buddhists sought to fit their own identity into larger conversations about normative masculinity in China.

As scholars have amply demonstrated over the last several decades, to be a successful Chan master during the Song dynasty (and beyond) required literary skill, and patronage from literati and rulers was often secured through the exchange of letters and poetry. Yet the rhetorical appeal to tropes of martial heroism nonetheless helped many Song-period Chan Buddhists to identify themselves most closely with the bravery and boldness of martial heroes, even as they relied on literary talent as a medium of communication. In other words, although literary skill was required of Chan masters, it was rarely singled out as a defining feature of Chan mastery or used to distinguish Chan Buddhists from rival elite traditions.[40] Instead, many Chan masters preferred to identify with a kind of martial masculinity that transcended literal military service, articulating a heroic form of distinctively Chinese buddhahood and encouraging would-be Chan masters to bravely stare death in the face—not by literally risking their lives on the battlefield, but by facing down the cycle of life and death itself through the valiant pursuit of awakening.

Picturing the Chan Master's Martial Masculinity

It was not only by writing texts that Chan Buddhists sketched the contours of normative "great manhood"; visual culture also provided an important medium through which a normatively male-gendered Chan identity was expressed. In this section, I examine how the culture of viewing and commemorating painted portraits of Chan patriarchs known for embodying the martial ethos of great manhood provided occasions for Song-period Chan Buddhists to negotiate the figural shape of Chan mastery.

By and large, portraits of Chan masters in the Song period were painted according to prevailing conventions of secular portraiture. Although the (typically) shaved heads and robes of the portrayed figures clearly signal their status as Buddhist monastics, in most cases these portraits bear little visual resemblance to other forms of Buddhist iconography, such as paintings or statues of buddhas and bodhisattvas. Yet, as Griffith Foulk and Robert Sharf have shown, Chan portraits were not simply visual reminders of Chan masters from earlier eras; they were objects of ceremonial worship in Chan monasteries as well.[41] Foulk and Sharf argue that "all such portraits, regardless of their aesthetic value or style, are of a type in respect to their religious significance: they all functioned as holy icons embodying the charisma of a Chinese Buddha."[42] At the same time, as Michele Matteini urges, considering Chan portraits in ritual context should not lead us to overlook the complex relationship "between ritual norm and visual form."[43] As we will see, the particular ways Chan masters appeared in their portraits did sometimes matter to the viewers of those portraits in Song-dynasty China.

To begin, let us consider an anecdote written by the famous Chan master Juefan Huihong (1071–1128). Huihong quotes the lines from Yongjia's *Song of Realizing the Way* that we considered in the previous section, in which the Chan master as great man wields the sword of wisdom, and comments:

> When I first read these lines, I thought that this person's [i.e., Yongjia's] spiritual bearing must be noble and unique, his majesty surpassing that of all other monks, severe and not to be trifled with. But when I saw his painted portrait—in which he sits submissively in his seat, his robe draped in casual good order, like a young teacher specializing in expounding the monastic code—I realized that his style of writing was like a saw and blade because his mind's wisdom was ferocious. One simply cannot search for such ferocity in bodily appearance.[44]

In this revealing passage, Huihong writes about his experience of reading Yongjia's *Song of Realizing the Way* and forming a mental picture of Yongjia as visibly heroic, majestic, and severe. We can understand his disappointment, then, at discovering a painted portrait in which Yongjia looked like any ordinary monk—indeed, like a monk specializing in study of the monastic code, a Buddhist archetype of civil masculinity that (as we have seen) was sometimes cast by Chan Buddhists as the antithesis of great manhood.

Only after being confronted by this disjuncture between the hero he imagined and the ordinary-looking person he encountered in painted form, Huihong tells us, did he fully recognize the insignificance of the body—and the primacy of the mind—in measuring someone's character and level of spiritual realization. Huihong's concluding reflections about the priority of mind over body accord nicely with the Chan tradition's orthodox stance. At the same time, his conclusions still leave the virtue of martial ferocity intact, even if he displaces this virtue from body to mind. Huihong's account also suggests that he and perhaps many others *did* expect an ideal Chan master, a prototypical great man, to look somehow or other visibly heroic. This expectation was shaped by textual rhetoric pervading Chan literature that relied on tropes of martial heroism drawn both from Buddhist scriptures and from the annals of China's most illustrious military generals.

Although no portrait of Yongjia survives from the Song, we do have Song-period portraits of the legendary Tang-period Chan master Linji Yixuan (d. 866). These offer a sense of Chan portraiture's visual conventions during this period and allow us to guess what Yongjia's portrait may have looked like. The influential *Record of Linji* (Ch. *Linji lu*)—attributed to Linji but actually written and edited over the course of the tenth and early eleventh centuries (and therefore attesting to Song rather than Tang interests and concerns)—made its own important contributions to the larger project of imagining Chan masters as martial heroes and "great men."[45] In one passage, Linji invites questions from the audience by saying, "Are there any skilled generals who forthwith can array their battle lines and unfurl their banners here before me? Let them try proving themselves before the assembly!"[46] In another passage, Linji harangues his listeners in the following terms for not believing in their own inherent buddhahood: "Great men [though you may be], you do not draw a man's breath."[47] In yet another passage, he tells his audience: "Followers of the Way, if you want to accord with the Dharma, you must simply begin by being great men. If you just shilly-shally along indecisively, that won't do."[48]

Linji was remembered as a ferocious Chan master, and he was famous for shouting at students rather than giving straightforward answers to their questions. Linji's fearsome reputation was reflected in some of the verse commemorations of his portrait written by Song-period Chan masters that come down to us detached from the original portraits, having been copied into their authors' discourse records. For example, Xiatang Huiyuan (1103–1176) describes Linji dripping with blood and surrounded by a landscape littered with corpses.[49] Tiantong Rujing (1163–1228), famously the teacher to Japanese Zen master Dōgen (1200–1253), opens a verse on Linji's portrait by remarking, "Holding up an empty fist, he frightens to death everyone under heaven."[50] Wuzhun Shifan (1178–1249) begins his own verse by writing, "Skilled at warfare, he yet wields no banner or spear."[51] By this he seems to mean something like Huihong's concluding reflection that Yongjia's ferocity resides in his mind rather than his body.

Curiously, the Song-period portraits of Linji that survive do not depict him raising a fist or looking particularly fearsome. One such portrait (fig. 2.1) represents Linji looking much as we might imagine the portrait of Yongjia encountered by Huihong to have looked: sitting calmly in an abbot's robe atop a wooden chair, his hands folded in his lap, and his shoes removed and arranged neatly below his crossed legs on a low platform. Yet the commemoration brushed in calligraphy onto this particular portrait and ascribed to Huihong's junior contemporary Dahui Zonggao (1089–1163) nonetheless combines an appraisal of Linji's painted appearance with allusions to the *Record of Linji* in order to evoke Linji's larger reputation for spiritual power.[52]

Here is Dahui's verse in full:

His complexion looks like it's been smeared with a pile of ash;
His shout resembles heaven-shaking thunder.
Although he's coarse and plain,
At least he doesn't "shilly-shally along indecisively."
Tut, tut, tut. What is it?
If he had not attained this [Chan] principle,
He would certainly have become a leader among bandits.[53]

In most elite Chinese contexts, speaking of someone's potential for banditry would have held an obviously pejorative connotation. But here Dahui clearly intends to *praise* Linji's reputed willingness to transgress established rules and conventions—a widely agreed-upon sign of authenticity among Chan Buddhists and an important feature of normative great manhood, as we have seen.

In several places in his collected writings, the famous Neo-Confucian philosopher Zhu Xi (1130–1200), known to have studied Dahui's writings as a young man before rejecting Buddhism as detrimental to Chinese society, comments on this particular verse and on Chan portraits generally.[54] In the first case, Dahui's comment on Linji's appearance leads Zhu to concede that the heroic character of Chan masters visible in their portraits attests to the tradition's vigor and to lament the relative lack of vigor among his fellow Neo-Confucians.[55] Elsewhere, however, Zhu's comments on the same verse by Dahui turn critical: "I have seen the painted portraits of the [Chan] patriarchs, and they are all depicted as manly heroes. Thus Master [Dahui Zong]gao said that if Linji had not become a monk, he would certainly have been a bandit leader. I also once saw the portrait [statue] of [Chan master] Guizong on Mount Lu, which was especially frightful; if he had not become a monk, he would certainly have been a great thief!"[56] Here Zhu implies that Chan masters' visual appearances reveal not commendable ferocity, but latent criminality. He suggests that Chan Buddhists' potentially subversive martial masculinity ought to *exclude* them from the ranks of the normatively law-abiding cultural elite.

Although we have no Song-period portraits matching descriptions of Linji as visually fearsome, textual evidence suggests that by the Yuan period (1279–1368)—and likely earlier than this—there were at least two discrete visual traditions for portraying Linji. In one tradition he was shown to be fearsome, and in the other, exemplified by portraits like figure 2.1, he looked more like an ordinary Chan abbot.[57] A handful of portraits of Linji that survive from Muromachi Japan (1392–1573) differ markedly from figure 2.1 and might offer clues about how the fearsome Linji was portrayed in Song-period China. In figure 2.2, for example, we see him seated on the ground rather than on a chair, with a beard and hair on the sides of his head rather than clean-shaven, eyes bulging with intensity, and mouth open apparently in mid-shout. This portrait, much more than figure 2.1, was clearly painted to render Linji's textual reputation for ferocity in visual form. Its depiction of a bearded Linji draws upon the association of facial hair with foreignness or barbarity in Chinese visual culture and calls to mind the widespread convention of painting the Chan patriarch Bodhidharma—who legendarily brought Chan from India to China—with conspicuously foreign features. Its visual portrayal of ferocity might also have evoked for Song-period viewers what Megan Bryson calls the "barbaric masculinity" associated with tantric deities like Mahākāla.[58] As Chan master Gulin Qingmao (1262–1329) suggests, portraits depicting a

FIGURE 2.1 Portrait of Linji Yixuan with inscription attributed to Dahui Zonggao. Myōshinji, Kyoto, Japan.

FIGURE 2.2 Portrait of Linji Yixuan, attributed to Shunpo Sōki (1416–1496) with inscription attributed to Oguri Sōtan (1413–1481). Tensho-in, Kyoto, Japan. Photograph by Kyoto National Museum.

fearsome Linji were likely intended to "precipitate [viewers'] spirits to take flight and guts to quiver."[59]

The doubling of Linji's visual identity evident in these two traditions of portraiture speaks to the Chan tradition's ambivalence about bodily appearance. In the case of Huihong's response to viewing the portrait of Yongjia, we see how the conventions of secular portraiture that governed the visual style of most Chan portraits might sometimes have reined in the rhetorical power of tropes of martial masculinity that filled Song-period Chan literature, reminding Huihong that such tropes are merely meant to evoke a ferocity of mind. Yet the case of Linji's portrait suggests that even the artistically conservative genre of painted Chan portraiture sometimes registered the martial heroism pervading textual representations of certain Chan masters, making way for an understanding of Chan mastery as a visibly heroic kind of great manhood.

* * *

"Buddhism's many critics" in medieval China, Bret Hinsch writes, "accuse[d] monks of a wide range of alarming practices that violated conventional masculine ideals. They pointed out that monks did not cultivate land, marry, respect filial piety, fulfill military service or corvée duties, or conduct lay rites."[60] In response to such criticisms, Hinsch notes, Buddhists sometimes sought to offer alternative ideals of specifically monastic masculinity and other times presented Buddhist monasticism as fulfilling established hegemonic Chinese ideals of masculinity in new ways. A famous example of the latter sort of adaptation centers on the normative virtue of filial piety. Pushing back against the notion that "leaving the family" to become a Buddhist monastic was unfilial, a number of Buddhist texts from medieval China presented the vocation of monasticism as counterintuitively representing the ultimate form of filial piety, since the Buddhist monastic community generated meritorious karma that could aid the monastic's parents in the afterlife.

When Chan Buddhists adopted the ideal of great manhood starting in the tenth century, they pursued a new strategy for rendering Buddhist monasticism—and Chan mastery in particular—legible and appealing to secular elites. In so doing, they succeeded in acquiring for themselves some of the cultural cachet that had long been invested in standard-bearers of hegemonic masculinity in Song-period China—namely, the legendary ministers and generals exemplifying civil and martial virtues, respectively.

In Chinese history, civil and martial virtue were understood to be complementary: both were needed for the ideal state to function. Yet the political and cultural power typically possessed by civil elites meant that the prestige of martial virtue was often subordinated to that of civil virtue. With this in mind, it is interesting to notice how, in the materials we have considered in this chapter, Chan Buddhists often chose to invoke tropes of martial bravery and to compare themselves to heroic generals when articulating what it means to be an ideal Chan master. Why did they do so?

This question is all the more puzzling in the particular context of Song-dynasty China, because the Song has long been considered an especially civil or "Confucian" dynasty.[61] Scholars of gender in China have also suggested that Song-dynasty culture tended to privilege literary or civil masculinity over martial masculinity.[62] Chan Buddhism, too, has been viewed as having become more literary and less down-to-earth during the Song. But the emphasis on martial masculinity in the Song-period Chan materials we have considered in this chapter complicates such a historiographical picture.

The figure of Chan master Linji provides a helpful focal point for considering the puzzle of martial masculinity in Song-dynasty Chan. The eminent scholar of Chan Yanagida Seizan famously proposed that the *Record of Linji* attests to a Chan movement unique to northern China during the late Tang period, which offered a simple and direct rhetorical style to appeal to the militaristic disposition of the region's non-Han rulers. This late-Tang northern tradition, Yanagida argued, was lost as the Tang gave way to the Song, and the more cultured Chan Buddhists from the south prevailed in shaping Song-period Chan identity and values.[63] In the decades following Yanagida's groundbreaking work on this and other topics in the historiography of Chan, we have learned that the *Record of Linji* dates to a period well after Linji's lifetime, and its popularity in the tenth and especially the eleventh centuries means the text illuminates more about Song-period Chan than it does about the late Tang.[64] I propose that Linji—as he is portrayed in the *Record of Linji*—is thus probably best viewed as a carefully crafted archetype of quasi-barbaric martial masculinity. I also suggest that the appeal of those character traits to educated Song-period literati has been underestimated.

The connection we find here between barbarity and martiality is not incidental. As Don J. Wyatt notes, "Traditional Chinese frequently regarded the foreign antagonists surrounding them and the barbarism they embodied as representing *wu* [martiality] in its most extreme form."[65] Analyzing legends about the early Song scholar and military man Liu Kai (947–1000) eating the raw livers of rebels whose capture he oversaw, Wyatt suggests that such stories were "aimed at cultivating dread . . . [and] intended to terrorize and demoralize both the external and domestic enemies of the Song. The intention was to project Liu Kai's capacity for confronting 'like with like' "—which is to say, barbarity with barbarity. Something similar might be said about the spiritual example offered by Linji.[66]

The appeal of martial masculinity to civil elites, in other words, may have derived in part precisely from the way it hovered at the edge of transgression. Linji, for example, straddles the boundary between heroic and threatening martial power, as well as the boundary between Chinese and "barbarian" ethnic identity. Yet, in occupying this ambiguous position, Linji makes visible fault lines within ideals of elite Chinese masculinity that we might otherwise miss. Zhu Xi's ambivalence about Chan portraiture also taps into this larger tension. On the one hand, military prowess was always considered necessary to maintaining the integrity of Chinese empire, even if some elites considered war a last resort. But the more ferociously Chinese military heroes were portrayed, the more they resembled the "barbaric" peoples whose purported lack of civility justified Chinese imperial hegemony in the first place. Similarly, the freer any man felt to buck convention and transgress elite norms of civilized masculinity, the more easily he might be taken for a thief or bandit—a kind of barbarian internal to the Chinese empire's borders threatening the sovereignty of the emperor. Understanding how Chan ideals of masculinity fit into Song-period Chinese culture thus requires not that we simply clarify typologies of civil versus martial masculinity, but that we identify in these two interconnected frameworks examples of how "masculinity is structured through contradiction," as Lynne Segal puts it.[67]

We have seen how powerful the trope of great manhood could be in articulating just what made the Chan tradition special. Yet when Juefan Huihong tells us about his uncertainty over how best to understand Yongjia's martial masculinity, we get the sense not of an innate coherence to the ideal of great manhood, but instead of an instability at the heart of this ideal. This instability emerged out of the conflicting array of interests and aspirations that were invested in Chan identity during the Song period. Chan Buddhists dealing with unresolvable tensions between universalism and elitism, mind and body, soteriology and social life, had themselves to sew Chan identity into a loosely coherent fabric. The seams of Chan identity could always come apart, but the Chan tradition's remarkable success in the Song invites us to analyze how exactly Chan Buddhists held them together.

NOTES

1. See, especially, Benjamin Brose, *Patrons and Patriarchs: Regional Rulers and Chan Monks During the Five Dynasties and Ten Kingdoms* (Honolulu: University of Hawai'i Press, 2015).
2. See T. Griffith Foulk, "Myth, Ritual, and Monastic Practice in Sung Ch'an Buddhism," in *Religion and Society in T'ang and Sung China*, ed. Patricia Buckley Ebrey and Peter N. Gregory (Honolulu: University of Hawai'i Press, 1993), 147–208; and Morten Schlütter, *How Zen Became Zen: The Dispute Over Enlightenment and the Formation of Chan Buddhism in Song-Dynasty China* (Honolulu: University of Hawai'i Press, 2008).
3. Albert Welter, *Monks, Rulers, and Literati: The Political Ascendancy of Chan Buddhism* (Oxford: Oxford University Press, 2006); Mark Halperin, *Out of the Cloister: Literati Perspectives on Buddhism in Sung China, 960–1279* (Cambridge, Mass.: Harvard University Asia Center, 2006).
4. John Powers, *A Bull of a Man: Images of Masculinity, Sex, and the Body in Indian Buddhism* (Cambridge, Mass.: Harvard University Press, 2009), chapter 1.
5. For example, it appears in *Mengzi* 3B2, in *Mengzi yizhu*, ed. Yang Bojun, 2 vols. (Beijing: Zhonghua shuju, 1988), 140–41; *Daode jing* 38, in *Laozi Daode jing zhu jiao shi*, ed. Lou Yulie (Beijing: Zhonghua shuju, 2008), 93; and *Han Feizi jijie*, ed. Wang Xianshen (Beijing: Zhonghua shuju, 1998), j.6, 135.
6. Miriam Levering, "Lin-chi (Rinzai) Ch'an and Gender: The Rhetoric of Equality and the Rhetoric of Heroism," in *Buddhism, Sexuality, and Gender*, ed. José Ignacio Cabezón (Albany: State University of New York Press, 1992), 137–56.
7. *Pujue Zonggao chanshi yulu*, X.1362.69:646a7–8; translation follows Ding-hwa E. Hsieh, "Images of Women in Ch'an Buddhist Literature of the Sung Period," in *Buddhism in the Sung*, ed. Peter N. Gregory and Daniel A. Getz Jr. (Honolulu: University of Hawai'i Press, 1999), 161–62.
8. *Conglin shengshi*, X.1611.86:698a11–12; translation follows Hsieh, "Images of Women," 162.
9. Hsieh, 162.
10. Wendi Adamek, *The Mystique of Transmission: On an Early Chan History and Its Contexts* (New York: Columbia University Press, 2007), 232–37.
11. Beata Grant, "Da Zhangfu: The Rhetoric of Heroism in Seventeenth-Century Chan Buddhist Writings," *Nan Nü: Men, Women, and Gender in China* 10, no. 2 (2008): 177–211.
12. Elise Anne DeVido, *Taiwan's Buddhist Nuns* (Albany: State University of New York Press, 2010), 68–70, 80–81, 87–91; Chün-fang Yü, *Passing the Light: The Incense Light Community and Buddhist Nuns in Contemporary Taiwan* (Honolulu: University of Hawai'i Press, 2013), 42, 70, 139, 211–12; Hillary Crane, "Becoming a Nun, Becoming a Man: Taiwanese Buddhist Nuns' Gender Transformation," *Religion* 37 (2007): 129–31; Ching-ning Wang, "A 'Great Man' Is No Longer Gendered: The Gender

Identity and Practice of Chan Nuns in Contemporary Taiwan," in *Buddhist Feminisms and Femininities*, ed. Karma Lekshe Tsomo (Albany: State University of New York Press, 2019), 123–29.

13. "Ban Liang liezhuan," in *Hou Hanshu* (Beijing: Zhonghua shuju, 1965), 6:47.1572. On Ban's life and career, see Li Feng, *Early China: A Social and Cultural History* (Cambridge: Cambridge University Press, 2013), 298. On the war between the Han and Xiongnu empires, see Li, *Early China*, chapter 12.
14. "Ban Liang liezhuan," 47.1571.
15. "Ban Liang liezhuan," 47.1571. Fu Jiezi was a general and Zhang Qian a diplomat, both involved in Han-period foreign relations. See Herbert A. Giles, *A Chinese Biographical Dictionary* (Shanghai: Kelly and Walsh, 1898), 229–30, 12–13.
16. "Ban Liang liezhuan," 47.1571.
17. See *Zuting shiyuan*, X.1261.64:336b3–16. Several Song-period Chan masters even made reference to the trope of the "swallow's chin and tiger's head" in writing verse commemorations of their own painted portraits. See *Foguo Yuanwu chanshi biyan lu*, *T*.1997.47:809a17–18; *Pujue Zonggao chanshu yulu*, X.1362.69: 648b11–13; and *Xutang heshang yulu*, *T*.2000.47:1061b17–18.
18. See *Su Shi shiji hezhu*, ed. Feng Yingliu (Shanghai: Shanghai guji chubanshe, 2001), 3:39.2012; Ronald Egan, "The Northern Song (1020–1126)," in *The Cambridge History of Chinese Literature*, ed. Kang-i Sun Chang and Stephen Owen (Cambridge: Cambridge University Press, 2010), 1:420; and Stuart Howard Sargent, *The Poetry of He Zhu (1052–1125): Genres, Contexts, and Creativity* (Leiden: Brill, 2007), 239.
19. *Zutang ji*, ed. Sun Changwu, Kinugawa Kenji, and Nishiguchi Yoshio (Beijing: Zhonghua shuju, 2007), 1:4.223.
20. *Zutang ji*, 1:8.364.
21. For example, *Jingde chuandeng lu*, *T*.2076.51:445a4–5; and *Foguo Yuanwu chanshi yulu*, *T*.1997.47:773c12–14.
22. *Jingde chuandeng lu*, *T*.2076.51:460c9–10.
23. *Dafang guangfo huayan jing*, 421, trans. Buddhabhadra, *T*.278.9:688c1–2.
24. *Zhengdao ge zhu*, X.1241.63:270c19–22.
25. The sword of Mo Ye is a legendary sword associated with the swordsmith of the same name, wife of swordsmith Gan Jiang. See Olivia Milburn, "The Weapons of Kings: A New Perspective on Southern Sword Legends in Early China," *Journal of the American Oriental Society* 128, no. 3 (2008): 423–37, 427.
26. See Welter, *Monks, Rulers, and Literati*, 161–62.
27. This is an allusion to a line attributed to Chan master Nanyue Huairang (677–744), discussing his reaction to the teachings of his master Mazu Daoyi (709–788). See *Jingde chuandeng lu*, *T*.2076.51:249c12–14.
28. Being in a dark room is a common Buddhist metaphor for a state of ignorance.
29. *Tiansheng guang denglu*, X.1553.78:501b9–11.
30. See Albert Welter, "Mahākāśyapa's Smile: Silent Transmission and the Kung-an Tradition," in *The Kōan: Texts and Contexts in Zen Buddhism*, ed. Steven Heine and Dale S. Wright (Oxford: Oxford University Press, 2000), 75–109.
31. *Foguo Yuanwu chanshi yulu*, *T*.1997, 47:773c5–6.
32. *Luohu yelu*, X.1577.83:394c20–395a6.

33. Halperin, *Out of the Cloister*, 197.
34. "Nanlin Baoguo si bei," in *Wuxing jinshi ji*, in *Shike shiliao xinbian*, series 1, 2nd ed. (Taipei: Xinwenfeng, 1982), 28:11.3a. Translation follows Halperin, 198.
35. As Halperin points out, Su Shi's brother Su Zhe (1039–1112) also wrote of his appreciation for the story of Yaoshan's dialogue with Li Ao. See Halperin, 69.
36. "Nanlin Baoguo si bei," in *Wuxing jinshi ji*, 11.3a. Translation follows Halperin, 198, with minor changes.
37. Halperin, 198. As Halperin notes elsewhere, the competition some literati felt with Buddhist monastics over a limited pool of talented men evinced a perceived "homology between groups that cast them as largely engaged in the same enterprise with the same goals" (189).
38. Kam Louie, *Theorising Chinese Masculinity: Society and Gender in China* (Cambridge: Cambridge University Press, 2002), chapter 1.
39. Raewyn Connell, *Masculinities*, 2nd ed. (Berkeley: University of California Press, 2005), 76.
40. On the contrary, as Jason Protass convincingly argues, literary skill was often seen by Song-period Buddhists as a worldly art inhibiting spiritual progress, even as many Buddhist monastics nonetheless participated in literary culture. See Jason Protass, *The Poetry Demon: Song-Dynasty Monks on Poetry and the Way* (Honolulu: University of Hawai'i Press, 2021), especially chapter 4.
41. T. Griffith Foulk and Robert H. Sharf, "On the Ritual Use of Ch'an Portraiture in Medieval China," *Cahiers d'Extrême-Asie* 7 (1993–1994): 149–219, 191–94.
42. Foulk and Sharf, "Ritual Use of Ch'an Portraiture," 208.
43. Michele Matteini, "On the 'True Body' of Huineng: The Matter of the Miracle," *RES: Anthropology and Aesthetics* 55–56 (2009): 42–60, 44.
44. *Zhizheng zhuan*, X.1235.63:173a1–4.
45. See Albert Welter, *The "Linji lu" and the Creation of Chan Orthodoxy: The Development of Chan's Records of Sayings Literature* (Oxford: Oxford University Press, 2008).
46. *Zhenzhou Linji Huizhao chanshi yulu*, T.1985.47:496b17–18; translation follows Ruth Fuller Sasaki, *The Record of Linji*, ed. Thomas Yūhō Kirchner (Honolulu: University of Hawai'i Press, 2009), 119, with alterations.
47. *Zhenzhou Linji Huizhao chanshi yulu*, T.1985.47:502b29–c1.
48. *Zhenzhou Linji Huizhao chanshi yulu*, T.1985.47:499a18–19; translation follows Sasaki, *Record of Linji*, 206, with minor alterations.
49. *Xiatang Huiyuan chanshi guanglu*, X.1360.69:590b24.
50. *Rujing heshang yulu*, T.2002A.48:131b12.
51. *Wuzhun Shifan chanshi yulu*, X.1382.70:270c1.
52. Based on the apparent incongruity between inscription and portrait, as well as a comparison of the calligraphy inscribed on this portrait with another surviving work of Dahui's calligraphy from the same year, Kinugawa Kenji speculates that this inscription may not be in Dahui's hand, and that the inscribed verse was originally written in commemoration of a more fearsome-looking portrait of Linji. See Kinugawa Kenji, "Zengaku sakki," *Hanazono Daigaku bungakubu kenkyū kiyō* 48 (2016): 87–142, 136–37.
53. This verse is also reproduced in *Pujue Zonggao chanshi yulu*, X.1362.69:647a6–9.

54. Daniel K. Gardner, *Learning to Be a Sage: Selections from the Conversations of Master Chu, Arranged Topically* (Berkeley: University of California Press, 1990), 11–12.
55. *Zhuzi yulei*, 8 vols. (Beijing: Zhonghua shuju, 1986), 1:4.80. See also Yanagida Seizan, "Bukkyō to Shushi no shūhen," *Zen bunka kenkyūjo kiyō* 8 (1976): 1–30, 7.
56. *Zhuzi yulei*, 8:126.3011. See also Yanagida, "Bukkyō to Shushi," 3–4; and Kinugawa, "Zengaku sakki," 134–37. On the large statue of Guizong at Mount Lu, see *Lushan ji*, *T*.2095.51:1034c29–1035a5.
57. *Gulin Qingmao chanshi yulu*, *X*.1412.71:256a24–b8.
58. Megan Bryson, *Goddess on the Frontier: Religion, Ethnicity, and Gender in Southwest China* (Stanford, Calif.: Stanford University Press, 2017), 63–64.
59. *Gulin Qingmao chanshi yulu*, *X*.1412.71:256b3–4.
60. Bret Hinsch, *Masculinities in Chinese History* (Lanham, Md.: Rowman and Littlefield, 2013), 50.
61. See, for example, Dieter Kuhn, *The Age of Confucian Rule: The Song Transformation of China* (Cambridge, Mass.: Harvard University Press, 2009), a recent historical survey of the Song.
62. For example, Patricia Buckley Ebrey, *The Inner Quarters: Marriage and the Lives of Chinese Women in the Sung Period* (Berkeley: University of California Press, 1993), 32–33.
63. Yanagida Seizan, *Rinzai roku no kenkyū* (Kyoto: Hōzōkan, 2017), 46–61.
64. See Welter, *"Linji lu"*; and Brose, *Patrons and Patriarchs*, chapter 6.
65. Don J. Wyatt, "Unsung Men of War: Acculturated Embodiments of the Martial Ethos in the Song Dynasty," in *Military Culture in Imperial China*, ed. Nicola Di Cosmo (Cambridge, Mass.: Harvard University Press, 2009), 200.
66. Wyatt, "Unsung Men of War," 199.
67. Lynne Segal, *Slow Motion: Changing Masculinities, Changing Men*, 3rd ed. (New York: Palgrave, 2007), 103; quoted in *Exploring Masculinities: Identity, Inequality, Continuity, and Change*, ed. C. J. Pascoe and Tristan Bridges (New York: Oxford University Press, 2016), 1.

Additional Primary Sources

Broughton, Jeffrey L., and Elise Yoko Watanabe, trans. *The Letters of Chan Master Dahui Pujue*. Oxford: Oxford University Press, 2017.

Cleary, Thomas, and J. C. Cleary, trans. *The Blue Cliff Record*. London: Shambhala, 2005.

Sasaki, Ruth Fuller. *The Record of Linji*. Edited by Thomas Yūhō Kirchner. Honolulu: University of Hawai'i Press, 2009.

Bibliography

Adamek, Wendi. *The Mystique of Transmission: On an Early Chan History and Its Contexts*. New York: Columbia University Press, 2007.

Brose, Benjamin. *Patrons and Patriarchs: Regional Rulers and Chan Monks During the Five Dynasties and Ten Kingdoms*. Kuroda Institute Studies in East Asian Buddhism 25. Honolulu: University of Hawai'i Press, 2015.

Bryson, Megan. *Goddess on the Frontier: Religion, Ethnicity, and Gender in Southwest China*. Stanford, Calif.: Stanford University Press, 2017.

Conglin shengshi 叢林盛事. Daorong 道融 (fl. 1197). *X*. vol. 86, no. 1611.

Connell, Raewyn. *Masculinities*. 2nd ed. Berkeley: University of California Press, 2005.

Crane, Hillary. "Becoming a Nun, Becoming a Man: Taiwanese Buddhist Nuns' Gender Transformation." *Religion* 37 (2007): 117–32.

Dafang guangfo huayan jing 大方廣佛華嚴經 [Sk. *Avataṃsaka-sūtra*]. Translated by Buddhabhadra [Ch. Fotuobatuoluo 佛馱跋陀羅, 359–429]. *T*. vol. 9, no. 278.

DeVido, Elise Anne. *Taiwan's Buddhist Nuns*. Albany: State University of New York Press, 2010.

Ebrey, Patricia Buckley. *The Inner Quarters: Marriage and the Lives of Chinese Women in the Sung Period*. Berkeley: University of California Press, 1993.

Egan, Ronald. "The Northern Song (1020–1126)." In *The Cambridge History of Chinese Literature*, vol. 1, edited by Kang-i Sun Chang and Stephen Owen, 381–464. Cambridge: Cambridge University Press, 2010.

Foulk, T. Griffith. "Myth, Ritual, and Monastic Practice in Sung Ch'an Buddhism." In *Religion and Society in T'ang and Sung China*, edited by Patricia Buckley Ebrey and Peter N. Gregory, 147–208. Honolulu: University of Hawai'i Press, 1993.

Foulk, T. Griffith, and Robert H. Sharf. "On the Ritual Use of Ch'an Portraiture in Medieval China." *Cahiers d'Extrême-Asie* 7 (1993–1994): 149–219.

Gardner, Daniel K. *Learning to Be a Sage: Selections from the Conversations of Master Chu, Arranged Topically*. Berkeley: University of California Press, 1990.

Giles, Herbert A. *A Chinese Biographical Dictionary*. London: Bernard Quaritch, 1898.

Grant, Beata. "Da Zhangfu: The Rhetoric of Heroism in Seventeenth-Century Chan Buddhist Writings." *Nan Nü: Men, Women, and Gender in China* 10, no. 2 (2008): 177–211.

Gulin Qingmao chanshi yulu 古林清茂禪師語錄. Gulin Qingmao 古林清茂 (1262–1329). X. vol. 71, no. 1412.

Halperin, Mark. *Out of the Cloister: Literati Perspectives on Buddhism in Sung China, 960–1279*. Cambridge, Mass.: Harvard University Asia Center, 2006.

Han Feizi jijie 韓非子集解. Edited by Wang Xianshen 王先慎. Beijing: Zhonghua shuju, 1998.

Hou Hanshu 後漢書. Fan Ye 范曄 (398–445). 12 vols. Beijing: Zhonghua shuju, 1965.

Hinsch, Bret. *Masculinities in Chinese History*. Lanham, Md.: Rowman and Littlefield, 2013.

Hsieh, Ding-hwa E. "Images of Women in Ch'an Buddhist Literature of the Sung Period." In *Buddhism in the Sung*, edited by Peter N. Gregory and Daniel A. Getz Jr., 148–87. Honolulu: University of Hawai'i Press, 1999.

Jingde chuandeng lu 景德傳燈錄. Daoyuan 道原 (fl. 1004) and Yang Yi 楊億 (974–1024). *T*. vol. 51, no. 2076.

Kinugawa Kenji 衣川賢次. "Zengaku sakki 禪學札記." *Hanazono Daigaku bungakubu kenkyū kiyō* 花園大学文学部研究紀要 48 (2016): 87–142.

Kuhn, Dieter. *The Age of Confucian Rule: The Song Transformation of China*. Cambridge, Mass.: Harvard University Press, 2009.

Laozi Daode jing zhu jiao shi 老子道德經注校釋. Edited by Lou Yulie 樓宇烈. Beijing: Zhonghua shuju, 2008.

Levering, Miriam L. "Lin-chi (Rinzai) Ch'an and Gender: The Rhetoric of Equality and the Rhetoric of Heroism." In *Buddhism, Sexuality, and Gender*, edited by José Ignacio Cabezón, 137–56. Albany: State University of New York Press, 1992.

Li Feng. *Early China: A Social and Cultural History*. Cambridge: Cambridge University Press, 2013.

Louie, Kam. *Theorising Chinese Masculinity: Society and Gender in China*. Cambridge: Cambridge University Press, 2002.

Luohu yelu 羅湖野錄. Xiaoying Zhongwen 曉瑩仲溫 (fl. 12th century). *X.* vol. 83, no. 1577.

Lushan ji 廬山記. Chen Shunyu 陳舜俞 (d. 1076). *T.* vol. 51, no. 2095.

Matteini, Michele. "On the 'True Body' of Huineng: The Matter of the Miracle." *RES: Anthropology and Aesthetics* 55–56 (2009): 42–60.

Mengzi yizhu 孟子譯注. Edited by Yang Bojun 楊伯峻. 2 vols. Beijing: Zhonghua shuju, 1988.

Milburn, Olivia. "The Weapons of Kings: A New Perspective on Southern Sword Legends in Early China." *Journal of the American Oriental Society* 128, no. 3 (2008): 423–37.

Pascoe, C. J., and Tristan Bridges, eds. *Exploring Masculinities: Identity, Inequality, Continuity, and Change*. New York: Oxford University Press, 2016.

Powers, John. *A Bull of a Man: Images of Masculinity, Sex, and the Body in Indian Buddhism*. Cambridge, Mass.: Harvard University Press, 2009.

Protass, Jason. *The Poetry Demon: Song-Dynasty Monks on Poetry and the Way*. Kuroda Institute Studies in East Asian Buddhism 29. Honolulu: University of Hawai'i Press, 2021.

Pujue Zonggao chanshi yulu 普覺宗杲禪師語錄. Dahui Zonggao 大慧宗杲 (1089–1163). *X.* vol. 69, no. 1362.

Rujing heshang yulu 如淨和尚語錄. Tiantong Rujing 天童如淨 (1163–1228). *T.* vol. 48, no. 2002A.

Sargent, Stuart Howard. *The Poetry of He Zhu (1052–1125): Genres, Contexts, and Creativity*. Leiden: Brill, 2007.

Sasaki, Ruth Fuller. *The Record of Linji*. Edited by Thomas Yūhō Kirchner. Honolulu: University of Hawai'i Press, 2009.

Schlütter, Morten. *How Zen Became Zen: The Dispute Over Enlightenment and the Formation of Chan Buddhism in Song-Dynasty China*. Kuroda Institute Studies in East Asian Buddhism 22. Honolulu: University of Hawai'i Press, 2008.

Segal, Lynne. *Slow Motion: Changing Masculinities, Changing Men*. 3rd ed. New York: Palgrave Macmillan, 2007.

Su Shi shiji hezhu 蘇軾詩集合注. Su Shi 蘇軾 (1037–1101). Edited by Feng Yingliu 馮應榴. 3 vols. Shanghai: Shanghai guji chubanshe, 2001.

Tiansheng guang denglu 天聖廣燈錄. Li Zunxu 李遵勗 (988–1038). *X.* vol. 78, no. 1553.

Wang, Ching-ning (Chang-shen Shih). "A 'Great Man' Is No Longer Gendered: The Gender Identity and Practice of Chan Nuns in Contemporary Taiwan." In *Buddhist*

Feminisms and Femininities, edited by Karma Lekshe Tsomo, 107–36. Albany: State University of New York Press, 2019.

Welter, Albert. *The "Linji lu" and the Creation of Chan Orthodoxy: The Development of Chan's Records of Sayings Literature*. Oxford: Oxford University Press, 2008.

——. "Mahākāśyapa's Smile: Silent Transmission and the Kung-an Tradition." In *The Kōan: Texts and Contexts in Zen Buddhism*, edited by Steven Heine and Dale S. Wright, 75–109. Oxford: Oxford University Press, 2000.

——. *Monks, Rulers, and Literati: The Political Ascendancy of Chan Buddhism*. Oxford: Oxford University Press, 2006.

Wuxing jinshi ji 吳興金石記. Lu Xinyuan 陸心源 (1838–1894). In *Shike shiliao xinbian* 石刻史料新编, series 1, 2nd ed., vol. 28, 10677–875. Taipei: Xinwenfeng, 1982.

Wuzhun Shifan chanshi yulu 無準師範禪師語錄. Wuzhun Shifan 無準師範 (1178–1249). X. vol. 70, no. 1382.

Wyatt, Don J. "Unsung Men of War: Acculturated Embodiments of the Martial Ethos in the Song Dynasty." In *Military Culture in Imperial China*, edited by Nicola Di Cosmo, 192–218. Cambridge, Mass.: Harvard University Press, 2009.

Xiatang Huiyuan chanshi guanglu 瞎堂慧遠禪師廣錄. Xiatang Huiyuan 瞎堂慧遠 (1103–1176). *X*. vol. 69, no. 1360.

Xutang heshang yulu 虛堂和尚語錄. Xutang Zhiyu 虛堂智愚 (1185–1269). *T*. vol. 47, no. 2000.

Yanagida Seizan 柳田聖山. "Bukkyō to Shushi no shūhen 仏教と朱子の周辺." *Zen bunka kenkyūjo kiyō* 禅文化研究所紀要 8 (1976): 1–30.

——. *Rinzai roku no kenkyū* 臨済録の研究. Kyoto: Hōzōkan, 2017.

Yü, Chün-fang. *Passing the Light: The Incense Light Community and Buddhist Nuns in Contemporary Taiwan*. Honolulu: University of Hawai'i Press, 2013.

Foguo Yuanwu chanshi biyan lu 佛果圜悟禪師碧巖錄. Yuanwu Keqin 圜悟克勤 (1063–1135). *T*. vol. 47, no. 1997.

Zhengdao ge zhu 證道歌註. Yanqi 彥琪 (fl. Northern Song). *X*. vol. 63, no. 1241.

Zhenzhou Linji Huizhao chanshi yulu 鎮州臨濟慧照禪師語錄. *T*. vol. 47, no. 1985.

Zhizheng zhuan 智證傳. Juefan Huihong 覺範慧洪 (1071–1128). *X*. vol. 63, no. 1235.

Zhuzi yulei 朱子語類. Zhu Xi 朱熹 (1130–1200). 8 vols. Beijing: Zhonghua shuju, 1986.

Zutang ji 祖堂集. Jing 靜 and Yun 筠 (fl. 10th century). Edited by Sun Changwu 孫昌武, Kinugawa Kenji 衣川賢次, and Nishiguchi Yoshio 西口芳男. 2 vols. Beijing: Zhonghua shuju, 2007.

Zuting shiyuan 祖庭事苑. Mu'an Shanqing 睦庵善卿 (fl. 1108). *X*. vol. 64, no. 1261.

THREE

Men of Virtue

Reexamining the Bodhisattva King in Sri Lanka

STEPHEN C. BERKWITZ

SCHOLARS IN BUDDHIST studies have ample material with which to examine how Buddhist men are constructed in literature and culture. In his book *A Bull of a Man: Images of Masculinity, Sex, and the Body in Indian Buddhism*, John Powers cites biographical narratives of the Buddha as the primary source for thinking about masculinity in Buddhist traditions. The Buddha's beauty, strength, and virtue are normally associated with his accumulation of merit over many lifetimes, and he emerges as the "ultimate man" whose very physical presence enables him to win over supporters and perform miraculous feats.[1] As the ultimate man, the Buddha simultaneously embodies both the ascetic ideal of the *brahman* (priestly or renunciant) class and the physically robust ideal of the *kṣatriya* (ruler and warrior) class.[2] He is an athletic, virile prince as well as a wonder-working renunciant who eschews material comforts. The Buddha's body displays his exceptional masculinity: not only does he possess the smooth, well-proportioned features associated with male beauty in early India but he also sports the thirty-two marks of the "great man" (P. *mahāpurisa*; Sk. *mahāpuruṣa*). These thirty-two marks similarly adorn Buddhist monarchs (P. *cakkavarti*; Sk. *cakravartin*), which reinforces the structural homology of buddhas and rulers as paragons of hegemonic masculinity.

While displaying exceptional physical beauty, the Buddha's body also reflects exceptional moral achievement. Susanne Mrozik has pointed out that Buddhist texts can contain seemingly contradictory messages concerning the body: warnings about its putrescence and the dangers of becoming attached to it coexist with praise for the irresistibly beautiful bodies of the Buddha and bodhisattvas.[3] Mrozik identifies the latter as a "physiomoral discourse" that generally ascribes positive value to bodies whose beauty signifies great moral accomplishments and that are productive for the ethical development of others.[4] In Buddhist traditions, the recognition of the varied kinds of work that physical bodies can do, from serving as objects of meditation to catalyzing veneration and moral action, enables us to explore more deeply the corporeal significance of Buddhist masculinities.

This chapter approaches the subject of Buddhist masculinities by examining a specific and somewhat enigmatic figure: the bodhisattva king in Sri Lankan Buddhism. The conflation of these two ideals—the bodhisattva and the human ruler—invites us to reflect on how images of masculinity have been used to envision great men in Buddhist traditions. The form of masculinity seen in the Sri Lankan bodhisattva king differs from the concept of the early Buddhist bodhisattva renunciant whose masculinity (as pointed out by Dessislava Vendova in chapter 1) trumps that of a ruler by epitomizing power over oneself that leads to liberation. Sri Lankan bodhisattva kings may have aspired for liberation and buddhahood, but their descriptions typically gave less attention to spiritual perfection. The bodhisattva king from medieval Sri Lanka exhibits a masculinity that differs from the heroic Chan monks (as discussed in chapter 2 by Kevin Buckelew) or Tibetan demon-tamers (as discussed by Joshua Brallier Shelton in chapter 4). These Buddhist figures occupied a different social space than did kings, with whom they could occasionally even compete for sociocultural dominance. The image of the bodhisattva king in Sri Lanka blended religious and temporal powers that were enhanced by the use of masculine imagery in textual and material cultures. This chapter will focus on inscriptional and literary representations of Buddhist kingship in Sri Lanka between roughly the tenth and sixteenth centuries of the Common Era. This material will show that the move to associate kings with bodhisattvas was by no means invariable, but its occurrence at certain periods of Sri Lankan history suggests that masculine ideals could provide the basis for theorizing about power and virtue in Buddhist traditions.

Theravāda Bodhisattvas

The fact that bodhisattvas—future buddhas or beings on the way to awakening—are found in Theravāda texts and traditions sometimes goes unrecognized.[5] Associated more commonly with vows, precepts, and ordinations in Mahāyāna Buddhism, the bodhisattva (P. *bodhisatta*) has often been taken as the key factor that differentiates the Mahāyāna from the so-called Hināyāna (lesser vehicle) traditions of mainstream Indian Buddhism.[6] Yet even within the Mahāyāna (great vehicle) there has been a range of conceptions and associations given to the bodhisattva. In some older texts, such as the first-century CE *Inquiry of Ugra* (Sk. *Ugraparipṛcchā*), the bodhisattva personifies a rare spiritual path marked by values of renunciation and detachment from worldly life, whereas in the eighth-century CE *Entrance to the Way of Awakening* (Sk. *Bodhicaryāvatāra*) the bodhisattva is a universal path conditioned by highly developed compassion and wisdom.[7] In the rhetoric of some Mahāyāna texts, it is precisely the altruistic spiritual path of the bodhisattva leading to buddhahood that marks this tradition as superior to the "lesser" Buddhist ones. Conversely, as Joshua Brallier Shelton observes in his chapter, we see the Mahāyāna bodhisattva compared unfavorably to the tantric *siddha* ("accomplished one") in the life story of Padmasambhava, who is said to have subjugated demons opposing the establishment of Buddhism in Tibet that neither king nor bodhisattva-scholar could handle.

As Jeffrey Samuels has noted, however, one also finds evidence of bodhisattvas in Theravāda literature, from stories narrating the Buddha's previous lives to aspirations and assertions made by certain kings, monks, and scribes in Theravāda lands.[8] Because the Theravāda bodhisattva is primarily associated with the Buddha's previous lives, wherein he strived to perfect ten virtues and earn sufficient merit to become a buddha who would assist others in attaining liberation and freedom from suffering, such a figure has been interpreted as an extraordinarily virtuous and determined individual. Given that buddhas appear relatively rarely in the world according to the Theravāda, and only after nearly innumerable lifetimes of striving, the bodhisattva in Theravāda is by definition a unique and special being that is not easily replicated.

In the Pāli *jātaka* stories, which appear in both canonical and noncanonical works throughout the Theravāda world, the Bodhisattva often appears as a human king who through various trials develops one of the ten perfections (P. *pāramī*; Sk. *pāramitā*): giving, morality, renunciation, wisdom, energy, forbearance, truth, resolution, loving-kindness, and equanimity.[9] The juxtaposition of bodhisattva and king as an exceptional Buddhist agent who acts in the world (as opposed to being withdrawn from it) commonly appears in the *jātakas*' depiction of a ruler who provides for his subjects, gives alms generously, and protects his kingdom from harm and danger.[10] Such notable bodhisattva kings in Theravāda literature include King Vessantara, King Sutasoma, and King Mahājanaka, and they are held to represent great virtues and illustrate some of the incredible lengths to which the Bodhisattva went in his past lives to travel the path leading up to buddhahood. They appear as the protagonists in some of the more popular *jātaka* stories, exemplifying what it took for the Bodhisattva to eventually become the Buddha.

As such, these accounts locate the Theravāda bodhisattva chiefly in the realm of narratives about past heroes who performed great deeds. This means that the Theravāda bodhisattva path was an exceptional one upon which relatively few people embarked. Nevertheless, even in Theravāda Buddhism one finds a more prescriptive account of the bodhisattva to go along with its narrative accounts. In Dhammapāla's commentary on the *Basket of Conduct* (P. *Cariyāpiṭaka*), the perfections of the bodhisattva are outlined and analyzed for the sake of one wishing to undertake them—that is, how they are practiced and accomplished by a great being who wishes to achieve the supreme awakening of buddhahood.[11] This outline of the bodhisattva path is, however, uncommon in Theravāda Buddhism, as the normative view has traditionally been that buddhas are extremely rare, and few people have attained the requisite qualities to undertake this goal.

The Paradigmatic Bodhisattva King: Sirisaṅghabodhi's Self Sacrifice

References to bodhisattva kings in written works seem to begin with the account of King Sirisaṅghabodhi (r. 251–253) in the early sixth-century *Great Chronicle* (P. *Mahāvaṃsa*), in which the legendary king is described as offering his own body to a malevolent creature (P. *yakkha*; Sk. *yakṣa*) who was causing people in the region to sicken and die. The *Great Chronicle* states that the king was a "Great Being" (P. *mahāsatta*) whose virtues made the *yakkha* quit harming the people of his kingdom.[12] Scholars tend to read this epithet as signaling that Sirisaṅghabodhi was understood to be a bodhisattva.[13] After renouncing the throne, Sirisaṅghabodhi continued his self-sacrificing ways, offering his own head to a poor villager so that the villager could redeem the bounty placed on it by the king's wicked successor.

Sirisaṅghabodhi's fulfillment of the bodhisattva ideal is elaborated upon in the Pāli and, especially, Sinhala versions of the *History of the Hatthavanagalla Monastery* (P. *Hatthavanagalla-vihāra-vaṃsa*), a narrative that celebrates this king and the founding of a monastery where he died. The fourteenth-century Sinhala text describes this king recalling the sacrifices of the Bodhisattva in *jātaka* stories and wishing to imitate the compassion and self-sacrifice of the future Buddha.[14] King Sirisaṅghabodhi's reflection on what the original Bodhisattva did in his previous lives leads him to likewise abandon his throne and retire from the life of a householder. After reflecting on the perfections achieved by the Bodhisattva and leading to his buddhahood, Sirisaṅghabodhi resolves to fulfill those perfections himself. The narrative describes how he retires to the forest and inadvertently leaves his throne to an evil-minded treasurer. Before he does so, he offers his own body to relieve the suffering of his people from a drought and again from an epidemic. The theme of this king's willingness to sacrifice his life for the benefit of others is established in the text early on.

Lest anyone doubt the king's true nature, *Attanagalu's History in Sinhala* (Si. *Eḷu Attanagalu Vaṁśaya*) describes Sirisaṅghabodhi as a "bodhisattva king."[15] His wish to renounce power and wealth is said to reflect his intentions to become a bodhisattva. An influential Theravāda analysis of basic (P. *pāramī*), intermediate (P. *upapāramī*), and ultimate (P. *paramatthapāramī*) perfections distinguishes these three levels by the sacrifice of one's belongings, limbs, and life, respectively.[16] The increasing levels of self-sacrifice by a bodhisattva become relevant for Sirisaṅghabodhi's story. The renunciation of his throne imitates a common deed undertaken by the Bodhisattva in the *jātaka*s and would be recognizable as such. As the narrative progresses, the wicked king who grabs his abandoned throne is said to feel threatened by Sirisaṅghabodhi's virtues and the lifespan he should enjoy for generating so much merit. Consequently, he issues an edict promising one thousand gold coins to whomever can bring him the ascetic Sirisaṅghabodhi's head. A poor traveler encounters the former king near the latter's forest residence and shares the news of the reward for the former king's head. Sirisaṅghabodhi, overjoyed, resolves to give his head to the traveler, who may thereby earn the gold coins while the former king can arrive at the perfection of giving and omniscience.[17] The sacrifice of his life for the sake of others is an unmistakable sign of a bodhisattva performing an ultimate perfection of virtue needed for future buddhahood.

Although the traveler initially refuses to commit a wicked act, Sirisaṅghabodhi tells him to hold out his arms. The bodhisattva king then draws a line with water around his own neck, grabs his bundle of hair, and makes a resolution (Si. *adhiṣṭhānaya*) to pull his own head clean off his body. He does so and dies on the spot, while his head falls into the travelers' hands. This location, we are told by the text, is later chosen as the site of a monastery and a relic shrine. The successor king, who is said to have seen the evil of his ways, sets about to honor the late Sirisaṅghabodhi by cremating his corpse and building a circular relic house on the spot of his funeral pyre, where all beings could honor the bodhisattva king.[18] The existence of several texts in Pāli and Sinhala about King Sirisaṅghabodhi clearly indicates that, despite his short reign of three years over the island, this king's resemblance to a bodhisattva made him into a figure of great renown and respect among the Buddhist population. These narratives and the relic shrine built to honor this king represent early efforts to celebrate the idea of a bodhisattva king as a pious individual who would be willing to sacrifice the throne and his very life to help others.

The narrative of Sirisaṅghabodhi appears to have been influential enough to lead many medieval Sri Lankan kings to adopt the name *Sirisaṅghabodhi* as part of their honorary titles.[19] The title appears in several inscriptions dedicated to different kings in the medieval period. Although his reign was said to have lasted only a few years, his personal virtues left a powerful impression on later generations. King Sirisaṅghabodhi appears to have been an attractive ideal with which other kings could associate themselves to earn public praise. Yet the association with this bodhisattva king only goes as far as a kind of eulogistic trope in *praśasti* writing, the genre of panegyric literature that was developed across South Asia to enhance the fame of ruling kings. Later Sri Lankan kings would have understandably wished to be credited with the virtues of abundant piety and extensive generosity like Sirisaṅghabodhi. However, there are few accounts of extraordinary acts of self-sacrifice made by later kings, or any descriptions of their remains being enshrined and venerated in *stūpas*. Sirisaṅghabodhi appears as a paradigmatic bodhisattva king, one whom later kings would have wished to be associated with in terms of their personal virtues, but not necessarily as a role model to imitate. In other words, the story of Sirisaṅghabodhi helped popularize the idea of bodhisattva kingship, but later Sri Lankan kings who sought this title would revise what qualities and actions should be embraced by those who assumed the mantle of a Theravāda bodhisattva king.

Praising Buddhist Kings

A famous eleventh-century line from the Jētavanārāma Slab-Inscription of King Mahinda IV asserts, "None but *bodhisattas* would become kings of Sri Lanka."[20] Based largely on this statement, both Sri Lankan and Western scholars have suggested that the medieval era in Sri Lanka was marked by the perception that the kings of the island were bodhisattva kings. References portraying kings as bodhisattvas have often been interpreted to mean that they possessed a greater sanctity for having been regarded as a bodhisattva, and that they are descendants from the same Śākya lineage into which the Buddha was allegedly born.[21] Explicit links between medieval Sinhala kings and bodhisattvas were made in textual depictions of King Sirisaṅghabodhi and in various inscriptions, all of which are sometimes taken as evidence of so-called Mahāyāna influences.[22] However, little attention has been given to understanding what this idea of a "bodhisattva king" actually meant in premodern Sri Lanka, and how it functioned in various historical and cultural contexts. I contend that the notion of the bodhisattva king is both overdetermined and undertheorized in studies of Buddhist kingship, and thus it is necessary to address these deficiencies by looking at some of the different ways that kings and bodhisattvas were related and sometimes conflated in premodern Buddhist texts. In the process of doing so, we shall see that the bodhisattva king often served as a trope to enhance the masculine power of Buddhist kings.

The late historian Leslie Gunawardana took a more cautious view of Sri Lanka's bodhisattva kings than many other scholars have done. While recognizing that the inscription in question seems to confirm that kings of Sri Lanka had to be bodhisattvas or men destined to be buddhas, he noted that we should not conclude that all kings were actually considered to be bodhisattvas by their subjects.[23] The existence of textual and epigraphic sources that allude to the identity of Sri Lankan kings and bodhisattvas still falls short of the kind of conclusive evidence required to posit that premodern kings were typically viewed and treated as spiritually exceptional future buddhas. Nor do we find clear examples of bodhisattva kings being worshipped by their contemporaries as living, quasi-divine beings who could bestow supernatural favors upon them. Instead, we see certain Sri Lankan kings from around the fourth through the sixteenth centuries being praised intermittently for possessing the virtues or titles associated with bodhisattvas, elevating them to the highest position among the Buddhist laity.[24]

Such efforts to equate kings and bodhisattvas in medieval Sri Lanka need not be taken literally as historical facts that are attested by certain texts, whether written on palm leaves or inscribed in rock. The portrayals of kings as bodhisattvas typically appear in the context of *praśasti* writing in inscriptions and manuscript texts intended to celebrate and enhance the virtues of living kings.[25] Such compositions were highly conventional and formulaic, often depicting kings in grandiose terms by comparing them with superhuman figures such as gods and bodhisattvas. Although such writing would not in itself prevent literal interpretations of bodhisattva kings, it is equally possible and even preferable to interpret such discourse on kings in more figurative ways. In fact, as we shall see, it makes more sense to read the comparisons of kings with bodhisattvas as examples of eulogistic writing about kings as pious Buddhist men.

The eulogistic praise of kings in Sri Lanka appeared in the historical record first in inscriptions carved in stone and metal and then subsequently in written texts, particularly poetic verse. I have noted elsewhere how Sinhala authors adopted the *praśasti* genre in Sri Lanka and transformed the style of eulogistic writing that originated in the mainland subcontinent and relied on the Sanskrit language to express praise for ruling kings.[26] Writing in the Sinhala language and celebrating Buddhist virtues are two of the ways in which *praśasti*s in Sri Lanka were distinctive. Much of this *praśasti* writing in Sri Lankan inscriptions appeared between the ninth and thirteenth centuries, although the island contains short donative inscriptions that date back before the beginning of the Common Era. Inspired by the *praśasti*s composed in Cōḷa and Pallava inscriptional praise, Sinhala *praśasti*s from this period typically contained statements that praise the king's genealogy, his physical appearance, his moral qualities, and his noteworthy deeds.[27] This conventional praise celebrated the king's masculine attributes in superlative ways, making him appear extraordinary and deserving of his position as the ruler of society. These inscriptions, usually composed in the Sinhala language of the island, included descriptions of the king that would enhance his power and invited comparisons with divine figures and bodhisattvas.

The popular notion that there was a fusion of the ideals of Buddhist kingship and the bodhisattva in medieval Sri Lanka overlooks two important facts.[28] First, these ideals were not uniform or consistent for any sustained period. And, second, the evidence linking Sri Lankan kings with the bodhisattva ideal is sporadic at best. Aside from the Jētavanārāma Slab-Inscription, only a handful of documented inscriptions explicitly associate kings with bodhisattvas. Most of them liken a particular king to a bodhisattva in terms of the virtues he was said to possess. For instance, King Niśśaṅkamalla (r. 1187–1196) is said to have been attached to the virtuous qualities of a bodhisattva king who, "like a parent, protects the world and the religion."[29] Elsewhere, King Vijayabāhu I (r. 1055–1110) is said to have surpassed not only the gods in his prowess, wealth, and wisdom but also the bodhisattva in his benevolence.[30] In another inscription, Mahinda IV is described as having the determination of a bodhisattva to repair a monastic building.[31] In these few statements, the king's association with a bodhisattva seems to be chiefly metaphorical. The virtues of care and generosity—here coded as masculine—are illustrated paradigmatically by describing kings as bodhisattvas that protect and provide for their subjects. Such a comparison served to enhance the fame and prestige of a living king, in much the same way that comparisons to gods would be used to elevate his reputation.[32]

In one notable exception, the Oruvaḷa Sannasa, the deed of a grant for the village of Oruvaḷa, describes on a copper plate how a living king should really be seen as a bodhisattva. "Should in the future a king of our great lineage appear," it notes, "may he wear his crown fifty-five times in Laṅkā as did our great Bodhisattva, the great king Parākrama Bāhu."[33] In describing King Parākramabāhu VI (r. 1412–1467) as an "incarnate bodhisattva" (Si. *bodhisatvāvatāra*) due to his great merit and boundless authority, the inscription expresses the expectation that he will one day become a buddha. This statement seems to confirm that a particular king could actually be regarded as a bodhisattva, chiefly because of his great virtues and his ultimate destiny for buddhahood. The king is recalled posthumously in this inscription as a long-serving monarch who possessed great merit and whose wheel of command rolls throughout the universe.[34] Parākramabāhu VI, however, was exceptional in this regard. In the vast majority of instances, the literal association of king and bodhisattva seems to be rare in the epigraphic record in Sri Lanka. Instead, kings are typically represented figuratively as extraordinary beings such as gods and bodhisattvas in *praśasti* inscriptions. In the metaphorical logic of eulogistic inscriptional writing, to be compared with a god or a bodhisattva meant being attributed with great power and great merit.

Inscriptional praise of Buddhist kings developed into a common form of textual expression between the ninth and thirteenth centuries in Sri Lanka. Local authors drew upon the examples of *praśasti*s composed in kingdoms across the mainland in languages including Sanskrit and Tamil. Carved into stone pillars and onto copper plates, Sinhala *praśasti*s eulogized the power and virtues of ruling kings, while locating them in renowned dynastic genealogies and comparing them to divine and quasi-divine beings. These inscriptions generally conform to the standard *praśasti* model found in Sanskrit epigraphy from roughly the same period. This entails fixing a genealogical succession, noting the kingly traits of the dynasty and eulogizing the ruling lord, before listing the gift or gifts bestowed by the king, as well as any imprecations against those who violate its conditions.[35] By imitating these examples from the subcontinent, Sri Lankan authors sought to attribute the fame and power of mainland kings to the ruling kings on the island. They incorporated the language of divine kingship from the mainland while adding references to bodhisattvas in order to signal the specifically Buddhist virtues of their kings. With the passage of time, Sinhala inscriptions became longer and more elaborate, and they tended to focus more upon the personal qualities of the king than on any gifts he had bestowed.[36] The kings' majestic features became the subjects of ornate praise, and often these rulers were portrayed as renowned overlords to whom other kings paid respect and tribute. In short, the inscriptional praise of Buddhist kings in Sri Lanka bears the early traces of what Sheldon Pollock has called the "aestheticization of power," whereby Sanskrit literary expressions were used to declare a king's qualifications to rule.[37] In Sri Lanka, the linguistic medium used was the Sinhala language, but ruling kings were likewise celebrated for their extraordinary features in stylistically embellished ways, with their generosity, beauty, and power eulogized in aesthetically rich inscriptional writing. However, the method of offering praise to ruling kings would begin to shift by the early thirteenth century, when inscriptions carved in rock began to decline, and poetic works in palm-leaf manuscripts started to become the primary medium of eulogistic writing. Therein the qualities of bodhisattva kings became expressed and elaborated upon in poetic compositions.

The Bodhisattva King in Literature

Beginning around the fourteenth century, Sri Lankan poets praised their ruling kings as great men who possessed extraordinary masculine qualities in aesthetically rich verse. Their eulogistic style drew upon the aims of inscriptional *praśastis*, but they employed the Sinhala poetic dialect of *eḷu* to express in pleasing language the virtue and virility of kings. The *eḷu* dialect used a smaller range of letters and a highly affected vocabulary to create distinctive forms of words and a uniquely Sinhala form of poetics. Written on palm-leaf manuscripts that were more portable than stone pillars, these Sinhala poetic texts appear designed to be recited in royal courts. Such literary works often celebrated contemporary kings as great men modeled at once after the heroic figure of the bodhisattva in Buddhist narratives and the quasi-divine, libertine images of kings from post-Gupta India.[38] Attributed with moral and physical excellence, these kings were described and praised in Sinhala literature as both bodhisattvas and masculine heroes that ruled over all spheres of human society. The juxtaposition of their morality and strength—virtues required of good Buddhist kings—made it appropriate to portray kings as manly bodhisattvas who inspired reverence and obedience. Poets celebrated their ruling kings in elaborately poetic language, identifying and praising the extraordinary characteristics that set them apart from all other men. Such poetic eulogies frequently compare such kings to gods and bodhisattvas, as both types of beings were generally seen to embody qualities that surpassed those of ordinary men.

One of the leading exemplars for a masculine bodhisattva king in medieval Sri Lankan literature was that of King Kusa in the thirteenth-century poetic work *Crest-Gem of Poetry* (Si. *Kavsiḷumiṇa*). Attributed to King Parākramabāhu II (r. 1236–1270), the *Crest-Gem of Poetry* retells the *jātaka* story of the Buddha's previous life as an ugly, mischievous king in an aesthetically rich poetic style, befitting a Sinhala adaptation of the Sanskrit *mahākāvya* genre of formalistic "great poetry" that was celebrated in royal courts throughout southern Asia. Departing from the original Pāli narrative, the bodhisattva king in the *Crest-Gem of Poetry* appears as a masculine hero whose power and virility are depicted in his romantic dalliances with attractive women and his military conquest over enemy kings.[39] In this work, the great moral attainments of a bodhisattva endowed him with physical beauty and strength, turning him into a hero worthy of acclaim and admiration. By reimagining the future Buddha as a handsome and powerful king whose accomplishments extend to the sexual and martial realms, rather than as a self-sacrificing ascetic, the *Crest-Gem of Poetry* offered subsequent authors a model for casting contemporary kings in the same mold. Therein, this King Kusa is said to display, among other things, a splendid chest that decorates the main gate to his palace when he appears there with his jeweled ornaments.[40] He is also praised for his extensive fame, which is evocatively compared to saffron paste decorating the round breasts of the maidens of the ten directions, and which extinguishes his angry, arrogant foes like the mythical submarine fire that burns up the waters at the ocean's floor.[41] As a mighty bodhisattva king, the figure of Kusa in the *Crest-Gem of Poetry* (the "best of men") represents a praiseworthy hero that embodies the worldly masculine power attributed more generally to kings in South Asian literature.

Subsequently, Sri Lankan kings become increasingly portrayed in literature like the handsome and powerful Kusa of the *Crest-Gem of Poetry.* Such monarchs, especially Parākramabāhu VI, were often said to have been born in the dynastic lineage of the Buddha, but they were typically praised extensively for their divine attributes. These poetic works are filled with figurative descriptions comparing kings and their virtues with various gods such as Śakra for prosperity, Kuvera and Anaṅga for beauty, Viṣṇu and Rāma for strength, and Bṛhaspati for knowledge.[42] Oftentimes, Sri Lankan kings are said to resemble the gods in terms of their appearance and characteristics, exemplifying their superhuman, masculine natures. Reflecting wider trends in the divinization of kingship in medieval South Asia, Sinhala authors likewise portrayed their kings not only as the embodiments of powerful gods but also as righteous bodhisattvas.[43] Their moral superiority was complemented and evidenced by their great power, wealth, and beauty. Occasionally, however, the gods were used comparatively to establish the superiority of a king who, according to the poet, even put them to shame. Either way, the panegyrical style of Sinhala court poetry typically drew upon images of extraordinary beings to elevate the fame and stature of a living king.

In this sense, Sinhala poets often connected kings with bodhisattvas in much the same way that the authors of inscriptions did centuries earlier. Kings may thus be said to resemble bodhisattvas or "buddha-aspirants" (Si. *budukuru*) just like they were said to resemble gods. The fifteenth-century *Crown of Poetry* (*Kāvyaśēkhara*) praises Parākramabāhu VI as one who "knows the entirety of the Good Dharma, with the delightful splendor of a bodhisattva."[44] This king is similarly praised in the Sinhala *Message of the Goose* (*Haṃsasandēśaya*) for possessing the desirable traits of a bodhisattva who edifies and attracts the minds of other beings.

> Making the minds of beings familiar with the customs of King Manu,
> Applying on the eyes of women the collyrium of his delightful physical beauty,
> Dispelling the suffering of various beings with his pure knowledge,
> This king carries at all times the manner of a bodhisattva.[45]

It would appear, then, that the "manner of a bodhisattva" comprised the masculine attributes of morality, beauty, and wisdom that a virtuous king embodied. His pleasing appearance is said to decorate the eyes of the women who cannot help but look and lust after him. By comparing Parākramabāhu VI to a bodhisattva, Sinhala poets celebrated his praiseworthy qualities, which could poetically be compared to those of a future buddha—the highest state that a layperson could hope to achieve.

Other works composed by different poets also extolled Parākramabāhu's bodhisattva-like attributes in Sinhala verse. The *Account of Parākramabāhu VI* (Si. *Pärakumbā Sirita*), written by an anonymous courtier, dedicates 140 stanzas to praising the living king in the *praśasti* style of panegyric writing. Many stanzas in this work celebrated the king's superlative qualities by comparing him to gods and other masculine metaphors of beauty and strength.

> Like the moon in terms of gentleness, and the Milky Ocean in terms of
> profundity,
> Like the lord of elephants in terms of power, and Mt. Meru in terms of
> steadfastness,

Like the Teacher of the Gods in terms of knowledge, and Viṣṇu in terms of might,
May King Parākramabāhu, lord of prosperity, be victorious![46]

In verses like these, the praise given to the ruling king emphasizes his many masculine virtues in divine terms. The poet draws upon kingly epithets and tropes used in ancient India, including comparing Parākramabāhu to the moon in terms of its qualities of gentleness and beneficence.[47] Evoking these qualities, the metaphor of the moon is used to highlight the physical beauty of the king, as well as the beauty created by his wealth. Such depictions of his characteristics carry over to those where he is described as an attractive and generous bodhisattva, which is another superlative figure with whom to compare and praise a king. This attribution comes in a verse that highlights the king's majestic, crowned appearance and describes him as a "buddha-aspirant."[48] The suggestion here is that the king's glorious appearance is akin to that of a bodhisattva wearing a gold crown covered with dazzling gems, an association that further glorifies the king. This association is somewhat recursive, in that the bodhisattva's highly adorned appearance, which visually distinguishes the worldly bodhisattva from most buddhas, is based on royal models. The comparison of the king to a bodhisattva in this verse is made not owing to the king's moral virtues but, rather, to his physical appearance, though his beauty could be seen as a karmic reward for his virtue.

One of the more compelling stanzas that compares Parākramabāhu VI to a bodhisattva appears in the fifteenth-century *Message of the Cuckoo* (Si. *Kōkilasandēśaya*). While, again, this represents a fleeting comparison that is overshadowed by the uses of other metaphors in the work, it nevertheless signals the attributes that serve to recall those of a bodhisattva. As opposed to highlighting the king's physical appearance, this attribution focuses more upon his praiseworthy moral conduct:

This Lord of Men, who is a buddha-aspirant, filling his ears,
With the flavor of the meaning of the Tripiṭaka Dharma, as preached by the Omniscient One,
While continually increasing his virtue, delighted the bees of alms-recipients,
With the pollen of the six-colored gems and the red water lilies of gifts.[49]

Here the poet associates the king with a bodhisattva based largely on his adherence to the Dharma and his munificence in giving alms. The king is lauded for his attributes of piety and generosity by asserting that he wishes to become a buddha in the future. By identifying Parākramabāhu with a bodhisattva, this text and several others confer upon the king some of the highest virtues that can be ascribed to a Buddhist ruler. Majestic, handsome, powerful, and generous, the king as described by the Sinhala poetry of the fifteenth century enjoyed an enhanced reputation as a masculine hero that ruled over all spheres of life.

In this sense, the notion of the bodhisattva king in Sinhala Buddhist literature appears to be related to the divine king as seen in the same poetic works. The debt that these works display to the *praśasti* genre of inscriptional writing is clearly evident in their usage of divine figures with which to compare ruling kings. As noted earlier, Sinhala poetic praise of ruling kings frequently draws upon images of gods such as Śakra and Viṣṇu to magnify the kings' power and greatness. Equally common is the use of divine figures to describe the king's physical qualities of beauty and majesty. In this way, Sinhala poets emulated Indic authors, who likewise portrayed kings as extraordinary, godlike beings through their accomplished use of metaphorical language.[50] Allusions to kings as bodhisattvas should also be seen as poetic metaphors designed to celebrate the ruling king's extraordinary virtues. The bodhisattva figure often functions as another useful metaphor in Sinhala poetic verse to illustrate a king's generosity and majesty. Akin to images of Indic gods that enhanced the reputations of kings in the subcontinent, the bodhisattva appeared as a prominent metaphor derived from the immediate contexts of Sri Lankan Buddhist culture. As such, Sinhala poets drew upon novel, contextually based metaphors to conceptualize local kings in a manner that made sense to a local Buddhist audience and that was distinct from most Indian contexts during this historical period.[51]

In other words, the poetic use of the bodhisattva to describe and praise kings, usually alongside similar comparisons made between the kings and gods, reflected moves made to render ruling kings as great men whose power and majesty were richly deserved. The comparisons to bodhisattvas were made to depict them as glorious and meritorious men who wear crowns. In the context of eulogistic verse, to describe kings as bodhisattvas appears more to celebrate their royal virtues than to label them as quintessentially moral beings who vow to fulfill perfections and attain buddhahood. Since bodhisattvas were widely recognized by Buddhist audiences to possess great stores of merit and physical beauty built up over numerous previous lives, they were seen as effective metaphors for kings in panegyric verse. Furthermore, since the bodhisattva was a distinctively Buddhist figure, poetic comparisons drawn between them, gods, and kings allowed Sri Lankan poets to indigenize the rhetorical flourishes of divine kingship borrowed from neighboring Hindu contexts and influences.[52] Local Buddhist kings could thus possess extraordinary strength, wisdom, generosity, and beauty akin to bodhisattvas as well as Indic gods. Poets often strung together series of metaphors comparing the same kings to both bodhisattvas and gods for the sake of celebrating their extraordinary qualities.

Making Great Men

In this chapter, I have argued that the notion of the bodhisattva king was frequently deployed in Sri Lankan inscriptions and Sinhala poetry as a metaphorical image to enhance the masculine virtues of the ruling king—specifically, his beauty, generosity, and power. Uncritical readings of inscriptions such as the Jētavanārāma Slab-Inscription of King Mahinda IV have led many scholars to posit that premodern Sri Lankan kings were actually seen as contemporary bodhisattvas and attributed with the range of virtues appropriate for future buddhas. The attribution of bodhisattva qualities, however, was made to make kings appear not literally as future buddhas but simply as more splendid and powerful men fit to rule over others. In the eyes of bards and poets, bodhisattva kings represented the apex of meritorious individuals who had earned their prowess, beauty, and wealth by the virtuous deeds they performed in their current and previous lives. The very idea of Sri Lanka's bodhisattva kings, more often than not, was linked to theologies of divine kingship developed in tandem with Hindu conceptions and was used to enhance the fame and power of kings to strengthen the image of their reigns both at home and abroad.[53] These kings were *godlike* rather than gods, and, likewise, the comparisons to bodhisattvas were more suggestive and figurative in nature.

Theorizing the Sri Lankan bodhisattva king presents us with some challenges that other authors in this volume also face. Megan Bryson helpfully guides this endeavor by suggesting that a connecting thread for understanding Buddhist masculinities is to make note of their hegemonic practices. Citing Raewyn Connell's notion of "hegemonic masculinity," Bryson observes that different masculine models underline the plurality of male models and roles in Buddhist traditions, and that these various figures together form a "matrix of masculinity" that uphold patriarchal systems in different Buddhist cultures. In this sense, a variety of masculine figures ranging from ascetics to kings, *siddhas* to laymen, may all compete for dominance in Buddhist communities while reinforcing the cultural dominance of men. Furthermore, Connell points out that hegemonic masculinities can be constructed in ways that do not correspond closely to the lives of actual men.[54] Sri Lankan bodhisattva kings appear in this way as ideal figures that were meant to be idolized and venerated for the great men that they were represented to be. The texts that praised bodhisattva kings effectively raised them up above other rulers and, in the process, solidified the dominant roles that men would occupy throughout the history of the island and religion.

Generally speaking, Sri Lankan Buddhist kings were described as gods and bodhisattvas in order to accentuate their qualities of power, glory, benevolence, and masculine beauty. Authors drew upon Indic deities such as Śakra, the mythical "Lord of the Gods," to emphasize a certain king's royal appearance, but they also referenced crowned bodhisattvas to make essentially the same point. King Parākramabāhu VI is in one work said to contain the "physical splendor of all the gods as if fashioned remarkably in one place" (Si. *savdev rusiri ekatänä mävu väni amutu*).[55] Importantly, this comparison is figuratively made "as if" the king contained the physical splendor of all the gods combined and expressed in his singular form. As the wearer of the crown, this king carries the appearance of a crowned bodhisattva as depicted in the literature and iconography of South Asian Buddhism:

> The gold crown that has come to the top of the head of this king, who is a buddha-aspirant,
> Colored by the light of the nine gems, is endowed with the splendor
> Of a tall and very firm mountain peak that radiates with lightning,
> Or one hundred pure rainbows upon that mountain peak.[56]

The king appears here as a buddha-aspirant because of his splendid, crowned appearance, which is compared to the peak of a mountain surrounded by lightning or rainbows. It is his body, not his moral virtues, that resembles a bodhisattva. Combining immovable strength and dazzling beauty, the physical appearance of this bodhisattva king is said to live up to his epithet.

Generally speaking, the cultural construction of masculinity in premodern Sri Lanka looked mainly toward kings and their bodies for discursive elaboration. In theorizing the male body, Todd Reeser has pointed out that its connections to culture and discourse is one of the main ways that cultures construct masculinity, and that they do so for various reasons and to different ends.[57] The bodies of kings in premodern Sri Lanka were constructed in large part through the metaphorical relations drawn by bards and poets between royal bodies and the physical features of gods and bodhisattvas. Their strength and splendor were key masculine qualities that defined kings and made them appear greater than other humans. Much like textual accounts of buddhas and monks, where their beautiful bodies reflected their worthiness and their intangible inner qualities that set them apart from others, the praise for bodhisattva kings served to indicate and celebrate their greatness.[58] Sri Lankan kings could be compared to bodhisattvas and gods because it was presumed that their magnificent, masculine qualities were the results of the many good deeds that they performed. Their moral superiority was indicated by their attractive physiques and their meritorious natures. Kings possessed physical appearances and moral virtues held to resemble gods and bodhisattvas because of what they accomplished in their past and present lives. In the cultural logic of Sri Lankan Buddhism, the superior power and beauty of kings was held to be properly expressed in masculine terms through select, conventional tropes and metaphors that made them appear as beings superior to other men and, hence, even greater than other beings.

NOTES

1. John Powers, *A Bull of a Man: Images of Masculinity, Sex, and the Body in Indian Buddhism* (Cambridge, Mass.: Harvard University Press, 2009), 22–25.
2. Powers, *Bull of a Man*, 230.
3. Susanne Mrozik, *Virtuous Bodies: The Physical Dimensions of Morality in Buddhist Ethics* (New York: Oxford University Press, 2007), 83–86.
4. Mrozik, *Virtuous Bodies*, 99.

5. Although the label "Theravāda" has recently been subject to scholarly discussion and reexamination, we may reaffirm that its identity has long been associated with textual and interpretive traditions preserved in the Pāli language and rhetorically associated with an allegedly unbroken monastic lineage that comes down from the Buddha's original disciples. For more scholarly analysis of what "Theravāda" means, see the essays in Peter Skilling, Jason A. Carbine, Claudio Cicuzza, and Santi Pakdeekham, ed., *How Theravāda is Theravāda? Exploring Buddhist Identities* (Chiang Mai: Silkworm, 2012).
6. I will use the term "bodhisattva" as it appears in Sinhala, because it is the linguistic medium of many of the texts cited herein, and also because it is more familiar to Western readers than the Pāli equivalent.
7. Barbara Clayton, "The Changing Way of the Bodhisattva: Superheroes, Saints, and Social Workers," in *The Oxford Handbook of Buddhist Ethics*, ed. Daniel Cozort and James Mark Shields (Oxford: Oxford University Press, 2018), 147.
8. Jeffrey Samuels, "The Bodhisattva Ideal in Theravāda Buddhist Theory and Practice: A Reevaluation of the Bodhisattva-Śrāvaka Opposition," *Philosophy East and West* 47, no. 3 (July 1997): 399–415, 402–4.
9. The Bodhisattva also takes the form of other kinds of humans, gods, and animals in Theravāda literature.
10. Naomi Appleton, *Jātaka Stories in Theravāda Buddhism: Narrating the Bodhisatta Path* (Surrey: Ashgate, 2010), 104.
11. See Ācariya Dhammapāla, *A Treatise on the Pāramīs: From the Commentary on the Cariyāpiṭaka*, trans. Bhikkhu Bodhi (Kandy: Buddhist Publication Society, 1996).
12. A. P. Buddhadatta, ed., *The Mahāvaṃsa: Pali Text Together with Some Later Additions* (Colombo: M. D. Gunasena, 1959), xxxvi, 82–90.
13. R. A. L. H. Gunawardana, *Robe and Plough: Monasticism and Economic Interest in Early Medieval Sri Lanka* (Tucson: University of Arizona Press, 1979), 173. It is worth noting that the *Mahāvaṃsa* commentary describes Sirisaṅghabodhi as a "righteous king" (P. *dhammikarājānaṃ*), but this text does not offer an explanation of the term *mahāsatta*. See *Vaṃsatthappakāsinī: Commentary on the Mahāvaṃsa*, ed. G. P. Malalasekera (London: Pali Text Society, 1935), 2:669.
14. Ratmalane Dharmakirti Shri Dharmarama, ed., *Pāḷi Hatthavanagallavihāravaṃsaya hā Eḷu Atvanagalu Vaṁśaya* (Peliyagoda: n.p., 1921), 45.
15. Dharmarama, *Pāḷi Hatthavanagallavihāravaṃsaya*, 56.
16. Dhammapāla, *Treatise on the Pāramīs*, 56–57.
17. Dharmarama, *Pāḷi Hatthavanagallavihāravaṃsaya*, 58–59.
18. Dharmarama, 63–64.
19. Gunawardana, *Robe and Plough*, 173. See also D. M. D. Z. Wickremasinghe, ed. and trans., *Epigraphia Zeylanica* (London: Oxford University Press, 1912), 1:213.
20. Wickremasinghe, *Epigraphia Zeylanica*, 1:240.
21. Lakshman S. Perera, *The Institutions of Ancient Ceylon from Inscriptions,* vol. 2, part 1 (Kandy: International Centre for Ethnic Studies, 2003), 167–68.
22. John Clifford Holt, *Buddha in the Crown: Avalokiteśvara in the Buddhist Traditions of Sri Lanka* (New York: Oxford University Press, 1991), 57–61.

23. Gunawardana, *Robe and Plough*, 172–73.
24. Gunawardana, 173.
25. Stephen C. Berkwitz, "Reimagining Buddhist Kingship in a Sinhala *Praśasti*," *Journal of the American Oriental Society* 136, no. 2 (2016): 325–41, 330–31.
26. Berkwitz, "Reimagining Buddhist Kingship," 327.
27. Stephen C. Berkwitz, "Divine Kingship in Medieval Sri Lanka: Dynamics in Traditions of Power and Virtue in South Asia," *Entangled Religions* 8 (2019): 15.
28. Holt, *Buddha in the Crown*, 57–58. This argument is also referenced in Lewis Doney, "Early Bodhisattva Kingship in Tibet: The Case of Tri Songdétsen," *Cahiers d'Extrême-Asie* 24 (2015): 29–48, 31.
29. D. M. D. Z. Wickremasinghe, ed. and trans., *Epigraphia Zeylanica* (London: Oxford University Press, 1928), 2:176.
30. Wickremasinghe, *Epigraphia Zeylanica*, 2:215–16.
31. Wickremasinghe, *Epigraphia Zeylanica*, 1:227–28.
32. Note that in *Niśśaṅkamalla's* Galpoṭa Slab-Inscription, it is said: "Though kings appear in human form, they are human divinities and must, therefore, be regarded as gods." See Wickremasinghe, *Epigraphia Zeylanica*, 2:121. Interestingly, although this lengthy, important inscription goes on to say that impartial kings "should be welcomed as the appearance of the Buddha," it does not explicitly instruct its readers to regard kings as a bodhisattva.
33. S. Paranavitana, ed. and trans., *Epigraphia Zeylanica* (London: Oxford University Press, 1933), 3:68–69.
34. Paranavitana, *Epigraphia Zeylanica*, 3:68–69.
35. Sheldon Pollock, "The Sanskrit Cosmopolis, 300–1300: Transculturation, Vernacularization, and the Question of Ideology," in *Ideology and Status of Sanskrit: Contributions to the History of the Sanskrit Language*, ed. J. E. M. Houben (Leiden: Brill, 1996), 211.
36. Berkwitz, "Reimagining Buddhist Kingship," 329.
37. Sheldon Pollock, *The Language of the Gods in the World of Men: Sanskrit, Culture, and Power in Premodern India* (Berkeley: University of California Press, 2006), 133–34.
38. Stephen C. Berkwitz, "Strong Men and Sensual Women in Sinhala Buddhist Poetry," in *Religious Boundaries for Sex, Gender, and Corporeality*, ed. Alexandra Cuffel, Ana Echevarria, and Georgios T. Halkias (London: Routledge, 2019), 63–64.
39. Stephen C. Berkwitz, "An Ugly King and the Mother Tongue: Notes on Kusa Jātaka in Sinhala Language and Culture," *Parallax* 18, no. 3 (2012): 56–70, 60–61.
40. Velivitiye Sorata, ed. *Kalpalatā Vyākhyā Sahita Kavsiḷumiṇa* (Galkisse: Abhaya Prakasakayo, 1966), v. 469.
41. Sorata, *Kavsiḷumiṇa*, vv. 40–41.
42. D. G. Abhayagunaratna, ed., *Pärakumbā Sirita* (Colombo: Religious and Cultural Affairs Department, [1929] 1997), vv. 104–8.
43. Daud Ali, "Kingship," in *Brill Encyclopedia of Hinduism*, ed. Knut A. Jacobsen (Leiden: Brill, 2011), 3:95.
44. Ratmalane Dharmakirti Shri Dharmarama, ed., *Kāvyaśēkhara Mahākāvya* (Kelaniya, Sri Lanka: Kelaniya Visvavidyalaya Mudranalaya, [1935] 1966), I. 8.

45. K. D. P. Wickramasinghe, ed., *Haṃsa Sandēśaya* (Colombo: M. D. Gunasena, 1995), v. 32:

manura da	*sirit sata sita sita äňda*	*līya*	
manana da	*rusiraňdana liya äsa äsa*	*līya*	
pirisi	*ňda*	*näṇin sat vaga duk dura*	*līya*
ämasa ňda	*me rada bō sat siri isi*	*līya*	

46. Abhayagunaratna, *Pärakumbā Sirita*, v. 42:

Tariňdu	*guṇayen gämbarin*	*kiriňdu*
Kiriňdu	*balayen diriyen*	*giriňdu*
Giriňdu	*nuvaṇin vikumen*	*siriňdu*
Siriňdu	*dina pärakumbuja*	*niriňdu*

47. Jan Gonda, *Ancient Indian Kingship from the Religious Point of View* (Leiden: Brill, 1966), 26.
48. Abhayagunaratna, *Pärakumbā Sirita*, v. 40.
49. P. S. Perera, *Kōkila Sandēśaya* (Colombo: S. Godage and Brothers, [1906] 2009), v. 139:

savan desū tevaḷā daṁ at rasi	*na*
savan purā niraturu susiri vaḍami	*na*
savan akuru me niriňdu tiḷiṇa tambara	*na*
savan miṇi ronin yadi biňgu keḷe naňda	*na*

50. Berkwitz, "Divine Kingship in Medieval Sri Lanka," 26.
51. On the effects of context-specific uses of metaphor, see Zoltán Kövecses, *Where Metaphors Come From: Reconsidering Context in Metaphor* (Oxford: Oxford University Press, 2015), 127–31.
52. Berkwitz, "Divine Kingship in Medieval Sri Lanka," 35.
53. Berkwitz, 43.
54. Raewyn Connell and James W. Messerschmidt, "Hegemonic Masculinity: Rethinking the Concept," *Gender & Society* 19, no. 6 (2005): 829–59, 838.
55. Abhayagunaratna, *Pärakumbā Sirita*, v. 91.
56. Abhayagunaratna, v. 40:

Vidu liya	*tara sara tuňgu siňgu siri ga*	*ta*
Udu iňdu	*sävu siya äta ehi muňdun a*	*ta*
Budu kuru	*me niriňdu ran kiruḷa ga pa*	*ta*
Räňdu	*nava miṇikän e mä vilasin yu*	*ta*

57. Todd W. Reeser, *Masculinities in Theory: An Introduction* (Malden, Mass.: Wiley-Blackwell, 2010), 91.
58. Powers, *Bull of a* Man, 227–28.

Additional Primary Sources

Ariyapala, M. B., trans. *Kavsiḷumiṇa: The Crown Jewel of Sinhala Poetry in English Prose.* Colombo: Godage International, 2004.

Cone, Margaret, and Richard F. Gombrich, trans. *The Perfect Generosity of Prince Vessantara: A Buddhist Epic.* Bristol: Pali Text Society, 2011.

Disanayaka, Kusum, trans. *Sasa Dā Vata: Bodhisattva as a Hare*. Colombo: Godage International, 2004.

Geiger, Wilhelm, trans. *The Mahāvaṃsa: Or the Great Chronicle of Ceylon*. Assisted by Mabel Haynes Bode. Oxford: Pali Text Society, [1912] 2001.

Suraweera, A. V., trans. *Rājāvaliya: Translation Into English with an Introduction*. Ratmalana: Vishva Lekha, 2000.

Bibliography

Abhayagunaratna, D. G., ed. *Pärakumbā Sirita*. Colombo: Religious and Cultural Affairs Department, [1929] 1997.

Ali, Daud. "Kingship." In *Brill Encyclopedia of Hinduism*, vol. 3, edited by Knut A. Jacobsen, 90–96. Leiden: Brill, 2011.

Appleton, Naomi. *Jātaka Stories in Theravāda Buddhism: Narrating the Bodhisatta Path*. Surrey: Ashgate, 2010.

Berkwitz, Stephen C. "Divine Kingship in Medieval Sri Lanka: Dynamics in Traditions of Power and Virtue in South Asia." *Entangled Religions* 8 (2019). https://er.ceres.rub.de/index.php/ER/article/view/8312 (accessed November 29, 2022).

——. "Reimagining Buddhist Kingship in a Sinhala *Praśasti*." *Journal of the American Oriental Society* 136, no. 2 (2016): 325–41.

——. "Strong Men and Sensual Women in Sinhala Buddhist Poetry." In *Religious Boundaries for Sex, Gender, and Corporeality*, edited by Alexandra Cuffel, Ana Echevarria, and Georgios T. Halkias, 63–77. London: Routledge, 2019.

——. "An Ugly King and the Mother Tongue: Notes on Kusa Jātaka in Sinhala Language and Culture." *Parallax* 18, no. 3 (2012): 56–70.

Buddhadatta, A. P., ed. *The Mahāvaṃsa: Pali Text Together with Some Later Additions*. Colombo: M. D. Gunasena, 1959.

Clayton, Barbara. "The Changing Way of the Bodhisattva: Superheroes, Saints, and Social Workers." In *The Oxford Handbook of Buddhist Ethics*, edited by Daniel Cozort and James Mark Shields, 135–61. Oxford: Oxford University Press, 2018.

Connell, Raewyn, and James W. Messerschmidt. "Hegemonic Masculinity: Rethinking the Concept." *Gender & Society* 19, no. 6 (2005): 829–59.

Dhammapāla, Ācariya. *A Treatise on the Pāramīs: From the Commentary on the Cariyāpiṭaka*. Translated by Bhikkhu Bodhi. Kandy: Buddhist Publication Society, 1996.

Dharmarama, Ratmalane Dharmakirti Shri, ed. *Kāvyaśēkhara Mahākāvya*. Kelaniya: Kelaniya Visvavidyalaya Mudranalaya, [1935] 1966.

——. *Pāḷi Hatthavanagallavihāravaṃsaya hā Eḷu Atvanagalu Vaṁśaya*. Peliyagoda: n.p., 1921.

Doney, Lewis. "Early Bodhisattva Kingship in Tibet: The Case of Tri Songdétsen." *Cahiers d'Extrême-Asie* 24 (2015): 29–48.

Gonda, Jan. *Ancient Indian Kingship from the Religious Point of View*. Leiden: Brill, 1966.

Gunawardana, R. A. L. H. *Robe and Plough: Monasticism and Economic Interest in Early Medieval Sri Lanka*. Tucson: University of Arizona Press, 1979.

Holt, John Clifford. *Buddha in the Crown: Avalokiteśvara in the Buddhist Traditions of Sri Lanka*. New York: Oxford University Press, 1991.

Kövecses, Zoltán. *Where Metaphors Come From: Reconsidering Context in Metaphor.* Oxford: Oxford University Press, 2015.
Malalasekera, G. P., ed. *Vaṃsatthappakāsinī: Commentary on the Mahāvaṃsa*, vol. 2. London: Pali Text Society, 1935.
Mrozik, Susanne. *Virtuous Bodies: The Physical Dimensions of Morality in Buddhist Ethics.* New York: Oxford University Press, 2007.
Paranavitana, S., ed. and trans. *Epigraphia Zeylanica*, vol. 3. London: Oxford University Press, 1933.
Perera, Lakshman S. *The Institutions of Ancient Ceylon from Inscriptions,* vol. 2, part 1. Kandy: International Centre for Ethnic Studies, 2003.
Perera, P. S. *Kōkila Sandēśaya.* Colombo: S. Godage and Brothers, [1906] 2009.
Pollock, Sheldon. *The Language of the Gods in the World of Men: Sanskrit, Culture, and Power in Premodern India.* Berkeley: University of California Press, 2006.
——. "The Sanskrit Cosmopolis, 300–1300: Transculturation, Vernacularization, and the Question of Ideology." In *Ideology and Status of Sanskrit: Contributions to the History of the Sanskrit Language,* edited by J. E. M. Houben, 197–247. Leiden: Brill, 1996.
Powers, John. *A Bull of a Man: Images of Masculinity, Sex, and the Body in Indian Buddhism.* Cambridge, Mass.: University of Harvard Press, 2009.
Reeser, Todd W. *Masculinities in Theory: An Introduction.* Malden, Mass.: Wiley-Blackwell, 2010.
Samuels, Jeffrey. "The Bodhisattva Ideal in Theravāda Buddhist Theory and Practice: A Reevaluation of the Bodhisattva-Śrāvaka Opposition." *Philosophy East and West* 47, no. 3 (July 1997): 399–415.
Skilling, Peter, Jason A. Carbine, Claudio Cicuzza, and Santi Pakdeekham, eds. *How Theravāda is Theravāda? Exploring Buddhist Identities.* Chiang Mai: Silkworm, 2012.
Sorata, Velivitiye, ed. *Kalpalatā Vyākhyā Sahita Kavsiḷumiṇa.* Galkisse: Abhaya Prakasakayo, 1966.
Wickremasinghe, D. M. D. Z., ed. and trans. *Epigraphia Zeylanica*, vol. 1. London: Oxford University Press, 1912.
——. *Epigraphia Zeylanica*, vol. 2. London: Oxford University Press, 1928.
Wickramasinghe, K. D. P., ed. *Haṃsa Sandēśaya.* Colombo: M. D. Gunasena, 1995.

PART TWO
Mighty Masters

CONTEMPORARY WESTERN MASS culture stereotypes Buddhist men as peaceful, or even effeminate, thereby subordinating Buddhist masculinities to hegemonic forms of masculine aggression and machismo. The next three chapters challenge this stereotype by showing how Buddhism has also generated powerful, martial, and macho masculinities that play hegemonic roles in different contexts. Joshua Brallier Shelton takes up Stephen C. Berkwitz's focus on Buddhist royal masculinity to examine depictions of the semilegendary Padmasambhava, a tantric master credited with introducing Buddhism to Tibet. As Shelton shows, later hagiographies elevate Padmasambhava's demon-slaying tantric masculinity over the king's masculinity, thereby ousting rulers from their previous position at the apex of hegemonic masculinity. Rebecca Mendelson brings us several centuries into the future with her analysis of martial masculinities among lay Rinzai Zen practitioners in twentieth-century Japan. Mendelson argues that Rinzai masculinity converged with other hegemonic forms of masculinity in imperial Japan, which contributed both to Rinzai's popularity among lay people and to Japan's imperial aggression. Finally, Bee Scherer discusses the machismo and sexual ethics of the Diamond Way, a contemporary lay movement of the Karma Kagyu Sect of Tibetan Buddhism. The founder and leader of the Diamond Way, the Danish lama Ole Nydahl, engages in gender stereotyping, heteromachismo, and mild homophobia, which both conform to and diverge from Indian and Tibetan Buddhist sexual ethics. By drawing attention to martial and macho forms of Buddhist masculinity, this section aims not to promote these masculinities as hegemonic ideals, but rather to demonstrate the full range and diversity of hegemonic masculinities throughout the Buddhist world.

FOUR

The Siddha Who Tamed Tibet

Padmasambhava's Tantric Masculinity

JOSHUA BRALLIER SHELTON

FEW FIGURES ENJOY such an elevated status in the Tibetan Buddhist tradition as the demon tamer Padmasambhava, the "Second Buddha" of Tibet. With over fifty different accounts of his life written across nearly eight centuries, the proliferation of materials about this extraordinary *siddha* (Sk. for "accomplished one"; T. *grub thob*) illustrates Padmasambhava's importance as a tantric master for Tibetans up to the present day. Tibetans credit this eighth-century Indian adept with taming the demonic forces of the Tibetan landscape in order to establish Buddhism in their homeland. While all Tibetans venerate him as Guru Rinpoche, their "Precious Guru," the Nyingma (or "ancient") sect claims him as their founder. Stories of his life gradually spread across geographic borders to become a central fixture in pan-Tibetan and Himalayan mythology.

The earliest versions of Padmasambhava's life story in Tibetan literature depict him as a demon tamer, and the violent subjugation of demonic forces in Tibet becomes central to his character throughout all subsequent iterations of his narrative.[1] While there is a robust history of storytelling surrounding Tibet's Precious Guru, within the Tibetan literary tradition two versions of his tale are the most enduring and substantial: Nyangrel Nyima Öser's (1124–1192) *Copper Island Biography of Padmasambhava* (T. *sLob dpon padma 'byung gnas kyi rnam thar zang gling ma*, hereafter *Copper Island*) and Orgyen Lingpa's (b. 1323) *Testament of Padmasambhava* (T. *Padma bka' thang yig*, hereafter *Testament*).

Copper Island is the first full-length narrative of Padmasambhava's life, revealed as a treasure (T. *gter*) text in the twelfth century by the Nyingma visionary Nyangrel Nyima Öser. Orgyen Lingpa also revealed his opus *The Testament of Padmasambhava* as a treasure text nearly two centuries later.[2] Both texts signaled significant moments in Nyingma history: newer schools were taking root amid the "later dissemination" (T. *phyi dar*) of Buddhist texts and practices from India to Tibet. This gave rise to an increasingly competitive sectarian environment, in which the Nyingmas had to argue for their continued relevance. It was here that Nyangrel revealed the first substantive hagiography of Padmasambhava, which Orgyen Lingpa extended significantly with his revelation two centuries later.

The *Testament* is quite a bit longer and more embellished than *Copper Island*, but the narrative arc across the stories is substantively the same. Born magically from a lotus, Padmasambhava is adopted by King Indrabodhi and installed as heir to the throne of Uḍḍiyāna. His life story parallels the Buddha's, yet with distinct tantric twists. Whereas the Buddha renounces the luxuries of royal life to wander on his quest for enlightenment, Padmasambhava orchestrates his own exile through more unconventional and violent means. While engaging in the tantric "practice of yogic conduct" (T. *brtul zhugs spyod pa*) on the roof of the royal palace, the young hero deliberately murders a minister's son in order to be exiled from the kingdom. Following his exile, Padmasambhava roams charnel grounds and obtains initiations from *ḍākinīs* (a class of tantric female deities), launching his career as a siddha, an accomplished tantric master.

According to these narratives, Padmasambhava's renown spreads through India and beyond as he subdues demons and humiliates kings, eventually reaching central Tibet, where the emperor Tri Songdétsen (742–796) hears of his magical, demon-taming prowess. Tri Songdétsen has been trying to build Samyé, the first Buddhist monastery in his empire, with the aid of the Indian scholar-translator Śāntarakṣita. But what the two accomplish by day demons come to tear down by night. Exasperated and helpless, the king dispatches an invitation to Padmasambhava to help quell the demonic forces obstructing the construction. Padmasambhava accepts the invitation and sets off from Nepal, carving his way through the Tibetan landscape, subjugating the demonic forces opposing Buddhism, and binding them under oath to protect the Buddha's doctrine. In the implicit logic of these narratives, by taming the land deities of Tibet, Padmasambhava makes possible the conversion of the land and its people to Buddhism. It also, importantly, marks him as a *masculine* figure, given the explicitly gendered dimensions of subjugation activity within the Tibetan landscape. Sources from the same period as the two texts I explore here (ca. twelfth-fourteenth centuries) often depict the Tibetan landscape as a female demoness that required taming by a male tantric master—notably, Padmasambhava. Thus, Padmasambhava's taming activity reinforces his masculinity as potent and capable.[3]

Once Padmasambhava arrives in Tibet, he aids Tri Songdétsen and Śāntarakṣita in completing Samyé and implanting Buddhism within the Tibetan geographic, cultural, and historical landscape. Before departing from Tibet to tame more demons in other lands, Padmasambhava is shown burying treasures in the Tibetan landscape and the minds of his disciples, to be revealed in future times when the Dharma begins to wane in order to revitalize Buddhism in Tibet.

Anglophone scholarship on Padmasambhava has explored his historicity, his relationship to mythmaking about Tibet's imperial period, and his central role in subjugation and violence in Tibetan ritual and myth.[4] Despite this abundance of analysis, scholars have yet to unearth and thematize how gender factors into Padmasambhava's literary persona as a supreme tantric hero. In this chapter I make three interventions in Tibetological scholarship on Tibet's Second Buddha. First, I argue that masculinities analysis reveals the hitherto unacknowledged gendered dimensions of the famed trio of "scholar, tantric master, and Dharma king" (T. *mKhen slob chos gsum*), a necessary alliance for Buddhism to flourish in Tibet; political, economic, and sociological analyses alone fail to capture that gender is a structural condition for this configuration of power, one that is brokered between men *as men*. Second, I contend that Padmasambhava's twofold capacity for taming (T. *'dul ba*) the demons of the Tibetan land and menacing kings marks his masculinity as explicitly tantric. And, third, I suggest a methodology for responsibly excavating masculine praxis from premodern Tibetan texts.

Masculinity in Buddhist Studies

Just as the broader field of gender studies has moved in recent decades from a primary focus on women and sexuality to include the study of men and masculinity, Buddhist studies scholars are just beginning to take up the issue of masculinity.[5] Tibetan sources rarely explicitly comment upon or thematize masculine praxis because, while authors call attention to the femaleness of their subject when writing about women's lives, the maleness of the dominant group remains unmarked and therefore normative.[6] Since men are the primary subjects and authors of religious writings in Tibet, there is no perceived need to signal their maleness, given the androcentric bias of patriarchal systems, discourses, and representations.[7]

Even though references to maleness do not appear in the "literal and denotative" expression of a text, "deeper and broader insights" about masculinity can still be discovered through sustained interrogation.[8] In light of this, the present chapter begins a recovery project of the equally (and entirely) gendered position of men in Tibetan Buddhist literature by way of one of its most revered male figures. Here I will suggest a methodology for charting a genealogy of masculinity with respect to the ideal of the Buddhist tantric siddha as elaborated in two major Tibetan sources.

Critically reading medieval Tibetan texts for information on masculinity requires methodological precision and close attunement to primary sources. In suggesting a preliminary methodology for this task, I take my cue from José Cabezón, whose philological precision and depth of analysis provide an important example for scholars examining classical Buddhist texts with a gender studies approach. I heed Cabezón's charge to be alert to the risk of reading Tibetan literary formations of gender as reinforcing—or even expressing—our own contemporary gender constructs. Rather, I am interested in lifting out expressions of gender we find within the Tibetan literary tradition by paying close attention to the twofold work of the textualist that Cabezón advocates: (1) philology, analysis of the text's literal features; and (2) criticism, analysis of the text's literary dimensions. While I analyze literal features by attending carefully to grammar in my close readings, this chapter engages primarily with the literary dimensions of the early narratives of Padmasambhava, following Cabezon's injunction to engage in "sustained interrogation that, unsatisfied with merely re/presenting the text's literal or denotative meaning, searches for deeper and broader insights."[9]

Ultimately, I argue that Padmasambhava's violent demon taming and humiliation of the Tibetan king Tri Songdétsen illustrate an adaptably flexible tantric masculinity that harnesses gendered technologies of power to displace the king from the top of the social hierarchy without challenging the institutional power of the king himself. Siddha masculinity trumps kingly masculinity by means of tantric prowess, without usurping the king's temporal power—or the scholastic expertise of the bodhisattva monk Śāntarakṣita, who suggested inviting Padmasambhava to Tibet. As we will see, only once the proper gender hierarchy is acknowledged between the peaceful bodhisattva scholar, the demon-taming siddha, and the Dharma-championing king, the trio of scholar, master, and king (T. *mKhen slob chos gsum*) can form a powerful masculine alliance capable of installing Buddhism in Tibet. Masculinity analysis unveils a nexus of gendered concerns at the heart of this famous triad.[10]

Padmasambhava, Hegemonic Masculinity, and Tantric Violence

As discussed in Megan Bryson's introduction to this volume, Raewyn Connell's theoretical framework for gender analysis has substantially shaped the field that has coalesced under the rubric of critical studies of men and masculinity (CSMM).[11] This chapter builds on Connell's assertion that masculinity has been marked historically by contestations for power and ascendancy in the social order, and that these contestations are a continually adaptive process witnessed in the dynamic interactions of the "reproductive arena."[12] Masculinity theorists have highlighted the importance of power antagonisms between men as a central site for establishing hegemonic masculinity. The concept of hegemonic masculinity provides a lens to analyze the power dynamics that enable individual men—by "doing" their gender such that it is legible within historically embedded models of manhood—simultaneously to secure and justify possessing the highest positions in a social hierarchy, positions that structure the lives of everyone around and beneath them.

Violence is a crucial component of the creation, operation, and adaptation of hegemonic masculinities. Connell notes that violence establishes, sustains, contests, and is supported by dominance.[13] It also serves a function in gender politics between men, drawing boundaries and making exclusions: who has the legitimate authority to use violence (and get away with it); who is immune to violence; what type of violence is used against those who are not immune; and the extent, type, and duration of violence all speak to the various positions men hold in a given hierarchy and how those positions shift and adapt within and across contexts. Drawing from Antonio Gramsci's influential theorization of hegemony, Connell suggests that the greater the violence, the less stable the social order; violence functions as a tool for establishing new hegemonic systems, maintaining those systems when threatened, or overthrowing those systems.[14] Hegemony is much more effective and enduring (demonstrating its greater hold over the social order) when it operates through the *threat* of violence instead of actual violence: consent, suggestion, and persuasion are often experienced as noncoercive, and therefore we assent more readily to social sanctions. This theorization of violence in hegemony bears significantly on our exploration of Padmasambhava due to the centrality of subjugation in early narratives of his life. The threat of violence—and the suggestion of its imminence—reinforces his power to bend kings to his will and to prevail over demons where the milder, peaceful methods of the monastic bodhisattva fail.

A reading of Padmasambhava's masculinity must account for his violence, since he is famous for his capacity to engage in *dülwa* (T. *'dul ba*), which means both converting and forcibly subjugating, and sometimes even killing. The Tibetan king Tri Songdétsen calls upon the tantric master to subjugate and convert the indigenous spirits of Tibet that oppose the introduction of Buddhism. Padmasambhava frequently adopts violence as a necessary method of *dülwa* to instill Buddhism in the minds (and land) of those who oppose it, as seen in his youthful killing of a minister's son. Later, during his missionary activity in India, he "liberates" (again *dülwa*, here as a tantric euphemism for killing) the greedy king Norbu Öden for combating Buddhism. On his way to Tibet he boils a demoness in a lake until her skin peels off because she tries to prevent him from spreading Buddhism to her homeland.

Jacob Dalton, who theorizes violence in tantric ritual and myth by contextualizing it historically, notes that the Buddhist tradition has a long history of engaging with the "extraordinary ethical complexities surrounding violence, moral convolutions that require interminable struggle and may remain irresolvable even when ethical clarity is absolutely demanded." Dalton argues that what distinguishes the tantras from other Buddhist genres is their introduction of "a whole new ethos of extreme behavior and transgressive violence" that locates its genesis in the necessarily violent subjugation of the demon Rudra.[15] Thus, to Dalton, beginning with tantra's origin myth of Rudra's subjugation, through the development of its technologies of violence in ritual exorcism, the history of tantra is intimately tied to violence.

When we put Dalton's observation into conversation with Connell's insights into the role of violence as a central technique for challenging an old hegemonic order to institute a new one, it becomes clear that Padmasambhava's violent demon subjugations, set alongside his humiliation of kings, is a crucial component of his tantric masculinity. In other words, violence and subjugation mark Padmasambhava's masculinity in decidedly tantric terms. The tantras, rooted in the myth of a cosmic order requiring Buddhist violence to stop demonic threats against the flourishing of all sentient beings, champion the use of provocative methods—antinomianism, violence, magic—to subjugate and convert the enemies of Buddhism. But those methods are only available to those qualified to engage them: the siddhas, and Padmasambhava is the siddha par excellence.

Thus, when viewed through the lens of hegemonic masculinity, Padmasambhava's tantric activity (magic, violent subjugation/conversion) becomes a vivid mark of his masculinity, a gendered position that is conspicuously unmarked in the texts, produced as they were in a patriarchal context. Padmasambhava's use of violence—or strategic opting out of overt violence in favor of nonviolent, magical methods to convince kings of his authority—is a central technique in the literary crafting of his masculinity as a hegemonic ideal.

As Megan Bryson emphasizes in her introduction to this volume, what reads as legibly and authoritatively male is not transhistorical.[16] A culturally exalted form of masculinity will only attain hegemonic status if there is a correspondent relationship between the "cultural ideal" (the "best" way to be a man) and "institutional power, collective if not individual" (the "best" men receive the most social recognition, better pay, greater deference, and more freedom).[17] Thus, by virtue of his extraordinary capacity for subjugation and power to humiliate kings, Padmasambhava is able to challenge the institutional stability of kingship as the pinnacle of the male hierarchy. By commanding individual power over the king, who sits at the summit of institutional authority, Padmasambhava harnesses the potency of institutional sanction (the king ultimately submits to his superiority and bows to him) without threatening the institution itself—he does not displace king qua king, merely king qua most powerful *man*.

This helps us understand how early narratives of Padmasambhava portray him as able to continually reassert dominance in the hegemonic order, especially in contestations with kings, who would otherwise occupy the highest place in the social hierarchy.[18] As we see in a close reading of the episode wherein Padmasambhava meets the famed Tibetan king, masculinity analysis allows us to identify strategic violence and kingly humiliation as specifically gendered technologies of hegemony.

Hegemonic Masculinity in Tibetan *Namtar*: An Intertextual Method

Heeding Connell's injunction that masculinity is simultaneously constructed and witnessed in interpersonal exchanges (rather than simply manifested via "natural"—i.e., biological—imperatives), I draw her sociological model into the domain of Buddhist literary analysis by closely reading interactions between characters in Tibetan literature for the gendered information they contain. I take my cue from gender theorists in investigating interactions and relationships between characters in narrative literature for insight into the gender ideologies at play in the historical moment of a text's production. These theorists encourage us to interrogate texts to lift out and thematize the unstated, often intimated, ideations of gender that shape the horizon of possibilities, discourses, and enactments contained within them.[19] This is evident in the characters' relationships with one another, their bodily comportments, the narrative descriptions of their dress, the activities they engage in (and how the narrator frames such activities), the level of deference they receive, their relative ease in occupying or moving through various spaces, and the way they treat other people.[20]

Narrative literature is a key site for the development of Padmasambhava's legend, and in a Tibetan context we witness this quite readily in the genre of *namtar* (T. *rnam thar*), or "stories of complete liberation." *Namtar* are principal sources for mythmaking in Tibetan literature and for portraying an ideal religious life. Recently, Tibetologists have shifted our attention away from positivist concerns with mining *namtar* for "objective" historical data points, encouraging us instead to consider the processes by which religious figures, and the narrative depictions of them, emerge, expand, and proliferate, gaining social traction over time.[21] This aligns with a broader turn in studies of hagiography, spearheaded by scholars such as Patrick Geary, who has argued that hagiography is an important site for harvesting a society's ideals and values when read across collections of texts.[22] I thus take a cue from Tibetologists Kurtis Schaeffer and Andrew Quintman, who have used Geary's insights to strong effect in recognizing the importance of intertextuality in the formation and presentation of idealized religious figures: reading across different texts helps to illuminate the larger milieu of ideological and discursive networks that produced and shaped revered figures in a given sociohistorical context.[23] And, as Joan Scott advanced in her watershed essay, gender is a useful category of analysis in the work of comprehending the complex intersections of forces that shape, produce, and demarcate social history.[24]

The Siddha Who Tamed Tibet: A Close Reading of Padmasambhava's Tantric Masculinity

Drawing upon Geary's insights into intertextual analysis, I turn to the two most substantial narratives of Padmasambhava's life: Nyangrel Nyima Öser's *Copper Island Biography of Padmasambhava* and Orgyen Lingpa's *Testament of Padmasambhava*, due to their significant role in crafting Padmasambhava's legend.[25] Both texts were produced during times of heightened sectarian competition and political upheaval; the influx of new tantric Buddhist material from India amid the "later dissemination" period (T. *phyi dar*) gave rise to new Buddhist schools that competed for resources and patronage from shifting regional powers. Crafting Padmasambhava as a mighty hero not only bolstered the Nyingma claim to relevance but also presaged a new age of religious activity by strategically (re)imagining the past. Connell's remark on the role of violence in establishing new hegemonic social orders thus helps us understand the centrality of violence in Padmasambhava's tale.

I read *Copper Island* alongside the *Testament* with particular attention to the embellishments that we witness in the *Testament*: What becomes emphasized in the story, and what fades away? In particular, what types of shifts do we notice in Padmasambhava's gendered interactions with other characters—notably, kings—and what can this tell us about Padmasambhava's tantric masculinity? I look specifically to kings because of the longstanding literary tradition of siddhas' interactions with them; as two models of idealized manhood in a Tibetan Buddhist context, the siddha and the king stand as masculine archetypes whose gendered praxis reveals data about the imbrication of cultural gender ideals with literary representations.[26]

Both *Copper Island* and the *Testament* contain numerous episodes of Padmasambhava encountering, provoking, and humiliating kings: his adopted father Indrabodhi; Ārṣadhara, king of Zahor and the father of Padmasambhava's Indian consort princess Mandārava; Nāgaviṣṇu, the Indian despot trying to destroy Bodhgaya, seat of the Buddha's enlightenment; and, famously, Tri Songdétsen. I focus here on that initial, explosive encounter between Padmasambhava and Tri Songdétsen, both because it is a famous episode in Tibetan literary history, and because it showcases the central role of masculinity in brokering power relations between two of Tibet's most famous men.

In *Copper Island* and the *Testament,* Padmasambhava succeeds in taming all of India and converting it to Buddhism. After his wide-ranging success in quelling demonic forces and winning virgin princesses as his tantric consorts, the narrative gaze shifts to Tibet, where the Tibetan emperor Tri Songdétsen has recently resolved to bring Buddhism to Tibet and construct the first Buddhist monastery. Though the plot arc is the same in both narratives, the account in *Copper Island* is predictably much shorter, given that it was the first complete *namtar* of Padmasambhava in Tibetan history. Tri Songdétsen sets out to construct the first Buddhist monastery in his empire and hears of an Indian master Śāntarakṣita, whom he invites to "tame (T. *'dul*) the earth" for the construction site, so that building will proceed smoothly.[27] Tri Songdétsen sends an escort to accompany Śāntarakṣita to the court. When the bodhisattva scholar arrives, he bows first to Tri Songdétsen as emperor, acknowledging his status. Tri Songdétsen then pays respect to Śāntarakṣita as a famed bodhisattva, after which they proceed to the planned construction site. Notably, in the *Testament* (but not in *Copper Island*), Tri Songdétsen first sets out to erect Samyé without assistance and fails. Recognizing the need for help, he dispatches messengers to invite Śāntarakṣita, who is "famous for preaching the uncontentious Dharma."[28]

In both accounts, Śāntarakṣita's orientation toward peaceful methods for taming the construction site is made explicit, along with his need to be escorted to the imperial court. Whereas Stephen Berkwitz's chapter in this volume explores how the status of bodhisattva was ascribed to kings in the Theravāda context of Sri Lanka, in the life story of Padmasambhava the bodhisattva and the king are separate but complementary figures. Moreover, when Śāntarakṣita is named a bodhisattva (T. *byang chub sems dpa'*) in this story, rather than a siddha, he undeniably represents a Mahāyāna ideal. His peaceful Mahāyāṇa methods, relative to the siddha's tantric ones, are less potent. Śāntarakṣita acknowledges: "Since the gods and demons of Tibet are inhumane and savage, and because I subdue with *bodhicitta*, I am unsure I will succeed."[29] This line plays on the multivalent meaning of the Tibetan term *dülwa* (T. *'dul ba*) as both "subduing" and "converting," and Śāntarakṣita's ambivalence toward his own success foreshadows the need for a more potent means of subduing/converting, a more powerful method to tame the earth for construction. Despite the mutual respect between Śāntarakṣita and Tri Songdétsen in which both recognize their complementarity, this peaceful partnership fails to tame the malevolent spirits surrounding them. Their masculine alliance is ultimately ineffectual in installing Buddhism in Tibet, given its incapacity to engage in the violent means necessary to overcome a capable and determined enemy.

At this early point in the story, we are already primed for the disappointing failure of the peaceful methods available to the monastic scholar and benevolent king, and the need for a figure willing to use force and "wrathful means" (T. *drag po*).[30] Thus Śāntarakṣita, the monastic Mahāyāna bodhisattva, suggests inviting Padmasambhava, the mighty tantric master, to Tibet. Despite Śāntarakṣita's high degree of wisdom and compassion, he cannot match the power of the land's demonic forces. Violence and wrath as skillful means are available only to the tantric master, not to the peaceful bodhisattva. And yet the bodhisattva plays a significant role as precursor to the tantric adept, humbly acknowledging his limitations and later teaming up with Padmasambhava to translate Indian Buddhist texts and teach the young monks at Samyé.

When the narrative shifts to Padmasambhava, we find the great master already clairvoyantly aware of the impending invitation, resting confidently in his capacity to succeed where the king and bodhisattva failed. In accepting Tri Songdétsen's invitation, but sending messengers ahead of him, Padmasambhava subtly underlines his ascendancy: unlike the monastic bodhisattva Śāntarakṣita, the tantric master requires no escort—he can singlehandedly overcome the rough terrain and malevolent forces that he knows await him. As Padmasambhava begins the journey from Nepal to Tibet, both *Copper Island* and the *Testament* identify specific features of the

Tibetan landscape and name the baleful spirits residing within them, forces opposing the Dharma with violence and intimidation.

Where the equanimous balance between the king and bodhisattva fails to meet such threats, Padmasambhava's remarkable agility and might prevail. At each point of demonic resistance, Padmasambhava displays a different magical aptitude—often with force, but not always—that renders each demonic spirit totally helpless and often humiliated. Each of these encounters brings to light and expands Padmasambhava's adaptable potency, and each one advances a unique set of masculine attributes. Sometimes it is merely "by [Padmasambhava's] blessings" that the earth deities' thunderbolts "disperse, and their strength evaporates."[31] On other occasions, Padmasambhava uses force, displaying a penchant for violence.

Copper Island and the *Testament* portray the same degree of violence in Padmasambhava's encounters with demons, emphasizing the relevance of magical tantric abilities in subduing nonhuman evil forces. We witness this when Padmasambhava encounters the massively formidable super-yak form of Yarlha Shampo, one of the most famously powerful mountain deities of Tibet. He employs *mudrā* (T. *phyag rgyas*), or tantric gestures, to bind and shackle the deity before "beating and hacking him" (in *Copper Island*), or "flogging his body and mind" (in the *Testament*).[32] Padmasambhava only stops when the demon "offers the heart of his life," after which the demon "turn[s] into a young boy with white silken braids."[33] Subdued and sworn by oath to protect the Dharma, Yarlha Shampo becomes emasculated and domesticated by the unparalleled magical power of the male siddha.

Each of the encounters showcases Padmasambhava's seemingly limitless ability to conquer even the most ferocious and terrifying enemies with a wide range of powers, both mundane and magical, at his disposal. As he nears the court, the pace of his taming activities accelerates in both texts, subduing ever-greater numbers and varieties of spirits with a single *mudrā*, effectively condensing his remarkable power. In the process we witness the dynamic and spontaneous emergence of as many methods as are required to meet any given threat. The effect is a gradually crystallized vision of idealized violent methods cohering in a single gendered subject, the siddha, characterized by a total absence of vulnerability and capable of endless variation in overcoming any obstacle.

The verb most frequently used to describe his taming activity as he carves his way through the land is *dülwa*, which, as we have seen, carries semantic valences of both subjugation and conversion. Indeed, in a Tibetan context both meanings are understood to be complementary, perhaps even indistinguishable: the land must be tamed in order for its people to be converted. Here masculinity analysis helps uncover the gendered dimensions of Padmasambhava's activity—specifically, the ferocious and virile masculinity that he expresses. Subjugation of the Tibetan landscape is explicitly gendered: as noted at the beginning of this chapter, sources from the same period (twelfth to fourteenth centuries) often depict the Tibetan landscape as a demoness that required taming by a male tantric master, Padmasambhava.[34] Thus, his taming activity reinforces not only his magical Buddhist power, but his masculine power as well: potent, capable, and fearsome.

Padmasambhava's supreme masculinity, impervious to threat and limitlessly adaptable, comes as a prelude to his meeting with the Tibetan king Tri Songdétsen, who has invited him precisely for his demon-taming powers. The encounter is recorded in both *Copper Island* and the *Testament*, though the *Copper Island* account is again much shorter. In it the Tibetan king initially resists paying homage to Padmasambhava: "The king thought, 'I am the ruler of the black-headed Tibetans, the lord of every animal. What's more, I am a king who protects the Dharma, so the master should bow to me!' "[35]

Padmasambhava quickly disabuses the king of his misconception, spontaneously singing a song (T. *mgur*) in which he identifies himself immediately as a siddha, a master of the five sciences of classical Indian Buddhism, an immortal *vidyādhara* ("awareness holder"), a chief, a hero, and a sorcerer.[36] The king, in contrast, is cast as a "red-faced demon" who is full of pride and infatuated with his great dominion.[37] These epithets are gendered male with the masculine nominalizers *bo* and *po*, but the masculinity they express reveals sharp contrasts between the ideals of manhood they represent: Padmasambhava's masculinity encompasses learning and courage, along with temporal, magical, and spiritual power. The king, in contrast, is menacing, bloated with conceit, belying an ineffectual man concerned more with his status than what he can do with it.

Padmasambhava concludes his song with a jab: "I will not prostrate to the king of Tibet, but I will 'pay homage' to the clothing you wear," whereupon he raises his palm, emits rays of light (T. *'od zer*), and burns off the king's clothing.[38] The king, recognizing his arrogance and humbly accepting Padmasambhava's supremacy, fervently prostrates to him and installs the tantric master upon a golden throne. Reading this scene through the lens of hegemonic masculinity involves analyzing the power antagonism when siddha and king meet, and how that power antagonism is negotiated. Padmasambhava, who has just dazzlingly showcased his capacity for violence against demons, here restricts it to magically burning off the demon-faced king's clothing. He does not employ overt violence in establishing superiority, but, rather, the masculine technology of humiliation, by mocking the notion of obeisance, then laying bare the king's foolish conceit for all to see. In refraining from the violence the reader has just seen him enact on the Tibetan landscape, Padmasambhava punctuates his power by strategically opting out of violence against the demon-faced king.

This dynamic between overt violence and calculated humiliation becomes even more explicit when Padmasambhava meets Tri Songdétsen in the *Testament*. The Tibetan syntax and language reinforce Padmasambhava's ascendancy over the king before the two even exchange any words: although Tri Songdétsen extends the invitation, it is in fact Padmasambhava who orchestrates the encounter. The Tibetan literally states, "Padmasambhava made a meeting with the ruling king."[39] The verb *dzépa* (T. *mdzad pa*), the basic action verb *to do*, appears here in its honorific form, underlining Padmasambhava's revered status. Thus, although the king invited the siddha to Tibet, it was actually by the siddha's power that the meeting was even able to take place.

Whereas *Copper Island* portrays the king as initially arrogant, the *Testament* nearly mocks him, relating: "The king of Tibet was surrounded by his ministers, giving the impression of a glittering brood of pigeons."[40] Padmasambhava pauses here, and we gain insight into his interior dialogue (T. *thugs dgongs la*), in which he contemplates his superiority to the king. This monologue begins with "Regarding me" (T. *nga ni*), which is notable in Tibetan, given how rarely the first-person pronoun is used in what is commonly a humilific register. Padmasambhava goes on to list various criteria that establish his authority as clearly and unequivocally superior to the king's, adopting the honorific form of verbs for himself—another notably uncommon practice in the Tibetan language. Taken together, Padmasambhava determines that, "though the king will be unhappy about it," and, although he is "a great king," the mighty siddha is in fact "*incapable* of bowing first."[41]

Rather, Tri Songdétsen should extend the first sign of respect and acknowledge the proper hegemonic hierarchy.

Meanwhile, Tri Songdétsen balks at the thought of bowing to the siddha, noting the "awkwardness of the stalled encounter" and reflecting that "as Śāntarakṣita has already offered me, the king, a prostration, so too should this master."[42] He is the king, after all! And it was customary that kings should always receive the first prostration as a way of acknowledging the social hierarchy. Padmasambhava's "I Am Great and Mighty" song serves to disabuse the king of this notion, charting the full breadth of his own supreme mastery. Here is a brief sampling of stanzas from the end of the song, in which Padmasambhava's mastery crescendos dramatically:

> Bringing joy to the six classes of beings,
> I also take the eight types of gods and demons as my servants.
> I am the king Pema Jungné, the Lotus-Born One.
> The doctrine I teach captivates the three realms.
>
> . . .
>
> Deeply interested in my future lives,
> I set my gaze on the Three Jewels.
> I am the queen Pema Jungné.
> The doctrine I teach is buddhahood at the moment of death.
>
> Encouraging the aspirations of the pious,
> I bring happiness and comfort to people in their future lives.
> I am the chief Pema Jungné.
> The doctrine I teach severs the erring mind at its root.
>
> Wielding the weapons of *bodhicitta* and compassion,
> I slay the enemy—discursive thought and wrong view.
> I am the warrior Pema Jungné.
> The doctrine I teach turns back the warfare of *saṃsāra*.
>
> By bestowing the wealth of the three generosities,
> I settle my fortunate children in the Dharma.
> I am the old man Pema Jungné.
> The doctrine I teach is an elderly man wagging his finger.

Leading as a protectress of the three ethics,
I traverse the path of liberation in the higher realms.
I am the old woman Pema Jungné.
The doctrine I teach is an elderly woman wagging her finger.[43]

In addition to being an immortal master of the five sciences (earlier in the song), Padmasambhava also declares himself the supreme manifestation of nearly every conceivable social role, from monk (Sk. *bhikṣu*, T. *gra ba*) to *geshé* scholar (T. *dge bshes*), doctor to astrologer, sorcerer to king, queen to hero, old man to old woman, young woman to child, infant to one who cannot become sick. Padmasambhava's mastery is bound by no category—significantly, not even conventional categories of gender. Whereas the preceding chapter of the *Testament* described his tremendous adaptability in overcoming demonic obstructions, here we witness a gendered adaptability that incorporates both femaleness and maleness in order to punctuate his extraordinary capacity as a siddha to adapt and master even the capacities traditionally ascribed to women.[44]

The insertion of "I" (T. *nga*) into the meter in the final line of each stanza alters the cadence and rhythm of the Tibetan text, dramatically underscoring Padmasambhava's significance and positionality. Shifting through the gamut of conceivable social positions, Padmasambhava lays individual claim to mastery in all categories. The expansion of the meter in the quatrain's fourth line reinforces his mastery, detailing the qualifications granted by each one of these positions. The use of the first-person pronoun—a rarity in Tibetan *namtar*—further emphasizes its significance with every meter. The implication is clear: Padmasambhava unifies this remarkable diversity of mastery into a cohesive subject, understood to be infinitely adaptable and equally powerful. Padmasambhava is the man who can also be a woman, the king who can also be a queen. None of those positions on their own, however, could hope to rival the spectacular fluidity of his siddha masculinity.

Tri Songdétsen falls in stark contrast to Padmasambhava. At the end of the siddha's song, Padmasambhava turns on the king, saying: "[Yet] *you* are king of this meager borderland country known as Tibet, a king to a country with no virtue."[45] Jabbing at the king's foolish arrogance, disdaining the ruler who is bloated on his pride, Padmasambhava resolves: "*I* will not bow to a king like *you*."[46] The contrast of the "I" (T. *nga*) and "you" (T. *khyod*) is dramatic. The thirty-stanza song of Padmasambhava's might, with the provocative inclusion of "I" in each meter, has primed the reader for a stark contrast between the "I" of the siddha and the "you" of the king: How dare the king presume superior status when meeting a siddha as dynamic and powerful as Padmasambhava? Padmasambhava concludes his evisceration by scorching off Tri Songdétsen's clothing with a "miraculous flame" shooting forth from his fingers, laying bare the king's foolish arrogance—and naked body!—for all to see.[47] The king and his entire assembly simply "cannot bear" the weight of Padmasambhava's power and throw themselves into fervent prostrations.[48]

What *Copper Island* suggests, the *Testament* makes explicit: Padmasambhava's masculinity is a supremely adaptable matrix of superiority. The plot of the narrative is stalled by this contest between the siddha and king and can only advance once it is resolved in favor of the tantric master. This is a crucial moment in the development of Padmasambhava's gender, casting him to the level of unrivaled and unquestionable superiority in relationship to the arrogant but good-natured king and peaceful bodhisattva scholar. It is Padmasambhava's remarkable tantric power to tame violent demons and subdue even the mightiest kings (i.e., his masculine technologies of power) that allows him to reshape the hierarchy between kings and tantric Buddhist masters. Whereas the Mahāyāna bodhisattva Śāntarakṣita readily assents to the king as the strongest in the land, paying obeisance without question, the tantric siddha Padmasambhava's virile adaptability readily trounces the king's bloated pride of place. Padmasambhava's refusal to bow cannot be understood in solely political, class, or temporal terms; it is a masculine provocation, buttressed by his magical power and his adaptable masculinity.

In both accounts, Śāntarakṣita recedes into the narrative background, making no appearance until Padmasambhava has overseen the successful completion of Samyé, at which point the bodhisattva reemerges as a teacher and translator alongside the tantric master. The implication is clear: the restrained and peaceful monastic masculinity of the Mahāyāna bodhisattva can only effectively function in a sociopolitical matrix that has been stabilized and tamed by the tantric master. Similarly, the king cannot realize the successful completion of his aspiration to install Buddhism in Tibet until he, too, surrenders to Padmasambhava's uncontestable tantric prowess. Significantly, though Padmasambhava ousts the king from the peak of the social hierarchy, he does not presume upon any kingly duties; the business of governance and patronage famously remains the province of Tri Songdétsen.[49] Upon establishing the appropriate hierarchy between them, these three men proceed to forge a powerful masculine alliance to establish Buddhism within the Tibetan land and among its people.

* * *

Untangling the complex web of gendered associations in *Copper Island* and the *Testament of Padmasambhava* offers insight into Padmasambhava's particular masculine acts, as well as the overarching picture of his gendered positionality. Of course, Padmasambhava's *namtar* cannot be analyzed for straightforward documentary evidence about the structure and operation of gender orders in medieval Tibet as they were lived on the ground by real people. Here I agree with José Cabezón's injunction not to assume that a text's portrayal of a character can tell us much about the mundane realities of actual people. This is especially true of Tibetan *namtar*, given that they are texts about extraordinary beings. What can be mined from these texts, however, is the development of ideals and tropes about gender and sexuality in the Nyingma imaginaire and the texts' portrayal of "ideal pictures of what life *should* be like."[50]

In my analysis I have endeavored to render visible what has been previously invisible. The unmarked nature of maleness means that the dynamics of masculinity often operate without recognition. This analysis also tracks the various degrees of power afforded to privileged and marginalized gender positions in two beloved Tibetan texts, a point that is especially salient in the *namtar* literature, for a key component of the genre is its intended effect to inspire greater devotion in the reader.[51] Thus, attuning to the dynamics of masculinity within Tibetan *namtar* begins to reveal important—and previously unarticulated—forces that shape the normative ideals of the social hierarchy.

Padmasambhava's encounter with, and humiliation of, the Tibetan emperor Tri Songdétsen illuminates a dialectical process whereby Padmasambhava's supremacy in all spheres, encapsulated by his violence and magic, grants him the power to reshape hierarchy and claim hegemonic status. Padmasambhava can overcome any obstacle with ease by whatever means necessary. This is the vision of masculinity that Nyangrel produced in his glorified reimagining of the Tibetan empire's golden age following a tumultuous period. His reimagining was both compelling and convincing enough for Orgyen to successfully employ and expand it two hundred years later, and for it to survive in Tibetan literary tradition throughout subsequent generations.

The importance of male hierarchies and masculine alliances has far-ranging implications for the study of Tibetan Buddhist traditions: the patron-priest relationship (T. *mchod yon*) is a central aspect of Tibetan political and religious history that endured for centuries, most famously with the installation of the Dalai Lama's Ganden Potrang government under Mongolian patronage. Beyond that, numerous other aspects of Tibetan religious life can be enriched by scholarly attunement to masculinity dynamics: the layout of temples, the matter of who gets to walk first in a procession, the seating arrangements at a ritual ceremony, the dynamics of scholarly debate in the monastic courtyard, the relationship between tantric master and initiated disciple, and the abuse of students by wayward teachers.

Tracing the continued development of Padmasambhava's figure across time periods and through diverse genres of Tibetan literature to see what aspects of his tantric masculinity are deployed in various contexts would bring to light the various tropes different authors find compelling in their own contexts. Theoretically, this might illuminate Padmasambhava's adaptability as a religious figure, capable of being drawn into diverse contexts and deployed to suit the needs of authors within their sociohistorical contexts. It would also reveal what has remained stable through time: those aspects of his character that have resisted change. Viewed in this perspective, Padmasambhava's representational fluidity could come into relief; the largesse of the tantric master and the large body of tantric literature in which he is situated provides the tantric Buddhist author with a large repertoire of traits, characteristics, behaviors, and themes from which to draw in order to craft a character compelling to their particular audience(s). Such a view of Padmasambhava would further insulate him from the tendency to reify a particular configuration or literary presentation as *the* "authentic" or "genuine" picture of him and allows for a larger, more fluid picture of the tantric master, as befits his own adaptable tantric masculinity.

NOTES

1. The earliest textual reference to Padmasambhava appears in the *Testimony of Ba* (T. *dBa' bzhed*), which portrays him as an itinerant Indian sorcerer wielding water magic. However, this account is neither narratively nor thematically about Padmasambhava as a protagonist, and it contains no information about his life. The first full-length narrative of Padmasambhava is Nyangrel Nyima Öser's *Copper Island*. For more on the earliest textual evidence of Padmasambhava's legend, see Jacob Dalton, "The Early Development of the Padmasambhava Legend in Tibet: A Study of IOL Tib J 644 and Pelliot tibétain 307," *Journal of the American Oriental Society* 124, no. 4 (2004): 759–72.
2. Much can be said about these two famous works of Tibetan literature. Daniel Hirshberg's *Remembering the Lotus-Born* illuminates the broader twelfth-century sociohistorical context of Nyangrel's watershed text, pointing to the relevance of sectarian competition for royal patronage and the role of memory in (re)telling the story of Tibet's Golden Age of empire. Daniel Hirshberg, *Remembering the Lotus-Born: Padmasambhava in the History of Tibet's Golden Age* (Somerville, Mass.: Wisdom, 2016). Lewis Doney has engaged in a careful and precise philological study tracing the numerous recensions and redactions of these two most substantial biographies. By revealing the historically embedded process by which subsequent redactors shift, adapt, and recast the narrative, Doney highlights the power of Padmasambhava's narratives to "convince others of their particular vision of the past . . . by fixing a vivid reimagining of a lost world in the minds of their audiences." Lewis Doney, "A Richness of Detail: Sangs rgyas gling pa and the *Padma bka' thang*," *Revue d'Etudes Tibétaines* no. 37 (December 2016): 66–97, 70.
3. For an extensive treatment of the implications of the supine female demoness (T. *srin mo*) tied to the Tibetan landscape and the gendered implications of her forceful conquest, see Janet Gyatso, "Down with the Demoness: Reflections on a Feminine Ground in Tibet," *Tibet Journal* 12, no. 4 (1987): 38–53.
4. See Anne-Marie Blondeau, "Analysis of the Biographies of Padmasambhava According to Tibetan Tradition," in *Tibetan Studies in Honour of Hugh Richardson*, ed. Michael Aris and Aung San Suu Kyi (Warminster: Aris and Phillips, 1980); Hirshberg, *Remembering the Lotus-Born*; and the work of Jacob Dalton and Lewis Doney.
5. Notable monographs in this area include Charlene E. Makley, *The Violence of Liberation: Gender and Tibetan Buddhist Revival in Post-Mao China* (Berkeley: University of California Press, 2007); John Powers, *A Bull of a Man: Images of Masculinity, Sex, and the Body in Indian Buddhism* (Cambridge, Mass.: Harvard University Press, 2009); and Ward Keeler, *The Traffic in Hierarchy: Masculinity and Its Others in Buddhist Burma* (Honolulu: University of Hawai'i Press, 2017).
6. For a nuanced look at the explicitly feminized female voice alongside the unmarked dominance of male characters, see Sarah Jacoby, *Love and Liberation: Autobiographical Writings of the Tibetan Buddhist Visionary Sera Khandro* (New York: Columbia University Press, 2014).

7. As masculinities theorist Björn Krondorfer notes, the veiled and unmarked nature of dominant and hegemonic masculinities "makes it difficult to bring into speech the very phenomenon we try to analyze." Björn Krondorfer, "God's Hinder Parts and Masculinity's Troubled Fragmentations: Trajectories of 'Critical Men's Studies in Religon,' " in *God's Own Gender? Masculinities in World Religions*, ed. Daniel Gerster and Michael Krüggeler (Baden-Baden: Ergon-Verlag, 2018), 287.
8. José Ignacio Cabezón, *Sexuality in Classical South Asian Buddhism* (Somerville, Mass.: Wisdom, 2017), 8.
9. Cabezón, *Sexuality*, 8.
10. Makley, *Violence of Liberation*, offers a fine-grained analysis of contemporary masculinity dynamics in eastern Tibet, highlighting strategic alliances between lamas and tribal leaders in Labrang to showcase how shifting political and religious interests can forge new gender relations.
11. For a sophisticated and wide-ranging discussion of the emergence of CSMM as a critical field of study positioned deliberately against the anti-feminist men's rights movement, see Chris Beasley, *Gender and Sexuality: Critical Theories, Critical Thinkers* (Thousand Oaks, Calif.: Sage, 2005).
12. Connell defines the reproductive arena as "the bodily structures and processes of human reproduction." She continues: "I call this a 'reproductive arena' and not a 'biological base' to emphasize that we are talking about a historical process involving the body, not a fixed set of biological determinants." Raewyn Connell, "The Social Organization of Masculinity," in *Exploring Masculinities*, ed. C. J. Pascoe and Tristan Bridges (New York: Oxford University Press, 2016), 138.
13. Raewyn Connell, *Masculinities*, 2nd ed. (Berkeley: University of California Press, 2005), 83. Connell's theory includes not just interpersonal or physical violence, but also institutional and systemic violence.
14. For a sophisticated application of the theory of hegemony in a Tibetan cultural context, see Carl S. Yamamoto, *Vision and Violence: Lama Zhang and the Politics of Charisma in Twelfth-Century Tibet* (Leiden: Brill, 2012).
15. Jacob Dalton, *The Taming of the Demons: Violence and Liberation in Tibetan Buddhism* (New Haven, Conn.: Yale University Press, 2011), 10.
16. Connell updated her model of hegemonic masculinity in light of postcolonial critique: masculinity is not monolithic, even when it can operate hegemonically across, through, and within a variety of contexts. Thus, masculinities theorizing must attune jointly to the localized texture of specific gender relations within discrete communities, while also tracking the global migration of hegemonic ideals via colonial and imperial forces. Raewyn Connell, "Masculinities in Global Perspective: Hegemony, Contestation, and Changing Structures of Power," *Theory and Society* 45, no. 4 (2016): 303–18.
17. Connell, *Masculinities*, 77.
18. On the social superiority of the divine Tibetan king, see Charles Ramble, "Sacral Kings and Divine Sovereigns: Principles of Tibetan Monarchy in Theory and Practice," in *States of Mind: Power, Place and the Subject in Inner Asia*, ed. David Sneath (Bellingham: Western Washington University Press, 2006).

19. See Eve Kosofsky Sedgwick, *Epistemology of the Closet* (Berkeley: University of California Press, 1990); Lee Edelman, *Homographesis: Essays in Gay Literary and Cultural Theory* (New York: Routledge, 1994); and Roderick A. Ferguson, *Aberrations in Black: Toward a Queer of Color Critique* (Minneapolis: University of Minnesota Press, 2004).
20. While this chapter engages in a masculinities analysis of Padmasambhava via a close reading of his encounter with the Tibetan king and bodhisattva scholar, Padmasambhava's interactions with female characters also inform his masculine position and so, too, must factor into our understanding of his gender relations in narrative literature. Given current space constraints, such analysis much remain a horizon for later exploration.
21. For example, see Jacoby, *Love and Liberation*; Amy Holmes-Tagchungdarpa, *The Social Life of Tibetan Biography: Textuality, Community, and Authority in the Lineage of Tokden Shakya Shri* (Lanham, Md.: Lexington, 2014); Andrew Quintman, *The Yogin and the Madman: Reading the Biographical Corpus of Tibet's Great Saint* (New York: Columbia University Press, 2013); Yamamoto, *Vision and Violence*; and Kurtis R. Schaeffer, *Himalayan Hermitess: The Life of a Tibetan Buddhist Nun* (New York: Oxford University Press, 2004).
22. Patrick Joseph Geary, "Saints, Scholars, and Society: The Elusive Goal," in *Saints: Studies in Hagiography*, ed. Sandro Sticca (Binghamton, N.Y.: Center for Medieval and Early Renaissance Studies, 1996).
23. Quintman, *Yogin and the Madman*; Schaeffer, *Himalayan Hermitess*.
24. Joan W. Scott, "Gender: A Useful Category of Historical Analysis," *American Historical Review* 91, no. 5 (December 1986): 1053–75.
25. See note 2.
26. Quite a bit of ink has been spilled regarding the siddhas, tantric heroes of antinomianism, realization, and subversion. They became stock figures in tantric narrative literature in Indian Buddhism (as well as non-Buddhist tantric traditions), and their fame spread into Tibet, where it took hold in the Tibetan literary imagination for centuries, up to the present day. Siddhas were famous for their contestations with kings, and various schools of thought debated whether siddhas were actually interested in political or temporal authority while engaging in subversive ritual practices, or whether their tantric practices were more metaphorical, intended to critique a certain configuration of the ruling class. For the former position, see Ronald M. Davidson, *Indian Esoteric Buddhism: A Social History of the Tantric Movement* (New York: Columbia University Press, 2002) and *Tibetan Renaissance: Tantric Buddhism in the Rebirth of Tibetan Culture* (New York: Columbia University Press, 2005); for the latter, see Christian Wedemeyer, *Making Sense of Tantric Buddhism: History, Semiology, and Transgression in Indian Buddhism* (New York: Columbia University Press, 2014).
27. Nyang ral, 36.
28. U rgyan gling pa, 285.
29. Nyang ral, 36.
30. This evokes the centuries-long archetypal struggle in Tibetan literature between the wild and magical siddha and the reasoned, disciplined monk, a struggle long articulated by scholars of Tibetan literature but yet to be analyzed from a

gender studies perspective. See David M. DiValerio, *The Holy Madmen of Tibet* (New York: Oxford University Press, 2015).

31. U rgyan gling pa, 297.
32. Nyang ral, 43. This deity is a significant figure in indigenous Tibetan traditions, the name of a mountain (and the deity residing there) where the first king of Tibet, Nyatri Tsenpo, descended to earth to rule. The fact that Padmasambhava beats, subdues, and tames him further emphasizes his capacity to bend kings to *his* will.
33. Nyang ral, 63.
34. See note 3.
35. Nyang ral, 45.
36. The five sciences are composition, art, medicine, logic, and philosophy. In Tibetan these terms are *'chi mad rig 'dzin* (Sk. *vidyādhara*), *gtso bo* (chief), *dpa bo* (hero), and *mthu mkhan* (sorcerer). Nyang ral, 45.
37. In Tibetan these terms are *gdong dmar srin po* (red-faced demon), *glob ba dga'* (infatuated), and *mang thag che ba* (great dominion). Nyang ral, 47.
38. Nyang ral, 47.
39. U rgyan gling pa, 302.
40. U rgyan gling pa, 302.
41. U rgyan gling pa, 303.
42. U rgyan gling pa, 303.
43. U rgyan gling pa, 303. This translation of a small selection of stanzas and all other quoted translations from the text are my own. My complete translation of Padmasambhava's "I Am Great and Mighty" song will appear in *Longing to Awaken: Buddhist Devotion in Tibetan Poetry and Song* (Charlottesville: University of Virginia Press, forthcoming).
44. As Tristan Bridges and C. J. Pascoe have shown, in androcentric, patriarchal systems, powerful men often draw gendered characteristics from women and subordinated or marginalized masculinities to shore up their own hegemonic authority. This does not weaken their claim to masculinity, but in fact strengthens it. The same is not true for those occupying marginalized or subordinated gendered subject positions, who are routinely disciplined for straying beyond the confines of normative gender expectations. Thus, while Padmasambhava can articulate the superiority of his own masculinity by claiming traditionally female roles—even identifying as a woman!—this does not suggest gender fluidity. Quite the contrary, it further punctuates his power as a supreme man. Tristan Bridges and C. J. Pascoe, "Hybrid Masculinities: New Directions in the Sociology of Men and Masculinities," *Sociology Compass* 8, no. 3 (2014): 246–58.
45. U rgyan gling pa, 307 (emphasis added).
46. U rgyan gling pa, 307.
47. U rgyan gling pa, 307.
48. U rgyan gling pa, 307.
49. For insight into the depiction of Tri Songdétsen's rule in early sources, see Lewis Doney, "Early Bodhisattva-Kingship in Tibet: The Case of Tri Songdétsen," *Cahiers d'Extrême-Asie* 24 (2015): 29–48.

50. Cabezón, *Sexuality*, 12.
51. Janet Gyatso, *Apparitions of the Self: The Secret Autobiographies of a Tibetan Visionary* (Princeton, N.J.: Princeton University Press, 1999), 102–3.

Additional Primary Sources

Kunsang, Erik Pema, trans. *The Lotus-Born: The Life Story of Padmasambhava*. Boston: Shambhala, 1993.

Toussaint, Gustave-Charles, trans. *The Life and Liberation of Padmasambhava*. Translated from the French by Kenneth Douglas and Gwendolyn Bays. Berkeley, Calif.: Dharma, 1978.

Bibliography

Beasley, Chris. *Gender and Sexuality: Critical Theories, Critical Thinkers*. Thousand Oaks, Calif.: Sage, 2005.

Blondeau, Anne-Marie. "Analysis of the Biographies of Padmasambhava According to Tibetan Tradition." In *Tibetan Studies in Honour of Hugh Richardson*, edited by Michael Aris and Aung San Suu Kyi, 45–52. Warminster: Aris and Phillips, 1980.

Bridges, Tristan, and C. J. Pascoe. "Hybrid Masculinities: New Directions in the Sociology of Men and Masculinities." *Sociology Compass* 8, no. 3 (2014): 246–58.

Cabezón, José Ignacio. *Sexuality in Classical South Asian Buddhism*. Somerville, Mass.: Wisdom, 2017.

Connell, Raewyn. *Masculinities*, 2nd ed. Berkeley: University of California Press, 2005.

—. "Masculinities in Global Perspective: Hegemony, Contestation, and Changing Structures of Power." *Theory and Society* 45, no. 4 (2016): 303–18.

—. "The Social Organization of Masculinity." In *Exploring Masculinities*, edited by C. J. Pascoe and Tristan Bridges, 136–44. New York: Oxford University Press, 2016.

Dalton, Jacob. "The Early Development of the Padmasambhava Legend in Tibet: A Study of IOL Tib J 644 and Pelliot tibétain 307." *Journal of the American Oriental Society* 124, no. 4 (2004): 759–72.

—. *The Taming of the Demons: Violence and Liberation in Tibetan Buddhism*. New Haven, Conn.: Yale University Press, 2011.

Davidson, Ronald M. *Indian Esoteric Buddhism: A Social History of the Tantric Movement*. New York: Columbia University Press, 2002.

—. *Tibetan Renaissance: Tantric Buddhism in the Rebirth of Tibetan Culture*. New York: Columbia University Press, 2005.

DiValerio, David M. *The Holy Madmen of Tibet*. New York: Oxford University Press, 2015.

Doney, Lewis. "Early Bodhisattva-Kingship in Tibet: The Case of Tri Songdétsen." *Cahiers d'Extrême-Asie* 24 (2015): 29–48.

——. "A Richness of Detail: Sangs rgyas gling pa and the *Padma bka' thang*." *Revue d'Etudes Tibétaines* no. 37 (December 2016): 66–97.
Edelman, Lee. *Homographesis: Essays in Gay Literary and Cultural Theory*. New York: Routledge, 1994.
Ferguson, Roderick A. *Aberrations in Black: Toward a Queer of Color Critique*. Minneapolis: University of Minnesota Press, 2004.
Geary, Patrick Joseph. "Saints, Scholars, and Society: The Elusive Goal." In *Saints: Studies in Hagiography*, edited by Sandro Sticca, 1–22. Binghamton, N.Y.: Center for Medieval and Early Renaissance Studies, 1996.
Gyatso, Janet. *Apparitions of the Self: The Secret Autobiographies of a Tibetan Visionary*. Princeton, N.J.: Princeton University Press, 1999.
——. "Down with the Demoness: Reflections on a Feminine Ground in Tibet." *Tibet Journal* 12, no. 4 (1987): 38–53.
Holmes-Tagchungdarpa, Amy. *The Social Life of Tibetan Biography: Textuality, Community, and Authority in the Lineage of Tokden Shakya Shri*. Lanham, Md.: Lexington, 2014.
Hirshberg, Daniel. *Remembering the Lotus-Born: Padmasambhava in the History of Tibet's Golden Age*. Somerville, Mass.: Wisdom, 2016.
Jacoby, Sarah. *Love and Liberation: Autobiographical Writings of the Tibetan Buddhist Visionary Sera Khandro*. New York: Columbia University Press, 2014.
Keeler, Ward. *The Traffic in Hierarchy: Masculinity and Its Others in Buddhist Burma*. Honolulu: University of Hawai'i Press, 2017.
Krondorfer, Björn. "God's Hinder Parts and Masculinity's Troubled Fragmentations: Trajectories of 'Critical Men's Studies in Religon.'" In *God's Own Gender? Masculinities in World Religions*, edited by Daniel Gerster and Michael Krüggeler, 283–300. Baden-Baden: Ergon-Verlag, 2018.
Makley, Charlene E. *The Violence of Liberation: Gender and Tibetan Buddhist Revival in Post-Mao China*. Berkeley: University of California Press, 2007.
Nyang ral nyi ma 'od zer. *Ba dpon padma 'byung gnas kyi rnam thar zang gling ma*. Khreng tu'u: Si khron mi rigs dpe skrun khang, 1989. Buddhist Digital Resource Center (BDRC), https://www.bdrc.io/ (accessed January 2, 2023), W7956.
Powers, John. *A Bull of a Man: Images of Masculinity, Sex, and the Body in Indian Buddhism*. Cambridge, Mass.: Harvard University Press, 2009.
Quintman, Andrew. *The Yogin and the Madman: Reading the Biographical Corpus of Tibet's Great Saint*. New York: Columbia University Press, 2013.
Ramble, Charles. "Sacral Kings and Divine Sovereigns: Principles of Tibetan Monarchy in Theory and Practice." In *States of Mind: Power, Place and the Subject in Inner Asia*, edited by David Sneath, 129–49. Bellingham: Western Washington University Press, 2006.
Schaeffer, Kurtis R. *Himalayan Hermitess: The Life of a Tibetan Buddhist Nun*. New York: Oxford University Press, 2004.
Scott, Joan W. "Gender: A Useful Category of Historical Analysis." *American Historical Review* 91, no. 5 (December 1986): 1053–75.
Sedgwick, Eve Kosofsky. *Epistemology of the Closet*. Berkeley: University of California Press, 1990.

U rgyan gling pa (a.k.a. gTer chen u rgyan gling pa). *O rgyan gu ru padma 'byung gnas kyi skyes rabs rnam par thar pa rgyas par bkod pa padma bka' thang yig*. 2nd ed. Khreng tu'u: Si khron mi rigs dpe skrun khang, 2014.
Wedemeyer, Christian. *Making Sense of Tantric Buddhism: History, Semiology, and Transgression in Indian Buddhism*. New York: Columbia University Press, 2014.
Yamamoto, Carl S. *Vision and Violence: Lama Zhang and the Politics of Charisma in Twelfth-Century Tibet*. Leiden: Brill, 2012.

FIVE

Building a Nation on the Dharma Battlefield

Lay Zen Masculinities in Modern Japan

REBECCA MENDELSON

BEFORE A MEDITATION retreat for lay Zen practitioners at Engakuji in 1918, prospective participants were exhorted: "When presenting your understanding before the master, be as though you are facing a hero's battlefield and exchanging swordplay; you must absolutely not yield to the master or be timid."[1] These instructions appeared in the monthly journal *Zendō*, a popular publication aimed at Zen practitioners of all stripes. They signaled the unprecedented accessibility of Zen-style meditation training to laypeople, as well as a rhetoric of martial masculinity that served as a pervasive trope at Engakuji and reflected an ideal ethos for self-cultivation in early twentieth-century Rinzai Zen.

The metaphors and ideals of martial masculinity—depicted as crucial to effective Zen practice—were not new to Rinzai Zen or to Engakuji, whose relationship to samurai dated back centuries. Modern Rinzai Zen's ideals of martial masculinity were notable both for their prominence in Rinzai practice and rhetoric, and for the ways they converged with other historical exigencies and trends of the era. Such trends included a broad-based Japanese interest in self-improvement practices that were often gendered and tied to nation-building, as well as widespread interest in *bushidō* ("way of the warrior") rhetoric and *kendō* ("way of the sword") practice. Early twentieth-century *bushidō* and *kendō* were depicted as age-old Japanese traditions even while being products of their time; the term *kendō* itself was a twentieth-century invention. Both "ways" promoted ideals of martial masculinity and were embraced by many lay Zen practitioners alongside their practice of sitting meditation (J. *zazen*).

Through the interrelated lenses of ideology and materiality, this chapter examines the autobiographical accounts of modern lay Rinzai Zen practitioners to elucidate modern Rinzai Zen constructions of masculinity and their implications vis-à-vis Japan's shifting gender norms. Post–Meiji Restoration Japan saw an array of ideal gender roles, with ideal masculinities ranging from "a 'feminized' masculinity centered on the image of the Japanese gentleman" to "its antithesis represented by a 'masculinized' masculinity that rejected Western material culture," according to Jason Karlin.[2] Here, Karlin draws on the historical Chinese *wen-wu* (J. *bun-bu*) dyad as articulated by Kam Louie. This paradigm juxtaposes the mentally oriented ideal of "cultural attainment" (*wen*) with the physically oriented ideal of "martial valor" (*wu*) as two dimensions of Chinese masculinity, expressed diversely in both premodern and modern China.[3] Most broadly, modern lay Japanese Rinzai Zen embraced both dimensions, as its early Meiji exemplars included both "gentlemen" (e.g., elite state-makers and members of the intelligentsia) and former samurai, sometimes in the same person. However, as suggested by the autobiographical accounts I will discuss, modern Rinzai Zen practitioners idealized and embodied martial masculinity above all.[4]

This elevation of martial masculinity was commensurate with broader Japanese trends in nation-building, its gendering, and its intersection with self-cultivation practices. As Karlin notes, "In modern Japan, gender identity became closely intertwined with the processes of national consolidation and mobilization."[5] Indeed, a central state goal during and after the Meiji periods was "building a strong nation populated by physically robust subjects"—an enterprise bolstered by self-cultivation practices, which were frequently gendered.[6] In this way, lay Rinzai Zen's popularization and practitioners' embodiment of martial masculine ideals contributed to the modern Japanese imperial project. Following Raewyn Connell and James Messerschmidt's assertion that hegemonic masculinity "embodied the currently most honored way of being a man," we can say with certainty that martial masculinity was hegemonic in early twentieth-century Japan.[7] Within that context, Rinzai Zen practice was a "mechanism" of hegemony and a form "of social practice linking bodily processes and social structures."[8] Rinzai Zen practitioners embodied martial ideals through Zen kōan practice, monastic life, and other practice contexts, in which ideals of ferocity and heroism pervaded rhetoric and ethos.

For both monastic and lay practitioners, such martial ideals were intimately connected not only with prescriptions for cultivating strong national subjects but also with religious ideals and soteriological goals (e.g., attaining enlightenment through fierce practice and through penetrating kōans).

In modern Japan, a palpable tension existed between, on the one hand, Zen's popularization and professed inclusivity and, on the other, its androcentrism, which ran deep in both ideology and practice. Previously the prerogative of Zen monastics, meditation intensives and other forms of rigorous Zen practice were popularized in late nineteenth- and early twentieth-century Japan to an unprecedented degree, as the dramatic proliferation of lay Zen-centered groups, activities, and literature attests.[9] Lay Zen contexts signaled a shift away from gender-normative monasticism toward practice that was ostensibly open to anyone, regardless of gender, occupation, social status, or monastic status. For example, lay practitioner Iizuka Iwao observed at Engakuji a relatively diverse and inclusive community of practitioners circa 1920, comprising people young and old, Parliament members and government ministers, businessmen and military officers, novelists and painters, teachers and students, rich and poor alike.[10] Women, too, participated in lay Rinzai Zen practice across Japan to an unprecedented degree.[11]

Despite some degree of popularization, however, the body of Rinzai Zen practitioners remained overwhelmingly male, educated, and of middle or upper socioeconomic class.[12] Numerous factors, both practical and ideological, contributed to the dearth of female practitioners and persistence of androcentrism in modern Japanese Rinzai Zen. Ideologically, women occupied an ambiguous place amid Rinzai Zen's enduring ideals of male celibacy and monasticism, despite a new modern standard among Japanese Buddhist sects of clerical marriage.[13] Moreover, heroic ideals of masculinity and their performance pervaded modern Rinzai Zen for both monastic and lay practitioners.

Modern Rinzai Masculinity: Rhetoric and Ideals

Ferocity and Heroism: The "House Wind" of Modern Lay Rinzai Zen Practice

Congruent with martial ideals of masculinity in modern Japan, Rinzai Zen masters and lay practitioners articulated and ritually embodied a "rhetoric of heroism" that channeled an idealized martial ethos from multiple centuries and locales: their own era, Song-dynasty China, and Edo-period Japan. In short, heroism, ferocity, and determination persisted as ideals in modern Japanese lay Rinzai Zen, even while modern practitioners' language and prototypes diverged from those of their premodern and early modern forebears. Ferocity has constituted a central ideal in Rinzai Zen (Linji Chan) since its earliest centuries. Per Miriam Levering's work on Song-era Chan androcentrism, the qualities of ferocity and determination, as well as their embodiment by the "great man" or "great hero" (Ch. *da zhangfu*; J. *daijōbu*), played a central role in Chan master Dahui Zonggao's (J. Daie Sōkō; 1089–1163) rhetoric of heroism.[14] Building on Levering's work, Kevin Buckelew's chapter in this volume illustrates how the trope of great manhood was widespread in Song-dynasty Chan, where it helped Chan Buddhists formulate an ideal of martial masculinity that appealed to many literati. In early modern Japan, Rinzai master Hakuin Ekaku (1686–1768)—from whom modern Japanese Rinzai Zen practitioners traced their lineage and who disproportionately influenced succeeding generations' approach to kōan practice—popularized the "three essentials" of the Great Overpowering Will, Great Ball of Doubt, and Great Root of Faith.[15]

Terminologically, modern Japanese references to the "great hero" as a Rinzai paragon were rare. Rinzai master Mamiya Eijū (1871–1945)—known for his focus on training laypeople—stated that the great man ideal was not limited to men, and that "there are many strong-minded [mannish], admirable women."[16] However, he called for referring to female counterparts as "female hero" (J. *jojōbu*). Here, Eijū's formulation followed the androcentrism of the premodern great man ideal, in which exceptional women could become a female great man, but the standard was inevitably male.

Despite their lack of explicit references to the great man, modern Japanese authors employed other terms to characterize the "house wind" (J. *kafū*, or teaching style) of modern Rinzai Zen masters that contributed to the continued idealization of ferocity, heroism, and other features of martial masculinity. D. T. Suzuki describes the prototypical *rōshi* (master) in the context of would-be monastic novices' trials prior to entering training: "It seems as if no soft spots were left in the heart of the Zen master. What he generally doles out to his monks is 'hot invective and angry fist-shaking.' "[17] Rinzai Zen master Katsumine Daitetsu (1828–1911)—known for his dedication to teaching lay disciples and founding one of Japan's earliest Rinzai Zen lay groups,

Kōzen Gokokukai in 1893—was occasionally called Demon Daitetsu (Oni Daitetsu). Of Katsumine's characteristic ferocity, which he exhibited while touring Japan to raise funds for the impoverished Rinzai temple Nanzenji (of which Katsumine became the abbot in 1882), the author of his obituary, Enomoto Shūson, recounts: "He wielded his will, and when he gave a sermon [J. *teishō*] on the *Blue Cliff Record*, he smashed the bookstand, and the Demon Daitetsu would show his face."[18]

Such descriptions were not limited to exceptional masters. In their autobiographical accounts of Zen practice, many modern lay Rinzai Zen practitioners characterized their practice (actual and aspirational) with variations on the term *mō*, commonly translated as "ferocity," "intensity," or "severity." Permutations of *mō* included "ferocity" (J. *mōretsu*), "bravery" (J. *yūmō*), and "strenuous effort" (J. *shōjin yūmō*). In particular, *mōretsu* served as a buzzword among early twentieth-century university students who practiced Rinzai Zen, and many lay Zen practitioners in modern Japan threaded the terms *valor* (*yūmō*) and *intrepid spirit* (J. *yūmōshin*) throughout their autobiographical accounts.

Against the Grain of "Depraved" Youth: Ferocious Practitioners

Modern Rinzai masters and practitioners did not simply invoke ferocity as a centuries-old religious ideal. In their early twentieth-century context, cultivating ferocity was considered socially pragmatic and trumpeted as an attribute of a strong body and mind that could contribute to a strong nation, or *kokutai* (literally, "national body"). Moreover, as intellectuals and religious leaders expressed concerns about the moral decrepitude of twentieth-century youth and its effects on national strength, practices that cultivated ferocity and strength of character served as a critical corrective. In his essay "A Recommendation for Quiet Sitting" (first published in 1900), D. T. Suzuki minces no words: "In recent days the character of our Japanese youth has become noticeably depraved."[19] The solution for Suzuki—and for the Engakuji master Shaku Sōen, on whose notions Suzuki based his essay—was Zen-style "quiet sitting" (J. *seiza*). Suzuki was not alone in worrying about young people's deterioration of character amid Japan's modernization, nor was he alone in prescribing self-cultivation practice as a remedy. Enomoto, the author of Katsumine Daitetsu's obituary, bemoaned in 1911: "Gentlemen who have sturdy bodies and strong hearts and young men who love their country and lament what is happening in the world are few; the whole world has become a place of idleness for weak men with no willpower. Wouldn't anyone with a heart lament [such a situation]?"[20]

Here, Enomoto expresses concern about modern deterioration of character, insinuates a connection between patriotism and one's strength of body and mind, and distinctly genders these qualities. Enomoto then lauds Katsumine as a "Meiji-era exemplar of the spiritual world and pioneer of the Buddhist world" who helped to ameliorate the situation by teaching more than one thousand lay students and founding the lay group Kōzen Gokokukai.

Against the image of weak-willed, unpatriotic, and amoral youth of late Meiji Japan, the members of Tokyo Higher Commercial School's Zen group Nyoidan appeared in an entirely different light, exemplifying the contemporaneous ideals of patriotism alongside "traditional" Rinzai Zen values of ferocity and great effort.[21] In this way, lay Rinzai Zen—with its ideal ethos of heroism and martial masculinity—became an attractive path for young people. University students' accounts suggest that many envisioned their Zen practice as a form of self-cultivation (J. *shūyō*) that could contribute to national strength.

Nyoidan alumnus Shimada Hiroshi, among Nyoidan's earliest practitioners, articulated his fellow Zen practitioners' love of school and nation and the ferocity for which they strove in their endeavors: "It was a group [of people] who burned the flame of love for their school and country [J. *aikōshin aikokushin*]. Thus, the era's motto was the word 'ferocity' [*mōretsu*]. That is to say, we practiced [the Way] fiercely but also played fiercely. In daily life, we were fierce like wild beasts, but also [engaged] fiercely in spiritual self-cultivation [J. *seishinteki shūyō*]."[22] For Nyoidan members, this spiritual self-cultivation meant attending Zen practice intensives (J. *sesshin* or *zazenkai*) at one of the group's practice sites in Tokyo and Kamakura. These intensives varied in their degree of formality but were consistently characterized by fierce striving. *Sesshin*, modeled on monastic meditation intensives, were the most structured and typically lasted between three and seven days. For *sesshin*, the students either practiced alongside Engakuji's monastics in the latter's training hall (J. *sōdō*) or held their own intensive, following the *sōdō* schedule and rules and supervised by a monastic. Of the winter Rōhatsu *sesshin*—held in honor of the Buddha's awakening and known for its rigors—Nyoidan alumnus Masumoto Yoshitarō affirmed that it was especially fierce (J. *mōretsu*).[23] Even in less formal practice settings, such as staying in one of Engakuji's subtemples for one month or longer during school breaks, students described great rigor and exertion in their practice. For example, in July 1918, eighteen students from Tokyo Higher Commercial School and a Hokkaidō University professor together followed a daily practice schedule that lasted from 3 a.m. until 9 p.m. and included a lecture by the master, three opportunities for *sanzen* (one-on-one encounters with the master), and many hours of *zazen*.[24] There were also several Nyoidan members who lived long-term at Kaizenji in quarters suitably nicknamed the "Strenuous Effort Quarters" (Jikyōryō) by their teacher, Sakagami Shinjō.[25]

Such practitioners—a far reach from the stereotypically disaffected youth of the day—were a self-selecting population and might have had ferocious tendencies even before beginning Zen practice. Regardless of their starting point, however, many students described developing ferocity and discipline through sustained Zen practice and through internalizing their teachers' rhetoric and ideals. For example, early Nyoidan member Ōta Tetsuzō disparaged his own tendencies: "My life at Kaizenji was short, and I was well known as a lazy person, so it wasn't [the case] that I diligently exerted myself for the sake of the Way."[26] Despite this self-deprecating portrayal (not unusual in Japanese Zen practitioners' autobiographical accounts), Ōta chose to live at Kaizenji and therefore to practice regularly, listening to sermons and engaging in *sanzen* during Sakagami Shinjō's monthly week-long visits to Kaizenji. Other practitioners did not explicitly attribute their personal transformation to Zen practice but nonetheless described spirited engagement with it. In Zen-related accounts from this era, practitioners frequently used the term *nesshin* ("zealous" or "fervent"). For example, Tasaki Masayoshi (1880–1976) started practicing fervently following his summer exams in 1905, "gradually [turning] from the world of the abacus to the world of kōan."[27] Tasaki used similar language to describe the efforts of Nakahara Shūgaku (1878–1928), one of Nyoidan's monastic leaders, in teaching the student practitioners.[28]

Such allusions to fervent, ferocious practice appear throughout these brief testimonials and are even more striking in their prevalence in the diaries of a practitioner, Shimokawa Yoshitarō (1884–1934), whose unusually detailed account of Zen practice shows how he idealized ferocity and strength, grappled with what it means to be a man, and explored these themes as they related to Zen practice.[29] Shimokawa was a lawyer and local politician who embarked on spiritual pursuits and began keeping diaries in 1911, found his way to Zen in 1912, and subsequently practiced Zen seriously for more than twenty years. Throughout 1911, Shimokawa repeatedly articulated his drive to pursue spiritual cultivation and to develop an "immovable mind" through *zazen*.[30] In his first journal entry of 1912, Shimokawa laid out his New Year's goals for both spiritual self-cultivation (J. *seishin shūyō*) and physical training (J. *nikutai senren*): for the former, he pledged to cultivate "perfect sincerity, [his] own worth, immovability, and fortitude," and, for the latter, he sought to bathe in cold water and practice abdominal breathing and the way of quiet sitting.[31] Thereafter, he experimented with Okada-style breathing practices and Christian-style selflessness, and his close friend Satō Teiichi urged him to try Zen practice in Kamakura, which was home to the Rinzai temple Engakuji.[32]

A series of losses propelled Shimokawa further into spiritual inquiries and Zen practice. Tragically, his friend Satō took his own life in June 1912, one month after Satō encouraged Shimokawa to practice Zen.[33] Later, Shimokawa connected his loss of Satō and other loved ones to his spiritual efforts and Zen practice, which he began a few months after Satō's death. At this point, Shimokawa's descriptions of Zen practice grew more gendered, explicitly connecting it with masculine strength and emotional resilience. The day after Satō's death, Shimokawa stated: "Thus, I had lost my mother, I had lost my lover, I had lost my friend. From now on, I will try to be a strong man" (J. *tsuyoi otoko*).[34] Similarly, Shimokawa reiterated many times that becoming strong was a central motivation for his practice, while reflecting that "it is hard to be a man."[35] He also used the gendered term *gōki*—which could be translated as "fortitude" or "manliness"—in the context of his aspirations.[36] For Shimokawa, the ideal of a man was General Nogi Maresuke (1849–1912), who was born a samurai and served central roles in Japan's imperial aggression via the first Sino-Japanese War (1894–1895), invasion of Taiwan (1895), and Russo-Japanese War (1904–1905). Three months after Satō's death, Nogi committed ritual suicide following the funeral of Emperor Meiji, and Shimokawa wrote afterward: "My sorrow for the General Nogi incident is unbearable. [He was] the archetype of a warrior [J. *bushi*], a flower of a man. Undeniably, I revere the general's spirit."[37] Shimokawa's reverence for Nogi as the archetypal warrior foreshadowed his approach to Zen, which he initiated the following month.

Shimokawa's diaries affirm that his practice was characterized from the start by determination and intensity, which he expressed through permutations of the term *ferocity* (J. *mōretsu*), in line with student practitioners' descriptions of ideal Zen ethos. Shimokawa first practiced zazen in October 1912, when he attended a meditation intensive (J. *zazenkai*) with two friends at the Tokyo temple Zeshō'in. There, Shimokawa's first master, Mineo Daikyū, assigned Shimokawa the kōan "one's original face."[38] Shimokawa took immediately to *zazen* and kōan practice, returning daily for *zazen* at Zeshō'in for the next six days. From the start, Shimokawa understood that logic and reasoning was useless with kōan practice and "vowed deeply in [his] heart" to practice: "I will work so that my mind becomes cool and quiet; I must stop judging the entangling vines."[39] While attending monastic-style *sesshin* over the next two months at Zeshō'in, it bothered Shimokawa immensely that he could not grasp the kōan fully and express its meaning beyond intellectual description, and he renewed his determination to do so; before long, he "penetrated" it (to be discussed later in the chapter). Particularly in his early days of Zen practice, Shimokawa repeatedly used the term *mōretsu* and described his aspiration to develop a courageous spirit (J. *yūmōshin*).[40]

In the early months and years of Shimokawa's Zen practice, thoughts of Satō surfaced repeatedly, and the meaning of life and death remained a central theme throughout his diaries.[41] He explicitly discussed Satō, suicide, and death, and his descriptions of spiritual practice itself reflected his preoccupation with life and death—a common trope in Rinzai Zen. Notably, Shimokawa used the term *ferocity* (J. *mōzen*) in the context of grappling with the issue of life and death.[42] He described the qualities of practice, which for him started with "thinking deeply about the things that occur every day. From there, it's piling on layer upon layer of self-cultivation [*shūyō*]. It's self-cultivation for halting one's will and killing the self. Without doing away with the emphasis on oneself, it's useless; if we don't die, we cannot live."[43]

The ideological and rhetorical dimension of martial masculinity in modern Rinzai Zen was significant. For both lay and monastic practitioners, heroism and warfare were prominent tropes, drawing from centuries of religious ideals and further amplified in the historical context of Japan's imperialism. Heroism and warfare were not limited to ideology, as many practitioners embodied these distinctly masculine ideals, within and beyond the Zen meditation hall.

Modern Rinzai Masculinity: Physical Practice and Embodiment

There were two key modes by which Zen practitioners embodied and reinforced martial masculinity and ideals of heroism: through *kendō* ("way of the sword") practice, as distinct from but related to Zen practice, and through practitioners' main form of Rinzai Zen meditation practice, kōan work.

"The Unity of Sword and Zen": Kendō, Zen, and Martial Masculinity

Contrary to normative depictions of motivations for practicing Zen (e.g., to attain enlightenment), many modern Japanese lay practitioners came to Rinzai Zen for practical reasons. According to early twentieth-century practitioners' accounts, common motivations spurring lay Zen practice were to improve one's swordsmanship and to strengthen one's own character and the nation by practicing Zen as a form of self-cultivation (J. *shūyō*). Both paths centered on the physical body as site of cultivation, and both were highly gendered: Zen-as-*shūyō* frequently entailed performing men's and women's (highly binary) gendered ideals in modern Japan, and Zen-as-swordsmanship-cultivation connected directly to performing the masculinity of *bushidō*.

Engakuji practitioner Tsuji Sōmei regularly invoked the Dharma combat (J. *hossen*) involved in facing one's Zen master, and fellow practitioner Iizuka Iwao identified the master's quarters as the Dharma battlefield (J. *hō no jissenjō*).[44] Such metaphors went beyond rhetorical expressions of ferocity, extending to physical connections among practitioners, swordsmanship, and the military. Oleg Benesch and Yamada Shōji demonstrate that, in significant ways, the narrative of an unchanging, intimate relationship between Zen and the sword was an invented tradition produced and reinforced by modern Japanese ideologues.[45] In fact, the modern practice of *kendō* had developed as an amalgam of earlier swordsmanship practices, but its nomenclature was a modern product, not widely used until the early twentieth century.[46] However, scholars' emphasis on intellectual history tends to overlook the material dimension and to reduce the Zen-*kendō* relationship to a rhetorical strategy and form of Japanese nationalism. The Zen practitioners' accounts I will examine complicate such narratives and indicate that many modern lay Zen practitioners embodied the Zen-*kendō* relationship in numerous ways. *Kendō* led many young practitioners directly to Rinzai Zen practice, served as a vehicle for inscribing martial masculinity on the physical body, and reinforced Rinzai Zen's ideals of heroism and warrior ethos at a historical moment when warfare sustained an empire.

In this context, the Zen-*kendō* relationship took two main forms: in the physical practice settings, and in the body of the practitioner. Regarding physical space, there were many instances of porous boundaries among swordsmanship, Zen, and the military. For example, Zen practitioners occasionally held their retreats in *kendō* training halls.[47] Later, during the Pacific War, Engakuji's training hall for laypeople, Kojirin (Laypeople's Grove), served as a facility for the Japanese navy while the laymen themselves were called to battlefields, factories, or other sites to support the war effort.[48] Even before the war, the physical site of Kojirin itself embodied the Zen-sword connection, as the building served as a *kendō* training hall before its transformation into Japan's premiere lay Rinzai Zen practice space in the late 1920s. From 1877 until 1922, university students and other laypeople who practiced Zen at Engakuji meditated in various subtemples and, on occasion, alongside the clerics in the monastic hall. Despite intensifying efforts in the 1910s among laypeople to establish a dedicated meditation hall on Engakuji's grounds, it was not until 1922 that the subtemple Saiin'an became the Tokyo-area Rinzai laity's first dedicated training hall, replete with practice opportunities that mirrored those of monks, while maintaining distinction as a lay-centered training hall that embodied the "unity of Zen and sword."[49] Called by its generic name Kojirin, Saiin'an survived the Great Kantō Earthquake of 1923. However, an accidental late-night fire in March 1926 destroyed it, leaving student practitioners and other laypeople without a dedicated practice space.[50] In the face of this loss, students from numerous Tokyo-area universities banded together, approached the Yagyū-lineage *kendō* master in Tokyo who instructed many of them, and asked him for his training hall.[51] When he assented, the students solicited enough donations to transport the training hall from Tokyo to Engakuji's grounds in Kamakura. Kojirin was thus reborn from ashes, and, from 1928, lay practitioners at Engakuji have done *zazen* in a *kendō* training hall, where a photo of the Yagyū *kendō* master is mounted on the wall to this day.

Kojirin's history points to a second site of material overlap: that of the practitioners themselves. Early Meiji lay Rinzai Zen lore at Engakuji focuses on a small circle of elite, exceptional laymen, some of whom were born into samurai families. A foremost example is Yamaoka Tesshū (1836–1888), a venerated swordsman and exceedingly rare layperson who received Dharma transmission from Engakuji master Imakita Kōsen (1816–1892) and openly taught Buddhism as both a layperson and "de facto Rinzai [master]."[52] As the makeup of the lay Rinzai community shifted in the early twentieth century, the Zen-*kendō* connection shifted, too. A disproportionate number of Tokyo-area lay practitioners were university students and other young people, and, of these, a significant number came to Zen practice through their university *kendō* clubs.

The first generation of Nyoidan practitioners included many such students. For example, early Nyoidan members Tasaki Masayoshi (1880–1976) and his classmate Suga Reinosuke, both of whom graduated from Tokyo Higher Commercial School in 1905, spoke explicitly of the overlap between the *kendō* and Zen worlds. Tasaki started as a *kendō* practitioner and subsequently found his way to Nyoidan and Engakuji. He eventually became a fervent Zen practitioner, living in the aforementioned "Strenuous Effort Quarters" at Kaizenji and participating in frequent Zen intensives.[53] Tasaki regularly practiced Zen at Nyoidan events with his classmate Suga, who praised the "way of the sword" that Tasaki and the *kendō* club pursued. Suga discussed the formation of Nyoidan as a "self-cultivation organization" (J. *shūyōdan*) in the context of the Sino-Japanese War, Russo-Japanese War, and development of Japan as a nation-state. In contrast with the *kendō* club's efficacious self-cultivation practices, Suga reported that there was no "feeling of *shūyō*" in his university's *jūjutsu* club.[54] Later Nyoidan member Uhara Yoshitoyo (b. 1885) stated that his "motivation for starting Zen practice" stemmed from various factors, though he primarily entered Zen through *kendō*, which he had practiced from middle school onward and, during university, under *kendō* master Yamada Jirōkichi (1863–1930) with fellow Nyoidan member Shimada Hiroshi.[55] Uhara recounted that fellow *kendō* club members regularly practiced Zen at Kaizenji under Nakahara Shūgaku, and one of them invited Uhara to join them. Uhara's "mind moved from *kendō* to Zen," and his commitment deepened throughout his university years, as he practiced at both Engakuji and Kaizenji and resided in Kaizenji's "Strenuous Effort Quarters."[56]

The members of Waseda University's student Zen group, Saiindan, also referred to the plethora of *kendō* practitioners who found their way to Zen practice. Saiindan's wartime generation included Shiragami Eizō (1921–2001), who recounted that, from childhood, his *kendō*-practitioner father instructed him in the martial art. In *kendō*, Shiragami sought "the wondrous realm of Yamaoka Tesshū's unity of sword and Zen [J. *kenzen ichinyo*]."[57] Shiragami attributed his affinity with Zen both to *kendō* practice and to the experience growing up amid war. From a young age, he sought to remain calm in the face of enemies and the threat of death, and later in life he was strongly drawn to the Zen practices of "sitting alone, quietly, and feeling the encouragement stick [J. *keisaku*] on [his] back."[58]

Underlying this Zen-*kendō* affinity and overlap between the respective practice communities are at least three factors: first, the layer of martial rhetoric that has long pervaded "traditional" Rinzai Zen teachings and practice; second, the context of Imperial-Way Zen, referring to Zen's complicity with Japanese militarism prior to and during the Fifteen Years' War; and, third, modern Japan's *bushidō* boom.[59] Regarding the latter, Oleg Benesch highlights the role of politician and journalist Ozaki Yukio (1858–1954) in "recovering" and promoting an ancient warrior ideal as an exemplary form of masculinity in the 1880s, in the wake of the Meiji Restoration, as samurai lost power and prestige.[60] Although the concept of the "way of the warrior" (J. *bushidō*) had not previously existed as a stable entity, it was born anew as the traditional samurai code and gained momentum following the first Sino-Japanese War (1894–1895), in symbiosis with the popularization of martial arts. A range of intellectuals and religious professionals appropriated *bushidō* to bolster claims of authority, adding to its traction as an invented tradition. In relation to Zen, Benesch presents compelling evidence that modern Japanese intellectuals deliberately constructed and promoted narratives about Zen's historic influence on samurai: "Like martial artists, Buddhists came to use bushido to establish a connection with patriotically sound 'native' traditions. Meiji Buddhists often had their patriotism and devotion to the national cause called into question, and many came to rely on bushido to prove their 'Japaneseness.'"[61] Accordingly, "a new 'national' masculine ideal of the Japanese soldier who also embodied ancient martial virtues" emerged.[62]

An emblematic expression of modern Japanese *bushidō* masculinity is found in Nitobe Inazō's (1862–1933) *Bushido: The Soul of Japan*, which was first published in English in 1900 and became an international bestseller, particularly after Japan's 1905 victory in the Russo-Japanese War.[63] Nitobe's vision hinged on an essentialized gender binary; above all, he associated *bushidō* with masculinity and contrasted *bushidō* ideals with many of women's "intrinsic" qualities. He asserted: "Bushido being a teaching primarily intended for the masculine sex, the virtues it prized in woman were naturally far from being distinctly feminine."[64] Nitobe observed a tension between samurai women's "domesticity and Amazonian traits" cultivated by *bushidō*, and he subsequently resolved this tension by proclaiming that "the domestic utility of her warlike training was in the education of her sons."[65] Similarly, Nitobe highlighted self-sacrifice as a central *bushidō* ideal for both men and women, though the gendered forms that it takes were different: "Woman's surrender of herself to the good of her husband, home, and family was as willing and honorable as the man's self-surrender to the good of his lord and country."[66]

As discussed, Nitobe's bifurcated gender roles and idealization of *bushidō* masculinity were not the only configuration of gender roles in post-Meiji Restoration Japan. However, they incorporated elements from pre-Meiji ideology and practices and powerfully resonated with modern Japan's developing ideological orthodoxy, commensurate with the growing popularity of *kendō* and Rinzai Zen practice. Even while *kendō* and the Zen-*kendō* relationship were exaggerated as age-old traditions, the Zen-*kendō* relationship was indeed strong in modern Japan, as *kendō* provided a physical setting for modern Zen practitioners, motivation for many people's Zen practice, and visceral embodiment of an intimate Zen-samurai-swordsmanship relationship. In this way, the cultivation of ideal martial masculinity through practices like *kendō* and Zen was frequently, per Nitobe's vision, seen as a contribution to imperial Japan's strength.

Kōan Performance and Gender in Rinzai Zen

While *kendō* contributed powerfully yet indirectly to inscribing and reinforcing gender ideals in modern lay Japanese Rinzai Zen, kōan practice served as a direct means of doing so, as Rinzai Zen's primary spiritual tool and as an embodied mode of practice and pedagogy. Through kōan practice, practitioners performed encounters between legendary Chan masters and disciples, nearly all male, thus embodying and reinforcing ideals of heroism and martial masculinity. Ideally, kōan practice in Rinzai Zen unites body and mind, with profound implications for gender performance. During their practice, students meditate on the kōan (literally, "public case") that their teacher assigns to them, questioning and seeking to merge with the kōan—or with an abbreviated nub of it—during formal meditation sessions and throughout daily activities.[67] Students strive to understand the kōan's meaning not through cognition but ostensibly through transcending the rational mind, with the aspiration of intuiting the enlightened perspectives expressed in the kōan and achieving a state of nonduality. Physicality and embodied understanding are crucial dimensions of kōan practice and efficacy, not only during meditation sessions but also in *sanzen*, during which the master appraises the students' demonstrations of their understanding.

Concretely, kōan collections—and Chan patriarchal literature more generally—overflow with scenarios featuring male masters, disciples, and the occasional layperson. The cases themselves consistently elevate physical displays of courage and ferocity. Chan masters both praised such qualities in the abstract and illustrated them physically via striking, shouting, and berating their students (and sometimes receiving blows from students). These scenarios are often explained in religious terms: for example, later masters interpret earlier masters' blows as exemplifying Zen antinomianism and spontaneity, which disrupt the practitioners' psychophysical paradigm and spur transcendence of the dualistic world. Such religiously focused explanations are problematic because, first, they belie the conspicuous masculinity that practitioners perform each time they practice and demonstrate these kōans. Second, they may presume that kōans serve as a spiritual tool that can be wholly transcended once the student penetrates the kōan, and that the students' subsequently enlightened state obliterates gender binaries and any distinctions between self and other.[68]

An extreme example of physical displays of ferocity comes from case 66 in the *Blue Cliff Record* (Ch. *Biyan lu*; J. *Hekiganroku*), known as "Getting Gantō's Sword." The main case reads:

> Gantō asked a monk, "Where are you coming from?" The monk said, "From the Western Capital." Gantō said, "After the rebel Kōsō passed through there, did you pick up his sword?" The monk said, "I did." Gantō approached with his neck outstretched and hollered, "Yaa!" The monk said, "The master's head has fallen." Gantō roared with laughter.
>
> Later the monk went to Seppō. Seppō asked him, "Where are you coming from?" The monk said, "From Gantō." Seppō asked, "What did he say?" The monk told the foregoing story. Seppō hit him thirty blows with his staff and drove him out.[69]

This kōan is then followed by a verse by Setchō (980–1052, Ch. Xuedou Chongxian) that includes the line "Thirty blows of the mountain cane is still getting off lightly; to take the advantage is to lose the advantage."[70]

In practice, Zen students must embody viscerally each element of the kōan in both case and commentary, from the sword's significance to that of the master's blows (a common trope in kōans). They must then display this understanding to the master "as if" they were Gantō, Seppō, or Setchō, physically expressing the ethos, which here is explicitly violent. In other words, students perform the normative masculinity of swords, simulated decapitation, shouts, and blows. Even if students do not perform them literally, they ideally channel and express the intentions behind the acts and the premodern masters' ostensibly enlightened states. Along a continuum of violence and martial masculinity, the figures of "Getting Gantō's Sword" occupy one extreme—in contrast, for example, to masters who perform enlightenment through silent sitting. However, tropes of striking and shouting recur with remarkable frequency through kōan collections and other Chan patriarchal literature that, taken together, reinforce an ethos of normative masculinity hinging on ferocity, courage, and performative violence. Masters reward spontaneous physical acts and boldness, and they regularly justify brute force in the name of spiritual benefit. Both premodern exemplars and modern practitioners share a language of "penetrating" kōans that is inherently violent and also connotes phallic sexuality.

Among modern lay Rinzai Zen practitioners, detailed accounts of advanced kōan practice and performance are scarce, due to Rinzai Zen taboos around disclosing details of kōan practice, and to the seeming rarity of lay practitioners who progressed to advanced kōan practice, relative to the number of laypeople who worked on a single kōan for the duration of their Zen career. However, practitioners' accounts attest to the persistence of tropes of heroism and ferocity in kōan practice. One such account is Shimokawa's, which sheds light on how he embodied martial ideals in his Zen practice.

Zen practice assumed for Shimokawa life-or-death significance, which fueled his relentless engagement with kōans. In his diaries, he described his efforts to rouse his ferocious spirit (J. *yūmōshin*) in practice and, in the case of his first kōan, to work on it even while walking in the road.[71] Initially, Shimokawa's descriptions of *sanzen* were brief, terse, and understated—even when he passed through his initial kōan in 1913, four months into his Zen practice.[72] Later in his diaries, however, Shimokawa started providing great detail about his kōan practice, illuminating the physicality of his encounters with Zen masters.[73] For example, in entries describing a meditation intensive at Kaiseiji in Nishi-no-miya on January 7–13, 1920, Shimokawa discussed the kōan "Xinghua's 'Hold to the Center.' " The case begins: "A monk asked Xinghua Cunjiang, 'What should one do when things come from every direction? The master said, 'Hold to the center.' The monk bowed."[74]

Shimokawa described his interactions in the *sanzen* room with his master: "The Master directly strikes the student with the stick. The student takes a stooped posture and runs around, in pain, trying to escape the room."[75] Here, the master's strike and student's pain is both literal and performative. Presumably these interactions demonstrated Shimokawa's penetration of the kōan, as he proceeded to the next kōan in the collection *Entangling Vines* (J. *Shūmon kattōshū*), Guishan's "Water Buffalo." In "Water Buffalo," the Chan master Guishan Lingyou, discussing his potential rebirth as a water buffalo, asked the monastic assembly: "If you call it a monk from Mount Gui, it's still a buffalo, and if you call it a buffalo, it's still a monk of Mount Gui. So tell me then, to get it right, what should you call it?" Shimokawa's *sanzen* records signal a high degree of embodiment, his notes reading: "Becoming a cow; behavior is running around the room, saying 'Muuuu,' " then, simply, "becoming cow-nature."[76]

Vis-à-vis embodiment in kōan practice, Shimokawa's descriptions accord with Rinzai masters' exhortations for practitioners to become one with the kōan, merging with the Zen/Chan exemplars' acts, states of mind, and ethos, per classical Chan literature and received tradition. For understanding ritual and gender performance in this context, Robert Sharf offers a helpful lens: understanding the Chan master's performance of enlightenment in terms of "play," whether in large public rituals or in private encounters with disciples.[77] The notion of "play" can accommodate ritual performance generally—in which "the form/content, subject/object, and self/other dichotomies are intentionally confounded"—and the Mahāyāna Buddhist concept of emptiness in particular.[78] Sharf highlights an "as if" component of play that does not concern belief: "One does not believe that the wafer is flesh, nor that the icon is buddha; belief has little to do with it. One simply proceeds as if it were the case."[79] Extending these notions to the *sanzen* context, the Rinzai Zen master is performing buddhahood (enlightenment), while the Zen student aspires to do so. Shimokawa's master proceeded as if he were Xinghua

Cunjiang and as if his teaching were no different than Xinghua's enlightened teaching, and Shimokawa proceeded as the monk: struck by Xinghua and comprehending, viscerally, Xinghua's teaching, "Hold to the center."

Authors examining Rinzai kōan practice in other contexts have demonstrated its potential for subverting patrilineage and the ritual performance of masculinity.[80] However, if "becoming one with" Chan patriarchs' acts and ethos is fundamental to kōan practice in Rinzai Zen, and if Rinzai Zen religious attainment is filtered through a highly embodied practice and an androcentric framework that reinforces ideals of heroism and martial masculinity, this would suggest that Shimokawa's and his contemporaries' Rinzai kōan practice is inescapably androcentric. Indeed, extant accounts of such practitioners express a highly consistent pattern in modern Japanese Rinzai Zen, in which teachers, practitioners, and practice contexts worked together to promote and reinforce a ritualized confrontation between master and disciple, both rhetorical and embodied, and in which kōan practice was a central vehicle for reinforcing this ethos.

* * *

Within lay Rinzai Zen in early twentieth-century Japan, the ideals of heroism and martial masculinity extended beyond rhetoric, as practitioners embodied through their kōan practice the masculine ideals of heroism, ferocity, and determination so intimately associated with Chan patriarchs and other Buddhist exemplars, and as many practitioners paired their Zen practice with swordsmanship. As Raewyn Connell and James W. Messerschmidt note, "Hegemonic masculinities can be constructed that do not correspond closely to the lives of any actual men. Yet these models do, in various ways, express widespread ideals, fantasies, and desires."[81] The average Japanese man was not "the archetype of a warrior, a flower of a man" like Shimokawa's assessment of General Nogi, and relatively few Rinzai Zen practitioners reached the stage of advanced kōan practice in which they enacted the martial machismo of past masters. However, such ideals of heroism resonated powerfully with modern Japanese Zen practitioners, particularly as these ideals converged with other practices and frameworks that valorized similar models of masculinity, such as *bushidō* ideology and the practice of martial arts, as well as nation-protecting self-cultivation practices.

Autobiographical accounts affirm that Zen's convergence with contemporaneous practices and frameworks produced numerous modes of inscribing and reinforcing these martial ideals. Moreover, this convergence of ideals of masculinity with actual communities of practitioners arguably served as a factor in lay Rinzai Zen's popularization in early twentieth-century Japan. Its congruence with mainstream Japanese ideals of martial masculinity—and the implication that practitioners can contribute to building a strong nation through cultivation practices in which they embody martial masculinity—likely attracted many people to Zen practice. At the same time, the valorization within lay Rinzai Zen of martial masculinity, embodiment of heroic ideals through kōan practice, and overlap with martial arts practices and communities—particularly in the context of university Zen and *kendō* clubs, most of which were off-limits to women—was inherently exclusionary and in tension with modern Zen's "rhetoric of equality."

NOTES

1. "Koji sesshinkai sankai kokoro'e," *Zendō*, no. 97 (August 1918): 59. Engakuji, a large Rinzai Zen training temple in Kamakura, was the hub of lay Zen in late nineteenth- and early twentieth-century Japan.
2. Jason G. Karlin, *Gender and Nation in Meiji Japan: Modernity, Loss, and the Doing of History* (Honolulu: University of Hawai'i Press, 2014), 20.
3. These definitions come from Kam Louie, *Theorising Chinese Masculinity: Society and Gender in China* (Cambridge: Cambridge University Press, 2002), 4.
4. Japanese Rinzai Zen has long encompassed a tension between its rhetorical rejection of literature and its creation and transmission of sophisticated literary traditions. This tension has produced ambivalence about the *bun* ideal, while Rinzai Zen's idealized antinomianism more easily accommodates the *bu* ideal.
5. Karlin, *Gender and Nation*, 21.
6. Barbara R. Ambros, *Women in Japanese Religions* (New York: New York University Press, 2015), 116.
7. Raewyn Connell and James W. Messerschmidt, "Hegemonic Masculinity: Rethinking the Concept," *Gender & Society* 19, no. 6 (December 2005): 829–59, 832.
8. Connell and Messerschmidt, "Hegemonic Masculinity," 834, 851.
9. See Rebecca Mendelson, "Fierce Practice, Courageous Spirit, and Spiritual Cultivation: The Rise of Lay Rinzai Zen in Modern Japan" (PhD diss., Duke University, 2020), especially 40–108.
10. Iizuka Iwao, *Sanzen no shiori* (Tokyo: Kōyūkan, 1920), 40.
11. See, for example, *Zendō*, no. 1 (August 1910): 55; "Onna no zazen," *Zendō*, no. 123 (December 1920): 51; and Hiratsuka Raichō, *In the Beginning, Woman Was the Sun:*

The Autobiography of a Japanese Feminist, trans. Teruko Craig (New York: Columbia University Press, 2006), 83–139.

12. This evidence comes from a diverse range of sources, including Zen groups' name registers, photographs, and practitioners' testimonials.
13. In comparison to other Japanese Buddhist sects, the Rinzai sect's idealization of male monasticism and celibacy has proved especially persistent, and the sect was among the last to adopt regulations recognizing clerical marriage. See Richard M. Jaffe, *Neither Monk nor Layman: Clerical Marriage in Modern Japanese Buddhism* (Princeton, N.J.: Princeton University Press, 2011), 214, 236.
14. Miriam Levering, "Lin-Chi (Rinzai) Ch'an and Gender: The Rhetoric of Equality and the Rhetoric of Heroism," in *Buddhism, Sexuality, and Gender*, ed. José Ignacio Cabezón (Albany: State University of New York Press, 1992).
15. These translations come from Victor Sōgen Hori, *Zen Sand: The Book of Capping Phrases for Kōan Practice* (Honolulu: University of Hawai'i Press, 2003), 6.
16. Mamiya Eijū, "Jikishin kore dōjō," *Zendō*, no. 122 (November 1920): 15.
17. Daisetz Teitaro Suzuki, *The Training of the Zen Buddhist Monk* (Boston: C. E. Tuttle, [1934] 1994), 10. The Japanese term that Suzuki uses is *nekkatsu to shinken*; for the original, see Suzuki Daisetsu, *Zendō seikatsu*, trans. Yokogawa Kenshō (Tokyo: Iwanami Shoten, 2018), 44.
18. Enomoto Shūson, "Meiji Zenkai iketsu: Katsumine Daitetsu Zenji risshiden," *Seikō: risshi dokuritsu shinpo no tomo* 20, no. 4 (April 1911): 7–11, 9.
19. Daisetz Teitaro Suzuki, *Selected Works of D. T. Suzuki, Volume 1: Zen*, ed. Richard M. Jaffe (Berkeley: University of California Press, 2015), 2. This essay was first published in 1900.
20. Enomoto, "Meiji Zenkai iketsu," 7.
21. Tokyo Higher Commercial School was later renamed Hitotsubashi University, as it is known today.
22. Hitotsubashi Nyoidan, *Tetsu nyoi* (Tokyo: Hitotsubashi Nyoidan, 1931), 257. Shimada graduated from Tokyo Higher Commercial School in 1908.
23. Nyoidan, *Tetsu nyoi*, 273. During Rōhatsu *sesshin* in some Rinzai Zen monasteries, practitioners were expected to remain awake—or at least upright—for seven full days and nights.
24. Nyoidan, 196.
25. Nyoidan, 263. This seems to be a reference to the phrase *Kunshi wa motte mizukara tsutomete yamazu*, which means: "The gentleman, through his strenuous effort, is not even breathing."
26. Ōta Tetsuzō, "Shinjō rōshi to watashi," in Nyoidan, 269–72. Ōta Tetsuzō graduated from Tokyo Higher Commercial School in 1911.
27. Nyoidan, 254.
28. Nyoidan, 255.
29. Shimokawa Yoshitarō, *Koji Zen*, ed. Matsuoka Yuzuru (Tokyo: Shimokawa Kōryū, 1935). Shimokawa's diaries were published posthumously in this book, entitled *Lay Zen* (*Koji Zen*) because of the centrality of lay Zen practice in his life and writings. His teachers included several prominent Rinzai Zen masters, including Mineo Daikyū (1860–1954) and Nakahara Nantenbō (1839–1925); Iida

Tōin (1862–1937), a physician who taught Zen as a layperson and received Dharma transmission in both Rinzai and Sōtō Zen lineages; and Ōishi Masami (1855–1935), a politician and another rare Rinzai Zen layperson who received Dharma transmission.

30. On self-cultivation and the "immovable mind" (*fudōshin*), see Shimokawa, *Koji Zen*, 17–20.
31. Shimokawa, 24.
32. Shimokawa, 30, 36.
33. Shimokawa, 38–41. Later, Shimokawa notes that that academic year, a total of three classmates (including Satō) died.
34. Shimokawa, 43.
35. Shimokawa, 62, 54.
36. Shimokawa, 62.
37. Shimokawa, 50.
38. Shimokawa, 57. Rinzai Zen masters frequently assign this kōan, known as *honrai no menmoku*, to practitioners as a first kōan.
39. Shimokawa, 57.
40. Shimokawa, 63, 66, and 232. For his full description of *sesshin*, see 62–64.
41. Shimokawa, 65, 281.
42. Shimokawa, 282.
43. Shimokawa, 64.
44. Trevor Leggett, *Three Ages of Zen: Samurai, Feudal and Modern* (Rutland, Vt.: C. E. Tuttle, 1993), 101; Iizuka, *Sanzen no shiori*, 21. Reflecting the Rinzai Zen context as well as the sociohistorical context, Leggett translates *hossen* as "spiritual warfare," and Tsuji calls it "the most important and solemn occasion in Zen training."
45. Oleg Benesch, *Inventing the Way of the Samurai: Nationalism, Internationalism, and Bushidō in Modern Japan* (Oxford: Oxford University Press, 2014); Yamada Shōji, *Shots in the Dark: Japan, Zen, and the West*, trans. Earl Hartman (Chicago: University of Chicago Press / International Research Center for Japanese Studies, 2009).
46. Alexander Bennett, *Kendo: Culture of the Sword* (Oakland: University of California Press, 2015), 125–28; G. Cameron Hurst, *Armed Martial Arts of Japan: Swordsmanship and Archery* (New Haven, Conn.: Yale University Press, 1998), 78–79, 158–61.
47. For example, Nyoidan convened a meditation intensive in a *kendō* training hall in 1930. Hitotsubashi Nyoidan, *Tetsu nyoi*, 226.
48. Waseda Daigaku Saiindan, *Saiin: Waseda Daigaku Saiindan sōritsu shijūgo shūnen kinenshi* (Tokyo: Waseda Daigaku Saiindan, 1967), 18; Tamamura Takeji and Inoue Zenjō, *Engakuji-shi* (Tokyo: Shunjūsha, 1964), 757.
49. For a detailed account of Kojirin's development, see Mendelson, "Fierce Practice," 124–51.
50. Saiindan, *Saiin*, 2, 133.
51. Saiindan, 2, 133.
52. Janine Anderson Sawada, *Practical Pursuits: Religion, Politics, and Personal Cultivation in Nineteenth-Century Japan* (Honolulu: University of Hawai'i Press, 2004), 166–71.
53. Nyoidan, *Tetsu nyoi*, 253–55, 271.

54. Nyoidan, 243–44. *Jūjutsu* is a broad term that denotes several forms of Japanese martial arts, ranging from traditional techniques that samurai used in battle to aikido and karate as we know them today.
55. Nyoidan, 261.
56. Nyoidan, 262.
57. Saiindan, *Saiin*, 89–90. This appears to be the same person as Shiragami Ikkuken, who had various connections to the world of *kendō* and *kendō*-related publications.
58. Saiindan, 89–90.
59. Regarding Zen's complicity with Japanese militarism, see Christopher Ives, *Imperial-Way Zen: Ichikawa Hakugen's Critique and Lingering Questions for Buddhist Ethics* (Honolulu: University of Hawai'i Press, 2009); and various works by Brian Victoria, including *Zen at War* (New York: Weatherhill, 1997).
60. Oleg Benesch, "Myths of Masculinity in the Martial Arts," in *The Routledge Companion to Gender and Japanese Culture*, ed. Jennifer Coates, Lucy Fraser, and Mark Pendleton (New York: Routledge, 2020), 264–65; Benesch, *Inventing the Way*, 45–56.
61. Oleg Benesch, "Reconsidering Zen, Samurai, and the Martial Arts," *Asia-Pacific Journal: Japan Focus* 14, no. 17 (September 2016): 1–23, 11, 15–16.
62. Benesch, "Myths of Masculinity," 265.
63. Benesch, *Inventing the Way*, 90–97. This work was critiqued by contemporaneous intellectuals such as Inoue Tetsujirō (1856–1944), another vociferous proponent of *bushidō* ideology.
64. Nitobe Inazō, *Bushido: The Classic Portrait of Samurai Martial Culture* (New York: Tuttle, 2004), 96.
65. Nitobe, *Bushido*, 95–96. This sentiment reflected "good wife, wise mother" (J. *ryōsai kenbo*) ideology—prevalent in imperial Japan—and an assumption that women's foremost role was bearing, rearing, and educating her children.
66. Nitobe, 99–100.
67. Kōan practice is significant in Rinzai Zen for both monastic and lay practitioners, although it is not the only practice. Early twentieth-century lay practice included seated meditation intensives (J. *zazenkai* or *sesshin*) and listening to Zen masters' sermons, while monastic practice additionally emphasized ritual, liturgy, and daily work at the monastery. Rinzai teachers occasionally assigned nonkōan meditation practices to students, such as counting the breaths. An increased emphasis on kōans is a hallmark of modern Rinzai Zen.
68. Such scholars as Victor Hori have contested what Hori calls an "instrumentalist" approach to kōan practice, as it presupposes that some kind of "pure," unmediated religious experience is possible. See G. Victor Sōgen Hori, "Kōan and Kenshō in the Rinzai Zen Curriculum," in *The Kōan: Texts and Contexts in Zen Buddhism*, ed. Steven Heine and Dale S. Wright (Oxford: Oxford University Press, 2000), 280–84.
69. This translation is by Thomas Cleary, in Tenkei Denson and Hakuin Ekaku, *Secrets of the Blue Cliff Record: Zen Comments by Hakuin and Tenkei*, trans. Thomas Cleary (Boston: Shambhala, 2000), 347 (formatting adapted).
70. Tenkei and Hakuin, *Secrets of the Blue Cliff Record*, 349.
71. Shimokawa, *Koji Zen*, 64.

72. Shimokawa, 79.
73. Shimokawa maintained these records most actively through 1922, although they go until at least 1926. See especially Shimokawa, 179–90, 191–200, 291–97, 301–5, 307–13, 315–17, 322–24, 326–28, 338–40, 360–64, 375–77, 380–81, 392–95, 446.
74. This is case 59 from the collection *Shūmon kattōshū*, or *Entangling Vines*. This translation comes from Thomas Yūhō Kirchner, *Entangling Vines: Zen Koans of the Shūmon Kattōshū* (Kyoto: Tenryu-ji Institute for Philosophy and Religion, 2004), 72–73.
75. Shimokawa, *Koji Zen*, 323. The "Master" here was either Nakahara Nantenbō or Nantenbō's disciple, Iida Tōin.
76. Shimokawa, 323.
77. Robert H. Sharf, "Ritual," in *Critical Terms for the Study of Buddhism*, ed. Donald S. Lopez Jr. (Chicago: University of Chicago Press, 2005), 253–57.
78. Sharf, "Ritual," 257.
79. Sharf, 257.
80. Ben Van Overmeire, " 'Mountains, Rivers, and the Whole Earth': Koan Interpretations of Female Zen Practitioners," *Religions* 9, no. 4 (2018): n.p.
81. Connell and Messerschmidt, "Hegemonic Masculinity," 838.

Additional Primary Sources

Nitobe Inazō. *Bushido: The Classic Portrait of Samurai Martial Culture*. New York: Tuttle, 2004.

Suzuki, Daisetz Teitaro. *The Training of the Zen Buddhist Monk*. Boston: C. E. Tuttle, [1934] 1994.

Tsuji Sōmei. "Treading the Way of Zen: The Autobiography of Tsuji Somei." Translated by Trevor Leggett. In Trevor Leggett, *Three Ages of Zen: Samurai, Feudal and Modern*, 91–141. Rutland, Vt.: C. E. Tuttle, 1993.

Bibliography

Ambros, Barbara R. *Women in Japanese Religions*. New York: New York University Press, 2015.

Benesch, Oleg. *Inventing the Way of the Samurai: Nationalism, Internationalism, and Bushidō in Modern Japan*. Oxford: Oxford University Press, 2014.

——. "Myths of Masculinity in the Martial Arts." In *The Routledge Companion to Gender and Japanese Culture*, edited by Jennifer Coates, Lucy Fraser, and Mark Pendleton, 261–69. New York: Routledge, 2020.

——. "Reconsidering Zen, Samurai, and the Martial Arts." *Asia-Pacific Journal: Japan Focus* 14, no. 17 (September 2016): 1–23.

Bennett, Alexander. *Kendo: Culture of the Sword*. Oakland: University of California Press, 2015.

Connell, Raewyn, and James W. Messerschmidt. "Hegemonic Masculinity: Rethinking the Concept." *Gender & Society* 19, no. 6 (December 2005): 829–59.

Enomoto Shūson 榎本秋村. "Meiji Zenkai iketsu: Katsumine Daitetsu Zenji risshiden" 明治禅界偉傑: 勝峰大徹禅師立志傳. *Seikō: risshi dokuritsu shinpo no tomo* 成功—立志獨立進步之友 20, no. 4 (April 1911): 7–11.

Hiratsuka Raichō. *In the Beginning, Woman Was the Sun: The Autobiography of a Japanese Feminist*. Translated by Teruko Craig. New York: Columbia University Press, 2006.

Hitotsubashi Nyoidan 一橋如意団. *Tetsu nyoi* 鉄如意. Tokyo: Hitotsubashi Nyoidan, 1931.

Hori, G. Victor Sōgen. "Kōan and Kenshō in the Rinzai Zen Curriculum." In *The Kōan: Texts and Contexts in Zen Buddhism*, edited by Steven Heine and Dale S. Wright, 280–315. Oxford: Oxford University Press, 2000.

——. *Zen Sand: The Book of Capping Phrases for Kōan Practice*. Honolulu: University of Hawai'i Press, 2003.

Hurst, G. Cameron. *Armed Martial Arts of Japan: Swordsmanship and Archery*. New Haven, Conn.: Yale University Press, 1998.

Iizuka Iwao 飯塚巖. *Sanzen no shiori* 参禅のしをり. Tokyo: Kōyūkan, 1920.

Ives, Christopher. *Imperial-Way Zen: Ichikawa Hakugen's Critique and Lingering Questions for Buddhist Ethics*. Honolulu: University of Hawai'i Press, 2009.

Jaffe, Richard M. *Neither Monk nor Layman: Clerical Marriage in Modern Japanese Buddhism*. Princeton, N.J.: Princeton University Press, 2011.

Karlin, Jason G. *Gender and Nation in Meiji Japan: Modernity, Loss, and the Doing of History*. Honolulu: University of Hawai'i Press, 2014.

Kirchner, Thomas Yūhō, trans. *Entangling Vines: Zen Koans of the* Shūmon Kattōshū. Kyoto: Tenryu-ji Institute for Philosophy and Religion, 2004.

"Koji sesshinkai sankai kokoro'e" 居士接心會参會心得. *Zendō*, no. 97 (August 1918): 59.

Leggett, Trevor. *Three Ages of Zen: Samurai, Feudal and Modern*. Rutland, Vt.: C. E. Tuttle, 1993.

Levering, Miriam. "Lin-Chi (Rinzai) Ch'an and Gender: The Rhetoric of Equality and the Rhetoric of Heroism." In *Buddhism, Sexuality, and Gender*, edited by José Ignacio Cabezón, 137–56. Albany: State University of New York Press, 1992.

Louie, Kam. *Theorising Chinese Masculinity: Society and Gender in China*. Cambridge: Cambridge University Press, 2002.

Mamiya Eijū 間宮英宗. "Jikishin kore dōjō" 直心是道場. *Zendō*, no. 122 (November 1920): 15.

Mendelson, Rebecca. "Fierce Practice, Courageous Spirit, and Spiritual Cultivation: The Rise of Lay Rinzai Zen in Modern Japan." PhD diss., Duke University, 2020.

Nitobe Inazō. *Bushido: The Classic Portrait of Samurai Martial Culture*. New York: Tuttle, 2004.

"Onna no zazen" 女の座禅. *Zendō*, no. 123 (December 1920): 51.

Sawada, Janine Anderson. *Practical Pursuits: Religion, Politics, and Personal Cultivation in Nineteenth-Century Japan*. Honolulu: University of Hawai'i Press, 2004.

Sharf, Robert H. "Ritual." In *Critical Terms for the Study of Buddhism*, edited by Donald S. Lopez Jr., 245–70. Chicago: University of Chicago Press, 2005.

Shimokawa Yoshitarō 下川芳太郎. *Koji Zen* 居士禅. Edited by Matsuoka Yuzuru 松岡讓. Tokyo: Shimokawa Kōryū, 1935.

Suzuki Daisetsu 鈴木大拙 (a.k.a. Daisetz Teitaro Suzuki). *Zendō seikatsu* 禅堂生活. Translated by Yokogawa Kenshō 横川顕正. Tokyo: Iwanami Shoten, 2018.

Suzuki, Daisetz Teitaro (a.k.a. Suzuki Daisetsu). *Selected Works of D. T. Suzuki*, vol. 1: *Zen*. Edited by Richard M. Jaffe. Berkeley: University of California Press, 2015.

——. *The Training of the Zen Buddhist Monk*. Boston: C. E. Tuttle, 1994 [1934].

Tamamura Takeji 玉村竹二 and Inoue Zenjō 井上禅定. *Engakuji-shi* 圓覺寺史. Tokyo: Shunjūsha, 1964.

Tenkei Denson and Hakuin Ekaku. *Secrets of the Blue Cliff Record: Zen Comments by Hakuin and Tenkei*. Translated by Thomas Cleary. Boston: Shambhala, 2000.

Van Overmeire, Ben. " 'Mountains, Rivers, and the Whole Earth': Koan Interpretations of Female Zen Practitioners." *Religions* 9, no. 4 (2018): n.p.

Victoria, Brian [Daizen]. *Zen at War*. New York: Weatherhill, 1997.

Waseda Daigaku Saiindan 早稲田大学済蔭団. *Saiin: Waseda Daigaku Saiindan sōritsu shijūgo shūnen kinenshi* 済蔭:早稲田大学済蔭団創立四十五周年記念誌. Tokyo: Waseda Daigaku Saiindan, 1967.

Yamada Shōji. *Shots in the Dark: Japan, Zen, and the West*. Translated by Earl Hartman. Chicago: University of Chicago Press / International Research Center for Japanese Studies, 2009.

Zendō 禅道. Zendōkai, 1910–1923.

SIX

Macho Buddhism (Redux)

Gender and Sexualities in the Diamond Way

BEE SCHERER

Positioning "Macho Buddhism" (2022 Introduction)

In November 2011, my article "Macho Buddhism" appeared in the inaugural issue of the journal *Religion and Gender* (using my first name's deadname before I made my nonbinary trans subjectivity public in 2014). With this article, I expanded on my conceptual-ethnographic research on the neotraditionalist Karma Kagyu Tibetan Buddhist movement the Diamond Way, and its founder and leader, the Danish Lama Ole Nydahl (b. 1941).[1]

The Diamond Way reaction to the publication of "Macho Buddhism" was prompt and equaled an excommunication. Prior to its publication, I was still invited to Diamond Way centers around the world with the courtesy status of an "International Traveling Teacher" (in the clunky Diamond Way jargon of that time); I also co-led a Karma Kagyu Tibetan and Buddhist Studies initiative called Institute of Tibetan and Asian Studies (ITAS) that I had cofounded in 2004 under the auspices of (one of) the Seventeenth Karmapa hierarch(s), His Holiness Thaye Dorje, in an Diamond Way–associated retreat center, Karma Guen, in the Axarquía foothills of the Spanish Sierra Nevada. I managed to continue my leadership at the ITAS against growing Diamond Way opposition until the end of 2012: after organizing the 6th International Buddhist Forum there (with a brief guest appearance by Nydahl, the last time we met), despite the forum's great success, I was made persona non grata at the Karma Guen retreat center for "criticizing Lama Ole" after eight years of spending approximately two to three months every year (i.e., all my winter, spring, and summer recess time) working pro bono for the higher education institute I cofounded there. As I reflected in a 2014 article:

> As many constructive theologians and "scholars-cum-practitioner" I have regularly found myself in an ethnographic state of identitarian fluidity between observer-participant, necessarily oscillating between insider and outsider and/or inhabiting hybrid and/or liminal spaces of ethnographic privilege and internal voice and visibility. In this context it is important to acknowledge that scholars of any religious tradition are not static focal points themselves . . ., but are continuously changing themselves and always and necessarily co-shaping the very discourses they study and analyse. Still, the observer-participant-co-shaper tension and the struggle to maintain authenticity and integrity as both ethnographer and Buddhist thinker & teacher has resulted in my current, slightly eccentric liminal state, where I am viewed as a friendly abject in the Diamond Way and a suspected sectarian analyser of a controversial contemporary Buddhist movement in a (now decreasing) part of academia. Perhaps, inimical double exclusion can be an indication of fairly balanced (and thus non-partisan) scholarship?[2]

I am grateful that "Macho Buddhism" remains a timely piece of scholarship. Orthodox, hegemonic, or toxic masculinities operate widely within (g)local and transnational Tibetan Buddhist (post)modernities. Such masculinities are vital building blocks of "aphallophobia," or the "fear to lose 'phallic' (in Lacan's terms) power, which drives toxic hegemonic masculinity and (binary cis-)heteropatriarchy."[3] In aphallophobia the threatening and oppressing phallos (i.e., phallus)—religious, or otherwise—is erected in aid of the continuous cisheteropatriarchal policing of fundamental biopolitical dogmata: gender binary (male-female) and gender hierarchy (male above female).[4]

Further, Tibetan Buddhism in the Global North can rightly be criticized as yet another playing field for the commodification of spirituality and (post-)Buddhism or even as a spiritual smokescreen for a consciously self-deluding and self-inflating complicity with late-capitalist neoliberalism, with its dominant demographics coming from a traditional white bourgeois puritanical habitus accompanied by a cisheterosexist and patriarchal sexual lexicon. Ann Gleig and Brenna Artinger's analysis of the "Buddhist Culture Wars" illustrates this well.[5]

In transnational Tibetan Buddhist movements, these demographics encounter inherited sexuality and gender habitus and lexica that are readable and recognizable in their own sexual and gender grammar, both in counterpuritanical iconoclasm and reactionary reinscriptions of (cishetero) patriarchal prudishness. Combined with the exploitation of ill-understood guru devotion, male leaders of such transnational Buddhist movements can use systemic masculine toxicity—an important dimension of the hegemonic masculinity that Connell theorizes—in targeting "angry white converts" for their proselytizing, as well as utilizing abuse apologetics in the form of paradigms of transgression (such as "crazy wisdom"), and the "Dharma-splaining" of sexual hedonism in tantric contexts, or harnessing the power of denial, taboo, and mystified (tantric vow) codependency to commit abuse.[6] Such sexual, mental, and physical abuse in contemporary transnational Tibetan Buddhism has only recently been given increasing attention by survivor movements (#metooguru) and nascent research on the topic.[7]

For instance, in the case of Chogyam Trungpa (1939–1987) and Shambhala, one could argue that there is an organizational legacy of abuse running through the decades as the movement's "family constellation" (intergenerational trauma), as a nexus of displaced secrets and enabling that include the explicit or tacit complicity of senior female leaders.[8] In the case of Rigpa's late leader Sogyal Lakar (1947–2019), despite the overwhelming evidence for physical and sexual abuse, modern transnational Tibetan leaders such as Dzongsar Khyentse Rinpoche (b. 1961) appear to have become complicit with victim-blaming and the performance of "angry privileged Tibetan men," Dharma-bashing allegedly uneducated Westerners without reflecting on their own complicity with cis/heteropatriarchal systemic abuse.[9]

In Nydahl's case, questions about his overt criticism of Islam have recently eclipsed the discussion of his machismo. Nydahl lost a four-year-long court case in Austria against being characterized as *islamfeindlich* (Islamophobic).[10] During this protracted case and prompted by further anti-Islam statements by Nydahl in Germany in April 2019, the German Buddhist Union (DBU) started expulsion proceedings against the Diamond Way that the organization preempted by leaving the DBU on June 17, 2019.[11] Nonetheless, perhaps Nydahl's macho attitudes and habitus deserve a fresh intersectional look: Nydahl's statements can be read as white savior syndrome regarding Muslim women; his right-wing rhetoric and his displaced sexism, dressed up as the sexualized-appreciative male gaze, constitute an inextricable nexus that appears to offer a particular form of an enchanted, right-wing, heteropatriarchal biotope (i.e., habitat) for entitled white (cishetero)men and their enablers.

Rereading "Macho Buddhism" remains urgent in light of these related phenomena: transnational Tibetan Buddhist leaders' performances, lexicon, and habitus of masculinity; the queering of (cisheteropatriarchal) oppression from a queer-feminist liberation "theology" (Dharmology) perspective; and the continued need for positive, inclusive, and nonoppressive forms of masculinity in transnational Tibetan Buddhist groups "after toxic masculinity."[12]

Bee Scherer Amsterdam, Netherlands, September 2022

Macho Buddhism: Gender and Sexualities in the Diamond Way

This chapter addresses masculinity in the postcolonial context of Tibetan Buddhism's globalization. It focuses on a particular Western lay convert Buddhist movement, the Diamond Way—part of the global Karma Kagyu (T. bKa' brgyud) school of Tibetan Buddhism, under the guidance of the Danish Buddhist master Lama Ole Nydahl (b. 1941). Focusing on sexual ethics, gendered normativities, and sexual diversity, I investigate three intersecting questions with methodological pluralism. The approaches of historical-textual Tibetan Buddhist studies demonstrate how Nydahl's teachings are located in the Tibetan Buddhist tradition. Qualitative ethnographic approaches and discourse analysis elucidate Nydahl's own performance and understanding of gender and sexualities, particularly hegemonic masculinity, and how Nydahl's example shapes normativities within the Diamond Way. Finally, I adopt the perspective of Buddhist theology or Buddhist critical-constructive thought, informed by queer theory, to critique Nydahl's chosen location within the Tibetan Buddhist tradition in the context of Buddhist modernity. This combination of historical, sociological, and theological approaches promises new insights in the multifaceted intersection of Buddhism and masculinity. Thus, issues of masculinity, sexual ethics, and sexualities serve as a way to question the location of this contemporary Tibetan Buddhist movement in the "tradition vs. modernity" debate.

The globalization of Tibetan Buddhism(s) developed its specific dynamics from the exile and diaspora experience of most of its spiritual and political elite after the communist Chinese occupation of Tibet in the 1950s. The initial impulse for organizational restructuring and spiritual centralization and unification of the Tibetan Buddhist community in exile gradually ebbed away, and contemporary Tibetan Buddhism emerged in the global village in its full diversity. From the late 1960s onward, immigrant, ethnic, or "baggage" Tibetan Buddhism was complemented by "import," "elite," or convert Buddhism.[13] Tibetan Buddhism also developed missionary features and can be partly described as "evangelical" or "export" Buddhism, in Jan Nattier's terminology.[14] Tensions have arisen between yogic, decentralized, and eclectic tendencies on the one hand, and monastic, centralized, and traditionalist currents on the other.[15] Unsurprisingly, Buddhist modernism, with its emphasis on detraditionalization, demythologization, and psychologization, features strongly in contemporary convert Tibetan Buddhism.[16] However, any dichotomist typology of contemporary Tibetan Buddhism along the line of convert vs. immigrant or modernist vs. traditionalist falls short.[17]

"Adherents" and "sympathizers" of contemporary Tibetan Buddhism form a patchwork of hybrid religious identities.[18] "Convert" is still a meaningful category for the sociological approach to global Tibetan Buddhism, but Tibetan Buddhist convert movements defy categorization as modernist or traditionalist. Nydahl's Diamond Way illustrates this point: in Roy Wallis's typology of new religious movements, it is a "world-affirming" group whose packaging of Tibetan Buddhism is modernist, but whose content (teaching) is mostly traditional.[19] It can be described as "neo-orthodox" in Peter Berger's terms.[20] In contrast, another contemporary "world-affirming" lay Karma Kagyu group, Chogyam Trungpa's Dharmadhatu and his Shambhala lineage, can be described as neotraditionalist in form, but iconoclastic and post-Buddhist in content.[21] Both examples illustrate that any binary categorization of Western Buddhist convert movements along the modern vs. traditional axis is too simplistic in the postcolonial context of globalization. Rather, tradition and modernity only serve as one set of poles in a multipolar continuum of individual expressions and performances, which illustrate different modes and degrees of hybridity. Views and performances of masculinity and sexuality in the Diamond Way serve as a case in point.

The founder of the Diamond Way, Ole Nydahl, is both a charismatic and controversial figure. Born into an educated Danish middle-class household,

Nydahl was a drug-smuggling hippie when he encountered Tibetan Buddhism in Nepal and reformed himself. He became a devoted student of the Sixteenth Karmapa hierarch of the Tibetan Karma Kagyu school. This branch of Tibetan Buddhism traces back to the unconventional practitioners (Sk. *mahāsiddhas*) of the Yoginī tantras from late medieval India; it is characterized by its emphasis on meditation and a close teacher-student relationship.[22] Since the 1970s, Nydahl has established more than six hundred lay Buddhist centers worldwide (including many centers in the Global South, particularly in Central and South America). After the Sixteenth Karmapa's death in 1981 and the subsequent schism within the Kagyu community over the recognition of the Seventeenth Karmapa in the early 1990s, Nydahl supported the highest lineage authority of the school—Shamar Rinpoche—against the other lineage holders and established himself as an authenticated lay teacher and lama, as well as a key political factor on that side of the schism.[23]

Nydahl's teachings and lifestyle have attracted criticism from Tibetan Buddhists and scholars.[24] Still, these criticisms regularly do not take emic Tibetan Buddhist paradigms into consideration. From a "hermeneutics of recovery" (in Paul Ricœur's terminology), most of his activities can be meaningfully interpreted as authentic and traditional, and occasionally as an expression of the typically Kagyu "crazy wisdom."[25]

Sexual Ethics in the Diamond Way

The Diamond Way is clearly sex positive.[26] Nydahl propagates a self-proclaimed non-neurotic approach to sexuality: while celibacy pertains to monks, it is not for a layperson like himself.[27] Nydahl was happily married to his wife, Hannah, until her death in 2007. He was also openly promiscuous, sleeping with many female students during his earlier teaching tours in the 1970s and 1980s. In 1990, he committed himself to a steady second intimate partner, Caty Hartung (until 2004). Nydahl propagates healthy and joyful (hetero)sexuality and an unabashed heteromachismo.[28]

Traditional Indian and Tibetan lay Buddhist sexual ethics regarding promiscuity are ambiguous and heterosexist, privileging the male layperson and providing ample loopholes.[29] In this context, Nydahl's promiscuity is not completely modernist. Nydahl sees sexual activity as an important part of a full, mentally healthy life.[30] He frames this joyfully lived (hetero)sexuality and his frequent sexual innuendos and jokes as part of his missionary work to keep neurotic and difficult people away from his centers.[31] This psychologization is not traditionalist and (hetero)sexual libertinism is hardly characteristic for Tibetan Buddhist convert groups in the West, where a rather puritanical atmosphere usually prevails.[32]

Nydahl also views another aspect of lay Buddhist sexual ethics as outdated cultural baggage: prohibitions against oral and anal sex. In the highly influential tradition of Vasubandhu's fourth-century scholastic compendium the *Treasury of Abhidharma* (Sk. *Abhidharmakośa*) and its autocommentary, Tibetan Buddhism has generally rejected any form of oral and anal intercourse on the grounds that it constitutes sexual misconduct.[33] Nydahl interprets such teachings as being culturally and historically contingent and mainly resulting from hygienic concerns.[34] With this interpretation, Nydahl is in line with other Tibetan Buddhist teachers in the West, including the 14th Dalai Lama, probably the highest representative of Tibetan Buddhist orthodoxy.[35]

Important insights into Nydahl's lifestyle can be found in his book *Der Buddha und die Liebe* (Buddha and Love), which places love, sexuality, and gender into the broader context of the Karma Kagyu tradition.[36] *Der Buddha und die Liebe*, as a partnership and human development guide for the Diamond Way (heterosexual) lay practitioner, expands considerably on the rather simple (but poignant) interpretation of Buddhist sexual ethics as "not harming sexually and not breaking hearts unnecessarily."[37] The book is both traditional and modernist, catering to the needs of convert Western laypeople. By placing questions of love and partnership in the tantric context, it provides numerous clues about Nydahl's own lifestyle. He sees himself in the tradition of the aforementioned *mahāsiddhas*: precursors of the Tibetan Kagyu tradition and their "crazy yogi" successors in Tibet who used transgressive and unconventional methods (including sexuality) in their teachings, which also characterizes modern-day crazy yogis such as Chogyam Trungpa.[38] Although Nydahl makes it clear that he does not teach sexual tantra as such, and, when he and a female student sleep together, they do so as equals, the tantric yogi template provides an emic paradigm for interpreting Nydahl's sexualized teaching and lifestyle. On the other hand, several convert Tibetan Buddhist groups have been marred by scandals concerning abuse of power. Allegations of sexually abusing students have been made against Trungpa, Kalu Rinpoche, and Sogyal Rinpoche, to name just a few; Nydahl displays high awareness of these issues and frequently comments on these scandals.[39] Consistent with universally accepted Buddhist sexual ethics, Nydahl condemns any form of coercion.[40] The minutes of the German-speaking center meeting in October 2006 record allegations of unwanted intimacy and sexual bullying in a few Diamond Way Centers; Nydahl and the organization have taken these allegations very seriously. Nydahl's overt and self-described non-neurotic approach to (hetero) sexuality is only partially modernist, although his personality and style certainly attract less traditional students as Buddhist converts.

Hegemonic Heteromachismo

Nydahl combines yogic unconventionality and his approach to sexuality with traditional heteromachismo, which underlies both his own upbringing in 1950s Denmark and mainstream Tibetan culture. Despite the tantric dissolution of gender binaries in advanced meditation practice and the acknowledgment of the fluid middle in Tibetan medicine, Nydahl retains a thoroughly hegemonic heteronormative outlook on sex and gender.[41] Although tantric meditation both acknowledges and deconstructs "male" and "female" as inner polarities rather than outer realities, Nydahl follows mainstream Tibetan and pre- or, rather, counterfeminist Western gender stereotyping. He combines this essentialist interpretation of gender binaries and differences with popular pseudoscientific evolutionary-biological views, attributing to males the tunnel vision of the Neolithic hunter while the female "remained in the caves and cared for the offspring."[42]

Nydahl's propagation of a counterfeminist, conservative gender stereotype is consistent with heteronormative elements of the Tibetan Buddhist tradition.[43] His personal admiration of and praise for the opposite sex also aligns with Buddhist doctrines. Particularly in the Yoginī tantras (which are held in highest esteem in the Kagyu traditions), the female enlightened principle is seen as the source of deepest inspiration and even holds the key to the (male heterosexual) practitioner's development.[44] Additionally, the initiations (Sk. *abhiṣeka*) into the Yoginī tantric systems, which are an intrinsic part of more advanced Karma Kagyu practices, come with promises (Sk. *samaya*) that include the vow to see every female being on the highest level as a *ḍākinī* (i.e., goddess) and to never speak badly to or about a woman.

Nydahl takes these "highest yoga" promises very seriously, and his views on gender and sexuality are to be interpreted in this context; he is not prepared to leave tantric understanding of gender and sexuality on a mere symbolic and archetypal level, as did his wife, Hannah.[45]

Nydahl himself projects a hypermasculine image befitting his self-identification as a Dharma-protector.[46] Critics of the Diamond Way linked to the countercult movement of Protestant churches in Switzerland and Germany have not only taken offense at his high-libido sexual activities, but also his persistent (albeit merely rhetorical and metaphorical) linking of high-adrenaline sports (e.g., motorcycling, bungee jumping, and sky diving) and sexuality to experiences of enlightenment.[47] A hermeneutics of suspicion can easily see here the encouragement of a general hedonism, sexual (hyper)activity, and extrovert masculinity/femininity. Nydahl's hypermasculinity and heteromachismo seem to have promulgated a peculiar type of Diamond Way style. In the 1980s, Nydahl's followers already appeared conspicuously distinct from their fellow Western Kagyu converts. Recounting tensions at a large Kagyu course in Germany in 1985, Nydahl humorously characterized his students as "former troublemakers and hard cases" in contrast to another lama's "Bhagwanese and flower children."[48] More recently, Nydahl has explicitly acknowledged the problematic perception of Diamond Way heteromachismo and linked this issue to the important student-teacher relationship and guru devotion.[49] When asked why there is a preference for and predominance of "young macho he-lions" in the Diamond Way, Nydahl answered:

> Every teaching and teacher attract their own people. Our special merit is giving access to many fresh minds which would probably not otherwise be attracted to the Dharma. Other religions should be glad that we take the difficult non-sheep! Also we are not the only Kagyus. People who wish to become monks and nuns may go to France and receive excellent training.
>
> By the way: Caty [and eighteen additional names] and a dozen other of our exciting power-ladies would enjoy finding themselves within this category [i.e., "macho lion"].[50]

From the perspective of hegemonic discourses in countercult movements, the deep devotion that Nydahl inspires in his students must seem alarming. To the outsider, this level of personal loyalty shown to Nydahl appears to directly contradict the prevailing rhetoric of critical thinking that is supposed to characterize Buddhism(s), and that Nydahl himself uses as a tool for detraditionalization—for example, when he calls his students "non-sheep" and "fresh minds":

> Where but in Buddhism, however, shall sharp and critical people find the same transparency and effectiveness in their practices as from their computer? Those who will only trust what they can analyze logically and are embarrassed by exotic lifestyles especially need us to be bright. We simply have to keep a level of mental freshness these people can identify with, because where else can they go? It is always a pity when people end up with nihilism, political correctness, or drugs because they cannot find a spiritual way they can trust. . . . It is a healthy sign that my students think ever more independently and become increasingly critical towards any spirituality which is artificial and sugar-sweet. This ensures a clear and unshakable development and will attract other fresh minds.[51]

When uncritically imitating the lama's style, Nydahl's fresh minds can appear distinctively less fresh and independent. However, from a hermeneutics of trust, the tantric/mahāsiddhic guru devotion tradition of Tibetan Buddhism provides an interpretative frame—even for heteromachismo—when imitating the lama: the root or heart lama (Sk. *mūla-guru*, T. *rtsa ba'i bla ma*) is the sole source of spiritual development comprising blessing (the living authentic transmission), method (the tantric means), and protection (holding the view and applying it in daily life).[52] Gampopa (T. sGam po pa, 1079–1153)—founder of the Dagpo Kagyu (T. Dwags po bKa' brgyud) tradition, which includes the Karma Kagyu—particularly emphasized guru-devotion as the single white panacea (T. *dkar po chig thub*) for spiritual development.[53] Although it is generally seen as a sign of immaturity to imitate the teacher to the degree of copying personal traits, it is normally accepted as a transitory stage in personal development. The enthusiasm that Nydahl inspires in his followers shows that this identification works. The results of transitional, uncritical devotion and hypertrophic heteromachismo depends on the dynamic of the resultant spiritual transformation. Within this tradition, one can argue that the Karma Kagyu path offers the gradual way of spiritual development, and that, with more meditation experience, the sharpest edges of machismo are bound to disappear.

Queer as Kagyu?

Nydahl's view on gender and sexualities remains completely heteronormative. In relation to gay and lesbian sexuality he simply states, "Homosexual relationships I cannot fathom"; however, he relates this assertion to his own lack of experience.[54] Stating that his few gay students are "often gifted," but "do not have an easy life," Nydahl echoes the popular postenlightenment Western stereotype of the "gifted, but tragic homosexual" connected to the pathologization of same-sex desire and the invention of essentialist "homosexuality" in the nineteenth century.[55] He also speculates about the prevalence of strong jealousy in same-sex relationships and the assumed ego-enhancing quality of same-sex desire; these would allegedly constitute an obstacle for Buddhist practice, which aims to weaken and dissolve the ego into the experience of nonduality.[56] Nydahl seems to unwittingly echo Fritz Morgenthaler's mid-twentieth-century psychoanalytical theory of homosexuality privileging "autonomy," versus the "identity" or "integration" that underlies heterosexual relationships.[57]

Nydahl admits feeling uncomfortable with the idea of "two gentlemen kissing."[58] In his autohagiographical account *Riding the Tiger*, which recounts the early charismatic missionary phase of the Diamond Way movement, Nydahl uses "homosexuality" as a punch line to exemplify the (post)hippie generation's confused state of mind. In narrating his 1976 travels with the Sixteenth Karmapa in the United States, Nydahl relates that an audience of Trungpa's students included the poet Allen Ginsberg, who wanted to talk with the Karmapa about "homosexuality and pollution." In Nydahl's judgment, these were questions "with little substance" and "up in the air, like a cup of thin new-age tea."[59] Nydahl further recalls how in Denmark in 1981 he and his students upset a "sour intellectual newspaper" associated with "communists and homosexuals," which, again, was clearly not his cup of tea.[60]

Nydahl's homophobic subtexts are consistent with his projection of hegemonic hypermasculinity and his counterfeminist heterosexism, yet surprisingly out of sync with the great emphasis he places on Western democracy and human rights, especially when criticizing nondemocratic and oppressive religious expressions.[61] Nydahl's modernist (and potentially colonialist) recourse to secular, universal rights and values seems to contradict his squeamishness about homosexuality, since LGBTIQ+ (Lesbian, Gay,

Bisexual, Transgender, Intersex and Queer/Questioning) rights could be seen as an integral part of what Nydahl essentializes as human rights.

Still, Nydahl's views on homosexuality have adapted over the years from more or less overtly homophobic statements to his current neutral acceptance of homosexuality with implicit mildly homophobic undertones. He admits that he used to think homosexuals were "a bit funny" and has said, "When I was younger I thought that sexual orientation was the most important factor in shaping the character."[62] From the end of the 1990s, however, Nydahl stressed that he does not consider the issue of sexual orientation as terribly important anymore.[63] Still, in a question-and-answer-book published in Hungary in 1998, he more or less equates homosexuals with "sexual extremists."[64] In 2001, in an interview given to a German-language magazine in Los Angeles, Nydahl stated that homosexual relationships are "not advised" in Buddhism, since "they seem to bring more suffering, disease and disturbing emotions than normal relationships" (note the heterosexist qualifier "normal").[65] Even in more recent statements, Nydahl reinforces homophobic stereotypes when warning against "them" spreading diseases or even "chasing kids," assuming the popular conflation of pedophilia with homosexuality.[66] On the other hand, he attempts to communicate his newfound neutrality on the issue when he states that "the Buddha was clever enough to broadly steer clear of our bedrooms."[67]

Doctrinally, Nydahl explains homosexuality as the result of either aversion to the opposite sex in previous lives or strong partnership (karmic) bonds from previous lives, which are maintained even after the partners find themselves in the same sex/gender in their current lives.[68] As is not unusual within Tibetan Buddhism, these explanations are attributed to the historical Buddha, although no evidence for this claim can be adduced. Moreover, no premodern Tibetan source seems to contain such explanations, which is not surprising, given the lack of any identitarian concept of "homosexuality" in premodern Tibetan thought. It is reasonable to assume that Nydahl would have received these or similar explanations from his traditional Tibetan Buddhist masters, such as the Sixteenth Karmapa or Kalu Rinpoche, who had to react to new sets of questions raised in contact with Western modernity and the globalization of Tibetan Buddhism.

Nydahl's mild homophobia is largely consistent with mainstream Tibetan Buddhism. Any conclusions about sexual tolerance within the Tibetan cultural sphere based on the apparently condoned same-sex relations reported in some ethnographic accounts of warrior monks (T. *ldab ldob*) and practices in Tibetan Buddhist monasteries would be premature.[69] On a doctrinal level, Tibetan Buddhist sexual ethics clearly condemns same-sex activity as sexual misconduct (T. *log g.yem*). The genealogy of this sentiment suggests that the Tibetan assimilation of Indian Buddhism has mainstreamed existing notions about same-sex desire. In Tibetan culture, same-sex sexual contacts are prohibited as a breach of celibacy for monks and nuns, along with any other sexual activity. However, there is no evidence that same-sex sexuality between laypersons was prohibited in early Buddhism, and references to the condemnation of intragender sexuality begin only after (and possibly because) Indian society was exposed to sexually less liberal views during the rule of the Central Asian Kushans in the first to fourth centuries CE. For instance, Buddhaghosa (early fifth century CE), in his commentary on the *Collection of Long Discourses* (P. *Dīgha nikāya*; DA 853), classifies same-sex sexual activity as sexual misconduct (P. *kāmesu micchācāra*). Vasubandhu's *Treasury of Abhidharma*, which is seen as the normative source of scholastic views in Tibetan monastic traditions, prohibits opposite-sex anal and oral sex. Vasubandhu does not explicitly refer to same-sex intercourse, but same-sex anal and oral sex seems to be prohibited by analogy. The prohibition of same-sex intercourse is only made explicit in the Tibetan tradition by Gampopa, whose foundational text on the Dagpo Kagyu Buddhist path, the *Jewel Ornament of Liberation* (T. *dam chos yid bzhin gyi nor bu thar pa rin po che'i rgyan*, abbreviated as *Thar rgyan*), elaborates on sexual activities involving the prohibited orifices by including male-male sexuality: "Inappropriate (sexual) conduct is constituted by force, male-male, or male-third gender oral or anal intercourse."[70]

The contemporary, globalizing Tibetan Buddhist tradition can still be interpreted as mainly homo- and transphobic and has only slowly adapted to Western concepts of sexual orientation and gender identities in this regard. This process of reluctant adaptation is exemplified in the Dalai Lama's change in teaching style after the outcry he provoked with traditional homophobic teachings in San Francisco in the late 1990s and his subsequent meeting with representatives of LGBTIQ+ activism and queer Buddhists.[71] Within this ongoing process of adaptation, Nydahl admits to remaining "old-fashioned"; he appears to be more hesitant and conservative than Chogyam Trungpa was during the 1970s and 1980s.[72] Trungpa did not have any reservations about gay students and even appointed a bisexual student as his Vajra regent. This regent subsequently behaved irresponsibly in his sexuality and proved to be uncontrollable, having unprotected sex with both male and female students although he was clearly aware of his HIV+ status.[73] Nydahl uses Trungpa's tribulations to justify the turnaround in his own promiscuous behavior when entering into a more mellow ménage a trois in the 1990s:

> But then AIDS arrived on the scene; as a teacher I just had to set an example. There was a well known Buddhist group, Dharmadhatu, whose bisexual teacher knew since 1983 that he was HIV positive. But he didn't tell his students until 1988 and didn't protect them. Some became sick and some died. It was a terrible scandal. When this became public, I knew that something like this must never happen to the Diamond Way. Hence I became more settled. It is going very well with Hannah and Caty [his now deceased wife and his then second intimate partner, respectively].[74]

The negative experience within Trungpa's Vajradhatu influenced Nydahl's own performance of gender and sexuality; it also seems to have reinforced some of his prejudices against nonheterosexualities.

Nydahl's rather limited capability to comprehend the diversity of human sexualities and gender identities leads one to question if he is thereby limiting insight into the fluidity of reality, which includes gender and sexualities. This fluidity is crucial for Buddhist thought and can provide many liberating social impulses.[75] In line with Buddhist fluid interpretation of human identities, Nydahl expresses the view that sexual preference can change, but uses this only to reinforce his heteronormative stance. For example, he admits to being glad whenever one of his students changes his nonheterosexual preference to heterosexuality.[76] Nydahl assumes that he has very few gay and lesbian students, and Diamond Way courses have only marginal LGBTIQ+ visibility.[77] Still, some of Nydahl's closest students are openly gay and travel globally in his name throughout his centers as International Traveling Teachers.

Nydahl's heterosexist and binarist view on gender identity and performance is consistent with the prevalent androcentrism and heterosexism of Tibetan Buddhist orthodoxy. He is not prepared to transfer and adapt Tibetan Buddhist tantric teachings to queer identities as, for example, Jeffrey Hopkins did.[78] Nydahl firmly states that tantric sexual union practice is not for gay practitioners, though he does not transmit these highly advanced practices to any of his students.[79]

Another issue of contention is gay marriage. In those countries that recognize the Diamond Way as a church or official religion (Denmark, Austria, Poland, Hungary, and Russia), Nydahl is legally authorized to officiate at weddings. However, he refuses to officiate at same-sex ceremonies (which would be legally possible in Denmark and Austria). He also regularly conducts informal Buddhist wedding ceremonies at his courses around the world according to Buddhist tantric (heteronormative) ritual. All of these tantric ceremonies are open to heterosexual couples only; however, Nydahl offers and frequently conducts informal partnership blessings for his gay and lesbian students. He explains the difference in treatment of heterosexual and nonheterosexual couples with his own lack of understanding of gendered roles within same-sex relationship. In his view, the embodiment of polar gender roles is central for the tantric rite he uses for heterosexual couples.[80]

While there is evidence for the interpretation of Nydahl's current views on nonheterosexualities as reluctantly neutral or only mildly homophobic, the hegemonic heteromachismo among many of his students, especially in Central and Eastern Europe, is still creating a difficult and occasionally openly homo/transphobic atmosphere in the Diamond Way. This is exemplified by the fate of a tiny LGBTIQ+ group, which formed in 2008 on a now-defunct internal platform, Virtual Sangha.[81] In its short, two-year existence, it counted only forty-two members (0.44 percent of the Virtual Sangha's total members) and attracted homophobic cyber bullying and preemptive self-censoring, displayed discussion strings burdened by queer angst and shame, and was finally removed from this Diamond Way social networking site in 2010. Lost in Kagyu cyberspace, the queer Diamond Way voices seem to have fallen silent.[82]

* * *

The diachronic and synchronic approaches to masculinities and sexualities in the Diamond Way locate this particular Tibetan Buddhist convert movement between traditionalism and modernism. Nydahl's view on and performance of hegemonic masculinities and sexualities are consistent with his propagation of convert Buddhist neo-orthodoxy/praxy. Further, the Diamond Way's hybrid—and, in part, paradoxical—responses to modernity illustrate the need to question (or even to queer) the binary categorizations of modernism vs. traditionalism in describing Western Buddhist convert movements and, by extension, of new religious movements in the postcolonial context of globalization. Clearly, negotiating issues of gender and sexualities and, more broadly, negotiating religious identities in the contemporary global village and spiritual supermarket creates different shades of institutional and individual hybridity and eclecticism.

Nydahl's choices within the space afforded to him by both the Tibetan Buddhist tradition and modern discourses exhibit the peculiar tension, in which the Diamond Way navigates (post)modernity. This tension is exemplified by Nydahl's combination of sex-positivity and heteromachismo. Feminist critiques of Buddhism(s) successfully inform contemporary global Buddhist movements (in particular Socially Engaged Buddhism).[83] However, in questions of gender and sexualities, Nydahl's neo-orthodox/prax Dharma moves firmly and rather unimaginatively within traditional Tibetan Buddhist parameters, with the exception of the Diamond Way's decisively sex-positive, nonpuritanical position. However, Nydahl's self-proclaimed non-neurotic approach to sex is interpellated with his own overt heteromachismo and with the pre/counterfeminist gender stereotyping consistent with his own postwar upbringing in Denmark and with traditional Tibetan cultural sentiments. Although Nydahl's teachings on the subject of sexuality can be broadly viewed as sex-affirmative and emancipating, they support and favor heteromachismo and seem to privilege Nydahl's own gender performance of hegemonic hypermasculine heterobravado. Nydahl's meandering and squeamish statements on LGBTIQ+ matters exhibit a strained neutrality or mild homophobia and result in the prevalence of queer invisibility among his students in the Diamond Way.

From the position of Buddhist theology or Buddhist critical-constructive thought, Nydahl's self-confessed old-fashioned attitudes and his uneasiness about nonheterosexualities and nonbinary gender identities and performances appear as a missed opportunity.[84] In many Buddhist movements in the West, LGBTIQ+ practitioners successfully claimed or created a queer space.[85] In fact, queer theory, with its emphasis on the fluidity of identities, ideally converges with Tantric technologies of the self and the fluid constructions and deconstructions of identity in Tantric Buddhist philosophy and practice. One can argue that acknowledging the kinship between Tantric Buddhist philosophy and queer theory, and incorporating queering and queered paradigms into Buddhist convert discourses, would retain the authenticity of the teachings while adapting Buddhism for the West in a truly inclusive way.

NOTES

1. The research outputs of this project include: "Macho Buddhism: Gender and Sexuality in the Diamond Way," *Religion and Gender* 1 (2011): 85–103; "Globalizing Tibetan Buddhism: Modernism and Neo-Orthodoxy in Contemporary Karma bKa' brgyud Organizations," *Contemporary Buddhism* 13 (2012): 125–37; "Queer as Kagyu: Negotiating Dissident Identities in Neo-Orthodox Buddhist Spaces," in *Queering Paradigms*, vol. 3: *Bio-Politics, Place, and Representations*, ed. Kathleen O'Mara and Liz Morrish (Oxford: Peter Lang, 2013), 145–55; "Trans-European Adaptations in the Diamond Way: Negotiating Public Opinions on Homosexuality in Russia and in the U.K," *ONLINE—Journal of Religions on the Internet* 6 (2014): 103–25; "Conversion, Devotion, and (Trans-)Mission: Understanding Ole Nydahl," in *Buddhists: Understanding Buddhism Through the Lives of Practitioners*, ed. Todd Lewis (London: Blackwell Wiley, 2014), 96–106; "Interpreting the Diamond Way: Contemporary Convert Buddhism in Transition," *Journal of Global Buddhism* 10 (2015): 17–48; and "A Neo-orthodox Buddhist Movement in Transition: The Diamond Way," in *Visioning New and Minority Religions: Projecting the Future*, ed. Eugene V. Gallagher (London: Routledge, 2017), 156–65.
2. Scherer, "Trans-European Adaptations," 108.
3. In Lacanian theory, the phallus signifies the desire of the Other—in other words, it is the quality the paternal figure possesses that makes him an object of maternal desire and allows him to dominate the maternal figure. Jacques Lacan, *Feminine Sexuality: Jacques Lacan and the École Freudienne*, ed. Juliet Mitchell and Jacqueline Rose, trans. Jacqueline Rose (New York: Norton, 1983), 84–85; Bee Scherer, "Beyond Heteropatriarchal Oppression: Inhabiting Aphallic Anthroposcapes," in *Queering Paradigms VII: Contested Bodies and Spaces*, ed. Bee Scherer (Oxford: Peter Lang, 2018), 74.
4. Scherer, "Beyond Heteropatriarchal Oppression."
5. Ann Gleig and Brenna Artinger, "#BuddhistCultureWars: BuddhaBros, Alt-Right Dharma, and Snowflake Sanghas," *Journal of Global Buddhism* 22, no. 1 (2021): 19–48.
6. On the potential toxicity of hegemonic masculinity, see Raewyn Connell and James W. Messerschmidt, "Hegemonic Masculinity: Rethinking the Concept," *Gender & Society* 19, no. 6 (December 2005): 829–59, 840.
7. See the Henry R. Luce Foundation research project headed by Ann Gleig and Amy Paris Langenberg, https://www.religionandsexualabuseproject.org (accessed December 13, 2021); and Ann Gleig and Amy Paris Langenberg, "Sexual Misconduct

and Buddhism: Centering Survivors," The Shiloh Project, November 18, 2020, https://www.shilohproject.blog/sexual-misconduct-and-buddhism-centering-survivors/ (accessed December 13, 2021).

8. See, for example, Matthew Remski, "A Disorganized Attachment Legacy at Shambhala: Brief Notes on Two Letters and a 1993 Interview with Pema Chödrön," July 11, 2018, http://matthewremski.com/wordpress/a-disorganized-attachment-legacy-at-shambhala-brief-notes-on-two-letters-and-a-1993-interview-with-pema-chodron/ (accessed December 13, 2021).
9. Joanne Clark, "Dzongsar Khyentse & his Dance with Nihilism," Beyond the Temple, August 13, 2021, https://beyondthetemple.com/dzongsar-khyentse-his-dance-with-nihilism/.
10. Ursache\Wirkung Editors, "Ole Nydahl versus Ursache\Wirkung," Ursache\Wirkung, January 9, 2020, https://www.ursachewirkung.com/blog/3491-ole-nydahl-versus-ursache-wirkung.
11. See the note of resignation (in German): Nadia Wyder, Martina Wesemann, and Manfred Kessler, "Austritt aus der BDU e.V.," Dokumente und Informationen zum Austritt des Buddhistischen Dachverbands Diamantweg (BDD) aus der Deutschen Buddhistischen Union (DBU), June 17, 2019, https://dbu.diamantweg-buddhismus.de/BDD_Austritt_aus_der_DBU.html. A collection of sources about these events can be found at "Organisation Diamantweg," Recht, Bewahrung und Transfer des Wissens der Tibetischen Medizin, Ludwig-Maximilians-Universität München, https://www.transtibmed.ethnologie.uni-muenchen.de/recht/diamantweg/index.html (accessed November 29, 2022).
12. Bee Scherer, "Queering Buddhist Traditions," *Oxford Research Encyclopedia of Religion*, June 28, 2021, https://oxfordre.com/religion/view/10.1093/acrefore/9780199340378.001.0001/acrefore-9780199340378-e-765.
13. On "baggage," "import," and "elite" Buddhism, see Jan Nattier, "Who Is a Buddhist? Charting the Landscape of Buddhist America," in *The Faces of Buddhism in America*, ed. Charles S. Prebish and Kenneth T. Tanaka (Berkeley: University of California Press, 1998), 189. On convert Buddhism, see Martin Baumann, "Protective Amulets and Awareness Techniques, or How to Make Sense of Buddhism in the West," in *Westward Dharma: Buddhism Beyond Asia*, ed. Charles S. Prebish and Martin Baumann (Berkeley: University of California Press, 2002), 54.
14. Lionel Obadia, "Tibetan Buddhism in France: A Missionary Religion?," *Journal of Global Buddhism* 2 (2001): 92–122; Scherer, "Interpreting the Diamond Way," 27; Nattier, "Who Is a Buddhist?," 189–90.
15. Geoffrey Samuel, *Tantric Revisionings: New Understandings of Tibetan Buddhism and Indian Religion* (New Delhi: Motilal Banarsidass, 2005), 324–29.
16. David L. McMahan, *The Making of Buddhist Modernism* (Oxford: Oxford University Press, 2008), 42–59.
17. Baumann, "Protective Amulets," 54–59.
18. Thomas Tweed, "Who Is a Buddhist? Night-Stand Buddhists and Other Creatures," in *Westward Dharma: Buddhism Beyond Asia*, ed. Charles S. Prebish and Martin Baumann (Berkeley: University of California Press, 2002), 17–33.

19. Jens Hjort Andersen, "Tibetansk Buddhisme i Danmark," *Chaos: Dansk-Norsk Tidsskrift for Religionshistoriske Studier* 20 (1994): 138–54, 152; Scherer, "Interpreting the Diamond Way," 36–39.
20. Eva Sabine Saalfrank, *Geistige Heimat im Buddhismus aus Tibet: Eine empirische Studie am Beispiel der Kagyüpas in Deutschland*, (Ulm: Fabri Verlag, 1997), 224–28.
21. [Bee] Scherer, "The Globalization of Tibetan Buddhism: Contemporary Karma bKa' brGyud Movements Between Modernism and Tradition" (paper presented at the Globalization of Contemporary Buddhism Conference, Minzu University, Beijing, December 18–20, 2009).
22. Scherer, "Interpreting the Diamond Way," 21–23.
23. Scherer, 29.
24. Scherer, 25, 30, 35–39.
25. For Ricœur's hermeneutics, see Alison Scott-Baumann, *Ricœur and the Hermeneutics of Suspicion* (London: Continuum, 2009); and Scherer, 23, 31, 33–35.
26. This term was coined within the context of second-wave feminism in the 1980s. George Becker, "The Social Regulation of Sexuality: A Cross-Cultural Perspective," *Current Perspectives in Social Theory* 5 (1984): 45–69.
27. Christopher Kelleher, "Pure Light: An Interview with Lama Ole Nydahl," January 6, 2008, https://web.archive.org/web/20080708231942/http://www.rakemag.com/multimedia/video/pure-light.
28. Ole Nydahl, "Wo steht der Diamantweg-Buddhismus?," *Buddhismus Heute* 44 (Winter 2007): 7–8.
29. Paul Harvey, *An Introduction to Buddhist Ethics* (Cambridge: Cambridge University Press, 2000), 72.
30. Ole Nydahl, "Der heiße Thron," *Kagyü Life* 23 (1997): 21–39, 32; Ole Nydahl, "Keeping Buddhism Alive," *Buddhism Today* 4 (1998): 33.
31. Nydahl, "Der heiße Thron," 31–32.
32. See James William Coleman, *The New Buddhism: The Western Transformation of an Ancient Tradition* (Oxford: Oxford University Press, 2001), 181; and Samuel, *Tantric Revisionings*, 329.
33. Harvey, *Introduction to Buddhist Ethics*, 72–73.
34. Ole Nydahl, *Glubina slavyaskogo uma: Byddizm v voprosakh i otvetakh. Tom II* (*The Depth of the Slavic Mind: Buddhism in Questions and Answers*, vol. 2), trans. Vagid Ragimov, Piotr Kalachin, and Elena Leontyeva (Moscow: Diamond Way, 2015), 213–14 (transcript of an answer given in Ulan Ude, February 2006).
35. Anthony E. Richardson, "How My Teacher Taught Me Tibetan Buddhism: A Gay Practitioner Remembers," in *Queer Dharma: Voices of Gay Buddhists*, vol. 2, ed. Winston Leyland (San Francisco: Gay Sunshine, 2000), 178; Harvey, *Introduction to Buddhist Ethics*, 432–33.
36. Ole Nydahl, *Der Buddha und die Liebe* (Munich: Knaur MensSana, 2005). Translations have been published in a dozen languages; the English edition is *Buddha and Love: Timeless Wisdom for Modern Relationships*, trans. Kristina Slade and Enno Jacobsen (San Francisco: Diamond Way, 2012).
37. Nydahl, *Der Buddha und die Liebe*, 61.

38. Scherer, "Interpreting the Diamond Way," 23; Scherer, "Globalization of Tibetan Buddhism."
39. Nydahl "Der heiße Thron," 26–27; Ole Nydahl, "Verrückte Weisheit und der Stil des Verwirklichers," *Buddhismus Heute* 37 (2004): 48–57, 49. This section is omitted in the abridged English version of this "Crazy Wisdom" interview; Ole Nydahl, "Crazy Wisdom," *Diamond Way Time* 1 (2003): 48–54.
40. Harvey, *Introduction to Buddhist Ethics*, 72.
41. [Bee] Scherer, "Gender Transformed and Meta-Gendered Enlightenment: Reading Buddhist Narratives as Paradigms of Inclusiveness," *Revista de Estudos da Religião* 6, no. 3 (2006): 65–76, 74; Janet Gyatso, "One Plus One Makes Three: Buddhist Gender, Monasticism, and the Law of the Non-Excluded Middle," *History of Religions* 43, no. 2 (November 2003): 89–115, 100–104.
42. Nydahl, *Der Buddha und die Liebe*, 154–61; Ole Nydahl, "Frauen," *Buddhismus Heute* 42 (Winter 2006): 26–33, 29.
43. Nydahl, 151–96.
44. See the following benchmark studies: Miranda Shaw, *Passionate Enlightenment: Women in Tantric Buddhism* (Princeton, N.J.: Princeton University Press, 1994); Adelheid Herrmann-Pfandt, *Dakinis: Zur Stellung und Symbolik des weiblichen im tantrischen Buddhismus* (Marburg: Indica et Tibetica, 2001); and Serinity Young, *Courtesans and Tantric Consorts* (London: Routledge, 2004).
45. Asked about male-female, Hannah Nydahl declared "that they are mere archetypes, not to be taken so literal" (personal communication, May 2005, Karma Guen/Spain).
46. Scherer, "Interpreting the Diamond Way," 25, 34–35.
47. Georg Schmid, "Verschmelzen mit Karmapa: Faszination und Dynamik des Karma-Kagyü-Buddhismus," Relinfo, Evangelische Informationsstelle: Kirchen—Sekten—Religionen, 1998, https://www.relinfo.ch/lexikon/themen/besuche-bei-gemeinschaften/lama-ole-nydahl/verschmelzen-mit-karmapa/ (accessed November 30, 2022); Christian Ruch, "Buddha, Bungee, Bettgeschichten: Der Lifestyle-Buddhismus von 'Lama' Ole Nydahl," in *"Wenn Eisenvögel fliegen . . . :" Der Tibetische Buddhismus und der Westen*, ed. Ulrich Dehn and Christian Ruch (Berlin: Evangelische Zentralstelle für Weltanschauungsfragen EZW, Pamphlet No. 185, 2006), 32–36. For an overview and critique of the countercult movement, see George D. Chryssides, *Exploring New Religions* (London: Continuum, 1999), 342–65.
48. Ole Nydahl, *Riding the Tiger: Twenty Years on the Road—Risks and Joys of Bringing Tibetan Buddhism to the West* (Nevada City, Calif.: Blue Dolphin, 1992), 264.
49. Nydahl, "Wo steht der Diamantweg-Buddhismus?," 7–8.
50. Nydahl, 8 (author's translation).
51. Nydahl, "Keeping Buddhism Alive," 33.
52. On the guru in tantra, Vajrayāna, and especially Karma Kagyu, see Jim Rheingans, "The Eighth Karmapa's Life and His Interpretation of the Great Seal" (PhD diss., University of the West of England, Bath Spa University, 2008), 231–35. For a broader emic discussion, see Alexander Berzin, *Wise Teacher, Wise Student: Tibetan Approaches to a Healthy Relationship* (Ithaca, N.Y.: Snow Lion 2010).

53. David Jackson, *Enlightenment by a Single Means: Tibetan Controversies on the "Self- Sufficient White Remedy" (dkar po chig thub)*, Österreichische Akademie der Wissenschaften, Philosophisch-historische Klasse Sitzungsberichte 615; Beiträge zur Kultur- und Geistesgeschichte Asiens 12, 1994, 150–51.
54. Ole Nydahl, "Love and Partnership," *Buddhism Today* 1 (1996): 26–30, 30.
55. Nydahl, "Der heiße Thron," 32; Ian Marsh, "Queering Suicide: The Problematic Figure of the 'Suicidal Homosexual' in Psychiatric Discourse," in *Queering Paradigms*, ed. Bee Scherer (Oxford: Peter Lang, 2010), 141–45.
56. Nydahl, 32.
57. Fritz Morgenthaler, *Homosexualität, Heterosexualität, Perversion* (Frankfurt: Fischer, [1961, 1980] 1987), 95–139.
58. Ole Nydahl, "Was sagt der Buddhismus zu Homosexualität," Fragen an den Lama, March 19, 2008, http://www.lama-ole-nydahl.de/fragen/?p=163 (accessed October 6, 2008).
59. Nydahl, *Riding the Tiger*, 93.
60. Nydahl, 191.
61. Nydahl, "Der heiße Thron," 22–25; Ole Nydahl, "The Changing Face of the Sangha," *Buddhism Today* 7 (2000): 31–33.
62. Ole Nydahl, *Bungee mądrości: Buddyzm Diamentowej Drogi w pytaniach i odpowiedziach*, trans. Wojciech Tracewski (Gdańsk: Czerwony Słoń, 2003), 107; Ole Nydahl, "Was sagt der Buddhismus."
63. Ole Nydahl, *Glubina slavyaskogo uma: Byddizm v voprosakh i otvetakh. Tom I* (*The Depth of the Slavic Mind: Buddhism in Questions and Answers*, vol. 1), trans. Vagid Ragimov (Kiev: Dialog, 2005), 284 (transcript of an answer given in Novosibirsk, August 1999).
64. Ole Nydahl, *Egy Jogi 109 Válasza: Válogatás, Láma Ole Nydahl tanításaiból*, 3rd ed., trans. Peter Lahucsky (Budapest: Gyémánt Út Buddhista Közösség, [1998] 2004), 47.
65. Ole Nydahl, "Ein Interview mit Lama Ole Nydahl," interview by Martina Zemlicka, *Buddhismus Heute* 32 (2001): 14–23, 20.
66. Nydahl, "Ein Interview," 20; Nydahl, "Was sagt der Buddhismus"; Nydahl, *Glubina slavyaskogo uma I*, 284.
67. Nydahl, "Was sagt der Buddhismus."
68. Nydahl, "Was sagt der Buddhismus"; Nydahl, "Ein Interview," 20; Nydahl, *Bungee mądrości*, 107–18.
69. Melvyn C. Goldstein, "A Study of the Ldab ldob," *Central Asian Journal* 9, no. 2 (June 1964): 123–41; José Ignacio Cabezón, "Homosexuality and Buddhism," in *Homosexuality and World Religions*, ed. Arlene Swidler (Valley Forge, Penn.: Trinity Press International, 1993), 93; Harvey, *Introduction to Buddhist Ethics*, 424–25. On negative attitudes toward same-sex desire in contemporary Tibetan communities in exile, see P. Christiaan Klieger, "Engendering Tibet: Power, Self, and Change in the Diaspora," in *Tibet, Self, and the Tibetan Diaspora: Voices of Difference*, ed. P. Christiaan Klieger (Leiden: Brill, 2002), 151.
70. rigs pa ma yin pa ni/ brdeg cing spyod pa'o// yang na po'am/ ma ning gi kha'am bshang lam du spyod pa'o// sGam po pa, *Thar rgyan*, ed. Khenpo Sonam Gyatso (Benares: Central Institute for Higher Tibetan Studies, 1999), 74.

71. Dennis Conkin, "The Dalai Lama and Gay Love," in *Queer Dharma: Voices of Gay Buddhists*, vol. 1, ed. Winston Leyland (San Francisco: Gay Sunshine, 1998); Harvey, *Introduction to Buddhist Ethics*, 432–33.
72. Nydahl uses the term *altmodisch*. Nydahl, "Was sagt der Buddhismus."
73. Scherer, "Globalization of Tibetan Buddhism," 4–5.
74. Nydahl, "Ein Interview mit Lama Ole Nydahl," 21 (author's translation).
75. Scherer, "Gender Transformed."
76. Nydahl, "Ein Interview," 20.
77. Nydahl, "Was sagt der Buddhismus."
78. Jeffrey Hopkins, *Sex, Orgasm, and the Mind of Clear Light: The Sixty-Four Arts of Gay Male Love* (Berkeley, Calif.: North Atlantic, 1998).
79. Ole Nydahl, "Dakini to żeńska zasada oświecenia," trans. Wojtek Tracewski, *Diamantowa Droga* 23 (Autumn 1999), http://diamentowadroga.pl/dd23/dakini_to_zenska_zasada_oswiecenia (accessed November 30, 2022).
80. Ole Nydahl, personal communication, September 2011.
81. The URL for this group was http://virtualsangha.ning.com/, but this site is no longer active.
82. Bee Scherer, "Queer Voices, Social Media, and Neo-orthodox Dharma: A Case Study" (paper presented at the Association for Asian Studies Annual Meeting, Honolulu, March 31, 2011).
83. See in particular the work of Rita M. Gross, including *Buddhism After Patriarchy* (Albany: State University of New York Press, 1993); and Karma Lekshe Tsomo, ed. *Buddhist Women Across Cultures* (Albany: State University of New York Press, 1999). The Orientalist perspective of Western feminism has been criticized in, for example, Wei-Yi Cheng, *Buddhist Nuns in Taiwan and Sri Lanka: A Critique of the Feminist Perspective* (New York: Routledge, 2007).
84. Roger Jackson and John Makransky, eds., *Buddhist Theology: Critical Reflections by Contemporary Buddhist Scholars* (London: Routledge Curzon, 2000).
85. Wendy Cadge, "Lesbian, Gay, and Bisexual Buddhist Practitioners," in *Gay Religion*, ed. Scott Thumma and Edward R. Gray (Walnut Creek, Calif.: AltaMira, 2004); Roger Corless, "Coming Out in the *Sangha*: Queer Community in American Buddhism," in *The Faces of Buddhism in America*, ed. Charles S. Prebish and Kenneth T. Tanaka (Berkeley: University of California Press, 1998); Winston Leyland, ed., *Queer Dharma: Voices of Gay Buddhists*, vol. 1 (San Francisco: Gay Sunshine, 1998); Winston Leyland, ed., *Queer Dharma: Voices of Gay Buddhists*, vol. 2 (San Francisco: Gay Sunshine, 2000).

Additional Primary Sources

Books by Ole Nydahl

Buddha and Love: Timeless Wisdom for Modern Relationships. Translated by Kristina Slade and Enno Jacobsen. San Francisco: Diamond Way, 2012.

Entering the Diamond Way: Tibetan Buddhism Meets the West. Grass Valley, Calif.: Blue Dolphin, [1985] 1999.
Riding the Tiger: Twenty Years on the Road—Risks and Joys of Bringing Tibetan Buddhism to the West. Grass Valley, Calif.: Blue Dolphin, 1992.
The Way Things Are: A Living Approach to Buddhism for Today's World. Nevada City, Calif.: Blue Dolphin, 1996.

Magazine

Buddhism Today (1996–). Biannual magazine published by the Diamond Way Buddhist centers. https://buddhism-today.org/ (accessed November 30, 2022).

Bibliography

Andersen, Jens Hjort. "Tibetansk Buddhisme i Danmark." *Chaos: Dansk-Norsk Tidsskrift for Religionshistoriske Studier* 20 (1994): 138–54.
Baumann, Martin. "Protective Amulets and Awareness Techniques, or How to Make Sense of Buddhism in the West." In *Westward Dharma: Buddhism Beyond Asia*, edited by Charles S. Prebish and Martin Baumann, 51–65. Berkeley: University of California Press, 2002.
Becker, George. "The Social Regulation of Sexuality: A Cross-Cultural Perspective." *Current Perspectives in Social Theory* 5 (1984): 45–69.
Berzin, Alexander. *Wise Teacher, Wise Student: Tibetan Approaches to a Healthy Relationship.* Ithaca, N.Y.: Snow Lion 2010.
Cabezón, José Ignacio. "Homosexuality and Buddhism." In *Homosexuality and World Religions*, edited by Arlene Swidler, 81–101. Valley Forge, Penn.: Trinity, 1993.
Cadge, Wendy. "Lesbian, Gay, and Bisexual Buddhist Practitioners." In *Gay Religion*, edited by Scott Thumma and Edward R. Gray, 139–51. Walnut Creek, Calif.: AltaMira, 2004.
Cheng, Wei-Yi. *Buddhist Nuns in Taiwan and Sri Lanka: A Critique of the Feminist Perspective.* New York: Routledge, 2007.
Chryssides, George D. *Exploring New Religions.* London: Continuum, 1999.
Clark, Joanne. "Dzongsar Khyentse & his Dance with Nihilism." Beyond the Temple, August 13, 2021. https://beyondthetemple.com/dzongsar-khyentse-his-dance-with-nihilism/.
Coleman, James William. *The New Buddhism: The Western Transformation of an Ancient Tradition.* Oxford: Oxford University Press, 2001.
Conkin, Dennis. "The Dalai Lama and Gay Love." In *Queer Dharma: Voices of Gay Buddhists*, vol. 1, edited by Winston Leyland, 351–56. San Francisco: Gay Sunshine, 1998.
Connell, Raewyn, and James W. Messerschmidt. "Hegemonic Masculinity: Rethinking the Concept." *Gender & Society* 19, no. 6 (December 2005): 829–59.

Corless, Roger. "Coming Out in the *Sangha*: Queer Community in American Buddhism." In *The Faces of Buddhism in America*, edited by Charles S. Prebish and Kenneth T. Tanaka, 253–65. Berkeley: University of California Press, 1998.

Gam po pa. *Thar rgyan*. Edited by Khenpo Sonam Gyatso. Benares: Central Institute for Higher Tibetan Studies, 1999.

Gleig, Ann, and Amy Paris Langenberg. "Sexual Misconduct and Buddhism: Centering Survivors." The Shiloh Project, November 18, 2020. https://www.shilohproject.blog/sexual-misconduct-and-buddhism-centering-survivors/.

Gleig, Ann, and Brenna Artinger. "#BuddhistCultureWars: BuddhaBros, Alt-Right Dharma, and Snowflake Sanghas." *Journal of Global Buddhism* 22, no. 1 (2021): 19–48.

Goldstein, Melvyn C. "A Study of the Ldab ldob." *Central Asian Journal* 9, no. 2 (June 1964): 123–41.

Gross, Rita M. *Buddhism After Patriarchy*. Albany: State University of New York Press, 1993.

Gyatso, Janet. "One Plus One Makes Three: Buddhist Gender, Monasticism, and the Law of the Non-Excluded Middle." *History of Religions* 43, no. 2 (November 2003): 89–115.

Harvey, Paul. *An Introduction to Buddhist Ethics*. Cambridge: Cambridge University Press, 2000.

Herrmann-Pfandt, Adelheid. *Dakinis: Zur Stellung und Symbolik des weiblichen im tantrischen Buddhismus*. Marburg: Indica et Tibetica, 2001.

Hopkins, Jeffrey. *Sex, Orgasm, and the Mind of Clear Light: The Sixty-Four Arts of Gay Male Love*. Berkeley, Calif.: North Atlantic, 1998.

Jackson, David. *Enlightenment by a Single Means: Tibetan Controversies on the "Self-Sufficient White Remedy" (dkar po chig thub)*. Österreichische Akademie der Wissenschaften, Philosophisch-historische Klasse Denkschriften 615; Beiträge zur Kultur- und Geistesgeschichte Asiens 12, 1994.

Jackson, Roger and John Makransky, eds. *Buddhist Theology: Critical Reflections by Contemporary Buddhist Scholars*. London: Routledge Curzon, 2000.

Karma Lekshe Tsomo, ed. *Buddhist Women Across Cultures*. Albany: State University of New York Press, 1999.

Klieger, P. Christiaan. "Engendering Tibet: Power, Self, and Change in the Diaspora." In *Tibet, Self, and the Tibetan Diaspora: Voices of Difference*, edited by P. Christiaan Klieger, 139–54. Leiden: Brill, 2002.

Lacan, Jacques. *Feminine Sexuality: Jacques Lacan and the École Freudienne*. Edited by Juliet Mitchell and Jacqueline Rose. Translated by Jacqueline Rose. New York: W. W. Norton, 1983.

Leyland, Winston, ed. *Queer Dharma: Voices of Gay Buddhists*, vol. 1. San Francisco: Gay Sunshine, 1998.

——. *Queer Dharma: Voices of Gay Buddhists*, vol. 2. San Francisco: Gay Sunshine, 2000.

Marsh, Ian. "Queering Suicide: The Problematic Figure of the 'Suicidal Homosexual' in Psychiatric Discourse." In *Queering Paradigms*, edited by Bee Scherer, 141–59. Oxford: Peter Lang, 2010.

McMahan, David L. *The Making of Buddhist Modernism*. Oxford: Oxford University Press, 2008.

Morgenthaler, Fritz. *Homosexualität, Heterosexualität, Perversion.* Frankfurt: Fischer, [1961, 1980] 1987.

Nattier, Jan. "Who Is a Buddhist? Charting the Landscape of Buddhist America." In *The Faces of Buddhism in America*, edited by Charles S. Prebish and Kenneth T. Tanaka, 183–95. Berkeley: University of California Press, 1998.

Nydahl, Ole. *Buddha and Love: Timeless Wisdom for Modern Relationships.* Translated by Kristina Slade and Enno Jacobsen. San Francisco: Diamond Way, 2012.

——. *Bungee mądrości: Buddyzm Diamentowej Drogi w pytaniach i odpowiedziach.* Translated by Wojciech Tracewski. Gdańsk: Czerwony Słoń, 2003.

——. "The Changing Face of the Sangha." *Buddhism Today* 7 (2000): 31–33.

——. "Crazy Wisdom." *Diamond Way Time* 1 (2003): 48–54.

——. "Dakini to żeńska zasada oświecenia." Translated by Wojtek Tracewski. *Diamantowa Droga* 23 (Autumn 1999). http://diamentowadroga.pl/dd23/dakini_to_zenska_zasada_oswiecenia (accessed June 2011).

——. *Der Buddha und die Liebe.* Munich: Knaur MensSana, 2005.

——. *Egy Jogi 109 Válasza: Válogatás, Láma Ole Nydahl tanításaiból.* Translated by Peter Lahucsky. 3rd ed. Budapest: Gyémánt Út Buddhista Közösség, [1998] 2004.

——. "Frauen." *Buddhismus Heute* 42 (Winter 2006): 26–33.

——. "Der heiße Thron." *Kagyü Life* 23 (1997): 21–39.

——. *Glubina slavyaskogo uma: Byddizm v voprosakh i otvetakh. Tom I* (*The Depth of the Slavic Mind: Buddhism in Questions and Answers*, vol. 1). Translated by Vagid Ragimov. Kiev: Dialog, 2005.

——. *Glubina slavyaskogo uma: Byddizm v voprosakh i otvetakh. Tom II* (*The Depth of the Slavic Mind: Buddhism in Questions and Answers*, vol. 2). Translated by Vagid Ragimov, Piotr Kalachin, and Elena Leontyeva. Moscow: Diamond Way, 2015.

——. "Ein Interview mit Lama Ole Nydahl." Interview by Martina Zemlicka. *Buddhismus Heute* 32 (2001): 14–23.

——. "Keeping Buddhism Alive." *Buddhism Today* 4 (1998): 33.

——. "Love and Partnership." *Buddhism Today* 1 (1996): 26–30.

——. "Pure Light: An Interview with Lama Ole Nydahl." Interview by Christopher Kelleher, November 2007, January 6, 2008. http://www.rakemag.com/multimedia/video/pure-light. Archived at https://web.archive.org/web/20080708231942/http://www.rakemag.com/multimedia/video/pure-light (accessed January 18, 2022).

——. *Riding the Tiger: Twenty Years on the Road—Risks and Joys of Bringing Tibetan Buddhism to the West.* Grass Valley, Calif.: Blue Dolphin, 1992.

——. "Verrückte Weisheit und der Stil des Verwirklichers." *Buddhismus Heute* 37 (2004): 48–57.

——. "Was sagt der Buddhismus zu Homosexualität." Fragen an den Lama, March 19, 2008. http://www.lama-ole-nydahl.de/fragen/?p=163.

——. "Wo steht der Diamantweg-Buddhismus?" *Buddhismus Heute* 44 (Winter 2007): 7–8.

Obadia, Lionel. "Tibetan Buddhism in France: A Missionary Religion?" *Journal of Global Buddhism* 2 (2001): 92–122.

"Organisation Diamantweg." Recht, Bewahrung und Transfer des Wissens der Tibetischen Medizin, Ludwig-Maximilians-Universität München. Accessed

November 30, 2022. https://www.transtibmed.ethnologie.uni-muenchen.de/recht/diamantweg/index.html.

Remski, Matthew. "A Disorganized Attachment Legacy at Shambhala: Brief Notes on Two Letters and a 1993 Interview with Pema Chödrön." July 11, 2018. http://matthewremski.com/wordpress/a-disorganized-attachment-legacy-at-shambhala-brief-notes-on-two-letters-and-a-1993-interview-with-pema-chodron/.

Rheingans, Jim. "The Eighth Karmapa's Life and His Interpretation of the Great Seal." PhD diss., University of the West of England, Bath Spa University, 2008.

Richardson, Anthony E. "How My Teacher Taught Me Tibetan Buddhism: A Gay Practitioner Remembers." In *Queer Dharma: Voices of Gay Buddhists*, vol. 2, edited by Winston Leyland, 161–82. San Francisco: Gay Sunshine, 2000.

Ruch, Christian. "Buddha, Bungee, Bettgeschichten: Der Lifestyle-Buddhismus von 'Lama' Ole Nydahl." In *"Wenn Eisenvögel fliegen . . . :" Der Tibetische Buddhismus und der Westen*, edited by Ulrich Dehn and Christian Ruch, 32–36. Berlin: Evangelische Zentralstelle für Weltanschauungsfragen EZW, pamphlet no. 185, 2006.

Saalfrank, Eva Sabine. *Geistige Heimat im Buddhismus aus Tibet: Eine empirische Studie am Beispiel der Kagyüpas in Deutschland*. Ulm: Fabri Verlag, 1997.

Samuel, Geoffrey. *Tantric Revisionings: New Understandings of Tibetan Buddhism and Indian Religion*. New Delhi: Motilal Banarsidass, 2005.

Scherer, Bee. "Beyond Heteropatriarchal Oppression: Inhabiting Aphallic Anthroposcapes." In *Queering Paradigms VII: Contested Bodies and Spaces*, edited by Bee Scherer, 65–81. Oxford: Peter Lang, 2018.

——. "Conversion, Devotion, and (Trans-)Mission: Understanding Ole Nydahl." In *Buddhists: Understanding Buddhism Through the Lives of Practitioners*, edited by Todd Lewis, 96–106. London: Blackwell Wiley, 2014.

——. "Gender Transformed and Meta-Gendered Enlightenment: Reading Buddhist Narratives as Paradigms of Inclusiveness." *Revista de Estudos da Religião* 6, no. 3 (2006): 65–76.

——. "The Globalization of Tibetan Buddhism: Contemporary Karma bKa' brGyud Movements Between Modernism and Tradition." Paper presented at the Globalization of Contemporary Buddhism Conference, Minzu University, Beijing, December 18–20, 2009.

——. "Globalizing Tibetan Buddhism: Modernism and Neo-Orthodoxy in Contemporary Karma bKa' brgyud Organizations." *Contemporary Buddhism* 13 (2012): 125–37.

——. "Interpreting the Diamond Way: Contemporary Convert Buddhism in Transition." *Journal of Global Buddhism* 10 (2009): 17–48.

——. "Macho Buddhism: Gender and Sexuality in the Diamond Way." *Religion and Gender* 1 (2011): 85–103.

——. "A Neo-orthodox Buddhist Movement in Transition: The Diamond Way." In *Visioning New and Minority Religions: Projecting the Future*, edited by Eugene V. Gallagher, 156–65. London: Routledge, 2017.

——. "Queer as Kagyu: Negotiating Dissident Identities in Neo-Orthodox Buddhist Spaces." In *Queering Paradigms*, vol. 3: *Bio-Politics, Place, and Representations*, edited by Kathleen O'Mara and Liz Morrish, 145–55. Oxford: Peter Lang, 2013.

——. "Queer Voices, Social Media and Neo-orthodox Dharma: A Case Study." Paper presented at the Association for Asian Studies Annual Meeting, Honolulu, March 31, 2011.

——. "Queering Buddhist Traditions." *Oxford Research Encyclopedia of Religion*, June 28, 2021. https://oxfordre.com/religion/view/10.1093/acrefore/9780199340378.001.0001/acrefore-9780199340378-e-765.

——. "Trans-European Adaptations in the Diamond Way: Negotiating Public Opinions on Homosexuality in Russia and in the U.K." *ONLINE—Heidelberg Journal of Religions on the Internet* 6 (December 2014): 103–25.

Schmid, Georg. "Verschmelzen mit Karmapa: Faszination und Dynamik des Karma-Kagyü-Buddhismus." Relinfo, Evangelische Informationsstelle: Kirchen—Sekten—Religionen, 1998. https://www.relinfo.ch/lexikon/themen/besuche-bei-gemeinschaften/lama-ole-nydahl/verschmelzen-mit-karmapa/ (accessed November 30, 2022).

Scott-Baumann, Alison. *Ricœur and the Hermeneutics of Suspicion*. London: Continuum, 2009.

Shaw, Miranda. *Passionate Enlightenment: Women in Tantric Buddhism*. Princeton, N.J.: Princeton University Press, 1994.

Tweed, Thomas. "Who Is a Buddhist? Night-Stand Buddhists and Other Creatures." In *Westward Dharma: Buddhism Beyond Asia*, edited by Charles S. Prebish and Martin Baumann, 17–33. Berkeley: University of California Press, 2002.

Ursache\Wirkung editors. "Ole Nydahl versus Ursache\Wirkung." Ursache\Wirkung, January 9, 2020. https://www.ursachewirkung.com/blog/3491-ole-nydahl-versus-ursache-wirkung.

Wyder, Nadia, Martina Wesemann, and Manfred Kessler. "Austritt aus der BDU e.V." Dokumente und Informationen zum Austritt des Buddhistischen Dachverbands Diamantweg (BDD) aus der Deutschen Buddhistischen Union (DBU), June 17, 2019. https://dbu.diamantweg-buddhismus.de/BDD_Austritt_aus_der_DBU.html.

Young, Serinity. *Courtesans and Tantric Consorts*. London: Routledge, 2004.

PART THREE

Making Men

THROUGHOUT THE BUDDHIST world, Buddhism coexists with different cultural and religious traditions, which raises questions regarding what is distinctively Buddhist about forms of masculinity that develop in different times and places. This section examines the way Buddhism informs, and is informed by, ideas and processes of how to be a good man in contemporary Burma (a.k.a. Myanmar), contemporary Thailand, and the contemporary United States. It adopts a broad, inclusive understanding of Buddhism that extends beyond conventional monastic and academic boundaries. Ward Keeler draws on extensive ethnographic research to argue that Burman masculinity privileges monastic autonomy and independence over the web of social relations that enmeshes even the most powerful of laymen. He shows how Burmese gender stereotypes construct distinct notions of masculinity and femininity, and how the former is further shaded along the spectrum from dependence to independence. However, in nearby Thailand, Natawan Wongchalard notes the prominence of selfless devotion to others exemplified by the monkey deity Hanuman, the paradigmatic devotee of the hero-god Rama in the Thai Buddhist *Ramakien* (an adaptation of the Hindu *Rāmāyaṇa*). Wongchalard argues that the Thai heroes of the 2018 Tham Luang cave rescue were recognized as such because they embodied Hanuman's particular form of hegemonic Buddhist masculinity. Finally, Marcus Evans considers how Chan Buddhism informs depictions of manhood in *The Man with the Iron Fists* films written by RZA, the so-called Abbot of hip hop's

Wu-Tang Clan. As represented in the *Iron Fists* films, Chan Buddhism challenges the hegemony of Anglo-American racial discourses by foregrounding Afro-Asian brotherhood, while leaving the hegemony of masculinity unquestioned. These chapters collectively demonstrate that hegemonic Buddhist masculinities are inseparable from the societies and cultures that generate them, whether in Burma, Thailand, or the United States.

SEVEN

Being a Man vs. Being a Monk

Alternative Versions of Burmese Buddhist Masculinity

WARD KEELER

A SIGNIFIER LIKE *masculinity*, as structural linguistics taught us long ago, can convey meaning only by means of contrasts it makes with another signifier—in this case, *femininity*. Yet, in Burma, there are two versions of masculinity that contrast each other, even though both clearly fit under the rubric of what is expected of men, not women.[1] Masculinity's two versions pertain to laymen, on the one hand, and monastics, on the other. What is common to both versions of masculinity is an emphasis on power. Power, in turn, is manifested in an individual's autonomy, the ability to act independently, and men are expected to be deeply invested in their autonomy. Laymen exercise autonomy in their control over others. Monks exercise autonomy, in theory if not always in practice, in their control over themselves: detachment is the Buddhist rendering of autonomy. Men of both sorts stand in contrast to women, who are expected to be invested in attachment and neither expected nor often much permitted to demonstrate autonomy. The greater a person's attachments—their investment in their relations with others who are dear to them, as well as in their worldly possessions and pleasures—the less autonomy, and, in Buddhist terms, the less detachment they are seen to exercise, and thus less power is attributed to them.

In what follows I summarize generalized assumptions Burmans make about what characterizes men, and what characterizes monks, and how those characteristics differ from what characterizes women. These are generalizations, and Burmans (like people elsewhere) are ready to grant that specific individuals can diverge quite far from any norms or expectations linked to one or another of these gender categories. Such deviations may arouse surprise, disapproval, or indifference, depending on the observers' attitudes. Burmans have, like many Southeast Asians, exhibited a relative tolerance for various gender presentations.[2] Yet hegemonic understandings of masculinity—what men are like or should be like, determined in part by the paths they choose to follow—are generally agreed upon, hence hegemonic.

Hegemonic masculinity in Burma may be agreed upon, but it is not likely to be subject to much discussion. What is assumed, in any society, need not be examined, let alone questioned, and so getting at how masculinity is assumed to differ from femininity does not lend itself to formal statements. And any such statements, when made, must be seen as prescriptive rather than merely descriptive. Scholars can only infer these generalized attitudes from the accumulating experience of ethnographic observation. My own fieldwork in Burma extends over a number of years: stays of ten months in 1987–1988 and in 2011–2012, plus a number of shorter stays, from two to six weeks, in a number of other years (most recently in 2019–2020). The Burmese government has permitted me to stay at hotels or monasteries, not with Burmese families. I have, of course, chosen to live in monasteries, with the result that I have more experience sharing living space with monks than with laypeople, although I have a number of laypeople as friends and have always been free to see them at will.

I summarize in this chapter what I believe most Burmans would claim about masculinity's expected expression(s). I include fewer vignettes from life than I would normally, because it is not specific incidents that ground my understandings so much as noting, say, the style with which laymen interact or monks comment on their own and others' actions. Enactments of piety, or a hint of swagger, or consistent deference: these elements of people's behavior generate impressions of how gender roles are implemented, and they inform my inferences of how they fit into generalized ideas about interaction in Burma more broadly.

Monastic vs. Lay Masculinity

The two idealized forms masculinity takes in Buddhist Burma are, once again: 1) that of the layman performing a man's role in secular society; and

2) that of the monk performing a religious role either in a monastery or at a yet further remove from secular society, in the forest. The two roles appear so different that it would seem at first glance hard to reconcile them. A Burman layman is most praised, at least rhetorically, when he acts as the responsible head of household, a man who is sexually active (at least in the earlier stages of his marriage) and committed to providing for the material needs of his wife and children.[3] A monk, by way of contrast, must be completely asexual and committed to concentrating on his own spiritual advancement. He is expected to live among monastics and to spend time either studying texts or meditating.

The contradictory nature of these two different idealized versions of masculinity, lay and religious, goes a long way back. In an appreciative review of José Cabezón's *Sexuality in Classical South Asian Buddhism*, John Powers writes of such antinomies having been "perceived by the people who created and developed the literary character 'Buddha.' They attempted to construct a narrative of a man who was able to effortlessly and simultaneously enact two seemingly incompatible masculine ideals—the religiously inclined *brahman* and the warrior *kṣatriya*—and who was praised by exemplars of both for his perfect instantiation of their respective paradigms."[4] Putting aside how the roles of *brahman* and *kṣatriya* differed in ancient India, I will elaborate on how each of the two roles, lay and religious, is conceived in Burma today, and how they relate to each other.

Lay Masculinity and the Demonstration of Power in the World

Burmans assume that men possess greater strength than women. That strength is physical, certainly, but also mental. Men are capable of withstanding hardship and strain more consistently, it is thought, than women. It is because of men's ability to exert themselves that they are held responsible for providing materially for their family's well-being. At the same time, they are expected to be particularly invested in their own and their family's honor. From Burmans' perspective, a touch of hotheadedness is not surprising in a man, and indeed it may win him a certain degree of respect, since it suggests his confidence in his own powers relative to those of anyone he encounters or confronts.

In the past, most families considered a position in the civil service a particularly secure and honorable career for a man to have. A military career was worthy of respect, too, provided a man made his way up the ranks. Only relatively recently has becoming rich through business dealings gained a man prestige among Burmans, who had generally thought such a path undignified and best left to Sino-Burmese or Indo-Burmese men, who have always been looked upon with a certain contempt (not unmixed with envy).

In actual fact, a layman may choose to fulfill a related but rather different model of secular masculinity in which he is sexually promiscuous, liable to drink and gamble, and daring in his actions and speech. He will in that case win the disapproval of some observers but still garner the admiration of many other men (and fewer women), especially younger ones, who are less concerned with his Buddhist mores than with his display of power. Men who womanize, drink alcohol, and gamble face disapproval particularly because they are contravening Buddhist proscriptions. Yet there is a definite ambivalence in perceptions of them. Yes, they are squandering money that should go to supporting their families. But, at the same time, they are displaying manly qualities—sexual potency, a taste for pleasure and display, a willingness to test their karmic fate—that bespeak the strength justifying the privileges they enjoy. Their honor hinges as much on the performance of manliness as on the eminently respectable but far less showy demonstration of concern for the welfare of their dependents, or for Buddhist institutions and monastics, that they are also enjoined to display.

Men who take on this aggressive role, which may be seen as shading into thuggishness, do fail to conform to Buddhist ideals. That they nevertheless win respect in some quarters follows from the multivocality of power as a masculine ideal. Physical strength, sexual and financial profligacy, and a taste for violence are the most obvious and concrete manifestations of power. No amount of domesticating religious rhetoric or other moralizing rhetoric can quite overcome the impression they make, especially on young males looking for a patron or a role model, but also on other members of any community, including a Burman Buddhist one. Assertive, even swashbuckling, quick to anger, and indifferent to others' opinion and to any karmic consequences their actions might entail, they impose their will upon others and so show themselves powerful. They thereby act autonomously—because both controlling and unbowed—in a way that wins them real respect, however grudging.

Much more socially acceptable, of course, is for a man to demonstrate his Buddhist piety. A certain, but fairly small, number of Burman men regularly participate in religious activities. The rest seem to hold sincere and firm religious convictions: I have never heard a Burman man express real disbelief in any conventional Buddhist ideas. They do not, however, go to particular lengths as a rule to support a local monastery, provide alms to monks and novices doing their morning rounds, attend "Dharma talks" (sermons delivered by Buddhist monks, usually organized by a neighborhood administration, or a religious or other institution), or engage in meditation. Women engage in all of these activities much more frequently and much more enthusiastically. A few older men, particularly those whose middle-class wealth is assured, do become patrons of monks and monasteries. Such action brings them prestige and, I infer from occasions in which I have seen older men participate in such activities, the pleasure of meaningful social interaction in a socially honored role. Yet their numbers are relatively few.

Monastic Masculinity and the Demonstration of Power Over the Self

Much praised in public discourse are the men who choose to become monks. These are men who have most taken to heart the Buddha's teaching that the root of all suffering lies in desire, and that the escape from suffering lies in detachment. A man who gives up physical comforts and the pleasures of sexuality, and who is oblivious to worldly honors, best exemplifies the spiritual path to which every Buddhist should aspire. In this case, a man displays autonomy not so much in his ability to control others' actions (although he may well do that, too, should he become a noteworthy monk or abbot of a monastery), as much as in his ability to exercise control over himself. He is autonomous in the sense that he is impervious to the world's blandishments and any influence they might exert over his thoughts and actions.

I would have to say that, in light of my experience living in three monasteries in Burma, to attribute a truly ascetic lifestyle to many monks would be a polite exaggeration. The prohibition of sexual activity appears to be rigorously policed. A taste for consumer goods, however, does not appear to be held against monks by the Burman laypeople who support them. The fleet of cars commanded by the greatly respected Sitagu Sayadaw—monastic rules mean he cannot actually own them—does not appear to put his supporters off. People's conviction, furthermore, that monks truly do not feel invested in power appears unshakable.

The greatest prestige is accorded monks who took on the robe as boys. Assumed never to have had sex, their purity justifies their being labeled *nge hpyu*, "little, white." Men who choose in later life to take on the robe usually do so after having married, raised children, and entered a stage of life where they are expected to start preparing for their eventual withdrawal from everyday affairs and ultimate death. A man must obtain his wife's written permission to make this transition to monkhood, and public opinion is actually divided about it. On the one hand, by doing so he is abandoning the role of primary earner for his wife and anyone still dependent on their household; such a move strikes some observers as a dereliction of duty. On the other hand, it is considered appropriate for a man to pursue his spiritual advancement in his later years, and becoming a monk should therefore win him praise.

Burman relationships are virtually always hierarchical in nature, and that is as true for relations among monastics as laypeople. Formally speaking, the hierarchical ordering among monks depends only on the number of years in succession they have worn the robe. In actual practice, a number of other criteria enter into estimations of their relative status: the degree of their knowledge of Pāli scriptures, particularly as attested in the titles they have acquired by means of the examination system; the number, power, and wealth of their lay sponsors; and whether they have been members of the sangha since boyhood. Some monks become particularly famous for having memorized an impressive portion of the Pāli canon. Others derive fame because they are skilled preachers who give learned, or entertaining, Dharma talks. A senior monk who showed me exceptional kindness while I did my fieldwork in 2011–2012 had as a young monk impressed his superiors by memorizing a sixth of the Pāli canon—an extraordinary achievement. They planned to have him proceed on this path, perhaps eventually achieving the rare feat of memorizing it in its entirety. (Only about thirteen Burmese monks have accomplished this.) Yet when they discovered his talent as a public speaker, they counseled him to take up this role instead, and he has become famous for his lively and entertaining Dharma talks.

Somewhat more ambiguously respected are monks who can address laypeople's desire for good health, or life prognostications, or even intimations of forthcoming lottery numbers. Many are convinced that certain monks (by no means all) have such special skills. Reformist elements in contemporary Buddhist circles look askance at such claims, citing prohibitions in the Vinaya (the monastic code of conduct) against laying claim to magical powers. To such people, monks should devote themselves exclusively to the study of Pāli texts and to meditation.

In the past, textual study was the activity to which a monk was expected to devote himself. A monk with a great command of Pāli learning, conversant with a good number of texts out of the Pāli canon, wins great prestige. A monk who is well connected to wealthy donors or powerful political leaders (these two lay donors' roles often coincide) will also be looked upon as particularly prestigious and worthy of support. He is likely as a result to gather a fortune in laypeople's donations.

Nevertheless, in recent decades, meditation has come to seem to many people, both lay and religious, to be a monk's primary obligation. The practice has attracted enormous attention among Burmans since the 1950s. It is difficult to know how widely it was practiced prior to that time, and, as a matter of fact, to this day it is no doubt more talked about than engaged in. In any case, its practitioners garner great respect. Many people I spoke with in Mandalay, including monks, assured me that meditation was by far the best way for a practitioner of Buddhism, monastic or lay, to carry out the responsibilities—and benefit from the advantages—of being Buddhist. Although in the past monks who specialized in studying the Pāli canon concerned themselves relatively little with meditation, popular impressions of how monks should conduct their lives now make it incumbent upon them to lay claim to spending time in meditation frequently, or even daily.

A monk, therefore, who meditates for much of his time, especially if he does so in remote places, enjoys singular prestige. This will attract a great many donors, and large donations, paradoxically undermining the reputation for asceticism that first lay the foundation for his reputation. A way to resolve the contradiction does exist: the most powerful monks are said to have undertaken rigorous meditation practice in remote locations in the past. They cannot claim to do so in the present, since they could then not be seen intervening so actively in ongoing affairs, whether among monastics or in Burmese society at large. Still, their prestige requires that their biographies allude to the rigors of the meditative practices they undertook in the past. For example, a brief biography of the immensely famous and powerful Sitagu Sayadaw, U Nyanissara, available on his organization's website, includes the following entry:

> 1972 lived in seclusion in Thabaikaing Tawya Monastery, Paung Ts, Mon State and practiced meditation.[5]

In another recension of his biography, the next date to appear is 1975, when he is said to have started preaching the "Buddha Dharma" all over the country, implying that he had spent the years 1972 to 1975 in seclusion.[6]

The Sitagu Sayadaw actually instantiates, perhaps better than anyone in contemporary Burma, the highly respected figure of a monk whose charisma has won him an immense following.[7] Such fame has attracted extraordinary wealth to his complex of monasteries. When I first met him in 1988, he was famous for having sponsored projects to supply clean water to the many monasteries and nunneries that dot the hills in Sagaing, a town across the Irrawaddy River from Mandalay where his own monastery is located. In subsequent years, he became more powerful and well known by virtue of his good relations with certain important members of the ruling military clique, as well as other wealthy individuals. His constant international travel and meetings with the world's most prominent political and religious leaders (including popes and American presidents), as well as his founding and fostering of monasteries and Buddhist universities at sites in Burma and beyond, including in the United States, brought him still greater acclaim. In 2008, when the Irrawaddy delta region was laid waste by the cataclysmic Cyclone Nargis, he defied official strictures against traveling to the hardest-hit regions to deliver aid. His defiance, even more than the assistance he was able to purvey, won him great admiration. More controversially, he has recently joined in making racist statements against Muslims living in Rakhine State in western Burma.[8]

What is most important to note about the Sitagu Sayadaw's fame is the way that it lends itself to retroactive reasoning. That is, when a monk attracts great attention and lay supporters, he is believed to be possessed of special spiritual authority. As a consequence, it is thought that donations made to him are particularly sure to bring a lay donor great stores of merit. Impressions of a monk's exceptionally great spiritual status encourages still more laypeople to choose to support him. And so it goes. As he accrues more and more lay supporters he accrues more and more stature and wealth. This material wealth enables such a monk to support an ever-expanding network of subordinates: monks and novices, first of all, although a fair number of laypeople may become attached to a monastery in various supportive roles, as well. He becomes, in other words, an important patron, and this combination of spiritual accomplishments and material power accords him much respect, attributed retrospectively to his spiritual charisma.[9]

Needless to say, when great material resources, as well as personal and institutional prestige, are at stake, jockeying for position and dissension soon become manifest among a patron's subordinates, monastic or lay. This applies all the more pointedly in contexts such as Burman monasteries in which transitions are invariably fraught because there are few binding rules about how transitions, such as when an important abbot passes away, are to be handled.[10]

An altogether different figure who looms large in many Burman men's imagination of the ideal monk is of one who lives far away from all human settlement, eats only food he finds on his own (and need not cook, since monks are forbidden to prepare their own food), and spends most of his time in meditation in the forest. Many people believe that such monks were more plentiful in the past than at present, although many also believe they still exist, even if known only by report of others.[11] They are admired for their fearlessness—they are oblivious to the danger posed by the wild animals thought numerous in the forest—yet at the same time they are believed to exert an energy on their surroundings such that they are immune to threat, and wild animals never trouble their meditation practice.

The power of this image was made clear to me by a man of my acquaintance, in his early forties, when we met on a number of occasions during my fieldwork in Mandalay in 2011–2012. He told me that he hoped to become a monk when he turned forty-five. He and his wife never had children, although they had wanted to. He hoped that he could convince his wife not only to agree to his becoming a monk but also to become a nun herself. If he succeeded at this plan, he added, he did not want to live in an urban monastery such as the one where we met and where an uncle of his, having donned the robe late in life, resided; instead, he wanted to follow a monk he knew about who lived far from town, in the Shan Hills, where he meditated at almost all times, sleeping only a few hours a night and eating very little. On later occasions, when we met again in Mandalay, this man explained that he had not acted on his plans, due not to any opposition from his wife but out of his own lack of resolve: he simply wasn't strong enough to do it. Yet what impressed me was how much more respect he felt for the lone, meditating monk, without bonds to almost anyone else, than the many monks living in town. The isolated meditator represented for him the idealized model for a Buddhist man who found within himself the strength to pursue the path of the Buddha.

Hegemonic Masculinities

The two different ways of achieving ideal manliness, as a potent, progeny- and wealth-producing head of household able to protect and win prestige for his family and other dependents, or as a pleasure-avoiding ascetic—most laudably of all, one avoiding social relations of all sorts—appear completely opposed. The contrast would appear unbridgeable. (Indeed, in Burmese, the words for *person* and *monk* are mutually exclusive, such that you can ask, for example, "How many people were there?" or "How many monks were there?," but you cannot ask about both at the same time.) Yet they are linked by the plastic but ultimately unitary notion of power.

The contrast between these two apparently opposed versions of masculinity, both of which arouse respect among Burmans, suggests a counterexample to Raewyn Connell's famous contribution to the literature on masculinity, the concept of "hegemonic masculinity": a dominant version of masculinity within any group, some set of traits that enjoys a hegemonic hold on people's notion of what a man most needs to exemplify to be deserving of respect.[12] As Megan Bryson notes in her introduction to this volume, the plural may be the more appropriate number here, hegemonic masculinit*ies*, at least in the case of Buddhist conceptions.

The Burman case suggests that Connell and Bryson are both right: that multiple versions of masculinity can be hegemonic while still demonstrating an overarching affinity and so constituting a singular entity. In other words, we should ask what core values inform a range of versions masculinity can take while still remaining in some sense consistent. In Burma, I believe the two versions of idealized masculinity are linked in that they constitute different manifestations of power, a multivalent but compelling concept taken to be the defining characteristic of manliness. But different versions of masculinity constitute points on a spectrum of power that are then distinguished by degrees of attachment. In accordance with Buddhist views, diminishing degrees of attachment, in favor of autonomy, mark greater demonstrations of power and so justify greater claims to prestige. The ultimate form autonomy takes is not control over others but rather over the self, culminating in its most praiseworthy version: detachment.

A male head of household should be able to take charge: of himself, of his wife and children and other subordinates, and of matters of all sorts. He "takes responsibility." He is endowed with a special quality, *hpòun* (derived from the Pāli *puñña*, meaning "merit"), that males—or, at least, qualified males—enjoy. The authority of *hpòun* derives from his gender, his demeanor, and, ultimately, from the amount of merit he has accumulated over a series of lifetimes.[13] He is effective and deserving of respect to the degree that he enhances and makes appropriate use of that masculine charisma.[14]

A monk is deemed to possess still greater *hpòun* than a layman. It is common practice to refer to a monk of some stature as a *hpòun gyì*, "[an individual of] great *hpòun*." His power is exercised to a degree over laypeople, who must rely on him for officiating at rituals, particularly those regarding death, and above all by his acting as a "field of merit" to whom they can make donations. Such donations are likened to seeds cast in a field, yielding a harvest of karmic merit for all concerned.

Both of these masculine roles presume hierarchical relationships that bind either laymen or monks to their dependents.[15] Virtually all relationships among Burmans are conceived of as being hierarchical in nature. Hierarchical relationships refer not simply to inequality but rather to relationships, precisely. They bind together in relations of exchange people of differing sorts and statuses: in the case of laypeople, adult male heads of households in contrast to women and children; in a religious context, monks and novices in contrast to their lay supporters. These relationships do indeed assume and maintain inequality: few Burmans question the validity of a differential allocation of prestige among men and monks relative to their dependents. Yet that inequality implies the *interdependence* of the parties. Individuals of lesser standing offer up labor and deference; those of greater standing bestow in return gifts of material, affective, and spiritual support.

Exchange, however, very clearly does not apply to monks meditating alone in the forest. How do they fit into this same system of concepts surrounding masculinity? The figure of the monk devoted only to his own spiritual advancement constitutes the highpoint—the apogee on the continuum of ascending prestige—because informing the whole complex of ideas is the value of autonomy and its corollary, the devaluation of attachment. Autonomy refers in the case of laymen to their ability to act as they see fit as they direct the lives and actions of others. In the case of monks, it refers to their ability, first of all, to act as they see fit in relation to lay supporters. More importantly, it refers to their ability to deal relatively little with the world: their autonomy allows them to spend time in the study of Pāli texts and in meditation, relatively little invested in worldly matters and relationships. They thereby instantiate more fully, and more admirably, the detachment that Buddhism enjoins upon us all, but that Buddhism recognizes to be hard for most of us to implement in our lives.

Key to all of these understandings, once again, is power, masculinity's distinctive feature. If a man exercises power as a legitimate authority over members of his household and other subordinates, he is enacting a role appropriate to his masculine privileges and obligations, as hierarchical understandings enjoin him to do. A monk exercises power as a legitimate authority over his lay supporters when he provides them moral guidance, funerary ritual services, and the opportunity to gain merit by giving him donations. But, more significantly still, he exercises power over himself: his own desires, for food, for sexual pleasure, for all comforts and entertainments, as well as for secular power.

A monk meditating alone in the forest, therefore, represents power exercised over the self to the maximal degree. A life virtually devoid of social relations—or imagined to be such—looks like detachment taken to the hilt and so best instantiating the Buddhist validation of it, as well as the most impressive conceivable form that power, manifesting as autonomy, can take. Detachment is power exercised over the self, and this is taken to be the ultimate demonstration of power.

However, the very multivalent nature of power explains why the ostensibly disvalued actions of the headstrong, irascible, threatening, and threat-defying individual man will nevertheless win respect at least in some quarters. At the outset, at least, such a man does not obviously seek respect by "taking responsibility" for others, nor does he display a Buddhist commitment to detachment. Nevertheless, his very ability to disregard what others think of him; his willingness to impose himself on situations no matter how many people he offends or crosses; his showing himself, in other words, to be impervious to other people's anger, envy, hostility, and other negative forms public opinion may take, encourages others to attribute to him a degree of power that is, if hardly ingratiating, nevertheless impressive and compelling—which, for many people, is more important. Some of those impressed by his display of manly power may well wish to subordinate themselves to such a figure, who is likely to amass a following—of young toughs, frequently—of his own. They will try to engage him in hierarchical relations whereby he, as their superordinate, must take responsibility for them, in return for the labor and deference they offer him.

Any such accumulation of power, and a concomitant agglomeration of adherents, may lead to a man becoming a local leader, on one side or the other of the law. The biographies of Burmese kings follow much the same trajectory; indeed, it is the script that would-be "world-conquerors," as Tambiah describes them (Sk. *cakravartin*; P. *cakkavatti*), follow to become powerful kings in the classical Southeast Asian mode.[16] At either order of magnitude, local or much grander, the impression that power is demonstrated in transgressive acts helps explain the sense that violence augments masculinity. As Kevin Buckelew traces in Chinese Chan sources in his chapter in this volume, a "great man" may well be more readily associated with martial than meditative or peace-making skills. Many a Burman king has sought to burnish his fame by supporting the sangha, while also engaging in ferocious warfare with his neighbors.

Contemporary Attitudes Toward Masculinity

No set of assumptions about social relations is impervious to changing circumstances, and gender ideology in Burma has been affected by the thoroughgoing changes that have taken place in Burma over recent decades, especially with the shift from a military dictatorship to a quasi-civilian regime for the 2010–2020 decade, followed by a military coup in early 2021. Most relevant to a discussion of masculinity are shifting ideas about where prestige is believed to lie, attitudes that are clearly inflected by class. Middle-class families do not, as a rule, send their sons into the monastery. Some middle-class men decide to become monks later in life. Although these are few in number, my impression is that young men of the middle class are even less numerous in the sangha. They are much more likely to pursue the prestige attaching to education, bureaucratic posts, and wealth than that accruing to the status of a monk.

Consumerism is by no means new in Burma, but the economic lockdown that Ne Win and his regime imposed on the nation for many years after the coup he staged in 1962 greatly reduced opportunities to act on consumerist desires. The fitful but very real opening of the economy since 1988, and the transition, however partial, away from military rule during the 2010s, have led to much greater economic interaction with the outside world. As a result, conspicuous consumption has become a pervasive means of seeking social prominence, and materialist rather than spiritual values have come much more to the fore; conspicuous donation to monasteries has only increased. Yet, even as Buddhist conceptions of suffering's roots in desire would seem ever more clearly demonstrated in the everyday lives of people in Burma today—the tribulations of crony capitalism, horrendous traffic, and unbridled advertising are suddenly everywhere apparent—there is little evidence of any greater embrace of the doctrine. Among most young Burman males, these developments have not fostered any inclination to pursue detachment, even if the discourse of detachment remains a mainstay of people's remarks. Simply put, wealth has become a much more compelling means of obtaining masculine prestige, undermining any older validation of Buddhist spiritual accomplishments.

There is another, very dangerous, development in recent Burmese public discourse that implicates both lay and monastic understandings of masculine privilege and imagined threats thereto. Anti-Muslim sentiment can be traced back to the British colonial regime's practice of bringing poor South Asians to Burma as laborers. Only some of them were Muslim, but, at various points in Burmese history, certain parties have found fomenting anti-Indian and/or anti-Muslim feeling, at times to the point of violence, politically useful. The most recent instance of such ethnoreligious conflict started in 2012, with violence perpetrated against Muslims living in the western state of Rakhine. The reasons for that ongoing catastrophe are complex and cannot be covered here.[17] Yet anti-Muslim remarks crop up increasingly often elsewhere among Burmans, not just in Rakhine State. A constantly repeated claim is that Muslim men marry young Buddhist women, have many children by them, divorce them, and raise their children as Muslims, with the ultimate goal of making Burma a majority Muslim rather than Buddhist society. The statistical impossibility of this taking place counts for nothing. The reaction it fosters—panic among men that young women in their community will be seduced away from their authority—shows how vulnerable they feel their authority to be.

Many outside observers have been startled to learn that Buddhist monks have participated fulsomely in fomenting such anti-Muslim feeling and even to have incited violence. The reason lies at least partly in the unsteadying effect that all the recent political change has brought about. The military regime made it a point to display its leaders' piety by funneling support to the sangha. What will monks' circumstances be in the less constricted new Burma? Some monks (by no means all) find reassurance of their continued prominence and sustenance in putting themselves at the forefront of resistance to this imaginary threat to the primacy of Buddhism. Attracting attention and a following by making themselves appear powerful—alert, fearless, and aggressive, powerful in a particularly crude version of masculinity—they generate impressions of their indispensability by setting themselves up as essential defenders of the Buddhist faith.[18]

Obligations to Dependents vs. Obligations to One's Spiritual Advancement

Even aside from recent shifts in attitudes as to where prestige for both laypeople and monks lies, there is an inherent tension running through conceptions of masculinity I have set out thus far. If autonomy signals an individual man's power—his ability to impose himself upon any situation, and upon others, or even to rise above them—he is likely to favor his own freedom of movement over his obligation to take care of his subordinates. In the end, it is very difficult to find ways to constrain superordinates to fulfill the obligations of their privileged status. For a man to abandon his family in order to pursue other women, or to indulge a weakness for alcohol, or simply to escape his fatigue with family matters, makes it clear that he has forgotten the obligations that come with the privileges of being a male head of household, and he will suffer censure as a result. If he goes far away for very long periods of time but sends remittances home, he will show himself mindful of those obligations, although a fair number of men are inconsistent at best in their sending of such remittances. There are, of course, a great many variations on this theme of privileges and obligations as they get played out in the lives of individual men and the relations they have with their families, both natal and reproductive, and with any other subordinates, such as in an office or a business or a political party. If responses to a layman's decision late in life to take on the robe are ambivalent, it is because his motives are often suspected to be mixed.

Then there is the case of the Buddha. He did, after all, abandon his wife and young son. I have always been struck at the relative lack of emphasis, let alone analysis, this point seems to arouse in popular Buddhist discourse. I can only infer that, for Burmese Buddhists, this display of masculine autonomy, in detachment, was rightfully chosen over his obligations to his family. It appears to provide an incontestable model to which we should all aspire, since it enabled the Buddha to model the means for all of us to overcome suffering.

Comparing Masculinity and Femininity in Burman Buddhism

Does that *us* include women? The matter is complicated. To explain why, I must turn to the way that femininity is construed among Burman Buddhists. In contrast to the links I have traced between power and autonomy in conceptions of Burman masculinity, the terms most readily associated with femininity are *weakness* and *attachment*, or, perhaps better, a weakness for attachment. Paradoxically enough, this weakness is women's most valued trait.

Women are assumed to be heavily invested in the well-being of people they are close to. They *should* wish to tend to the well-being of their parents and of their children. They *should* concern themselves with the material affairs—this includes money—that are crucial to providing such care. They *should* busy themselves with all the affairs that connect people in their neighborhoods to one another. And of course they should take it upon themselves to cook food to donate to monks and novices as they go on their morning rounds. They will win special praise if they demonstrate themselves particularly pious by dint of the service they provide to the monastery (or monasteries) and monastics they and their family select for particular consideration.

Women, in sum, *should* show themselves to be, if not incapable of, at least little inclined toward, the very detachment that Buddhism prescribes. Their role as devout Buddhists is to support monks and novices, males who can devote themselves to their own autonomy (their detachment) precisely because women take care of the duties requiring its opposite. At home, they play much the same role vis-à-vis their husbands. These men's freedom of movement—in pursuit of money, or prestige, or whatever else it behooves a man to maximize—is predicated on the assiduousness with which their female subordinates remain bound to the activities and persons close to home, including their husbands. It would be altogether incorrect to infer that Burman women, because I have labeled them "subordinate," are submissive, let alone passive, actors in Burman social relations. Nevertheless, Burman gender ideology clearly distinguishes between the valued and disvalued roles for men, on the one hand, and women, on the other. A man's detachment is the mirror opposite of women's attachments.

The tensions intrinsic to being a woman and a Buddhist become particularly clear in the highly ambiguous status afforded nuns among Burmans. Much has been written about the disparity in status of monks and nuns in Buddhist societies, especially in Theravādin ones.[19] Since most Theravāda monastic leaders claim that the line of ordination of nuns originating during the Buddha's lifetime came to an end several centuries ago, nuns' standing equates only to that of novices (male monastics under the age of twenty), not that of monks. Women and their allies have made pioneering efforts to alter the situation, particularly in Thailand, by reintroducing nuns' ordination from the Mahāyāna lineage. However, few people in Burma I spoke to thought it a reasonable change, if they had even heard about it. At the same time, the differing legal status of nunneries as compared to monasteries—the latter enjoy an institutional identity abetting their survival beyond the death of an abbot, whereas the former are looked upon as the personal preserve of an abbess, which leads to their dissolution on her passing, often in a welter of conflicting claims—reflects less respect for the entire undertaking of women's renunciation.[20]

Even apart from their official standing, in the past Burman women who chose to become nuns suffered a fair degree of disapproval, or even disdain. The relative lack of respect they garner shows even in such apparently ordinary touches as the fact that monks, prohibited from preparing their own food, receive donations of cooked food when they go on alms rounds, whereas when nuns make alms rounds they receive raw food stuffs, often just a spoonful of uncooked rice they are expected to cook themselves. After all, cooking is something women do.

The grounds for the poor opinion of female religious seem clear. As women, they are expected to devote their lives to attending to the needs of their husbands, children, and other family members. Should they decide not to marry they nevertheless are expected to provide assistance to their parents and other older kin and to the sick, to provide childcare for married sisters who want to go to work, and so on—in sum, to take on whatever supporting roles other people to whom they are connected assign them. Leaving their kin behind in order to pursue their spiritual advancement, which wins praise for men, generally arouses criticism for women. Such an endeavor is not looked upon as in keeping with a woman's place.

The anthropologist Hiroko Kawanami, who has written the most extensively (and with much discernment) on Burman nuns, shows that not even women who have chosen to become nuns in Burma escape these pressures to enact the expected role of caregiver.[21] Their kin do not hesitate to call them back to tend to ailing kin or to come to the assistance of anyone in their network—something they would not do in the case of monks.[22] Public opinion is not uniform: some Burmans appear to look upon nuns with respect, and Kawanami suggests that that respect is gaining ground. The contrast between many monks, especially ones in their twenties or early thirties, who bend the rules of the Vinaya by sitting in tea shops after noon or playing sports, and the absence of any such infractions on the part of nuns, would appear to justify such respect. It is the weight of gender ideology, rather than any observed behavior, that sustains the relatively low esteem in which many Burman Buddhists continue to hold nuns.

Buddhism prescribes detachment: detachment, a version of autonomy, is most appropriately as well as most effectively pursued by men; women's responsibility lies in enabling men to hone their own autonomy in their endeavor of attaining detachment. Women who strike out in pursuit of their own detachment are seen as behaving inappropriately. It is as though (although here I exceed what anyone has told me explicitly) they are jumping the queue. Women who accumulate much merit in this life will be rewarded by being born a man in their next one—if they are lucky, a man spiritually strong enough to become a monk.

Characteristically for Burman social arrangements, flexibility obtains, and exceptions are observable in the degree of respect a few Burmese nuns win for themselves. An abbess in Mandalay has become very famous and has been able to build a large and impressive nunnery in the city because she came to the attention of an influential monk who hailed from a place near her natal village, and his sponsorship led eventually to her becoming connected to a powerful member of the Burmese military leadership.

* * *

In describing Burman Buddhist understandings of masculinity, I have pointed to an affinity between the autonomy associated with men's roles, whether lay or monastic, and the detachment that Buddhism urges upon us all. Yet the question remains of how much Burman Buddhist conceptions of masculinity draw from Buddhism versus Burman culture. Perhaps pre-Buddhist gender roles help explain why Buddhist ideas found such widespread acceptance in the region, and why they have remained vital over centuries, even as they lost ground in the Indian subcontinent. I say this particularly because I found during ethnographic fieldwork in Indonesia many similar links between autonomy, gendered masculine, and attachment, gendered feminine, both in predominantly Muslim Java and Hindu-Balinese Bali. It is true, however, that when I aired this idea to a Buddhist monk in Mandalay, he assured me I was wrong. Everything of note about Burman culture, he insisted, derived from Buddhism. And Java, he noted triumphantly, was Buddhist long before its inhabitants became Muslim.

NOTES

A fellowship at the Hansewissenschaftskolleg, in Delmenhorst, Germany, gave me the opportunity to write this chapter, and I gratefully acknowledge the support of Professor Susanne Fuchs and other members of the institute's staff. I revised the chapter while enjoying a fellowship at the Aarhus Institute of Advanced Study, funded by the European Union's Horizon 2020 Research and Innovation Programme under the Marie Skłodowska-Curie grant agreement no. 754513 and the Aarhus University Research Foundation. The fieldwork on which the chapter is based was supported by funds from the University of Texas at Austin.

1. The military regime decided to substitute the label "Myanmar" for "Burma" in the 1990s on the grounds that it was more inclusive. It is not: it is the equivalent, in the formal register of the Burmese language, of the colloquial "Burma." It would be rather like insisting that people say "the United States of America"

instead of "the United States." The final "r" in Myanmar, incidentally, is not pronounced: it is modeled after the Queen's English, wherein postvocalic "r" lengthens the preceding vowel but disappears.

2. See Barbara Watson Andaya, "Gender Legacies and Modern Transitions," in *Routledge Handbook of Contemporary Indonesia*, ed. Robert W. Hefner (London: Routledge, 2018), 31–42; Michael Peletz, *Gender Pluralism: Southeast Asia Since Early Modern Times* (New York: Routledge, 2009); and Anthony Reid, *Southeast Asia in the Age of Commerce: 1450–1680*, vol. 1: *The Land Below the Winds* (New Haven, Conn.: Yale University Press, 1988).
3. Following current scholarly convention, I use the word "Burmese" to refer to citizens of the nation-state, and I use the word "Burman" to refer to the ethnic Burmans, who make up about two thirds of the population of the country.
4. John Powers, "Indian Buddhist Concepts of Normative and Deviant Bodies: Can Ancient Sexual Mores Be Reconciled with Modern Sensibilities?," *Religion* 49, no. 4 (2019): 735–44, 740–41.
5. "A Short Biography of Sitagu Sayadaw Dr. Ashin Nyanissara, The Founder of Sitagu Missionary Association, the Principal of Sitagu Projects," Sitagu International Buddhist Missionary Association (SIBMA), https://thesitagu.org/index.php/home/founder-academics/bio (accessed May 12, 2020).
6. Sitagu Buddha Vihara newsletter, Sitagu Sayadaw 77th birthday issue, February 23, 2014, http://sitagu.org/austin/news/Newsletters/2014Spring/Sitagu%20Sayadaw%2077th%20birthday%20Publication%20%28Web%29.pdf.
7. The title *sayadaw* refers to the abbot of a monastery: *saya* means "teacher," and *daw* means "deserving of special respect."
8. *New York Times* reporter Hannah Beech includes mention of the Sitagu Sayadaw in her reporting of anti-Muslim rhetoric among monks in both Sri Lanka and Burma. See Hannah Beech, "Buddhists Go to Battle: When Nationalism Overrides Pacifism," *New York Times*, July 8, 2019, https://www.nytimes.com/2019/07/08/world/asia/buddhism-militant-rise.html.
9. The work of Guillaume Rozenberg focusing on the Thamanya Sayadaw provides a vivid picture of another such famous and influential abbot. See, for example, Guillaume Rozenberg, "How Giving Sanctifies: The Birthday of Thamanya Hsayadaw in Burma," *Journal of the Royal Anthropological Society* 10, no. 3 (2004): 495–515.
10. Full disclosure: the Sitagu Sayadaw opened a monastery on the outskirts of Austin, Texas, where I live, and so I was able on a couple of occasions in later years to meet him there. Under his auspices, the abbot of a Sitagu monastery in Burma helped me obtain a visa, making it possible for me to do long-term research in Burma in 2011–2012—an invaluable boon. Unfortunately, another abbot in the Sitagu complex of monasteries took a dislike to me (for reasons I was never able to learn), poisoning my relationship with the Sitagu Sayadaw. This fact was made clear to me by his brusque and dismissive demeanor when I last saw him in Sagaing.
11. Kamala Tiyavanich attests to similar beliefs among Thais; see Kamala Tiyanavich, *Forest Recollections: Wandering Monks in Twentieth-Century Thailand* (Honolulu: University of Hawai'i Press, 1997).

12. Raewyn Connell, *Masculinities*, 2nd ed. (Berkeley: University of California Press, 2005).
13. See Min Zin, "The Power of *Hpoun*," *Irrawaddy* 9, no. 9 (December 2001), https://www2.irrawaddy.com/article.php?art_id=2471 (accessed December 1, 2022); and Mikael Gravers, "Monks, Morality, and Military: The Struggle for Moral Power in Burma—and Buddhism's Uneasy Relation with Lay Power," *Contemporary Buddhism* 13, no. 1 (2012): 1–33, 1–2. The Pāli term *puñña* is equivalent to the Sanskrit *puṇya*.
14. Nash writes of *hpòun* that it is "close to the idea of grace, charity, election, destiny," although he does not link it explicitly to "charisma" until later in his ethnography of two villages where he did fieldwork in the late 1950s. Manning Nash, *The Golden Road to Modernity: Village Life in Contemporary Burma* (New York: John Wiley, 1965), 76, 272.
15. For a more extended analysis of the concept, see Ward Keeler, *The Traffic in Hierarchy: Masculinity and Its Others in Buddhist Burma* (Honolulu: University of Hawai'i Press, 2017); for the text that first drew the interest of many of us to the topic of hierarchy, see Louis Dumont, *Homo Hierarchicus: The Caste System and Its Implications*, trans. Mark Sainsbury, Louis Dumont, and Basia Gulati (Chicago: University of Chicago Press, 1980).
16. Stanley Tambiah, *World Conqueror and World Renouncer: A Study of Buddhism and Polity in Thailand Against a Historical Background* (Cambridge: Cambridge University Press, 1976).
17. The work of historian Jacques Leider presents the crisis in particularly nuanced and historically sensitive fashion. See Jacques Leider, "History and Victimhood: Engaging with Rohingya Issues," *Insight Turkey* 20, no. 1 (2017): 99–118.
18. For an excellent summary of the inducements some monks feel for engaging in racist discourse, see Jacques Bertrand and Alexandre Pelletier, "Violent Monks in Myanmar: Scapegoating and the Contest for Power," *Nationalism and Ethnic Politics* 23, no. 3 (2017): 257–79.
19. See Nirmala Salgado, *Buddhist Nuns and Gendered Practice: In Search of the Female Renunciant* (New York: Oxford University Press, 2013); and Karma Lekshe Tsomo, ed. *Eminent Buddhist Women* (Albany: State University of New York Press, 2014).
20. See Hiroko Kawanami, *Renunciation and Empowerment of Buddhist Nuns in Myanmar-Burma: Building a Community of Female Faithful* (Leiden: Brill, 2013).
21. Kawanami, *Renunciation and Empowerment.*
22. Sid Brown, in a fascinating account of a Thai nun's life, cites her kin's demands to provide such help as instrumental in her resolve to become a nun. See Sid Brown, *The Journey of One Buddhist Nun: Even Against the Wind* (Albany: State University of New York Press, 2001), 9, 68.

Bibliography

Andaya, Barbara Watson. "Gender Legacies and Modern Transitions." In *Routledge Handbook of Contemporary Indonesia*, edited by Robert W. Hefner, 31–42. London: Routledge, 2018.

Beech, Hannah. "Buddhists Go to Battle: When Nationalism Overrides Pacifism." *New York Times*, July 8, 2019. https://www.nytimes.com/2019/07/08/world/asia/buddhism-militant-rise.html.

Bertrand, Jacques, and Alexandre Pelletier. "Violent Monks in Myanmar: Scapegoating and the Contest for Power." *Nationalism and Ethnic Politics* 23, no. 3 (2017): 257–79.

Brown, Sid. *The Journey of One Buddhist Nun: Even Against the Wind*. Albany: State University of New York Press, 2001.

Connell, Raewyn. *Masculinities*. 2nd ed. Berkeley: University of California Press, 2005.

Dumont, Louis. *Homo Hierarchicus: The Caste System and Its Implications*. Translated by Mark Sainsbury, Louis Dumont, and Basia Gulati. Chicago: University of Chicago Press, 1980.

Gravers, Mikael. "Monks, Morality, and Military: The Struggle for Moral Power in Burma—and Buddhism's Uneasy Relation with Lay Power." *Contemporary Buddhism* 13, no. 1 (2012): 1–33.

Kawanami, Hiroko. *Renunciation and Empowerment of Buddhist Nuns in Myanmar-Burma: Building a Community of Female Faithful*. Leiden: Brill, 2013.

Keeler, Ward. *The Traffic in Hierarchy: Masculinity and Its Others in Buddhist Burma*. Honolulu: University of Hawai'i Press, 2017.

Leider, Jacques. "History and Victimhood: Engaging with Rohingya Issues." *Insight Turkey* 20, no. 1 (2017): 99–118.

Min Zin. "The Power of *Hpoun*." *Irrawaddy* 9, no. 9 (December 2001). https://www2.irrawaddy.com/article.php?art_id=2471 (accessed December 1, 2022).

Nash, Manning. *The Golden Road to Modernity: Village Life in Contemporary Burma*. New York: John Wiley and Sons, 1965.

Peletz, Michael. *Gender Pluralism: Southeast Asia Since Early Modern Times*. New York: Routledge, 2009.

Powers, John. "Indian Buddhist Concepts of Normative and Deviant Bodies: Can Ancient Sexual Mores Be Reconciled with Modern Sensibilities?" *Religion* 49, no. 4 (2019): 735–44.

Reid, Anthony. *Southeast Asia in the Age of Commerce: 1450–1680*, vol. 1: *The Land Below the Winds*. New Haven, Conn.: Yale University Press, 1988.

Rozenberg, Guillaume. "How Giving Sanctifies: The Birthday of Thamanya Hsayadaw in Burma." *Journal of the Royal Anthropological Society* 10, no. 3 (2004): 495–515.

Salgado, Nirmala. *Buddhist Nuns and Gendered Practice: In Search of the Female Renunciant*. New York: Oxford University Press, 2013.

"A Short Biography of Sitagu Sayadaw Dr. Ashin Nyanissara, The Founder of Sitagu Missionary Association, the Principal of Sitagu Projects." Sitagu International Buddhist Missionary Association (SIBMA). Accessed May 12, 2020. https://thesitagu.org/index.php/home/founder-academics/bio.

Sitagu Buddha Vihara newsletter. Sitagu Sayadaw 77th birthday issue, February 23, 2014. http://sitagu.org/austin/news/Newsletters/2014Spring/Sitagu%20Sayadaw%2077th%20birthday%20Publication%20%28Web%29.pdf.

Tambiah, Stanley. *World Conqueror and World Renouncer: A Study of Buddhism and Polity in Thailand Against a Historical Background.* New York: Cambridge University Press, 1976.

Tiyavanich, Kamala. *Forest Recollections: Wandering Monks in Twentieth-Century Thailand.* Honolulu: University of Hawai'i Press, 1997.

Tsomo, Karma Lekshe, ed. *Eminent Buddhist Women.* Albany: State University of New York Press, 2014.

EIGHT

Hanuman, Heroes, and Buddhist Masculinity in Contemporary Thailand

NATAWAN WONGCHALARD

IN MODERN THAILAND, hegemonic masculinity conflates the ideas of nationalism, Buddhism, and the monarchy, which together constitute a national ethos represented by the tricolor flag. Even though the concept itself is contentious and subject to historical change, hegemonic masculinity—among a multitude of other masculinities—remains perennially dominant. In addition to preserving social relations that support the three national ideals (nation, Buddhism, and monarch), hegemonic masculinity has also operated as a political strategy; it was instrumental in dealing with national crises, such as the confrontation with Western colonization in the mid-nineteenth century and the economic recession of the late 1990s. This chapter considers the hegemonic Buddhist masculinities on display in another crisis: the Tham Luang cave rescue of 2018. The heroes of the cave rescue, I argue, were perceived as embodying the ideal masculinity of Hanuman, the monkey god of the Thai Buddhist *Ramakien*, an adaptation of the Hindu *Rāmāyaṇa* epic.

Understanding the Buddhist masculinities at work in the Tham Luang cave rescue—including the Hanuman ideal—requires understanding the history of hegemonic masculinities in Thailand (a.k.a. Siam). Starting in the fifteenth century, the country operated by the *sakdina* system, which defines land rights according to a social hierarchy under monarchic rule.[1] The higher the social class or rank, the larger allocation of land. Royal lords could own up to one hundred thousand *rai* (approximately forty thousand acres), whereas common free men (as opposed to enslaved people) were allowed up to twenty-five *rai*. Free men had to serve particular feudal lords, and for half the year they were conscripted into labor and military service for the kingdom.[2] Such a system generated certain practices and dispositions that were expected of free men, who constituted the majority of men in Siam. For example, they were tattooed with their lords' names, and they had to report to their lords annually, perform martial training to prepare for wars, and pledge allegiance to their lords. Hence, the *sakdina* system, apart from being an indicator of one's power and status, determined men's social relations and statutory duties. Men's bodies were made a focal point of the country's economic production and national protection. Equally important, as clients or subjects of their patrons, free men were to strictly observe discipline and moral codes such as loyalty and subservience. As Siam became the modern nation-state Thailand, different rulers selectively appropriated some of these attributes and practices—which now defined hegemonic masculinity—for their political agendas.

The inception of the modern nation-state has more closely associated hegemonic masculinity with policy-making authorities and rulers, as these leaders incorporated hegemonic masculinity into the nation-building process. On the one hand, men's bodies, as resources for wars and labor, have remained pertinent since the *sakdina* period. Men's mental attention, on the other hand, was invested in Theravāda Buddhist ethics, which became popular in rural villages even before its official recognition.[3] Thai people believed that every male should spend a period of his life as a member of the monastic order to study Dhamma (Sk. Dharma). Dhamma learning would instill Buddhist morality in men, who would retain these values even after they returned to the laity. This rendered ordained men, generally speaking, more socially respectable than those who were not.[4] Even though Thailand has integrated into a global capitalist system, I would argue that masculine ideals in modern Thai society have not changed much with respect to Buddhist morality.

Global capitalism defines hegemonic masculinity in terms of qualities needed to succeed in the competitive market economy, such as courage, inner direction, certain forms of aggression, autonomy, mastery, technological skill, group solidarity, adventure, and considerable amounts of toughness of mind and body.[5] However, in the Thai context, men are also expected to act in ways that contribute to the welfare of their community or the nation. This requires that they live up to Theravāda Buddhist ideals, such as gratitude and selflessness in serving others. These values and practices not only benefit the nation, but they also help sustain hierarchical social positions, as was once central to the patronage relationships of the premodern *sakdina* system.

Historical and Cultural Contexts of Thai Hegemonic Masculinity

The Wild Tiger Corps: Manly Men Serving Buddhism, King, and Country

In a Thai historical context, despite the pervasiveness of hegemonic masculinity, other types of masculinity do exist and thrive. However, in times of national urgency, hegemonic masculinity is often invoked to resolve political, social, or economic problems. According to Adam Scalena, masculinity has been reconfigured and embedded in Thai nationalist discourse to serve primarily as a source of national strength and unity, and as a self-fashioning strategy for any newly emergent modern nation.[6] King Chulalongkorn (Rama V, 1853–1910) created a new type of bureaucratic organization for the nation-state that left his son, King Vajiravudh (Rama VI, 1881–1925), with two difficulties. On one front, he had to deal with a reformed bureaucracy that had become centralized, enlarged, and complicated to manage. On another front, he had to maintain his sovereignty and divine aura to preserve loyalty to the throne. To navigate this situation, King Vajiravudh adopted a "gendered strategy" that defined and valorized certain masculine ideals.[7] In so doing, he first established the paramilitary organization known as the Wild Tiger Corps (Th. Sue Pa), which primarily served as a reserve army in case of war. It was later mandated to maintain law and order and to assist in humanitarian activities. In its early phase, the organization consisted of only government officials; it later included civilians from all social classes. All of the individuals were men, making the organization a sort of fraternity, and (at least in the beginning) all members were Buddhist.[8] Projecting himself as a paternal-figure-cum-commander-in-chief of the organization, the king funded and managed the corps, and he also took part in designing the organization's pageants for constant public displays.[9]

In depicting Siam as a civilized and unified Buddhist nation, King Vajiravudh imparted the members of the corps, civil servants in particular, with certain martial values such as discipline, honor, and loyalty to the monarch as they participated in military training, drills, and other activities. His ultimate objective was to produce "manly men united under the pillars of God [i.e., Buddhism], king, and country."[10] Despite the serious commitment required, many civil servants voluntarily took part in the corps to show their patriotism. In addition, being corps members guaranteed exemption from military recruitment and increased their chances for professional success, as good performances in the corps led to career promotions. When such incentives were combined with increasing publicity, the corps attracted more members within a few years. In teaching the corps, the king exclusively selected historical events and popular myths including the legend of King Naresuan—the late sixteenth-century warrior monarch who freed Siam from vassalage to Burma—and reconstructed stories that incited martial values, national loyalty, and deference to the monarch.[11] Frequent public feats of marching and drilling enhanced the corps' public appeal and reinforced martial ideals of manliness.

The king even wrote a didactic drama, *The Heart of a Young Man* (Th. *Hua chai chai num*), to instruct young bureaucratic officials to embrace the ideals and values propagated by the Wild Tiger Corps.[12] Viewing domestic affairs as relevant and important to bureaucracy, the king constructed a new type of ideal man who practiced monogamy and was careful with his spending. *The Heart of a Young Man* depicts two contrasting male characters. One is an educated young man who is disappointed with his failed marriage with a modern woman, but who channels his energy toward achieving his career goals in the bureaucracy while also joining the Wild Tiger Corps; this character finally finds a happy home life after remarrying a traditional woman. The other male character is a polygamous middle-aged man who always finds himself in financial trouble due to his lavish spending and exorbitant expenses associated with his seven wives, four horses, and large network of friends. The king's overall message was explicit: for individual achievement and dynastic prosperity, Siamese men should be educated, devoted to their work, practice monogamy, be frugal, and embrace a healthy sense of camaraderie with other men.

Monks, Boxers, and Thugs

While King Vajiravudh redefined hegemonic masculinity for bureaucrats, Peter Vail's work on Thai boxing (Muay Thai) identifies hegemonic masculinity through the intersecting figures of the Thai boxer (Th. *nak muay*), thug (Th. *nak leng*, also "ruffian" or "hitman"), and monk.[13] Although the boxer and the thug are not one and the same, they embody similarities, such as the mastery of boxing or shooting skills, an ability to endure pain, and a sense of loyalty to their patrons or peer groups. Operating within male-dominated circles, they seek the approval of other males and need to negotiate within the hierarchy of power for material success. The monk, on the contrary, represents an entirely different social role in contrast to the rather violent field of boxing, while still sharing certain structural and practical features associated with the practice of boxing. For example, as Vail has keenly observed, monks are spatially marked through social withdrawal into all-male spaces. Monks enter monasteries, whereas boxers choose to confine themselves within their boxing camps. Both forms of isolation are employed for the purpose of self-discipline and training. In addition, both monks and boxers receive different names (Th. *chaya*, or "designation") from their masters or seniors while remaining in either the monkhood or the world of competitive boxing. Despite their many differences, these shared attributes allow monks and boxers to embody hegemonic masculinities in surprisingly similar ways.

Pattana Kitiarsa's ethnographic study of Thai boxing conveys similar ideas about hegemonic masculinity.[14] For Kitiarsa, Thai boxing is an activity where hegemonic masculinity is practiced, produced, and consumed. In the material realm, boxers, particularly those from a working-class background, are motivated to financially provide for their families; the endeavor could then become a source of self-esteem and pride. This role requires a great deal of physical and mental investment that can attest to their manliness. Like Vail, Kitiarsa sees the boxing ring as a contradictory space where rules are followed and sportsmanship is promoted; at the same time, however, it serves as a gambling den, where men exploit other men and wield their power in a hierarchical manner. In another study, Kitiarsa links his previous analysis of hegemonic masculinity with Buddhism.[15] He argues that similar characteristics of Thai boxing and Theravāda Buddhism, in their coexistence, constitute a hegemonic cultural nexus that has formed a basis for gendered ideological practices for Thai people in general. One similarity is that both are male-oriented institutions where models for manliness are produced and promoted. Moreover, the act of becoming a boxer or a monk can empower men with a degree of self-agency to achieve economic change and social mobility, while indoctrinating them, in the process, into the national hierarchical structure of patriarchy.

Unlike the autonomy that Ward Keeler discusses in the Burman monastic context, in Thailand monasticism promotes the well-being and contentment of the community or the nation at large, in addition to conferring individual benefits. Through monastic ordination, even for a short period, men complete their *luk phu chai* duty, which refers to the responsibility primarily associated with being born a male child in Thai society. Metaphorically, *luk phu chai* can also refer to a manly son. Given the strong symbolism that is attached to ordination, it has become important for Buddhist men to live up to this normative ideal of the *luk phu chai*—that is to say, ordination allows Thai men to perform their socially required masculine duty.

Monastic ordination also confers a measure of gravitas and maturity. A man who has not been ordained as a monk is said to be "raw," whereas one who has entered monkhood is "ripe."[16] The ripe man is preferable to the raw one. Having learned Dhamma and practiced worldly renunciation, the ripe man has the awareness and ability to properly deal with his unwholesome thoughts or sinful desires. The sanctity of monkhood, along with the concept of Dhamma, lends authority to men who may not be able to achieve other forms of hegemonic masculinity. This is reflected in the case of Coach Ek, who led the "Wild Boars" youth soccer team that was saved in the Tham Luang cave rescue.

Hanuman: Loyal Soldier, Selfless Devotee

The final facet of hegemonic Thai Buddhist masculinity that manifests in the Tham Luang cave rescue is the ideal embodied by Hanuman (Sk. Hanumān), a monkey god who appears in the ancient Sanskrit epic *Rāmāyaṇa*.[17] Like the larger narrative of the *Rāmāyaṇa*, Hanuman bridges the cultural and religious divide from Hindu India to Buddhist Thailand. While Hanuman remains an important figure in Hinduism and embodies Thailand's Hindu-Buddhist history, in contemporary Thailand he is understood primarily through a Buddhist lens, as a Buddhist figure.[18] The *Rāmāyaṇa* recounts the story of Rama (Sk. Rāma), the prince of Ayodhyā and the incarnation of the god Viṣṇu.[19] Rama leads a battle against Rāvaṇa (Th. Dasakanth), the demonic King of Laṅkā, because the latter has abducted Rama's wife, Sītā. During the course of his journey to Laṅkā, Rama allies with the monkey army in the town of Kiṣkindhā, where Hanuman is the city minister. Later, Hanuman subjects himself to Rama and becomes his devoted servant. It is due to Hanuman's fighting prowess, physical power, and selflessness in serving Rama that Rama finally wins the epic war. Like Rama, Hanuman is born of nobility: his father is the god of wind, Vāyu, and his mother is the princess Añjanā.[20] As a child, Hanuman received boons from many gods such as physical immortality, phenomenal strength, and the ability to shape-shift; these physical qualities, when combined with his loving and emotional devotion to his personal god Rama, make him a much-loved deity. In India, where the *Rāmāyaṇa* originated, Hanuman temples are found practically everywhere, and images of him are ubiquitous in everyday life. Hanuman is worshipped especially by wrestlers and other athletes, by students seeking success in their exams, by women wishing to conceive, and by people suffering from mental problems and illnesses.[21]

The Indian *Rāmāyaṇa* tradition is the foundation for Thailand's *Ramakien*, a Thai version of the *Rāmāyaṇa*. The *Ramakien* is not just a single text, but a narrative canon that has inspired masterpieces of literature, painting, sculpture, and stage performances. Like the *Rāmāyaṇa* in India, multiple versions of the *Ramakien* exist, both official and regional. However, it is acknowledged that King Rama I (the Thai king of the Chakri dynasty who was viewed as the embodiment of Rama; 1737–1809) was the first to compile and standardize the text in order to make it compatible with Thai beliefs and society.[22] This version of the *Ramakien* (1797) has become the most widely known. As a great advocate of Buddhism, Rama I assimilated the idea of the "Glory of Rama" into the Buddhist ideal of royal authority.[23] When he installed the Emerald Buddha in his new royal temple (Wat Phra Kaew) in 1784, it was accompanied by cultic activities, and a commission of a set of murals depicting some of the *Ramakien* episodes (figs. 8.1–8.2). In celebrations of the Buddha image that happened regularly, selected episodes from *Ramakien* were performed. As Reynolds observes, these visual and ritual affairs clearly affirmed the royal power of the reigning Chakri dynasty.[24]

King Vajiravudh (Rama VI), the founder of the Wild Tiger Corps, incorporated the *Ramakien* and its characters into his nation-building project. It was

FIGURE 8.1 Hanuman makes his body a bridge that enables his army to cross from Lanka. Room 154, Temple of the Emerald Buddha, Grand Royal Place, Thailand. Photo by Korakot Kamkaew.

Vajiravudh who initially adopted the royal name "Rama" as Rama VI; consequently, all of the Thai kings of the Chakri dynasty have been formally addressed by the designation "Rama."[25]King Vajiravudh was instrumental in promoting Hanuman symbolism in modern Thailand. Under his reign, Hanuman's appearance was displayed in his royal standard (Thong Phra Krabi Dhuj).[26] Representing military valor, protective power, and strong devotion to lord Rama, the Hanuman standard was often paired with another one depicting the divine bird Garuda (Sk. *garuḍa*). Both were presented side by side during important ceremonial occasions in which the king was dressed in his royal Thai army uniform.

Hanuman played a role in King Vajiravudh's modern form of Buddhist hegemonic masculinity. The monkey god was also incorporated into traditional Thai boxing dance ritual as well as in protective charms and tattoos.[27] Phachalin Jeennoon has shown that different versions of the *Ramakien* present

FIGURE 8.2 Hanuman brings a mutilated *yakṣa* head to Rama. Room 86, Temple of the Emerald Buddha, Grand Royal Place, Thailand. Photo by Korakot Kamkaew.

Hanuman's characteristics differently.[28] In the Rama I version, for instance, the *Ramakien* conveys a didactic message of loyalty to the monarchy and government officials; it also serves as a form of entertainment for public audiences. The Northern or Lanna version functions as a religious text and aims to teach certain moral lessons, whereas the objective of the Western Thai version is mainly to entertain. As such, the entertaining versions portray Hanuman as a womanizer and comical figure as well as a smart and loyal soldier. The latter characteristics are possibly the best-known attributes that have been kept intact from Hanuman's representation in the Sanskrit *Rāmāyaṇa*.

Despite some differences, Jeennoon concluded that Hanuman's outstanding characteristics resonated in all versions of the story. The most notable characteristics of Hanuman are of a "devoted, very smart and skillful fighter."[29] These traits are also considered the prerequisites of any soldier who wishes to serve the king, the Chakri dynasty, and the state. The *Ramakien* emphasizes Hanuman's warrior role more than in the *Rāmāyaṇa* so that

Rama can more fully embody the Buddhist ethos of nonviolence.[30] At the same time, the image of Hanuman as a playful Casanova, as depicted in the canonical version of Thai *Ramakien*, seems to reveal another cultural overtone of Thai patriarchy in which a man's sexual prowess and playfulness is both accepted and admirable. Hence, this allows for different conceptions of hegemonic masculinity to emerge, specifically the *nak leng* (thug) ideal identified by Peter Vail, who locates hegemonic masculinity at the intersection between *nak muay* (boxer), *nak leng*, and monk.

Given the negative images of *nak leng*, who are often linked to violence and crime, Vail admits that there are varying perceptions of the *nak leng* that sometimes conjure a sense of dangerous allure and romance in the public imagination.[31] This reveals that the *nak leng* is not always about thuggery but can also display loyalty, generosity, and big-heartedness, depending on contexts and personal relations. Vail's observation about *nak leng* corresponds to what I have argued elsewhere, namely, that *nak leng* is indeed a broadly cultural concept that brings together chivalry (Th. *supap burut*) and other qualities such as courage, decisiveness, leadership, fighting skills, and attractiveness to women.[32] Thak Chaloemtiarana defined *nak leng* as "a person who was not afraid to take risks, a person who 'lived dangerously,' kind to his friends but cruel to his enemies, a compassionate person, a gambler, a heavy drinker, and a lady-killer. In short, he was the kind of person who represented one central model of Thai masculinity."[33]

Hanuman, as portrayed in the various versions of the Thai *Ramakien*, overlaps with the figure of the *nak leng* and resonates vividly with Thak Chaloemtiarana's definition. When used for protective tattoos (Th. *sak yant*) among men who aspire to the *nak leng* model, Hanuman's image represents power, strength, protection, victory, invincibility, gallantry, support and popularity, and sexual attraction.[34]However, within the Theravāda Buddhist context of Thailand, the idea of *nak leng* is not exclusively limited to men or male attributes. Linguistically, the term *nak leng* extends to a wider and more complex appropriation of vernacular expressions which transcend age and gender boundaries. One example is that one can be said to possess a *nak leng* spirit or mentality, popularly referred to as having *jai nak leng* (literally, a heart of *nak leng*) as epitomized by Hanuman regardless of age or gender. When one observes closely how Hanuman symbolism plays out in popular representations such as songs, his role of providing generous assistance and support to his followers, dependents, and constituents (P. *parivāra*) can be clearly discerned.[35]

The notion of *parivāra* is significant here, as it connects hegemonic masculinity to a Buddhist concept of fraternity, suggesting the importance of social collectivism for the conservative nation. As Satira Racharin points out, cultivating and maintaining a sense of fraternity requires the three principles of compassion, comradeship, and giving.[36] Just like Hanuman serving Rama, Sītā, and his fellow soldiers, fraternity could be achieved when members in a hierarchical community practice compassion, comradeship, and giving in the treatment of their *parivāra*. King Vajiravudh (Rama VI) attempted this approach to fraternity through his organization of the Wild Tiger Corps and the Tiger Cubs. Whether these organizations achieved fraternity in the moral sense of the term is a different question.

The main point here is that the Buddhist Hanuman portrayed in the *Ramakien*, who represents hegemonic masculinity despite his vices, differs from the Hindu Hanuman whose celibacy and devotion to Rama have inspired the Bhakti (devotional) cult and yogic and ascetic practices.[37] Hanuman in the Thai imagination encourages individual performance of duties, public services, and volunteerism; especially where the monarchy is concerned, Hanuman further signifies loyalty, gratitude, and selfless sacrifice. The newly established Special Weapons and Tactics (SWAT) unit, which is affiliated with the Crime Suppression Division of the Royal Thai Police, is officially named Hanuman.[38] Their badge logo, which bears an image of the frontal part of Hanuman's head with two tridents on both sides, was officially bestowed by King Vajiralongkorn (Rama X; r. 2016–present) in a ceremonial reception. Such a ritual accentuates the unit's prestige and royal allure. The Hanuman unit, which was established in 2019, received much public recognition for its performance in the arrest of a school director who was involved in murder and robbery in Lop Buri in January 2020 and the shooting rampage at a shopping mall in Nakhon Rachasima in February 2020. Since then, it has continued to make a name for itself for cracking down on crimes and criminal gangs.

Heroes of the Tham Luang Cave Rescue

The Tham Luang cave rescue has become one of the most dramatic and perhaps the most talked-about rescue missions in recent Thai history.[39] The operation was a multinational collaboration involving working teams and volunteers from several countries. The entire international task force amounted to ten thousand people. All of these individuals came together to play their part in rescuing twelve players from the Wild Boars youth soccer team and their coach, who were trapped inside the Tham Luang cave complex for ten days. The initial incident took place on June 23, 2018, when the twelve boys between the ages of eleven and sixteen, and their coach, twenty-five-year-old Ekkapol Chanthawong, went into the cave after their training session.[40] While they were inside, early monsoon rains flooded the cave, blocking its entrance. Unable to leave, the Wild Boars were reported missing, and local search efforts began that night.

The next day, the missing Wild Boars made news headlines on virtually every media platform in Thailand, while the search operation shifted into full swing. In the days that followed, support came in from all over the country, while rescue teams and volunteers worked to find the boys. This gigantic team effort ran systematically for days under the leadership of Chiang Rai governor Narongsak Osottanakorn, while international attention and support also grew. On June 28, international teams joined in the effort, and on July 2 two British cave divers, John Volanthen and Richard Stanton, discovered all of the boys and their coach alive and well on a ledge about four kilometers from the entrance. However, the divers—international divers and Thai Navy Seals—were hindered by the limited oxygen inside the cave complex. Sergeant Saman Kunan, a former Thai Navy Seal diver, was one of the volunteer members of the research effort. On July 6, while placing air tanks throughout the cave to make more oxygen available during the rescue operation, Saman fell unconscious and died at the age of thirty-eight. The loss of Saman Kunan made the commander of the Navy Special Forces even more determined to make the mission a success. Finally, the official rescue operation took place from July 8 through July 10. The members of the soccer club were brought out of the cave and transported by ambulances and a helicopter to the city hospital, where they ultimately recovered.

Those involved in the operation, no matter what their contributions were and whether or not their efforts were voluntary, were deemed heroes. The notion of a hero, as far as the Tham Luang cave rescue is concerned, complements the making of hegemonic masculinity. Though the term *hero* can apply to a number of men and women who served selflessly in this mission, there are three Thai men whose central roles, as represented in popular media, embody hegemonic masculinity: Chiang Rai governor Narongsak Osottanakorn, who directed the rescue operation; Saman Kunan, the former

Navy Seal officer who died during his diving efforts; and Ekkapol Chanthawong, the coach of the Wild Boars team who was also stranded inside the cave. These men may be recognized for embodying the qualities that Patricia Sexton defines as hegemonic masculinity: courage, inner direction, certain forms of aggression, autonomy, mastery, technological skills, teamwork skills, a sense of adventure, and considerable amounts of mental and physical toughness. These qualities resonate with Hanuman's masculine characteristics, which connects the god to the three heroes of the Tham Luang cave rescue operation. Moreover, the three heroes display additional attributes that resonate with Hanuman's Buddhist character, but that are not present in Sexton's description.

Selflessness and Self-Sacrifice: Narongsak Osottanakorn and Saman Kunan

Hanuman's leadership skills are widely recognized, as he managed the entire army in the battle against the demon Rāvaṇa; however, his sacrifice and selflessness in serving Rama receive less attention. In the popular version of *Ramakien* composed by Rama I, Hanuman's selflessness manifests through his strong commitment to every dangerous, life-threatening assignment given by Rama. Hanuman always prioritizes the well-being of the nation and Rama over his own safety.[41] For example, when Rama asks three times who will go after Dasakanth (Sk. Rāvaṇa), the demon king who abducted his wife, Hanuman is the only soldier who volunteers.

What distinguishes Hanuman from other servants is his lack of desire for recognition or rewards. When Hanuman realizes that he is not capable of ruling the city of Ayudhya (a.k.a. Ayutthaya; Sk. Ayodhyā), half of which is awarded to him to rule by Rama after he helped the latter defeat Dasakanth, Hanuman seeks renunciation by becoming a monk and only leaves the monkhood when he is required to go into battle for Rama. In a Buddhist context, Hanuman's selflessness evokes the notion of nonself (P. *anattā*; Sk. *anātman*), which, along with impermanence (P. *anicca*; Sk. *anitya*) and suffering (P. *dukkha*; Sk. *duḥkha*), are the "three marks" (P. *tilakkhaṇa*; Sk. *trilakṣaṇa*) of existence that are foundational to Buddhism.[42] Nonself is the realization that the self does not have an essence; the mistaken attachment to an essential, eternal, discrete self leads to suffering. Hanuman's service to

Rama reflects this notion of nonself because Hanuman sees himself merely as a constituent of Rama's victory and the success of the nation. As such, he rejects positions that would make him an equal ruler to his master, Rama. Hanuman thus typifies the self-less Buddhist leader whose goal is to serve, as opposed to the self-centered leadership embodied by Dasakanth (Sk. Rāvaṇa).

As commander in chief of the Tham Luang rescue operation, Narongsak Osottanakorn (fig. 8.3) epitomizes Hanuman's leadership in several ways. A day after the soccer team's disappearance, Narongsak became aware of the herculean nature of the operation and started to request help from outside organizations and coordinate with the Thai Navy Seal team. Narongsak himself directed the official emergency administrative center, which became the heart of the mission. He had been in charge since day one, securing necessary supplies and making sure that each major plan was strictly followed. Following Saman Kunan's death on July 6, 2018, Narongsak decisively declared that the rescue must be made before heavy rains fell again, despite the

FIGURE 8.3 Narongsak Osottanakorn, the Chiang Rai governor (as of 2018) who was the commander of the Tham Luang cave rescue operation. Work Point News Twitter feed, July 13, 2018.

serious risks. That decision eventually led to the successful recovery of the boys between July 8 and 10.

Narongsak refused the popular tag of *hero* given to him as a result of the rescue operation. He said metaphorically that he was only one piece in a larger jigsaw puzzle, among many others, and that this great achievement was the result of teamwork. He went on to say that all of the public attention and accolades should be directed toward the members of all of the teams involved. When asked what he considered the key factors that led to the success of the operation, Narongsak mentioned a few specifics: first, he prioritized making and executing plans, and the need to make follow-up evaluations. Having to coordinate a large number of working teams, both national and international, to complete multiple tasks, he would accommodate each team to the best of his ability while trusting that each individual working team had the necessary knowledge and skills to perform their respective tasks. Another important factor was Narongsak's own technical knowledge from his background in civil engineering and geological exploration. In addition, Narongsak expressed his gratitude to King Vajiralongkorn (Rama X), citing the monarch's generosity in providing essential equipment as a key reason for the mission's success.[43]

As a government official, Narongsak is fully committed to his civil responsibilities as the governor of Chiang Rai province (as of 2018). His personal motto is "Klay Thukh [i.e., Pāli *dukkha*], Bumroong Sukh," which translates to "Relieve Suffering, Cultivate Joy." When asked what *klay thukh* or "relieve suffering" means, he responded that if any problem befell the Chiang Rai populace, it would be immediately reported to him; it would then be resolved within twenty-four hours. Likewise, for *bumroong sukh*, Narongsak said that "it was simply that people would feel so secure that they could eat and sleep properly."[44] In order to cultivate joy, Narongsak devoted as much of his time as he could to tending to people's problems and taking care of their collective well-being. He added that, as a government servant, he was willing to devote every hour, seven days a week, outside of his official working hours, to serve the people. In recognition of Narongsak's dedication and leadership, he received the Game Changer Award in 2018 from the Asia Society. Nevertheless, what gave him the most pride and honor was receiving a handwritten letter from King Vajiralongkorn, who expressed his admiration for Narongsak's contribution to the Tham Luang cave rescue operation.[45]

Such selfless devotion to public service was also embodied by Saman Kunan (fig. 8.4), the former Navy Seal officer who volunteered for the mission. Just before he boarded the flight to Chiang Rai to join the Tham Luang rescue team on July 5, 2018, Saman recorded a short video clip of himself saying that he, along with another diving team, was on the way to join the rescue effort: "We'll reach Chiang Rai by 4:00 p.m., so we will meet at Tham Luang this evening. May good luck be with us. We are going to bring the boys home."[46] The clip went viral on news media channels after his death had been reported. His self-sacrifice and bravery mean that Saman Kunan will always be remembered by the people of Thailand as the hero of Tham Luang. His friends recalled how Saman often offered a helping hand to those in need even after his retirement from the Navy Seals. They also spoke of how disciplined and capable he was as a serious triathlete.[47] According to Chuleeporn Kunan, Saman's wife, Saman was praised as a hero for who he was as he "loved helping others, doing charity work and getting things done."[48]

Saman has since become a national hero: the Tham Luang cave entrance has become a place for visitors to take photographs, and this site features a 3.2 by 2.5-meter bronze sculpture of him. Saman's funeral was royally sponsored, and he was posthumously promoted to the rank of lieutenant

FIGURE 8.4 Saman Kunan, an ex–Navy Seal official who lost his life during the Tham Luang cave rescue operation and his photo and coffin being carried by Navy Seal officials for the royal funeral. Thairath Online. July 7, 2018.

commander, a remarkable rise of seven ranks, by the king.[49] Songs like "Hero" (by Tik Shero), "Sgt. Sam, the Hero" (by Baew Samba), and "Tears Flowing in Mourning for Sgt. Sam" (by Yenjit Pornthevi) were composed in dedication to him, while both a marathon and a soccer match were organized to raise funds for his family. Additionally, the Buddhist members of the Wild Boars soccer team, including the coach, expressed their gratitude to Saman by being ordained as monks.

Khwam-Katanyu *(Gratitude) and Coach Ek*

The concept of nonself has another layer of meaning. If the self lacks inherent existence, what we see is thus a constitution of small elements that make up the whole and not a permanent essence. Phra Paisal Visalo (b. 1957), a well-respected monk who adopts socially engaged activities as his primary approach to Dhamma, draws from Thich Nhat Hanh's concept of interbeing. Phra Paisal Visalo writes that in the real world everything is related in causal relationships, just like a sheet of paper that has come into existence as a consequence of its interbeing with sunshine, trees, rain and other natural forces and elements.[50] From this perspective, a separate self is an illusion, and we have to be mindful of, and responsible for, anything that is part of our interbeing.

The concept of interbeing aligns with discourses of collectivism (vs. individualism) that are hegemonic in Thailand and many other Asian countries. Thai collectivism encompasses national ideals, Buddhism, and the monarchy. Thai Buddhist collectivism requires that, within the purview of Buddhist values, one has to coexist and interdepend on others to realize the benefits of a peaceful nation under the reign of a benevolent monarch. The practice of interdependence gives rise to what is referred in Thai as *khwam-katanyu*, or gratitude, which is a symbol of all "good people" in the country.[51] The concept of *khwam-katanyu* originally derives from one's personal relationships, such as relations between parents and children, teachers and students, or givers and takers. Once there is an exchange of giving and taking, the takers are culturally expected to pay back the gratitude they have received; they are then regarded as a *katanyu* person, one who is obliged to return someone else's debt or favor whenever it is possible to do so. Between parents and male children, the best act of *khwam-katanyu* the latter can perform for his parents is to be ordained as a monk. In Theravāda Buddhism, donning the robes of a novice or a monk, even for a short period of time, is equal to making the greatest merit. In this act, the ordained son has demonstrated their deepest feelings of gratitude toward their parents.

The Tham Luang cave rescue effort clearly illustrates how the ideas of nonself and interbeing operate, and Governor Narongsak's metaphor of the jigsaw puzzle could in fact be taken as an explanation of these concepts. What is noteworthy, as far as interbeing is concerned, is that it was not only the rescuers' teamwork that was the key factor in their success, but also the survivors, the twelve soccer players and the coach, who played their part in the operation. Coach Ek (Ekkapol Chanthawong), in particular, had a significant role as the team's leader. People thought that spending so many days in hunger and near-total darkness would make the boys weak and panicky. However, their lively exchanges in English with the divers proved otherwise. The media attention then turned to Coach Ek.

At first, some people blamed Coach Ek for his carelessness in leading the team into the cave. However, after photos and a video clip of the boys showed that they were alive and in good spirits, the nation (and the world) saw that the boys had managed to stay healthy.[52] It was soon revealed that Coach Ek, who had ordained as a monk for ten years, kept the boys calm by asking them to meditate while they were waiting for help. By following Coach Ek's directions to stay calm and maintain mental focus, the boys did not succumb to panic or despair. Instead, they dug channels to let excess water flow away, left marks on the cave walls, avoided using flashlights to save batteries, drank fresh water seeping through the cave stones, and practiced other mindful techniques.

Coach Ek's survival techniques, which he had mainly learned from his monastic experience, were widely praised by the media. Ultimately, this media attention transformed him into another national hero. Consequently, the media began to look into his personal life. To the surprise of many, he was born in Myanmar near the Thai border and belonged to the Tai Yai ethnic minority.[53] As an orphan, he was raised by his grandmother, who stayed in Myanmar even after Coach Ek moved to Thailand. Like many underprivileged children, he sought his schooling through the monastery, where he became a monk between the ages of ten and twenty. Due to his love of soccer, he trained to become a certified soccer coach and then got involved with the Wild Boars Academy.[54] Since leaving the monkhood at the age of twenty,

Coach Ek's life has revolved around the temple Phra That Doi Wow in Chiang Rai, where he regularly visits and assists with temple affairs before turning to his coaching routine in the evenings. When the news broke that Coach Ek and the Wild Boars were trapped inside Tham Luang, local people linked to either the soccer team or the temple came together to help, pray, or do whatever else they could to assist in the rescue mission.

Despite being in need of rescue himself, Coach Ek's role in practicing leadership that incorporated Buddhist methods was instrumental in keeping the boys mentally calm and physically resilient. News coverage of his lifelong personal engagement with Buddhism painted a unique picture of Coach Ek. He was now viewed as a *katanyu*: a man who has a strong sense of gratitude and who has completely performed his *luk phu chai*'s duty through his long-term commitment to the monastic order. He was seen as someone who fully engaged himself in Buddhism, both when he was robed as a monk and after his time in the monkhood was over. Having no parents, his frequent trips to Myanmar to visit his aged grandmother embody the practice of *khwam-katanyu*. Similarly, Coach Ek is seen as a mature man who, through Buddhism, has developed from a poor marginalized boy to a man of wisdom with the skills required to tend to his family's financial needs.

Coach Ek's image as a robed monk, standing alongside the eleven boys of the Wild Boars soccer club who were also ordained as novice monks, was published in conjunction with the story of their ordination ceremony (fig. 8.5).[55] This act was meant to pay tribute and express gratitude to Saman Kunan, the lost Navy Seal diver; consequently, it has become an iconic image. In the same photograph, the medical professional Pak Lohanchun is shown prostrating in front of Coach Ek to demonstrate his utmost respect. The image highlights Coach Ek's honored position and also includes him, an erstwhile noncitizen excluded from the nation, into the collective ideal of a great man in the Kingdom of Thailand. Shortly after the Tham Luang incident, in August 2018, Coach Ek received what he had been fighting for: legal status as a Thai citizen.[56]

Performing hegemonic masculinity, especially to the point of heroism, is a communal affair, as it necessitates interbeing. Likewise, communitarianism allows for *khwam-katanyu* to operate and serve its highest purpose of showing gratitude to the community and the nation through a succession of exchanges involving a give-and-take. The case of Coach Ek attests to this

FIGURE 8.5 Dr. Pak Lohanchun, a Navy Seal medical doctor, prostrating in front of Phra Coach Ek who was ordained along with the eleven boys trapped inside the cave on July 25, 2018. Laanews. July 25, 2018.

point, as he has belonged to communities in Thailand and Myanmar, and on soccer fields and in Buddhist temples. All of these spaces and the people involved in them constitute a large community in which Coach Ek's development, as a man and as a Buddhist Thai citizen, are clearly interdependent.

* * *

The epitome of manliness in a Thai cultural context, as has been signified by the Hanuman figure, embodies the divine masculine attributes of being a capable fighter on the one hand and a Buddhist practitioner on the other. This extends to the functions that are socially required as a citizen of the Thai nation, where a national ideology that represents the nation, the Buddhist religion, and the monarch is hegemonized and upheld. One reason for the continued hegemony of these forms of masculinity is that Thailand has been proud of its noncolonial past, unlike its neighboring countries, who were colonized by various imperial powers. Thailand's independence is understood to reflect the wisdom and intelligence of the monarchs, who have identified themselves with Rama, the Dhamma king of Ayudhya. In effect, a strong sense of nationalism among the majority of the populace of the kingdom has been continually materialized and sustained.

Another reason is that, since the military coup in September 2006, Thailand has experienced political upheaval and economic recession, which have had twofold impacts upon the ordinary people of the country. The populace has lost a sense of security and has developed skepticism toward political and social structures. This scenario requires a symbol, whether concrete or abstract, that can provide a sense of unity and protection. The Hanuman figure, including its forms of selfless, strong Buddhist masculinity, has become this symbol, as embodied in the three heroes of the Tham Luang cave rescue.

Connell's observation that hegemonic masculinity is achieved by only a minority of men may also ring true in a Thai context, especially when Buddhist notions of selflessness and gratitude are part of the hegemonic masculinity under consideration.[57] Heroic men like Governor Narongsak Osottanakorn and the Navy Seal diver Saman Kunan are exceptional, but their examples suggest the possibility for men to live up to these masculine ideals. The example of Coach Ek additionally shows how the Buddhist domain accommodates men from underprivileged backgrounds and allows them to move up socially by providing opportunities for financial gain and social inclusion. In short, Buddhism functions as a domain for Thai men to perfect their manly obligations.

NOTES

1. Charles F. Keyes, *Thailand: Buddhist Kingdom as Modern Nation-State* (New York: Routledge, [1987] 2019), 29–31.
2. Narupon Duangwiset, "Deconstructing the Myth of 'Masculinity' in Thai Society" [Thai], Sirindhorn Anthropology Center Conference 2017, January 1, 2017), https://www.sac.or.th/conference/2017/blog-post/.
3. Keyes, *Thailand*, 32–39.
4. Keyes, 36.
5. Patricia Sexton, cited in Mike Donaldson, "What Is Hegemonic Masculinity?," *Theory and Society* 22, no. 5 (October 1993): 643–57, 644.
6. Adam Nicholas Scalena, "State Masculinities in Siam, 1919–1925" (master's thesis, University of British Columbia, 2009), 5.
7. Scalena, "State Masculinities in Siam," 22–23.
8. Walter F. Vella, *Chaiyo! King Vajiravudh and the Development of Thai Nationalism* (Honolulu: University of Hawai'i Press, 1978), 37–38.
9. Vella, *Chaiyo!*, 41; Scalena, "State Masculinities in Siam," 18.

10. King Vajiravudh studied law and history at Christchurch College, University of Oxford, and he received military training from Royal Military College, Sandhurst. His nationalistic approach to Siam's bureaucratic reform was influenced by Western ideas. See Scalena, "State Masculinities in Siam," 11; and Vella, *Chaiyo!*, 34, 132–34.
11. Vella, 216–17; Scalena, 23–24.
12. Scalena, 30–38.
13. Peter Vail, "Violence and Control: Social and Cultural Dimensions of Boxing in Thailand" (PhD diss., Cornell University, 1998), 282.
14. Pattana Kitiarsa, "'Lives of Hunting Dogs': *Muai Thai* and the Politics of Thai Masculinities," *South East Asia Research* 13, no. 1 (2005): 57–90, 59.
15. Pattana Kitiarsa, "Of Men and Monks: The Boxing-Buddhism Nexus and the Production of National Manhood in Contemporary Thailand," New Mandala: New Perspectives on South East Asia, October 2, 2013, https://www.newmandala.org/pattana-kitiarsa-on-thai-boxing/.
16. Keyes, *Thailand*, 36–37.
17. The earliest version of this narrative is attributed to the sage Vālmīki around 500 BCE.
18. See Chirapat Prapandvidya, "Aspects of Hanuman in Thai Life," *Damrong Journal* 1, no. 1 (January–July 2001): 361–68, 361.
19. I use Sanskrit names to introduce characters from the better known *Rāmāyaṇa*, but in general I refer to Rama (Sk. Rāma) and Hanuman (Sk. Hanumān) without the Sanskrit diacritics to indicate these figures beyond the Sanskrit tradition.
20. N. N. Wig, "Hanuman Complex and its Resolution: An Illustration of Psychotherapy from Indian Mythology," *Indian Journal of Psychiatry* 46, no. 1 (2004): 25–28.
21. See Philip Lutgendorf, *Hanuman's Tale: The Message of a Divine Monkey* (New York: Oxford University Press, 2007).
22. This also implies that the text might have been a collaborative work of more than one poet working under the king's patronage.
23. See Frank E. Reynolds, "*Rāmāyaṇa*, *Rāmā Jātaka*, and *Ramakien*: A Comparative Study of Hindu and Buddhist Traditions," in *Many Rāmāyaṇas: The Diversity of a Narrative Tradition in South Asia*, ed. Paula Richman (Berkeley: University of California Press, 1991), 58.
24. Reynolds, "*Rāmāyaṇa*, *Rāmā Jātaka*, and *Ramakien*," 57–59.
25. Villa, *Chaiyo!*, 143.
26. The standard displays a white Hanuman figure on a red square flag. See Prapandvidya, "Aspects of Hanuman in Thai Life," 362.
27. Prapandvidya, 362.
28. See Phachalin Jeennoon, "An Analysis of Hanuman in Various Versions of the Ramakien" (master's thesis, Silpakorn University, 2004).
29. Jeennoon, "Analysis of Hanuman," English abstract.
30. Angela Marie May, "*Sak Yant*: The Transition from Indic *Yantras* to Thai 'Magical' Buddhist Tattoos" (master's thesis, University of Alabama at Birmingham, 2014), 57.
31. Vail, "Violence and Control," 299–300.

32. Natawan Wongchalard, "Heroes and Representations of Masculinity in Thai Action Films," *Manusya: Journal of Humanities* 22, no. 1 (2019): 34–53.
33. Thak Chaloemtiarana, *Thailand: The Politics of Despotic Paternalism* (Ithaca, N.Y.: Cornell Southeast Asia Program, [1979] 2007), 225; quoted in Keyes, *Thailand*, 80–81.
34. *Sak yant* is an ancient Thai art form of tattooing performed by learned Buddhist masters who are knowledgeable and experienced in Buddhist symbolism and the associated blessings. See Joanna Cook, "Tattoos, Corporeality, and the Self: Dissolving Borders in a Thai Monastery," *The Cambridge Journal of Anthropology* 27, no. 2 (2007–2008): 20–35, 22–23. For the Hanuman figure, there are nine popular designs. "Hanuman Tattoos" [Thai], Pon Design, YouTube video, 10:29, June 21, 2020, https://www.youtube.com/watch?v=hUuunu1o3Lg.
35. See for example, a song by Sambahthasib featuring Prangthip the Voice & Noom Hanuman, "Hanuman" [Thai], Toffy Jully, YouTube video, 4:09, June 27, 2016, https://www.youtube.com/watch?v=sIgIMcMH7WU; and a song by Tae Sila, "Hanuman (Thinking of You)" [Thai], Feedback Studio Record, YouTube video, 4:44, June 18, 2016, https://www.youtube.com/watch?v=G7M-YMJy5zc.
36. Satira Racharin, "The Concept of Fraternity in Buddhist Philosophy," in "On the occasion of the Graduation Ceremony 2019," special issue, *Mahachula Academic Journal* 6 (2019): 153–65.
37. Lutgendorf, *Hanuman's Tale*, 45–50.
38. "Getting to Know the Hanuman Unit and Its Royal Badge Logo" [Thai], Bangkokbiznews.com, June 4, 2020, https://www.bangkokbiznews.com/news/883634.
39. See "Summary of Major Event Timelines of the Tham Luang Cave Rescue of 13 Lives" [Thai], PPTV Online, July 10, 2018, https://www.pptvhd36.com/news/ประเด็นร้อน/85091.
40. "The Full Story of Thailand's Extraordinary Cave Rescue," BBC News, July 18, 2018, https://www.bbc.com/news/world-asia-44791998.
41. Jeennoon, "Analysis of Hanuman," 323–24.
42. Robert E. Buswell Jr., and Donald S. Lopez Jr., *The Princeton Dictionary of Buddhism* (Princeton, N.J.: Princeton University Press, 2014), 42–43.
43. See Narongsak's interview on "Disrupted World" [Thai], Thai PBS, YouTube video, 58:15, July 24, 2018, https://www.youtube.com/watch?v=5ISvrDmb6WM.
44. See Narongsak's interview in "Governor Narongsak: The Model of Thai Civil Officials" [Thai], Standard, YouTube video, 9:26, June 3, 2019, https://www.youtube.com/watch?v=h9WWusWKfGY&t=420s.
45. In October 2019, Narongsak was transferred to Lampang province where he attracted media attention again with his successful COVID-19 vaccination campaign, making Lampang the city with the second-highest (after Bangkok) number of people registered for COVID-19 vaccinations in 2021. See "Amazing! Over 220,000 People in Lampang Booked for Covid-19 Vaccine Shots" [Thai], Manager Online, May 10, 2021, https://mgronline.com/onlinesection/detail/9640000044769.
46. "Sgt. Sam's Final Words" [Thai], TNN Station, YouTube video, 1:20, July 6, 2018, https://www.youtube.com/watch?v=7PXBEC33kWA.

47. See "Sergeant Sam: The Unforgettable Hero of Tham Luang" [Thai], Channel 8 News, YouTube video, July 14, 2018, https://www.youtube.com/watch?v=XRKmAuAuLTw [no longer available].
48. "Thai Cave Rescue: The Man Who Died Helping Save the Boys Has Been Remembered as a Hero," ABC News, updated July 11, 2018, https://www.abc.net.au/news/2018-07-11/thai-cave-rescue-navy-seal-remembered/9978638.
49. See "Ex-Seal Saman Posthumously Promoted," *Bangkok Post*, July 14, 2018, https://www.bangkokpost.com/thailand/general/1503426/sanan-kunan.
50. See Phra Paisal Visalo, "Thich Nhat Hanh and New Dimensions of Buddhism" [Thai], Visalo, 2009, https://www.visalo.org/article/person18NhatHanh.htm (accessed December 1, 2022); and Thich Nhat Hanh, *Peace Is Every Step* (New York: Bantam, 1991), 95.
51. A Pāli Buddhist proverb, *Nimittung saturupanung katunyukatavetita*, underscores the importance of practicing gratitude, as it is considered a basic requirement of a virtuous person. Busakorn Watthanabut, Phramaha Phanuwat Sankham, and Phra Udomsittinayok, "Good People with Gratitude Base on Buddhist [*sic*]" [Thai], in "Mindfulness: Traditions and Compassionate Applications," special issue, *Journal of MCU Peace Studies* 5, no. 1 (2017): 77–86.
52. See Nick Glass, "The Miraculous Story of the Thai Cave Rescue," CNN, YouTube video, 10:44, July 14, 2018, https://www.youtube.com/watch?v=d7uhm_OlXj4.
53. "Disclosing Coach Ek's Life: The Spirit Lifter of the Wild Boars team" [Thai], MGR Online, July 5, 2018, https://mgronline.com/onlinesection/detail/9610000066916.
54. Somruethai Sapsomboon, "Coach Ek: Another Hero at Tham Luang" [Thai], KomChadLuek Online, July 3, 2018, https://www.komchadluek.net/news/people/333192.
55. Adul Samon, who is a Christian, was not ordained.
56. "Phra Coach Ek and Three Football Players of the Wild Boars Team Have Obtained Citizenship" [Thai], MGR Online, August 8, 2018, https://mgronline.com/local/detail/9610000079001.
57. See Raewyn Connell and James W. Messerschmidt, "Hegemonic Masculinity: Rethinking the Concept," *Gender & Society* 19, no. 6 (December 2005): 829–59.

Additional Primary Sources

Howard, Ron, dir. *Thirteen Lives*. Los Angeles: United Artists Releasing, 2022.

The Ramakien: The Thai Epic. Vālmīki. Translated by John M. Cadet. Tokyo: Kodansha International, 1971.

Tancharoen, Kevin, and Nattawut Poonpiriya, dir. *Thai Cave Rescue*. Aired September 22, 2022, Netflix.

Vasarhelyi, Elizabeth Chai, and Jimmy Chin, dir. *The Rescue*. New York: Greenwich Entertainment, 2021.

Waller, Tom, dir. *The Cave*. 2019. Santa Monica, Calif.: Lionsgate, 2022.

Bibliography

"Amazing! Over 220,000 People in Lampang Booked for COVID-19 Vaccine Shots" [Thai]. Manager Online, May 10, 2021. https://mgronline.com/onlinesection/detail/9640000044769.
Buswell, Robert E., Jr., and Donald S. Lopez Jr. *The Princeton Dictionary of Buddhism*. Princeton, N.J.: Princeton University Press, 2014.
Chaloemtiarana, Thak. *Thailand: The Politics of Despotic Paternalism*. Ithaca, N.Y.: Cornell Southeast Asia Program, [1979] 2007.
Connell, Raewyn, and James W. Messerschmidt. "Hegemonic Masculinity: Rethinking the Concept." *Gender & Society* 19, no. 6 (December 2005): 829–59.
Cook, Joanna. "Tattoos, Corporeality, and the Self: Dissolving Borders in a Thai Monastery." *Cambridge Journal of Anthropology* 27, no. 2 (2007–2008): 20–35.
"Disclosing Coach Ek's Life: The Spirit Lifter of the Wild Boars team" [Thai]. MGR Online, July 5, 2018. https://mgronline.com/onlinesection/detail/9610000066916.
"Disrupted World" [Thai]. Thai PBS, YouTube video, 58:15, July 24, 2018. https://www.youtube.com/watch?v=5ISvrDmb6WM.
Donaldson, Mike. "What Is Hegemonic Masculinity?" *Theory and Society* 22, no. 5 (October 1993): 643–57.
Duangwiset, Narupon. "Deconstructing the Myth of 'Masculinity' in Thai Society" [Thai]. Sirindhorn Anthropology Center Conference 2017, January 1, 2017. https://www.sac.or.th/conference/2017/blog-post/.
"Ex-Seal Saman Posthumously Promoted." *Bangkok Post*, July 14, 2018. https://www.bangkokpost.com/thailand/general/1503426/sanan-kunan.
"The Full Story of Thailand's Extraordinary Cave Rescue." BBC News, July 18, 2018. https://www.bbc.com/news/world-asia-44791998.
"Getting to Know the Hanuman Unit and Its Royal Badge Logo" [Thai]. Bangkokbiznews.com, June 4, 2020. https://www.bangkokbiznews.com/news/883634.
Glass, Nick. "The Miraculous Story of the Thai Cave Rescue." CNN, YouTube video, 10:44, July 14, 2018. https://www.youtube.com/watch?v=d7uhm_OlXj4.
"Governor Narongsak: The Model of Thai Civil Officials" [Thai]. Standard, YouTube video, 9:26, June 3, 2019. https://www.youtube.com/watch?v=h9WWusWKfGY&t=420s.
"Hanuman" [Thai]. Toffy Jully, YouTube video, 4:09, June 27, 2016. https://www.youtube.com/watch?v=sIgIMcMH7WU.
"Hanuman Tattoos" [Thai]. Pon Design, YouTube video, 10:29, June 21, 2020. https://www.youtube.com/watch?v=hUuunu1o3Lg.
"Hanuman (Thinking of You)" [Thai]. Feedback Studio Record, YouTube video, 4:44, June 18, 2016. https://www.youtube.com/watch?v=G7M-YMJy5zc.
Jeennoon, Phachalin. "An Analysis of Hanuman in Various Versions of the Ramakien." Master's thesis, Silpakorn University, 2004.
Keyes, Charles, F. *Thailand: Buddhist Kingdom as Modern Nation-State*. New York: Routledge, [1987] 2019.
Kitiarsa, Pattana. " 'Lives of Hunting Dogs': *Muai Thai* and the Politics of Thai Masculinities." *South East Asia Research* 13, no. 1 (2005): 57–90.

——. "Of Men and Monks: The Boxing-Buddhism Nexus and the Production of National Manhood in Contemporary Thailand." New Mandala: New Perspectives on South East Asia, October 2, 2013. https://www.newmandala.org/pattana-kitiarsa-on-thai-boxing/.

Lutgendorf, Philip. *Hanuman's Tale: The Message of a Divine Monkey*. New York: Oxford University Press, 2007.

May, Angela Marie. "*Sak Yant*: The Transition from Indic *Yantras* to Thai 'Magical' Buddhist Tattoos." Master's thesis, University of Alabama at Birmingham, 2014.

"Phra Coach Ek and Three Football Players of the Wild Boars Team Have Obtained Citizenship" [Thai]. MGR Online, August 8, 2018. https://mgronline.com/local/detail/9610000079001.

Phra Paisal Visalo. "Thich Nhat Hanh and New Dimensions of Buddhism" [Thai], Visalo, 2009. https://www.visalo.org/article/person18NhatHanh.htm (accessed December 1, 2022).

Prapandvidya, Chirapat. "Aspects of Hanuman in Thai Life." *Damrong Journal* 1, no. 1 (January–July 2001): 361–68.

Racharin, Satira. "The Concept of Fraternity in Buddhist Philosophy." In "On the Occasion of the Graduation Ceremony 2019," special issue, *Mahachula Academic Journal* 6 (2019): 153–65.

Reynolds, Frank, E. "*Rāmāyaṇa*, *Rāmā Jātaka*, and *Ramakien*: A Comparative Study of Hindu and Buddhist Traditions." In *Many Rāmāyaṇas: The Diversity of a Narrative Tradition in South Asia*, edited by Paula Richman, 50–63. Berkeley: University of California Press, 1991.

Sapsomboon, Somruethai. "Coach Ek: Another Hero at Tham Luang" [Thai]. KomChadLuek Online, July 3, 2018. https://www.komchadluek.net/news/people/333192.

Scalena, Adam Nicholas. "State Masculinities in Siam, 1919–1925." Master's thesis, University of British Columbia, 2009.

"Sergeant Sam: The Unforgettable Hero of Tham Luang" [Thai]. Channel 8 News, YouTube video, July 14, 2018. https://www.youtube.com/watch?v=XRKmAuAuLTw [no longer available].

"Sgt. Sam's Final Words" [Thai]. TNN Station, YouTube video, 1:20, July 6, 2018. https://www.youtube.com/watch?v=7PXBEC33kWA.

"Summary of Major Event Timelines of the Tham Luang Cave Rescue of 13 Lives" [Thai]. PPTV Online, July 10, 2018. https://www.pptvhd36.com/news/ประเด็นร้อน/85091.

"Thai Cave Rescue: The Man Who Died Helping Save the Boys Has Been Remembered as a Hero." ABC News, updated July 11, 2018. https://www.abc.net.au/news/2018-07-11/thai-cave-rescue-navy-seal-remembered/9978638.

Thich Nhat Hanh. *Peace Is Every Step*. New York: Bantam, 1991.

Vail, Peter. "Violence and Control: Social and Cultural Dimensions of Boxing in Thailand." PhD diss., Cornell University, 1998.

Vella, Walter F. *Chaiyo! King Vajiravudh and the Development of Thai Nationalism*. Honolulu: University of Hawai'i Press, 1978.

Watthanabut, Busakorn, Phramaha Phanuwat Sankham, and Phra Udomsittinayok. "Good People with Gratitude Base on Buddhist [*sic*]." [Thai]. In "Mindfulness: Traditions and Compassionate Applications," special issue, *Journal of MCU Peace Studies* 5, no. 1 (2017): 77–86.

Wig, N. N. "Hanuman Complex and Its Resolution: An Illustration of Psychotherapy from Indian Mythology." *Indian Journal of Psychiatry* 46, no. 1 (2004): 25–28.

Wongchalard, Natawan. "Heroes and Representations of Masculinity in Thai Action Films." *Manusya: Journal of Humanities* 22, no. 1 (2019): 34–53.

NINE

Buddhism and Afro-Asian Masculinities in *The Man with the Iron Fists*

MARCUS EVANS

AFTER WORKING ON both Jim Jarmusch's *Ghost Dog: The Way of the Samurai* (1999) and Quentin Tarantino's *Kill Bill: Vols. 1 and 2* (2003, 2004), the self-pronounced Abbot of hip-hop's Wu-Tang Clan, RZA (pronounced "Rizah"), created his own East-meets-West Hollywood films called *The Man with the Iron Fists* (2012) and *The Man with the Iron Fists 2* (2015).[1] These pay homage to the Hong Kong martial arts films by which RZA had mythologized the Wu-Tang Clan as lyrical warriors from Shaolin and virtually link the rappers from Staten Island to the Daoist and Chan Buddhist traditions of Wudang and Shaolin, based, respectively, in China's Hubei and Henan provinces. Set in the nineteenth century, the *Iron Fists* films star RZA as the Black American slave Thaddeus Smith, who travels through China as a lone blacksmith and an unsung hero wielding a pair of iron fists as weapons. Full of gory violence and misogynistic portrayals of Asian women, they unapologetically tell the hero's story from an androcentric perspective. In fact, RZA and the Black Keys' "The Baddest Man Alive"—*Iron Fists*' theme song—is about a tough and formidable man who is absolutely unafraid of anything: Satan, legal authorities, female apes and grizzlies, wicked witches, and the world's "meanest woman."[2]

This chapter focuses on the role Chan Buddhism plays in Thaddeus's journey. It is Chan monks who welcome him to China, who teach him an antiracist spirituality, and who inform his overall heroic identity formation, thereby making him into the hero he was destined to become. Thaddeus's encounter with Chan Buddhism in the *Iron Fists* films is reminiscent of RZA's personal encounter with the tradition—specifically, the martial tradition of Shaolin Buddhism—which began with his youthful reception of Hong Kong martial arts films. Thaddeus's narrative can be read as RZA's interpretation of his own deep connection to Asian culture via martial arts films that spiritually and racially resonated with him. While RZA's understanding of Buddhism, and the Shaolin tradition, has matured since his youth, it was a cinematic representation of East Asian culture and Buddhism that initially inspired him, as it did many other Black youths of his generation and beyond.[3]

In examining Buddhism and Afro-Asian masculinities in the *Iron Fists* films, I am not concerned with the "authenticity" of RZA's depiction of Buddhism, whatever that might mean for other scholars and practitioners of Buddhism. Instead, I am interested in how RZA, like other Black Americans, encountered and appropriated Buddhism through the transnational circulation of East Asian films and martial arts. This chapter's broader argument is that the Buddhism RZA virtually encountered in films was, for him, a mythic model for transforming the masculine self. His *The Man with the Iron Fists* films, which more and less reflect his lived experience of masculinity, make this Buddhism integral to one Black man's overall sense of being and becoming a heroic man.

This idea of being and becoming a man saturates RZA's public discourse and self-fashioning. In various interviews and media, it is implicit in the androcentric language he uses, none of which precisely explains what being a man means, other than that it signifies something of manliness. Commenting on the term *Wu-Tang*, for example, RZA says that it "means 'a man deserving of God,' or 'a man who deserves to be God,' or 'a man trying to find God within himself.' "[4] He is not referring to the fact that the Clan is comprised of nine men affiliated with the Five Percent Nation of Gods and Earths—an androcentric religion that teaches that Black men are Gods, descendants of the Original Man: the Asiatic Black Man—but how the very concept of Wu-Tang, in the Wudang Daoist tradition, is about a man's act of attaining a certain kind of self-realization.[5] Also consider RZA's remarks on Daniel Wu, who played a villain in the first *Iron Fists* film; in an interview, RZA notes that Wu is "a great brother, a great spirit. I really like him as a person, as a man."[6] While the specific meaning of "as a man" is unclear, RZA's use of the phrase signifies something admirable about Wu's manhood. Elsewhere, RZA disassociates masculinity from meat-eating only to show that veganism is fit for making a man. He tells us, for instance, "a few bits of wisdom: A man is known to be strong, as they say, and that man eats steak for strength. Steak comes from a cow and the male cow, a bull, is a very strong animal that can grow up to around 1,500 pounds and move tons. All the cow eats is grass. All the muscles he has, all the steak, every part of him that we're consuming, is all built from plants."[7]

RZA's understanding of being and becoming a man reflects his own self-making "orientational process," in which he projects ideas of manliness as "aspects of the world" and of himself, alongside any other identities (e.g., vegan or Buddhist) that he appropriates, practices, or portrays on the silver screen.[8] I have mainly framed this study in terms of RZA's androcentric understanding of himself and the world, but his masculine orientation is not indicative of a single hegemonic masculinity, as if RZA/Thaddeus is simply an object or agent of a unilateral structure of power that subordinates women to men. RZA's "life-history," borrowing from Raewyn Connell and James Messerschmidt, could reveal a few "unique trajectories" of race and masculinity at work, which not only shape his sense of manhood but also paradoxically correlate and compete as alternative masculinities against others.[9]

This chapter first considers RZA's racialized and androcentric reception of the Hong Kong martial arts films of the late 1960s and 1970s, whose representations of chivalrous knights and martial monks gave him cinematic mythic models of manliness to which his *Iron Fists* films pay homage. This notion of *cinematic mythic models* refers to how films have functioned as archetypes for RZA and the Wu in their own mythmaking projects. I use terms such as *cinematic East* or *cinematic mythic models* to insist on the virtuality of RZA's initial encounter with Asian culture and Buddhism, which he celebrates in the virtual world of his own *Iron Fists* films.[10] This section also details RZA's understanding of the process of being and becoming a man—in terms of struggling with or sacrificing something for another man, as well as disciplining, mastering, and transforming oneself. It also gives a preliminary understanding of how Buddhism matters in this man-making process. Second, I walk us through a retelling of the *Iron Fists* narrative, describing what Thaddeus's heroic journey entails and detailing the several ways in which Chan Buddhism shapes him into a heroic man. In doing so, I demonstrate the thematic parallels between RZA's encounter with the virtual cinematic world of East Asian martial monks and the masculinized formations of Thaddeus's journey. Finally, I consider the counterhegemonic implications of Thaddeus/RZA's Buddhist masculinity in the sociocultural context of Black encounters with East Asian martial arts and film. The conclusion addresses the larger theoretical concern of hegemonic and alternate masculinities, specifically in terms of what Connell and Messerschmidt describe as masculinities at their "local" and "regional" levels.[11]

Cinematic Mythic Models of Manhood

The *Iron Fists* films pay homage to RZA's favorite Shaw Brothers directors, Chang Cheh and Lau Kar Leung, whose martial arts films he describes as "masterpieces."[12] The scholar of Hong Kong cinema Man-Fung Yip says that both directors' films often imagine "an exclusively male order, a realm of homosocial relationships encompassing not only the *horizontal* ties between sworn brothers but . . . the *vertical* or *hierarchical* ones between masters and disciples."[13] Chang Cheh's films more strongly emphasize those horizontal brotherly ties. As David Desser describes, they feature few women and are instead replete with rebellious, loyal, filial, and righteous men who can endure horrific forms of violence, and who will sacrifice their own limbs and lives for the sake of their sworn brothers, if not for their patriarchal father figures.[14] Such men reflect those "robust qualities of manhood" that, says Stephen Teo, Chang Cheh had "coined into the slogan of . . . *yang gang*, meaning staunch masculinity."[15] The movies of his protégé Lau Kar Leung differ in several ways. First, his films often feature more women, sometimes in leading roles, although their presence may serve the purpose of demonstrating the feminine (Ch. *yin*) and masculine (Ch. *yang*) aspects of martial performances.[16] Second, in his efforts to disclose both the Daoist and Chan Buddhist underpinnings of martial arts, his films are often about the monastic and martial traditions of Wudang and Shaolin. Their stories do not always take place in an all-male Daoist or Buddhist monastery, but they do focus on those master/disciple relations that mediate both the transmission of martial traditions between men and the processes of a man's martial discipline and self-transformation.

The masculinized style of these productions was more and less inspired by classical Chinese literary tradition, dating back to stories from as early as the Tang (618–907) and Ming (1368–1644) dynasties. Teo says that although the "*yang gang* concept pushes masculinity more to the edges of psychological obsession," Chang Cheh's films provide a modern "intonation" of masculine "heroic prototypes" from *The Water Margin* (Ch. *Shuihu zhuan*), a Ming dynasty novel about a band of sworn brothers rebelling against the government.[17] Furthermore, the influence of Chan Buddhism and Daoism is explicit in the movies of Lau Kar Leung, and Teo says that Chan Buddhism may have also influenced Chang Cheh's *yang gang* style. Evoking the work of Meir Shahar, Teo speculates that the "term *yang gang* may have been derived from *jin gang*, the Chinese name of the Buddhist divine warrior Vajrapāni who . . . is often represented in naked chest with hard muscles and ferocious countenance. . . . The term *jin gang* is also often used to refer to a virile male hero."[18] Suffice it to say that, while the masculine styles of these directors' films may derive from many sources—including Chang Cheh and Lau Kar Leung's own sociocultural milieu—RZA received their productions in his own way, finding in them cinematic models of manhood by which he could make sense of his own racialized masculinity.

When asked about the first *Iron Fist*, RZA said he aspired to create a "great martial arts film" and "a source of good philosophy," just like Lau Kar Leung's *The 36th Chamber of Shaolin* (1978).[19] That movie, he says, "changed me, for real." It is a film about "the idea of self-discipline, of re-creating yourself" and "struggle."[20] *36th Chamber* stars the Chinese actor Gordon Liu (as San Te), who appears in most of Lau Kar Leung's productions. Based in some obscure time during the Qing dynasty (1644–1911), it tells of the self-transformation of a hot-tempered young rebel who, fleeing from the goons of oppressive government, escapes to the Shaolin temple in search of refuge and the martial skills to avenge his murdered comrades. Like many of Chang Cheh and Lau Kar Leung's films, this movie is about oppression, dealing with the theme of imperialism in a quasihistorical tale of the Manchu subjugation of the ethnic Han.[21] But the *36th Chamber* is also very much about discipline and self-transformation: it focuses on San Te's ordeal in Shaolin's thirty-five chambers of discipline. His disciplinary process, in fact, encompasses nearly the entire second act of the film. This includes San Te undergoing various modes of somatic training pertaining to agility, strength, and balance, as well as martial combat, while the highest level of discipline—the thirty-fifth chamber—involves learning and chanting the Buddhist sutras. But, by his sheer determination, San Te masters all thirty-five chambers and creates a thirty-sixth for training the laity. Overall,

36th Chamber embodies most of the qualities that RZA appreciated about the films of its genre.

First, RZA understood productions like the *36th Chamber* against a background of the Black American man's experience. From this racialized and androcentric perspective, the power and appeal of the cinematic East resides in cross-cultural similarities and differences that enabled him to reimagine his historical and cultural self as a Black man. RZA observed, for example, the films' themes of ethnic oppression. Seeing people of color, whose circumstances compared with those of Black Americans, RZA identified with the oppressed peoples (in film) as well as with the heroic men and martial monks who fought for them. Furthermore, this cinematic mythic world of the East differed from anything RZA knew in the West. It was a totally different place, time, and culture that expanded his historical and cultural worldview—and horizon of possibility—unlike American television and film, which for him reduced the Black man's history to either slavery in America or "savagery" in Africa.[22] In an interview about the *36th Chamber*, RZA notes that "the first time I saw [*36th Chamber*], it was the first film that I seen that had a history that was outside the scope of American history. Being a Black man in America, history don't never go no further than slavery."[23]

Second, RZA took to the themes of brotherhood. In the worldview of RZA and the Wu-Tang Clan, bonding between sworn brothers constitutes the ideal relation between men. RZA claims that "brotherhood in martial arts movies is almost unsurpassed. . . . You'd see how a man would just give his life for another hero."[24] Elsewhere he mentions that the martial arts films "molded my mentality of what brotherhood is."[25] It is safe to say that, for RZA, Lau Kar Leung and Gordon Liu's *The 8 Diagram Pole Fighter* (1984) is one of the most important films dealing explicitly with the theme of brotherhood. RZA says it would elicit tears from his male associates, who were moved by the strength of filial ties between seven sons and their father when they are betrayed and killed in an ambush.[26] The film resembles *36th Chamber* in that one of the surviving sons, Gordon Liu (as Yang Wulang), takes refuge in a Buddhist monastery, where he undergoes martial training and self-transformation. But, for RZA, brotherhood is essentially about male bonding, where one man sacrifices himself for the sake of another man with whom he may not have any familial relation. RZA says that, in *36th Chamber*, "one man gives up his life for his brother. . . . In the beginning [of the film], you thought the two guys got away [from their pursuers]; and only one guy [actually] made it [away], because his friend risked his life to make sure he made it."[27] RZA speaks here about how San Te was able to go to the Shaolin temple only because his friend, who was traveling with him, sacrificed himself for his sake.

Finally, RZA and many other Black American men of his generation shared an appreciation for Bruce Lee, whom they saw as an exemplary model of masculinity.[28] Kung fu heroes like Bruce Lee, as Amy Ongiri puts it, displayed "a body politics that stressed discipline, restraint, and self-determination rather than [a] cartoonish display of brute force" that was often used in American popular culture to stereotype Black men as hypermasculine, violent, or sexually adept.[29] The masculinity of the East Asian martial arts virtuoso sharply contrasted with the hypermasculinity of the Black heroes in the Black exploitation genre that paralleled the kung fu films in the 1970s.[30] But while RZA appreciated Lee, he preferred the films of someone like Lau Kar Leung, due to their apparent Chan Buddhist and Daoist philosophies.[31] Daoism had always philosophically undergirded Bruce Lee's martial style and movies, but Lau Kar Leung's films were often explicitly graced with a Chan Buddhist and Daoist presence. In his films, RZA could sometimes observe Wudang and Shaolin monks in their mythical and religious settings, unlike in Bruce Lee's films, which were always set in modern and secular situations.

The Chan Buddhism that RZA encountered in film presented the spiritual aspect of manhood. RZA says, for instance, that a chamber is "something [that] a man must go through" or "something [that] a man must conquer."[32] For him, a chamber makes, molds, or transforms a man, just as San Te underwent successive chambers at Shaolin to eventually become an enlightened hero. Furthermore, when San Te tried to bypass all thirty-four chambers to enter the thirty-fifth chamber of sutra-chanting, RZA recounts that this "took my mind to a whole new level as a man," in "trying to decipher" how monks in this chamber had the vital power (i.e., qi) to knock San Te "twenty feet away" without touching him. Again, exactly how this scene spoke to RZA "as a man" is not clear, but RZA goes on to say that what he liked about this moment was both the "martial thing" and the "Buddhism"; both Buddhism and martial arts are mutually constituted as an embodied masculine spirituality.[33] Moreover, it is this monk, San Te, who plays an important role in RZA's imaginary of manhood, arguably more so than the martial arts virtuoso himself, Bruce Lee. San Te is RZA's Oriental Monk, who virtually embodies the spiritual wisdom and martial manliness of the East.[34] In fact, Gordon Liu, who portrayed San Te, is the man whom RZA calls the greatest martial arts actor on screen since Bruce Lee.[35]

The Black Man's Journey to the East

Hong Kong kung fu films expanded RZA's historical horizons beyond slavery, which explains why he situates Thaddeus Smith, a former slave, in nineteenth-century China, placing him in the East against a history of the Black man's emasculation in America. Near the third act of the first *Iron Fists*, in a flashback to Thaddeus's backstory, we see him unexpectedly arrive in China by boat, after escaping an American plantation, where he accidentally killed a white man who refused to acknowledge his new status as a freed man (fig. 9.1). Thaddeus will undergo many problems in China, but his race will not hinder him from belonging and finding a purpose. In the East, he becomes a renowned hero, such that, at the end of *Iron Fists 2*, he reflects on his sojourn in China by saying: "I may not find peace in this strange land, but I will find usefulness. You know, it is funny how a man can be a deposed wretch in one land and a hero in another. I guess that's just the way of the Tao."[36]

Thaddeus's heroism is always configured in relation to his Asian male counterparts, who have their own heroic journeys, and with whom, toward the end of each film, he expresses sworn brotherhood. Just like in the East

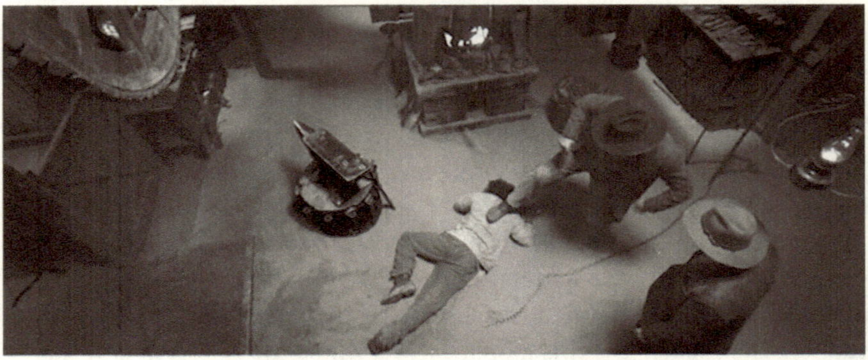

FIGURE 9.1 A flashback of Thaddeus in the slave quarters being harassed by two white men. *The Man with the Iron Fists* (2012).

Asian cinematic myths to which *Iron Fists* pay homage, this world is one of male bonding. Let us note, too, that while women in this world also demonstrate heroism, we discover them mainly as objects of heterosexual male pleasure and consolation, heroines who exist on a continuum of whores and housewives, if not simply as a yin to man's yang.[37] Furthermore, the brotherly bonds in themselves are not narratively convincing of any genuine or deserved camaraderie. But despite their superficiality—or how they are configured in relation to Asian women—Thaddeus always finds himself in situations that compel him to become a hero by sacrificing his bodily limbs or spiritual aims for the sake of another man.

In the first *Iron Fists* film, for instance, we initially see Thaddeus working as a lone blacksmith in place called Jungle Village, a town full of clan rivalry, violence, martial outlaws, and brothels. Suffering the consequences of having strayed from the Buddhist path—which we only learn about later in the film—Thaddeus earns his living by forging weapons, while hoping to elope someday with his ill-fated lover, a prostitute named Lady Silk. Hope fails, however, when goons of the film's main antagonist, Silver Lion, brutally hack off Thaddeus's forearms for aiding and refusing to disclose the whereabouts of an injured man named Zen Yi, who is Silver Lion's brother. Brotherhood and betrayal are central to the story of the first *Iron Fists*, insofar as it concerns all that transpires between Zen Yi and Silver Lion, men with whom Thaddeus seems to have no direct relationship. Silver Lion betrayed Zen Yi by killing their father, and, in an effort to ensure his authority over their father's clan, he tried to kill Zen Yi. Thaddeus initially assisted Zen Yi because he felt responsible for the death of Zen Yi's father. Thaddeus believed that he himself must have forged the weapons by which Zen Yi's father had been killed. But, after being maimed and reflecting on his past, Thaddeus, with the help of two other men, forges a pair of iron fists, which he adapts to his upper limbs by using his qi: the psychosomatic energy in both his body and in things external to him. With these fists, he helps Zen Yi and avenges his own Lady Silk, who was also killed by Silver Lion's henchman. But, by helping another man in crisis, this former slave becomes more of a brother to Zen Yi than Silver Lion. Zen Yi eventually says to him, "I have lost a father but gained a brother" and later returns to request Thaddeus's help in rescuing his wife.[38]

Following these events, Thaddeus, in *Iron Fists 2*, returns to the path of the Buddha, looking for peace as well as for an elixir that will revitalize his qi.

However, a violent turn of events leads him to Tsai Fu, a village of oppressed people. Aside from the terror of a man who feeds on the village girls' qi, a ruthless regime forces villagers to mine for silver and impales the insubordinate on the outskirts of town. For Thaddeus, this sort of violence recalls the terror of lynching in America, and such a similar mode of oppression paves a way for cross-racial male bonding. In Tsai Fu, for instance, Thaddeus crosses paths with a man named Li Kung, whose daughter retrieved Thaddeus's body from a river after he was ambushed and left unconscious and afloat en route to Tsai Fu. According to Li Kung, destiny drew Thaddeus to Tsai Fu, due to his own experiences of oppression back home. Although Thaddeus had quit forging weapons for the sake of the Buddha's path, he repays Li Kung for his hospitality by making weapons for a planned uprising, so long as doing so would not require him to directly do any violence. But sometime after suffering Li Kung's criticism for his Buddhist pacifism—and after talking to Li Kung's daughter about how her father is a "good man" who will sacrifice his life for her and for his people—Thaddeus sets aside his vow to abstain from violence. He puts his iron fists to work by saving Li Kung in an unfair duel to the death and by fighting along with the villagers against their oppressors. In the end, he saves Li Kung's daughter from the qi-imbibing monster, a rogue Buddhist monk named Lord Pi, by bursting his head with his fists.

Chan Buddhism in the Black Man's Journey in the East

The *Iron Fists* films make clear the importance of Chan Buddhism in Thaddeus's heroic journey. We are introduced to Thaddeus sometime after he abandons the Buddha's path, but by *Iron Fists 2* we see him leaving Jungle Village and returning to that path. The film opens with Thaddeus assessing his situation and expressing his intent to go back to the monks who found him upon his arrival in China: "They say Lord Buddha laughs at the world, and I'm sure he is laughing down at me. After leaving Jungle Village, I decided to return back to the monks. My challenge would be to find peace, reawaken my qi, and atone for my sins." Thaddeus also makes his Buddhist aims explicit in his dispute with Li Kung, insisting that he is on the path of the Buddha and forging weapons for killing other men has no place on the path. So how do we make sense, then, of the fact that, after spiritually assessing himself en route to the monks, he immediately finds himself gouging men's eyes out and splattering their guts, all to the tune of his own theme music, "The Baddest Man Alive"? The flashback scene in the first *Iron Fists* film offers plenty to consider regarding the way Chan Buddhism informs Thaddeus's masculinized and heroic identity; in it, Thaddeus comes to the Wu Chi Temple—a reimagining of the Shaolin temple—and undergoes discipline that prepares him to become an iron-fisted hero. Here we see that Chan Buddhism matters to Thaddeus in terms of race, master-disciple relations, and a masculinized self-transformation.

Buddhism serves as the spiritual vehicle of Thaddeus's liberation from his racialized suffering in America, the cloak by which destiny welcomes him home to the East, where he can become a hero. Thaddeus's very arrival in China is mediated by Chan Buddhism. For instance, following Thaddeus's shipwreck, it is a group of Chan monks who discover his body on the shore and take him to Wu Chi Temple (fig. 9.2). But in the process of removing him from the wreckage, we can see, among the ship's debris, a plaque reading "Destiny," the name of the boat on which Thaddeus arrives in China. The boat symbolizes Chan as the vehicle by which Thaddeus reaches the "other shore" of enlightenment—a common Buddhist metaphor. Also, that the figurative raft of Chan Buddhism mediates his "destiny" reflects RZA's interpretation on his own life experience, since RZA's friend and former Shaolin monk Sifu (master) Shi Yan Ming told him, while on a pilgrimage to Wudang and Shaolin in 1999, "History knows you already and history knows that you

FIGURE 9.2 Buddhist monks looking down at Thaddeus's body surrounded by his boat's debris. *The Man with the Iron Fists* (2012).

are a part of it. You are a part of this history."[39] Sifu also tells him, upon their arrival to the Shaolin Temple, "This is your home. Welcome home."[40] It is safe to interpret Thaddeus's arrival at the Wu Chi Temple as a spiritual homecoming. And while RZA believes himself destined to be a sort of cross-cultural conduit, introducing people of various racial backgrounds to Islam, martial arts, and Buddhism, in the film Thaddeus is destined to defy the historical and dehumanizing limits on his Black manhood by escaping slavery, coming to China, and becoming a hero.[41]

RZA draws on the tradition of Lau Kar Leung and situates Thaddeus within a master-disciple relationship, which is important because of who the master is, what he represents to RZA, and what he teaches to Thaddeus. The latter becomes a student of the Wu Chi abbot, who is played by Gordon Liu, who played San Te in *36th Chamber*. This is the martial monk who exemplifies RZA's model of manhood even more than the martial virtuoso Bruce Lee. Liu appears in the film immediately after the monks carry Thaddeus into the temple. More than a cameo, the monk of the cinematic myths is now the same monk under whom RZA, as Thaddeus, becomes a disciple. RZA himself says that San Te from *36th Chamber* is now the old wise Abbot of Wu Chi Temple.[42] RZA situates Thaddeus in the lineage of a man whose own ordeals in Shaolin's chambers taught him about processes of struggle, discipline, and self-transformation.

Thaddeus learns from the abbot some teachings specific to Chan Buddhism. The abbot, for instance, is a spiritually mature man whose realization of his own inherent buddhahood—his buddha-nature or buddha-mind—does not rely on the expediencies of imagery, speech, or texts. He explains to Thaddeus why he sits for long durations in silence: because words are traps for the truths they intend to convey. Therefore, "he who knows does not speak; this is called mind to mind, heart to heart." This reflects the saying of RZA's most beloved Chan personality: Bodhidharma, the fifth-century Chan Buddhist patriarch from India who legendarily brought Chan Buddhism to China and became associated with Shaolin. Famous for having sat in silent meditation for nine years in a cave on Mt. Song, the home of the Shaolin Monastery, Bodhidharma is purported to have said—in Red Pine's translation—that in order "to find a buddha, you have to see your nature. . . . If you don't see your nature, invoking buddhas, reciting *sūtras*, making offerings, and keeping precepts are all useless."[43] According to Sophia Chang, RZA's Korean Canadian friend and former business manager who planned his trip to Shaolin and Wudang, RZA always kept this Red Pine translation with him.[44]

Thaddeus also learns about the transracial universality of buddhahood, having heard the abbot say before a monastic assembly: "The Buddha is the enlightened one. The one who sees things clearly through his third eye, which is the mind. The buddha-nature, we all have it. But because of the design of our flesh, we do not go according to our nature. The five colors blind our eyes, thus when we see through the veil of [the] color of skin, then we see all men are the same, and all life is precious" (fig. 9.3). In the *36th Chamber*, San Te/Gordon Liu heard these words in the thirty-fifth chamber: "The five colors blind our eyes." Thaddeus/RZA now hears them, too, from the mouth of San Te/Liu, but he receives them against experiences of racism in America. The whole point of the sermon is that a man's innate buddhahood is not contingent upon his race. Advocating nondiscriminatory perception, the abbot recognizes Thaddeus's inherent sacredness, giving him a visibility and dignity unnoticed by his Anglo counterparts in America.

The sermon about nondiscrimination and the transracial universality of each man's buddhahood may also inform the cross-racial brotherly bonds that Thaddeus forms with Zen Yi and Li Kung. RZA often associates the Chan-inspired ideas of universal buddhahood and nondiscriminatory thinking with a transracial and transreligious discourse that enables cross-racial and cross-cultural exchanges. As early as 1999, for example, sometime after visiting Shaolin and Wudang, RZA maintained that the nondiscriminatory

FIGURE 9.3 Gordon Liu as the Wu Chi Temple's abbot, teaching about the universality of buddhahood. *The Man with the Iron Fists* (2012).

nature of Chan Buddhism and martial arts had enabled his relationship with Shi Yan Ming, a man who he considers not only as his *sifu* (his spiritual and martial teacher) but also as his brother.[45] In the *Iron Fists* films, Thaddeus's decision to save Li Kung was not based on Chan so much as on the idea of sacrificing oneself for a good man. But his abbot at Wu Chi Temple had already told him that he was destined to take all his learning from the temple into the outside world. This implies that everything Thaddeus undergoes in Jungle Village and Tsai Fu—his willingness to sacrifice himself for other good men—can be understood in view of his Buddhist background. Just like his own experiences of oppression, his learning about the transracial universality of buddhahood may predispose him to cross-racial bonding.

Enlightenment ensues after Thaddeus hears the abbot's exhortations about the transracial universality of buddhahood. He takes the initiative to kneel before a statue of the Buddha in the presence of other monks, and, in a bloody and excruciating gesture of self-mutilation, he shaves through the coarseness of his hair without any lubrication, demonstrating his determination to become a monk. His actions also mimic his abbot in the *8 Diagram Pole Fighter*, where Gordon Liu, as Yang Wulang, takes the same self-mutilating initiative to become a monk at a temple in the Wutai mountains, after his father and brothers were murdered. Since the monks refused to shave his head and acknowledge his desire to be a novice, Yang Wulang was forced to take this action himself, showing a determination to renounce worldly affairs. Thaddeus does exactly as Yang Wulang does in the cinematic myth: both men demonstrate their sincerity and self-transformation through a gruesome public display of self-tonsure. For Thaddeus, this means not only that he has set aside his worldly concerns but also that he has found a spirituality by which he can recreate his masculine self. Being in the East, he has already transcended limitations—in some respects—to freely exist as a Black man. Under the tutelage of his abbot and the senior monks, he must now learn how to master and transcend the limitations of his body, which would literally allow him to be the "man with the iron fists."

It is not until long after Thaddeus leaves Wu Chi Temple that unfortunate circumstances—losing his upper limbs—compel him to become the man with the iron fists, but it was at the temple where he learned the psychosomatic techniques that enable his bodily transformation into the masculinized hero. Under the tutelage of a senior monk, Thaddeus learns kinesthetic arts of qi energy, circulating in his body and in the external world. The senior monk uses a human-sized muscular brass mannequin to teach him about the energy channels running through his body while making the point that, "by learning to regulate breath, and controlling your qi, a man is capable of amazing feats," such as standing inverted on the tip of one finger (fig. 9.4). He goes on to say that "if one can find the source to one's own energy, you can transmit that energy to activate inanimate objects. You and the object become as one. It becomes a slave to your will, your mind, your qi." We know that this training sequence is important to Thaddeus's transformation into a masculinized, iron-fisted hero, because RZA juxtaposes it with a montage of Thaddeus in his forge, recalling what he learned while masterfully molding and adapting the iron fists as appendages to his own body.

Through this training process, Thaddeus learns how to manipulate not only inanimate objects but *hard* objects. Hardness signifies his masculinity. As Yvonne Tasker maintains about heroes in kung fu films, "The hero's masculine identity is" sometimes "constructed as hardness." Speaking of a film that is more or less analogous to RZA's *Iron Fists*, Tasker says that "in *The Chinese Boxer*, Wang Yu must make his hands like iron. The film's training sequences detail his disciplined struggle to become invincible, with images of him hardening his hands by placing them in a vat of heated iron fillings. . . . We identify with a masculine identity that is constituted before our eyes, enacted through these narrative images of physical hardening."[46] Thaddeus demonstrates his hardness when, recalling the energy channels represented by the brass mannequin, he uses his fists to literally

FIGURE 9.4 Thaddeus recalls the brass mannequin and the monks' teachings about qi energy. *The Man with the Iron Fists* (2012).

shatter a villain named Brass Body, a man who uses his qi to transform himself into a body of brass. However, while Thaddeus's assimilation of hardness symbolizes an invincibility and capacity to penetrate through the armor of others, he suggests that iron can also signify masculinity due to its malleability. As a blacksmith who knows about the transformation of things, he tells his protégé at his forge that "a good man is like iron" because iron is strong yet able to "adapt" and "change" (fig. 9.5).[47]

For RZA, this scene at the Buddhist temple is the most important in the first installment of *Iron Fists*, the one scene that he says he fought to keep in the film, and that he claims gives us "wisdom" amid everything else.[48] In it, Buddhism serves as the technology for Thaddeus's self-transformation. It mediates his arrival in China, addresses his racial emasculation in America, lends him exemplary models of manhood, legitimizes his cross-racial solidarities with Asian men, and teaches him to defy bodily limitations.

Here, Buddhism functions somewhat counterhegemonically, as in another RZA-associated movie, Jim Jarmusch's *Ghost Dog* (1999). Sharon Suh points out how in *Ghost Dog* a Black urban assassin's appropriation of "a Buddhist identity (albeit one funneled through the violence and moral codes of the Samurai warrior) functions as a form of self-invention and self-protection against the racialization of African American men through an ancient Samurai culture and ethos easily accessed by adopting Zen practices and a Samurai identity in the present."[49]

FIGURE 9.5 Thaddeus, in his forge, after successfully adapting the iron fists to his body. *The Man with the Iron Fists* (2012).

Iron Fists and Counterhegemonic Masculinities

RZA not only appropriates Chan Buddhism into a masculinized understanding of himself and the world; as we see in the case of Thaddeus, he also invokes Chan Buddhist doctrines against racism while strengthening, refining, and sacralizing Black masculinity. He contests a discursive history of anti-Black racism and, more and less, myths of Black masculinity as brute and virile. The irony of RZA's appeal to alternate masculinities from the virtual worlds of Asian men is that the latter have suffered myths of feminization, contrary to Anglo-American masculinity as "normative" and Black masculinity as hypermasculine. RZA's Buddhist masculinity, then, is not solely about male dominance; it is entangled in dominant discourses around Black, Asian, and Asian American men that triangulate them relative to a hegemonic form of Anglo-American manhood.[50] But this points us to the possibility of seeing when or how Black, Asian, and Asian Americans' appropriation of each other's masculinities have challenged both the hegemonic masculinity of the racialized third—that is, white masculinity—and the myths about their "surplus" or "insufficient" manhood. We cannot detail here such appropriations on both ends, but we can briefly return to how for some Black men, Asian martial arts have occasionally mediated the reimagining and making of the Black masculine self against dominant racist perceptions.[51]

As discussed, RZA's encounter with the Shaw Brothers' productions hearkens back to Black American encounters with East Asian martial arts and films. From the early 1970s, kung fu films became staples in Black American popular culture.[52] Sundiata Keita Cha-Jua lists various factors in the late 1960s and early 1970s that predisposed Black viewers to martial arts films, including the Pan-Africanist and Black internationalist discourses, which sought political and racial affinities between Blacks and Asians; the U.S. government's violent suppression of Black radical movements, which echoed in representations of ethnic suppression in kung fu films; and the cross-cultural significance of Bruce Lee, who acquired a heroic status in Black popular culture.[53] Cha-Jua's work brings forth much of the political and discursive underpinning of Blacks' gravitation toward East Asian martial arts and assumes—without clearly demonstrating why—the imagery of "colored men" in both the 1970s blaxploitation and kung fu genres challenged "white celluloid masculinity."[54]

However, Asian martial arts and film were also conduits for alternative religious discourses, or nonoccidental spiritualities, that were useful for reimagining or fashioning the self. In "China," a short story by the Black American Buddhist Charles Johnson, one man's theatrical viewing of *The Five Fingers of Death* (1972) inspires him to enter a local brotherhood of martial artists and to radically transform his lifestyle, his physique, and his worldview; he eventually abandons his local Christian church, opting instead for Chan Buddhist and Daoist philosophies.[55] Fan Che Wilkins maintains that "the metaphysical dimensions of kung fu films provide psychic and spiritual resources for aggrieved communities . . . in [a] relentless search for alternative ideas and practices that can contribute to transforming one's life" and further observed that kung fu films gave Black men, like the Wu, "insight into spiritual development and mental mastery as necessary prerequisites to a disciplined body capable of developing expertise in various martial arts techniques."[56] This spiritual or mind-body martial posture, Wilkins tells us, has likewise been appropriated by other hip-hop artists, like Jeru the Damaja, who have used this disposition as a means of contrasting and feminizing the hypermasculinities of hip-hop artists who pose as would-be gangsters, pimps, and players.[57]

In the most recent comprehensive study of this specific Afro-Asian phenomenon, Zachary Price discusses its spiritual and masculine implications. Price says that Black American males' appropriation of Asian martial arts is a racial kinesthetic practice and a counterhegemonic body politic for refashioning Black masculine subjectivity. Such appropriations occur against a history of Black men being hypermasculinized and "dismembered" by "lynching and castration" and other forms of racial violence.[58] The spiritual dimension of this kinesthetic appropriation is concomitant with the counterhegemonic project of refashioning masculinity, because spirituality is seen as integral to the martial practice itself. Price says that "because Buddhism, and hence spirituality writ large was actualized in the material practice of kung fu, from the point of view of the martial practitioner, they could themselves occupy the space of Buddha through the corporeal discipline of their bodies"; what is more, "Buddhism is endowed with the kinetics of bodily practice and is always raced and gendered."[59]

None of these points excuse what we may consider some of the most unsettling aspects of RZA's *Iron Fists* films, but they do tell us that there is something worth exploring behind their overt androcentrism and

Orientalism—or even their (mis)appropriation of Chan Buddhism. RZA's *Iron Fists* films provide us an example of how Asian martial arts, films, and religious discourses have been used by Black Americans to reimagine and counter dominant discourses of Black masculinity.

NOTES

1. RZA (Ruler Zig-Zag-Zig Allah) is also known as Bobby Digital and was born in 1969 as Robert F. Diggs. The Wu-Tang Clan is a hip-hop group cofounded by RZA. Their career began with their 1993 album debut, *Enter the Wu-Tang (36 Chambers)*.
2. RZA and the Black Keys, "The Baddest Man Alive," *The Man with the Iron Fists: Original Motion Picture Soundtrack*, track 1, Soul Temple Entertainment and Universal Studios, 2012.
3. For RZA on Chan Buddhism, see RZA, "RZA on the Tao of the Wu," interview by Gene Ching, *Kung Fu Magazine*, 2009, http://www.kungfumagazine.com/magazine/index.php?p=article&article=850 (accessed December 2, 2022); and "Tao of the RZA," interview by Rod Meade Sperry, Lion's Roar, December 14, 2014, https://www.lionsroar.com/the-tao-of-the-rza/.
4. RZA, "RZA Reflects on Wu-Tang at Wudang Mountain," interview by Gene Ching, *Kung Fu/Tai Chi Magazine*, April 2009, 10–13, 12.
5. For more on the Five Percenters, see Michael Muhammad Knight, *The Five Percenters: Islam, Hip-Hop, and the Gods of New York* (London: Oneworld, 2007).
6. RZA, "RZA on *The Man with the Iron Fists*," interview by Gene Ching, *Kung Fu/Tai Chi Magazine*, December 2012, 40–47, 47.
7. RZA, "Wu Tang Clan's RZA on Meat and Masculinity," interview by Chala Tyson Tshitundu, *Bon Appétit*, August 4, 2021, https://www.bonappetit.com/story/wu-tang-clan-rza-veganism.
8. Thomas J. Csordas, *The Sacred Self: A Cultural Phenomenology of Charismatic Healing* (Berkeley: University of California Press, [1994] 1997), 5.
9. Raewyn Connell and James W. Messerschmidt, "Hegemonic Masculinity: Rethinking the Concept," *Gender & Society* 19, no. 6 (December 2005): 829–59, 845.
10. This usage of "virtuality" more and less compares with Jane Naomi Iwamura's usage of "virtual orientalism" in *Virtual Orientalism: Asian Religions and American Popular Culture* (Oxford: Oxford University Press, 2011), 7.
11. Connell and Messerschmidt, "Hegemonic Masculinity," 849.
12. RZA, "Interview with The RZA," *The 36th Chamber of Shaolin*, special collector's edition DVD, dir. Lau Kar Leung (Santa Monica, Calif.: Dragon Dynasty, 2007).
13. Man-Fung Yip, *Martial Arts Cinema and Hong Kong Modernity: Aesthetics, Representation, Circulation* (Hong Kong: Hong Kong University Press, 2017), 85 (original emphasis).
14. David Desser, "Making Movies Male: Zhang Che and the Shaw Brothers Martial Arts Movies, 1965–1975," in *Masculinities and Hong Kong Cinema*, ed. Laikwan Pang and Day Wong (Hong Kong: Hong Kong University Press, 2005), 30.

15. Stephen Teo, *Chinese Martial Arts Cinema: The Wuxia Tradition* (Edinburgh: Edinburgh University Press, 2009), 94.
16. Stephen Teo, *Hong Kong Cinema: The Extra Dimensions* (London: British Film Institute, [1997] 2001), 104–6.
17. Teo, *Chinese Martial Arts Cinema*, 94.
18. Teo, 95. For a historical discussion of the Buddhist deity and warrior Vajrapāṇi, see Meir Shahar, *The Shaolin Monastery: History, Religion, and the Chinese Martial Arts* (Honolulu: University of Hawai'i Press, 2008), 37–42.
19. RZA, "RZA on the Tao of the Wu."
20. RZA, with Chris Norris, *The Wu-Tang Manual* (New York: Riverhead, 2004), 59, 63.
21. The Qing imperial rulers were ethnically Manchu, and they governed a Han ethnic majority.
22. RZA, "RZA on *The 36th Chamber of Shaolin*," interview by Gene Ching, *Kung Fu/Tai Chi Magazine*, January–February 2010, 60–61, 60. See also RZA, "The RZA—Kung Fu and Black Culture," YouTube video, 3:32, October 16, 2012, https://www.youtube.com/watch?v=6J-G48dcH4Y.
23. RZA, "Interview with The RZA."
24. RZA, "The RZA Revisited," interview by Chi Tung, *Asia Pacific Arts*, September 22, 2005, https://international.ucla.edu/apc/article/30251.
25. RZA, "Interview with The RZA."
26. See RZA, with Chris Norris, *Wu-Tang Manual*, 62; and *The Tao of the Wu* (New York: Riverhead, 2009), 57–58.
27. RZA, "Interview with The RZA."
28. Robin D. G. Kelley says that "martial arts films placed Bruce Lee among a pantheon of Black heroes that included Walt Frazier and John Shaft." See Robin D. G. Kelley, *Yo' Mama's Disfunktional! Fighting the Culture Wars in Urban America* (Boston: Beacon, 1997), 25.
29. Amy Abugo Ongiri, "'He wanted to be just like Bruce Lee': African Americans, Kung Fu Theater, and Cultural Exchange at the Margins," *Journal of Asian American Studies* 5, no. 1 (February 2002): 31–40, 36.
30. On Jim Kelly in Bruce Lee's *Enter the Dragon* (1973), see Yvonne Tasker, "Fists of Fury: Discourses of Race and Masculinity in the Martial Arts Cinema," in *Race and the Subject of Masculinities*, ed. Harry Stecopoulos and Michael Uebel, (Durham, N.C.: Duke University Press, 1997), 327–28; and Zachary F. Price, *Black Dragon: Afro Asian Performance and the Martial Arts Imagination* (Columbus: Ohio State University Press, 2022), 107–15.
31. See RZA, "RZA | Comic Con 2018 Full Panel (w/Ric Meyers)," YouTube video, 8:18, July 31, 2018, https://youtu.be/sFaqFUnGnjA?t=76.
32. RZA, "Interview with The RZA."
33. RZA, "RZA on *The 36th Chamber of Shaolin*," 60.
34. Jane Naomi Iwamura critically uses "Oriental Monk" for "a wide range of religious figures (gurus, bhikkhus, sages, swamis, sifus, healers, masters) from various ethnic backgrounds (Japanese, Chinese, Indian, Tibetan)" who serve as models of Eastern spirituality throughout several virtual platforms. See Iwamura, *Virtual Orientalism*, 6.

35. See RZA, "Wu-Tang's RZA Breaks Down 10 Kung Fu Films He's Sampled | Vanity Fair," YouTube video, 13:35, September 3, 2019, https://www.youtube.com/watch?v=RZ67KyHX-cY&t=233s.
36. *The Man with the Iron Fists 2*, directed by Roel Reiné (Universal City, Calif.: Universal Pictures Home Entertainment, 2015).
37. This polarity is reflected in both *Iron Fists* films by two sword-wielding knights, a man and woman duo called the Gemini Killers. On Lau Kar Leung's explorations of *yin* and *yang* in film see Teo, *Hong Kong Cinema*, 104–6.
38. *The Man with the Iron Fists*, directed by RZA (Universal City, Calif.: Universal Pictures Home Entertainment, 2013).
39. RZA, "RZA Reflects on Wu-Tang," 12.
40. RZA, with Chris Norris, *Wu-Tang Manual*, 55
41. RZA, "RZA Reflects on Wu-Tang," 12.
42. RZA, "On Set with the RZA: Casting Legends," bonus features, *Man with the Iron Fists.*
43. This comes from the "Bloodstream Sermon," in Red Pine, trans., *The Zen Teaching of Bodhidharma* (New York: North Point, [1987] 1989), 11.
44. Sophia Chang, "Magic Meditation: Wu-Tang's Kung Fu Zeal," Asian American Writers' Workshop, June 13, 2012, https://aaww.org/magic-mediation-wu-tangs-kung-fu-zeal.
45. See Gene Ching, "Hip Hop Fist: Wu-Tang Clan's RZA and His Sifu, Shaolin Monk Shi Yan Ming?," *Kung Fu Magazine*, 1999, http://www.kungfumagazine.com/magazine/article.php?article=100 (accessed December 2, 2022).
46. Tasker, "Fists of Fury," 319.
47. The phrase "A good man is like iron" was edited out of the film but remains in the film's trailer. See Universal Pictures All-Access, "*The Man with the Iron Fists 2*—Trailer—Own It Now on Blu-ray," YouTube video, 1:06, January 23, 2015, https://www.youtube.com/watch?v=KcbYBZsklGQ.
48. RZA, "RZA Interview Part 2," interview by Cecilia MacArthur, CKUT 90.3 FM, YouTube Video, 5:54–6:53, June 26, 2013, https://youtu.be/48tJchg65Fw?t=354.
49. Sharon A. Suh, *Silver Screen Buddha: Buddhism in Asian and Western Film* (London: Bloomsbury, 2015), 73.
50. Ellie M. Hisama addresses these triangulations and Wu-Tang's appropriation of Asian masculinities—that of martial monks. See Ellie M. Hisama, "We're All Asian Really: Hip Hop's Afro-Asian Crossings," in *Critical Minded: New Approaches to Hip Hop Studies*, ed. Ellie M. Hisama and Evan Rapport (Brooklyn, N.Y.: Institute for Studies in American Music, 2005), 2–6.
51. On the cross-cultural making of Black and Asian masculinities, see Daniel Y. Kim, *Writing Manhood in Black and Yellow: Ralph Ellison, Frank Chin, and the Literary Politics of Identity* (Stanford, Calif.: Stanford University Press, 2005); and Chong Chon-Smith, *East Meets Black: Asian and Black Masculinities in the Post-Civil Rights Era* (Jackson: University Press of Mississippi, 2015).
52. Frances Gateward, "Wong Fei-Hung in Da House: Hong Kong Martial Arts Films and Hip-Hop Culture," in *Chinese Connections: Critical Perspectives on Film, Identity, and Diaspora*, ed. Tan See-Kam, Peter X. Feng, and Gina Marchetti (Philadelphia: Temple University Press, 2009).

53. Sundiata Keita Cha-Jua, "Black Audiences, Blaxploitation and Kung Fu Films, and Challenges to White Celluloid Masculinity," in *China Forever: The Shaw Brothers and Diasporic Cinema*, ed. Poshek Fu (Chicago: University of Illinois Press, 2008), 199–223.
54. We can only make this judgement based on what is implied in the title of Cha-Jua's article "Black Audiences, Blaxploitation and Kung Fu Films, and Challenges to White Celluloid Masculinity."
55. Charles Johnson, "China," in *The Sorcerer's Apprentice: Tales and Conjurations* (New York: Plume, 1994), 61–95. This story was originally published in 1983. Tzarina T. Prater provides a commentary on "China" in an article about the postcolonial implications of Black encounters with Hong Kong martial arts films. See Tzarina T. Prater, " 'Old Man Your Kung Fu Is Useless': African American Spectatorship and Hong Kong Action Cinema," *Post Road*, no. 2 (2001): 185–204, 192–202.
56. Fanon Che Wilkins, "Shaw Brothers Cinema and the Hip-Hop Imagination," in *China Forever: The Shaw Brothers and Diasporic Cinema*, ed. Poshek Fu (Chicago: University of Illinois Press, 2008), 226, 227.
57. Wilkins, "Shaw Brothers Cinema," 238–39.
58. Price, *Black Dragon*, 5–6.
59. Price, 130.

Additional Primary Sources

Red Pine, trans. *The Zen Teaching of Bodhidharma*. New York: North Point, [1987] 1989.
Reiné, Roel, dir. *The Man with the Iron Fists 2*. Universal City, Calif.: Universal Pictures Home Entertainment, 2015.
RZA, dir. *The Man with the Iron Fists*. Universal City, Calif.: Universal Pictures Home Entertainment, 2013.
RZA, with Chris Norris. *The Tao of the Wu*. New York: Riverhead, 2009.
——. *The Wu-Tang Manual*. New York: Riverhead, 2004.

Bibliography

Cha-Jua, Sundiata Keita. "Black Audiences, Blaxploitation and Kung Fu Films, and Challenges to White Celluloid Masculinity." In *China Forever: The Shaw Brothers and Diasporic Cinema*, edited by Poshek Fu, 199–223. Chicago: University of Illinois Press, 2008.
Chang, Sophia. "Magic Meditation: Wu-Tang's Kung Fu Zeal." Asian American Writers' Workshop, June 13, 2012. https://aaww.org/magic-mediation-wu-tangs-kung-fu-zeal/.
Ching, Gene. "Hip Hop Fist: Wu-Tang Clan's RZA and His Sifu, Shaolin Monk Shi Yan Ming?" *Kung Fu Magazine*, 1999. http://www.kungfumagazine.com/magazine/article.php?article=100 (accessed December 29, 2021).

Chon-Smith, Chong. *East Meets Black: Asian and Black Masculinities in the Post-Civil Rights Era*. Jackson: University Press of Mississippi, 2015.

Connell, Raewyn, and James W. Messerschmidt. "Hegemonic Masculinity: Rethinking the Concept." *Gender & Society* 19, no. 6 (December 2005): 829–59.

Csordas, Thomas J. *The Sacred Self: A Cultural Phenomenology of Charismatic Healing*. Berkeley: University of California Press, [1994] 1997.

Desser, David. "Making Movies Male: Zhang Che and the Shaw Brothers Martial Arts Movies, 1965–1975." In *Masculinities and Hong Kong Cinema*, edited by Laikwan Pang and Day Wong, 17–34. Hong Kong: Hong Kong University Press, 2005.

Gateward, Frances. "Wong Fei-Hung in Da House: Hong Kong Martial Arts Films and Hip-Hop Culture." In *Chinese Connections: Critical Perspectives on Film, Identity, and Diaspora*, edited by Tan See-Kam, Peter X. Feng, and Gina Marchetti, 51–67. Philadelphia: Temple University Press, 2009.

Hisama, Ellie M. "We're All Asian Really: Hip Hop's Afro-Asian Crossings." In *Critical Minded: New Approaches to Hip Hop Studies*, edited by Ellie M. Hisama and Evan Rapport, 1–21. Brooklyn, N.Y.: Institute for Studies in American Music, 2005.

Iwamura, Jane Naomi. *Virtual Orientalism: Asian Religions and American Popular Culture*. Oxford: Oxford University Press, 2011.

Johnson, Charles. "China." In *The Sorcerer's Apprentice: Tales and Conjurations*, 61–95. New York: Plume, 1994.

Kelley, Robin D. G. *Yo' Mama's Disfunktional! Fighting the Culture Wars in Urban America*. Boston: Beacon, 1997.

Kim, Daniel Y. *Writing Manhood in Black and Yellow: Ralph Ellison, Frank Chin, and the Literary Politics of Identity*. Stanford, Calif.: Stanford University Press, 2005.

Knight, Michael Muhammad. *The Five Percenters: Islam, Hip-Hop, and the Gods of New York*. London: Oneworld, 2007.

Ongiri, Amy Abugo. " 'He wanted to be just like Bruce Lee': African Americans, Kung Fu Theater, and Cultural Exchange at the Margins." *Journal of Asian American Studies* 5, no. 1 (February 2002): 31–40.

Prater, Tzarina T. " 'Old Man Your Kung Fu Is Useless': African American Spectatorship and Hong Kong Action Cinema." *Post Road*, no. 2 (2001): 185–204.

Price, Zachary F. *Black Dragon: Afro-Asian Performance and the Martial Imagination*. Columbus: Ohio State University Press, 2002.

Red Pine, trans. *The Zen Teaching of Bodhidharma*. New York: North Point, [1987] 1989.

Reiné, Roel, dir. *The Man with the Iron Fists 2*. Universal City, Calif.: Universal Pictures Home Entertainment, 2015.

RZA. "Interview with The RZA." *The 36th Chamber of Shaolin*, special collector's edition DVD. Directed by Lau Kar Leung. Santa Monica, Calif.: Dragon Dynasty, 2007.

——. "RZA | Comic Con 2018 Full Panel (w/Ric Meyers)." YouTube video, 8:18, July 31, 2018. https://youtu.be/sFaqFUnGnjA?t=76.

——. "RZA Interview Part 2." Interview with Cecilia MacArthur, CKUT 90.3 FM, YouTube Video, 5:54–6:53, June 26, 2013. https://youtu.be/48tJchg65Fw?t=354.

——. "The RZA—Kung Fu and Black Culture." YouTube video, 3:32, October 16, 2012. https://www.youtube.com/watch?v=6J-G48dcH4Y.

——. "RZA on *The 36th Chamber of Shaolin*." Interview by Gene Ching, *Kung Fu/Tai Chi Magazine*, January–February 2010, 60–61.

——. "RZA on *The Man with the Iron Fists*." Interview by Gene Ching, *Kung Fu/Tai Chi Magazine*, November–December 2012, 40–47.
——. "RZA on the Tao of the Wu." Interview by Gene Ching, *Kung Fu Magazine*, 2009. http://www.kungfumagazine.com/magazine/index.php?p=article&article=850 (accessed December 29, 2021).
——. "RZA Reflects on Wu-Tang at Wudang Mountain." Interview by Gene Ching, *Kung Fu/Tai Chi Magazine*, March–April 2009, 10–13.
——. "The RZA Revisited." Interview by Chi Tung, Asia Pacific Arts, September 22, 2005. http://asiapacificarts.usc.edu/article@apa-the_rza_revisited_9780.aspx.html.
——. "Tao of the RZA." Interview by Rod Meade Sperry, Lion's Roar, December 14, 2014. https://www.lionsroar.com/the-tao-of-the-rza/.
——. "Wu-Tang's RZA Breaks Down 10 Kung Fu Films He's Sampled | Vanity Fair." YouTube video, 13:35, September 3, 2019. https://www.youtube.com/watch?v=RZ67KyHX-cY&t=233s.
——. "Wu Tang Clan's RZA on Meat and Masculinity." Interview by Chala Tyson Tshitundu, *Bon Appétit*, August 4, 2021. https://www.bonappetit.com/story/wu-tang-clan-rza-veganism.
RZA, and the Black Keys. "The Baddest Man Alive." *The Man with the Iron Fists: Original Motion Picture Soundtrack*. Soul Temple Entertainment and Universal Studios, 2012.
RZA, with Chris Norris. *The Tao of the Wu*. New York: Riverhead, 2009.
——. *The Wu-Tang Manual*. New York: Riverhead, 2004.
RZA, dir. *The Man with the Iron Fists*. Universal City, Calif.: Universal Pictures Home Entertainment, 2013.
Shahar, Meir. *The Shaolin Monastery: History, Religion, and the Chinese Martial Arts*. Honolulu: University of Hawai'i Press, 2008.
Suh, Sharon A. *Silver Screen Buddha: Buddhism in Asian and Western Film*. London: Bloomsbury, 2015.
Tasker, Yvonne. "Fists of Fury: Discourses of Race and Masculinity in the Martial Arts Cinema." In *Race and the Subject of Masculinities*, edited by Harry Stecopoulos and Michael Uebel, 315–36. Durham, N.C.: Duke University Press, 1997.
Teo, Stephen. *Chinese Martial Arts Cinema: The Wuxia Tradition*. Edinburgh: Edinburgh University Press, 2009.
——. *Hong Kong Cinema: The Extra Dimensions*. London: British Film Institute, [1997] 2001.
Universal Pictures All-Access. "*The Man with the Iron Fists 2* —Trailer—Own It Now on Blu-ray." YouTube video, 1:06, January 23, 2015. https://www.youtube.com/watch?v=KcbYBZsklGQ.
Wilkins, Fanon Che. "Shaw Brothers Cinema and the Hip-Hop Imagination." In *China Forever: The Shaw Brothers and Diasporic Cinema*, edited by Poshek Fu, 224–45. Chicago: University of Illinois Press, 2008.
Yip, Man-Fung. *Martial Arts Cinema and Hong Kong Modernity: Aesthetics, Representation, Circulation*. Hong Kong: Hong Kong University Press, 2017.

PART FOUR

Breaking Boundaries

WHILE MOST OF this volume focuses on hegemonic Buddhist masculinities, this section shifts to address challenges to hegemonic Buddhist masculinities, both in terms of Buddhist masculinities that transgress gender norms and Buddhist responses to transgressive masculinities. In an analysis of contemporary media representations of the effeminate monk Xuanzang in East Asia (China, Japan, and South Korea)—which continues the focus on Buddhism and media from the previous chapter by Marcus Evans—Geng Song shows how Xuanzang, the "Tang monk" featured in the wildly popular epic *Journey to the West*, has become a queer icon in contemporary East Asia based on modern understandings of Buddhism as a religion of peace, love, and compassion. Films, television series, and streaming series increasingly cast Xuanzang as a young man in the "little fresh meat" model, or as a woman. Finally, Amy Paris Langenberg brings us back to the early South Asian context where we began. Langenberg adopts a literary approach to trace how the Buddhist monastic code developed its rule that monks would be expelled from the monastic community for engaging in penetrative sex. As Langenberg argues, Buddhist monks defined monastic sexuality in contrast to the reproductively oriented, penetrative, sacralized sex of the *gṛhastha* (householder). This chapter highlights a complex interplay of competing hegemonies: while householder masculinity held sway for Brahmanical religion, Buddhist monastics crafted celibate masculinity as hegemonic for their community. By concluding with this consideration of how Buddhist masculinities can transgress hegemonic ideals, we invite readers to imagine new possibilities for Buddhist masculinities, femininities, and beyond.

TEN

The Afterlife of the Tang Monk

Buddhist Masculinity and the Image of Xuanzang in East Asia

GENG SONG

YOUNG MALE STARS with feminine beauty, colloquially known as "little fresh meat" (Ch. *xiao xianrou*), enjoy overwhelming popularity among the younger generation in today's China.[1] While this aesthetic trend exhibits the transnational influence of Japanese and Korean popular culture, it is at the same time informed by China's own masculinity discourse. One image that popularized this type of male beauty in film and television long before the little fresh meat vogue is that of the Tang Monk. Born as Chen Yi (602–664), the Tang-dynasty (618–907) monk Xuanzang or Sanzang (or Trepiṭaka, the Sanskrit honorific title for a monk who has mastered the Buddhist canon) endured considerable hardship traveling to India in the seventh century and translating into Chinese the Buddhist scriptures that he brought back. Xuanzang became a household name in China through the sixteenth-century vernacular novel *Journey to the West* (Ch. *Xiyou ji*), in which he, known as the "Tang Monk," is depicted as a gentle yet fearless, scholarly young man who is the prey of monsters and demons—both male and female—because of a legend promising that the consumption of his flesh would confer everlasting life. The character reappears in various adaptations of the stories of Xuanzang's pilgrimage, including films, TV shows, anime and manga, computer games, and memes, in China and beyond. This chapter explores the evolution of the handsome monk image from the past to the present, and from China to the wider world. Through the lens of this image's transformation, the chapter delves into the interactions and negotiations between

Buddhist discourse and other forms of social power in the construction of masculinity. In particular, it looks at how a Buddhist approach to gender is related to the fashions of male effeminacy and gender fluidity in East Asian popular culture.

The past two decades have witnessed burgeoning interest in the study of Chinese masculinities. A growing body of work addresses various aspects of Chinese masculinities in an attempt to reconstruct masculinity in a way that differs from the dominant Western model.[2] While these efforts are important and fruitful in many ways, we should bear in mind that the idea of an unchanging, monolithic "Chinese masculinity" is nothing but a fantasy. Buddhism, the first foreign religion and culture to be adopted in China, provides an important avenue for the study of the confrontation and reconciliation between different cultures and values in terms of masculinity. As men at the margins of society, Buddhist monks are an essential element in the *jianghu* (rivers and lakes)—an imagined spatial arena in Chinese literature and culture that is parallel to, or sometimes in a tangential relationship with, mainstream society—and they represent alternative subjectivities in traditional Chinese culture.[3] They therefore significantly enrich and supplement the archetypal *wen/wu* (literary attainment/martial prowess) matrix articulated by Kam Louie, which mainly summarizes gentry-class elite masculinity.[4] In addition, because they have given up their gender identity and fail to participate in patriarchal reproduction, monastics, especially Buddhist monks, have been cast as members of the yin world in the Confucianized yin/yang binary.[5] Throughout Chinese history, representations of religions and religious people often bespeak their subversion of and containment by society's dominant ideology. Late imperial vernacular literature represents celibate monks as either a parody of the Confucian scholar (the legitimate or even hegemonic form of masculinity) or his immoral and lustful Other. It was in this cultural context that the image of Xuanzang appears in *Journey to the West*.

From Xuanzang to the "Tang Monk"

As a young monk, Xuanzang was troubled by the numerous discrepancies and contradictions in available Buddhist scriptures, which were introduced to China from India during the Han dynasty (202 BCE–220 CE), and accordingly decided to travel to the fountainhead of Buddhism to seek the original, genuine Buddhist texts. After returning to China, he devoted the rest of his life to translating the scriptures he brought back in a monastery bestowed by the Tang emperor.[6] His adventurous travels to India, and, en route to it, several small countries to the west of China, are recorded in two seventh-century books: the *Great Tang Records on the Western Regions* (Ch. *Da Tang xiyuji*, 646), which is based on Xuanzang's own oral accounts and compiled by his disciple Bianji; and a biography of Xuanzang written by another of his disciples, named Huili (Ch. *Da Tang Da Ci'en Si Sanzang fashi zhuan*, 688). From a primarily religious perspective, these books eulogize, in a somewhat hyperbolic way, Xuanzang's moral power and his determination in pursuing the sutras.

Representations of Xuanzang's travels proliferated following his death, reaching new heights during the Ming dynasty (1368–1644) with the publication of Wu Cheng'en's (ca. 1506–1582) novel *Journey to the West*. The image of Xuanzang also began to deviate significantly from Tang sources in ways that, tellingly, reflected the stereotypical representations and associations of Buddhist monks in vernacular literature. He is often represented as a gentle, handsome, shy young man in line with the image of the scholar in the scholar-beauty romance genre.[7] One scene in *Journey to the West*, for instance, features Xuanzang and his disciples stranded in "Womanland," where the inhabitants are exclusively female and have never before seen a man. The queen of Womanland desires Xuanzang and tries to force him into marriage.[8] The panic-stricken Xuanzang is at a total loss as to what to do. In a variety play (Ch. *zaju*) version of this story, his disciple Monkey even teases the queen, saying, "My master is still a virgin, let me take his place!"[9] Such representations not only give voice to anxiety over and fantasies about the reversal of the gender order but also illustrate the peculiar association of Buddhist monks with sexuality in Ming-Qing (1368–1911) vernacular literature.

Wu's *Journey to the West* has been canonized as one of the "four masterpieces" of classical Chinese literature.[10] In the novel, Xuanzang (a.k.a. the Tang Monk) is protected and assisted by four disciples during his journey: Monkey (Ch. Sun Wukong, a.k.a. the Monkey King), Pigsy (Ch. Zhu Bajie), Sandy (Ch. Sha Wujing, a.k.a. Monk Sha), and the White Dragon Horse (a dragon prince who becomes Xuanzang's steed). Indeed, the Monkey King has been granted so much magic power and charisma that he outshines the Tang

Monk as the primary hero in the novel, so much so that Arthur Waley's abridged translation is entitled *Monkey*. Meanwhile, as a sidelined character, the Tang Monk is weak compared with the other half-human, half-spirit pilgrims that appear, embodying what C. T. Hsia calls a "deliberate caricature of a saintly monk" who thus "could not have borne any resemblance to his historical counterpart."[11]

In Wu's novel, the Buddhist scripture-seeking journey is significantly Confucianized. As a result, the image of Xuanzang conforms with Confucian values and aesthetics of manhood. Although in historiography Xuanzang became a monk voluntarily, in *Journey to the West* he seems to have had no other choice. While traveling to an official position, Xuanzang's father is murdered, and his pregnant mother is abducted by the killer. After she gives birth, she sends the baby (future Xuanzang) floating down the river, to protect him, and he ends up being raised in a Buddhist temple. After Xuanzang grows up, he learns of his family history, avenges his parents, and reunites with them (including his father, who had been saved by a Dragon King). However, Xuanzang insists on returning to the temple to pay his debt of gratitude to the Buddha and devotes the rest of his life to the pursuit of Dharma. In this way, Buddhist determination and sacrifice are combined with the Confucian mode of filial piety and gratitude. As Zhang Jinchi points out, Xuanzang has been turned into "a saintly monk with a Buddhist appearance outside but Confucian morals inside."[12]

Moreover, the motive of the pilgrims in *Journey to the West* has been modified according to Confucian ideology. According to the biography written by Huili, Xuanzang's pilgrimage was motivated solely by individual faith, and Xuanzang even defied an imperial decree prohibiting subjects from crossing national borders. In *Journey to the West*, however, the Tang Monk is not simply permitted to travel but is in fact sent to India by the Tang emperor to procure Mahāyāna Buddhist scriptures for the welfare of both the imperial family and the empire as a whole. In fact, the emperor even confers the title of "sworn brother" on the monk at a grand ceremony bidding him farewell. With the emperor's endorsement, the journey becomes a demonstration of unconditional loyalty to the sovereign in line with the dominant Confucian ideology. In the novel, the Tang Monk is known in foreign countries as "the younger brother of the Tang emperor," and his travels function as official diplomacy.

More importantly, the novel's image of Xuanzang is modeled on that of the typical Confucian scholar and thus deviates from the celibate monastic masculinity depicted in earlier historical records. His appearance and behavior are reminiscent of the rhetoric of the fragile scholar's body, which is characterized by "rosy lips, sparkling white teeth and [a] jasper-like face."[13] In the scene that takes place in Womanland, the Tang Monk is described from the queen's perspective:

> A noble manner,
> Distinguished features.
> White teeth as if made of silver,
> A square-cut mouth with lips of red.
> The top of the head flat, the forehead broad and ample;
> Fine eyes, a clear brow, and a long jaw.
> His ears had the round lobes of a great man;
> His body was that of one with no ordinary talent.
> A handsome, intelligent and gallant gentleman;
> The ideal consort for the graceful queen.[14]

This image is associated with the discourse of masculine purity. In the novel, the Tang Monk was in a past life the Elder Golden Cicada, a disciple of the Buddha in the Western Paradise. Once inattentive to a sermon given by the Buddha, he has been banished to Earth. Monsters and demons hunger for his flesh because he has lived a life of strict purity during his ten incarnations on Earth, never losing a single drop of his semen.[15] Their longing to consume his body is highly reminiscent of the little fresh meat discourse in present-day China, which presents men as desirable bodies.[16] At the same time, the Tang Monk is prone to making mistakes and wrong judgments and "neither withstands nor yields to the cannibalistic and sexual assault of the demons and monsters."[17] His embarrassment and panic when being seduced by female demons or humans suggest that he has not yet been spared from human desire. In a manner of speaking, his character signifies the weakness and general predicament of human beings on the journey toward enlightenment. As Zhang Jinchi acutely points out: "When facing women's seduction, Sun Wukong [Monkey] is insusceptible to the sea of desires and thus just does whatever he feels like. Zhu Bajie [Pigsy] never refrains from lust and thus is itching with desire [when he sees beautiful women]. As for Xuanzang, he is in between with obscure emotions. That explains his embarrassment and trepidation [when being seduced by women]."[18] When sexually provoked by the queen of Womanland, Xuanzang is described as "blushing from ear to ear" and being too embarrassed to look at her. Later, he even bursts into tears and desperately resorts to asking Monkey for help when the queen tries to force him into marriage.[19]

In fact, the motif of Womanland can be found in earlier scripture-seeking narratives. The earliest extant version of the story appears in a book entitled *The Story with Poems of How Trepiṭaka of the Great Tang Fetched Sūtras* (Ch. *Da Tang Sanzang qujing shihua*), which was probably written during the Southern Song dynasty (1127–1279).[20] In this book, however, the story is narrated in a way that illustrates Xuanzang's stoicism in the face of sexual temptation: "The monk declined again and again and determinedly took his leave. The women [in the palace] dissolved into tears and said dolefully, 'When will we see a man again after he leaves?' The queen then presented the monk with five luminous pearls and a white horse as farewell gifts."[21] It later turns out that the queen and other beautiful women are but a trial for Xuanzang set by the bodhisattvas Mañjuśrī and Samantabhadra to test his composure.[22] The story changes significantly, however, in a later Yuan variety play (*zaju*) version in which the monk appears shy, weak, and helpless when the queen tries to force him to marry her. The change reflects the tendency to ridicule and mock Confucian scholars in the popular entertainment of late imperial China.

The dyad of Xuanzang and Monkey in a sense represents the discourse of *wen/wu* masculinity in Confucian culture.[23] The historical Xuanzang displayed some *wu* qualities: according to the biographies written by his disciple, he survived several attacks by bandits and robbers. However, his image becomes that of the fragile and pedantic scholar in Wu's *Journey to the West*, a transformation reflecting the primacy of *wen* over *wu* following the Song dynasty, as well as the popularity of the kind of scholar-masculinity I outlined in *The Fragile Scholar*. In the novel, Monkey powerfully subdues demons and monsters in line with the martial spirit, while the Tang Monk, who is generally unable to tell evil from good, tries to stop him and even scolds and punishes him when Monkey resorts to violence. The Tang Monk's superiority over Monkey affirms his masculinity through two hierarchical roles:

that between teacher (and thus patriarch) and student and that between *wen* and *wu*.

The Prototype of "Little Fresh Meat": The Tang Monk in Film and Television

Journey to the West was among the very first Chinese literary masterpieces to be adapted into films. The first such film, *The Cave of the Silken Web* (Ch. *Pansi dong*), was produced in Shanghai in 1927. Since then, a large body of films, TV dramas, animations, and other forms of visual entertainment based on the stories of the Tang Monk and his disciples has emerged, making him one of the best-known figures among children and adults in China.

Setting the Standard: The Tang Monk in the 1986 Production

The TV drama series *Journey to the West*, which was produced by the official China Central Television (CCTV) in 1982 and premiered in 1986 (and is therefore referred to in China as the 1986 production), remains the most influential adaptation of the novel. It has aired numerous times since its premiere and is allegedly the most-watched TV drama series with the most reruns in the world.[24] A sequel that covers the remaining chapters of the original novel aired in 1999. One distinctive feature of both the 1986 production and its sequel is the heavy influence of the conventional aesthetic of traditional Chinese opera. Not only were most of the screenwriters and directors from Chinese opera circles, but most of the primary actors were also originally trained for the operatic stage. Three actors take up the role of the Tang Monk in the series: Wang Yue, Xu Shaohua, and Chi Chongrui (fig. 10.1).[25] At the time it was made, Wang and Xu were in their early twenties, and Chi, who had already made a name for himself in operas, had just turned 30. All three actors can be categorized into the young scholar (Ch. *xiaosheng*) role in traditional operas, characterized by a handsome appearance and refined manners.

Online articles and retrospective interviews reveal that there had been concerns about these casting decisions. The first actor, Wang, was still a

FIGURE 10.1 Wang Yue (top left), Xu Shaohua (bottom left), and Chi Chongrui (right) playing the Tang Monk in CCTV's 1986 TV drama series *Journey to the West* (source: http://images.baidu.com).

student at the Beijing Film Academy. When initially invited to play the role of the Tang Monk, he was worried about being labeled "a young scholar as soft as cream" (Ch. *naiyou xiaosheng*), a term widely used in the 1980s to criticize the lack of masculinity among Chinese men, especially when compared with their Western counterparts. His worry was alleviated only when the director, Yang Jie, commented that the character "looks Buddhist [and] handsome, but not feminine."[26] The actor who succeeded Wang, Xu Shaohua, was praised by the Hong Kong–based *Ta Kung Pao* newspaper as "the No.1 *xiaosheng* [actor playing the young scholar type] in China" for his debut performance in the 1983 film *Fox Spirit* (Ch. *Jing bian*). Yang allegedly urged Xu to gain weight to acquire both "the appearance of fortune" (Ch. *futai*)—as weight is traditionally associated with fortune and blessings in Chinese culture—that accords with the image of an achieved Buddhist master, and a baby face conveying youth and innocence. Xu is considered by many to be the best-looking of the three actors who played Xuanzang in the series, and even the best-looking of any actor who has ever played the role.

However, it is the story of the third actor, Chi Chongrui, that most foreshadows the little fresh meat discourse. Chi was born into a family of professional Peking opera actors and was selected by Yang to play the role of the Tang Monk after the two previous actors quit for personal reasons. He appeared in the final part of the series, and was thus jokingly referred to by the media as the only monk to procure the true sutras. After attaining overnight fame through the drama's phenomenal popularity, Chi faded from the entertainment scene after marrying the billionaire Chen Lihua in 1990. Chen, who is eleven years Chi's senior and was a divorcée with three adult children when the two met, is a successful businesswoman who ranked seventy-ninth in the list of the wealthiest people in China published by Hurun Report in 2020.[27] The obvious gap between the two in age, wealth, and social status has led to considerable tabloid nastiness, with accusations that Chi made a fortune with his "white face and smooth skin."[28] In a sense, Chi has become an icon of the little fresh meat rhetoric, which marks a reversal of the traditional male gaze upon women. For instance, one online article highlights the fact that the marriage was Chi's first, and thus that the purity of his masculinity resembles that of the monk in *Journey to the West*.[29]

The negotiation and discussion surrounding the image of the Tang Monk in the TV drama bespeak both the audience's and the actors' anxiety over the character's femininity, yet at the same time paradoxically demonstrate the resilience of traditional Chinese ideals of manhood. Although many subsequent attempts were made by other filmic and TV adaptations to "masculinize" the image, the Tang Monk's portrayal by the three aforementioned actors remains the most accepted by audiences across generations. Audience comments online indicate that viewers do not feel right about a tough or martial Tang Monk, with the 1986 TV production referred to as an exemplary depiction of the character. A classic scene that both the media and audiences revel in talking about is that which takes place in the Womanland queen's chamber, where the Tang Monk (played by Xu Shaohua) struggles between sexual desire and his faith. In the scene, the monk dares not look the queen in the eye, blushes and becomes soaked in sweat, and appears so fragile that the queen can easily push him onto the bed.

Compared with the original novel, a significant change in the 1986 production is the emotional link between the Tang Monk and his disciples,

Monkey in particular. Instead of being a severe teacher, the Tang Monk is sometimes portrayed in the drama as a gentle and amiable "brother," even demonstrating maternal care toward Monkey, such as in a scene in which he sews Monkey's tiger-skin skirt. Accordingly, the original domination of pupil by master is replaced by mutual love and a homosocial bond between men, a logical move in the context of the anti-feudal socialist literature and art in the early post-Mao period.

No More Little Fresh Meat: Tang Monks After 1986

A Chinese Odyssey (Ch. *Dahua xiyou*), a series of Hong Kong comedy films directed by Jeffrey Lau and starring Stephen Chow, is another influential adaptation of *Journey to the West*. Produced in 1995, the film duology comprises *A Chinese Odyssey, Pt. 1: Pandora's Box* and *A Chinese Odyssey, Pt. 2: Cinderella*. A third film was released in 2016 as a sequel to the series. Loosely based on the original novel, the films feature the scripture-seeking narrative along with Stephen Chow's signature style of slapstick, known as *mo le tau* (nonsense humor) in Cantonese. The films were a huge box office success in Hong Kong and other Chinese-speaking communities and, since being streamed online, have become overwhelmingly popular among the younger generation in China, exerting a great impact on their understanding of *Journey to the West*. They have also generated adaptations in other media, including comics and manga.

In the films, the Tang Monk is played by Hong Kong star Law Kar Ying. Originally a Cantonese opera star, Law was thirty-nine when he appeared in the films. By then a middle-aged comedian, he deviated from the little fresh meat image in appearance, and he portrays the Tang Monk as an extremely verbose, funny man. The most famous scene in the film series features the monk singing a song to the tune of "Only You" to persuade Monkey to fight for and protect him, only to irritate Monkey with his verbosity. The playfulness and comedic effects in the films are akin to parody and represent a backlash against the little fresh meat image. Rid of his androgynous appearance and romantic contact with female characters, what is left of the monk's image reflects the producer's interpretation of the character's essence—namely, a pedantic scholar. However, it seems that this type of image is acceptable only in the genre of spoof comedy. Notably,

FIGURE 10.2 The Tang Monk played by Nicholas Tse in *A Chinese Tall Story*.

when the same director produced another film, *A Chinese Tall Story*, in 2005, he recruited the Hong Kong star Nicholas Tse, who is very popular among female fans, to play the leading role of the Tang Monk (fig. 10.2). In this fantasy adventure film centered on the Tang Monk's romance before his journey of pilgrimage, the verbose middle-aged man is once again replaced by a handsome young man.

A more recent TV adaptation of the novel, with Zhang Jizhong as the producer and thus known as "the Zhang Jizhong production," is a sixty-six-episode drama series directed by Zhang Jianya that premiered in mainland China in 2011. The series, which was broadcast on numerous domestic TV channels and has been exported to such countries as Cambodia, Malaysia, and Indonesia, represents a new attempt to remasculinize the Tang Monk. The producer, Zhang Jizhong, reportedly said during a preshooting interview that he would not look for a "*xiao bailian*" (literally "young white face," implying a gigolo) to play the role of the Tang Monk, suggesting that the character in the 1986 production is too weak and effeminate. His remarks were strongly rebutted by Xu and Chi, who both played the monk in the 1986 drama. Chi remarked, "*Journey to the West* is a mythical novel based on the prototype of Xuanzang in the Tang dynasty. The Tang Monk in my mind is a man with perseverance and faith to procure the sutras. Many may think he is weak and cowardly, but in fact he is just too kindhearted. And exactly because of that, he needs three disciples to protect him."[30]

Nie Yuan was chosen to play the Tang Monk role in the Zhang Jizhong production (fig. 10.3). Given his soldierly bearing, Nie is regarded as an icon of valiant masculinity instead of the little fresh meat type. His image in the drama is more that of a traveler than a scholar. This characterization emphasizes Xuanzang's persistence and stoicism. Now able to distinguish between good and evil, the Tang Monk, as played by Nie, can rightfully justify his forgiveness of the monsters, as Buddhism discourages ignorance but encourages compassion.

Another TV drama, *A Sequel to Journey to the West* (Ch. *Xiyou ji houzhuan*), a fantasy series directed by Li Yuan that aired on Shaanxi Television in 2000, features Xuanzang as a martial monk. Played by Huang Haibing, a young actor who has also appeared in several costume dramas with a military theme, this Tang Monk is courageous, wise, and decisive. As the drama is set after the monk's successful completion of his scripture-seeking journey, he has become a god and, accordingly, is powerful enough to fight supernatural demons himself rather than relying on his disciples for protection and help. Romantic scenes are notably missing from this series, perhaps owing to the director's efforts to idealize Xuanzang as a holy monk and diminish his earthly desires. However, audiences have seen romantic potential in the interactions between Xuanzang and the pretty Bodhisattva and given free rein to their imagination through fan works. In fact, in mainstream heterosexual popular culture, audiences are sensitive to any romantic possibilities between the monk and female characters, and sometimes male characters, too (Monkey on most occasions).

This backlash against effeminacy and attempts to remasculinize the character have met a mixed response. On the one hand, some audience members applaud the new images for restoring the "real" historical Xuanzang, who is believed to have been tough, determined, and even martial. On the other, there have been criticisms targeting the liberty taken by dramas to alter the established image in a classic literary work. The Zhang Jizhong production, for instance, has been denounced online for "ruining a masterpiece." Internet commenters maintain that, for a Chinese audience, the room for

FIGURE 10.3 The Tang Monk (above, played by Nie Yuan) appearing as a traveler in the TV drama series *Journey to the West* (2011) and (below, played by Huang Haibing) fighting a villain in *A Sequel to Journey to the West* (2000).

improvement with respect to this character does not lie in his martial ability, but rather in the strength and power of his will. In fact, the monk's physical weakness only intensifies the hardships of the pilgrimage, and thus the power of his faith. In all of these discussions, the recurrent references to the 1986 production, both by the producers and commenters, affirm the standing of that TV drama series as the adaptation that solidified the popular imagination of Xuanzang.

In the years since, there have been numerous TV and film productions based on *Journey to the West*, both live action and animated, in China, Taiwan, and Hong Kong, and many of them have received significant public attention. Among them, the most prominent one is the film *Xuanzang*, a blockbuster jointly produced by a state-owned Chinese film company and an Indian company in 2016. Repackaging Xuanzang's story as a tale of "Chinese perseverance, ambition, and outreach," the film serves cultural diplomacy associated with the Belt and Road Initiative. Although the image of Xuanzang, played by the Chinese star Huang Xiaoming, is supposed to be "faithful" to history, the film flopped at the box office.[31] In addition, there has been a plethora of publications revolving around *Journey to the West*, including reprints and translations of Wu's novel, abridged versions for children, comics, and modern retellings of the stories. Xuanzang has even been hailed as an exemplary manager.[32] While for middle-aged and older audiences the new film adaptations are associated primarily with cultural nationalism and childhood nostalgia, the video games and web literature developed from them are gaining in popularity among younger generations.[33] These works feature new types of the monk image that reflect the shifting standard of masculinity at the intersection of commercialism, nationalism, and cosmopolitanism.

The Female Tang Monk: The Journey of *Journey to the West*

Journey to the West spread from China to neighboring countries such as Korea and Japan soon after its publication and was translated into Japanese and Korean. Over the years, the characters of Xuanzang and his disciples have been adapted and creatively represented by different forms of popular culture—literature, painting, film, television, anime, manga, and games—in these countries. This transnational interest in the novel's pilgrimage stories and characters has become a pan-East Asian cultural phenomenon, giving voice to mutually influenced expressions of masculinity.

Korean Odysseys: Old Monk, Young Woman

Owing to geographical proximity and close cultural ties, the stories of Xuanzang's pilgrimage spread to Korea very early on. In fact, a Chinese-language textbook published in Chosŏn Korea (1392–1910) is an important source for stories of the pilgrimage that pre-date the publication of Wu's novel.[34] The pilgrimage motif is so resonant in South Korea that the popular TV reality show *New Journey to the West* took its name from the classic text. According to Korean scholar Song Jin-ha, *Journey to the West* is generally treated as children's literature in South Korea today, with Xuanzang generally presented as a gentle yet strict old monk.[35] A primary example is *Fly, Superboard*, a South Korean animation based on cartoonist Heo Young-man's (b. 1947) work

FIGURE 10.4 Samjang in the South Korean animation *Fly, Superboard*.

Mr. Son (fig. 10.4). Premiering during the 1989–1990 season and reairing many times since, *Fly, Superboard* set a ratings record for a Korean animation. The animation features Samjang (the Korean pronunciation of Sanzang) as a faithful, kind, pacifist old monk. In being firm with Monkey, he behaves like a traditional Confucian teacher, whereas in studying martial arts in Shaolin Temple—intentionally learning only defensive moves—he also displays Buddhist compassion.

The most influential Korean TV production relating to the pilgrimage stories is the modern spin-off *A Korean Odyssey* (K. *Hwayugi*) (fig. 10.5). Its English title alludes to the cult classic *A Chinese Odyssey*. Written by the Hong sisters (Hong Jung-eun and Hong Mi-ran), who are renowned for TV drama screenwriting, the twenty-episode series produced by tvN was an immediate hit in Korea upon its premiere in 2017. As part of the Korean Wave, the drama was added to Netflix for international viewing at the end of 2017, with subtitles in Arabic, English, French, Polish, and traditional Chinese. It has also been broadcast in the Philippines (in 2018 and again in 2019), Malaysia (2018), and Thailand (2018) and has generated controversy among Chinese audiences in mainland China, Hong Kong, and Taiwan.

In the drama, which follows the characters of *Journey to the West*, the Tang Monk is reincarnated as a young woman. Jin Seon-mi (played by Oh Yeon-seo), whose name sounds like "truth-goodness-beauty," is a girl who can see ghosts and spirits. As a child, she accidentally frees Son Oh-gong (Lee Seung-gi), the Monkey King, who has been imprisoned by Heaven for his crimes. Jin eventually becomes the CEO of a real estate company that specializes in buying haunted houses, exorcising the spirits therein, and then reselling them. Meanwhile, Son Oh-gong, eager to reinstate his status as an immortal, is on the lookout for the reincarnation of Samjang because he has heard that anyone who eats Samjang's flesh can gain immortality. When he discovers that Samjang is none other than the little girl who released him years ago, he approaches her and tries to persuade her to die for him. In the process, Son falls madly in love with Jin, and the two fight off demons and monsters together. In the end, Jin dies to save the world, fulfilling her destiny to sacrifice herself for humanity.[36]

Although the setting is modern-day South Korea, the drama features many motifs from the original novel. For instance, in Wu's novel, the golden hoop (Ch. *jin'gu*) is a magic instrument that the bodhisattva Guanyin grants to the Tang Monk to ensure that his naughty yet powerful disciples obey his

FIGURE 10.5 A promotional poster for *A Korean Odyssey* featuring Jin Seon-mi in the center.

orders. Once worn on the head, the hoop cannot be removed, and when the monk chants the relevant incantations, the wearer suffers an intolerable headache. It is thus a magic weapon that the monk uses to discipline his followers. The hoop represents the potency of Buddhist incantations, Xuanzang's authority as a teacher in Confucian culture, and the supremacy of *wen* masculinity over *wu*. In *A Korean Odyssey*, however, it becomes a magical bracelet called *geumganggo* that an old lady, an incarnation of the bodhisattva, sells to Jin. The bracelet secures the obedience of anyone who wears it through the power of love. Jin gives it to Son as a gift, and when Son wears it he falls deeply in love with Jin. He constantly reminds her that if he takes the bracelet off, his love will disappear, and he may return to wanting to eat her flesh. Jin, for her part, is moved by Son's sincerity and thoughtfulness and struggles to guard her heart against any romantic feelings toward him because she is aware that Samjang's tragic destiny is to be a sacrifice for humanity.

For many audience members in the Chinese-speaking world, representing the Tang Monk as a woman sounds absurd or even offensive.[37] However, as early as the Qing dynasty (1644–1911), the Chinese commentator Wang Danyi declared that "the Tang Monk's benevolence and softness resemble characteristics of a woman."[38] The perception of the Tang Monk as feminine or androgynous aligns with the strand of Buddhist gender ideology that treats gender (and sex) as fluid.[39] This conception coincides with modern theorists' understanding of masculinity as a fluid identity that is performatively constituted.[40] It also dovetails with the analysis of performative masculinity in Rebecca Mendelson's chapter in this volume.

Further Feminization: The Tang Monk in Japan

Indeed, a female incarnation of Xuanzang can be found in much earlier representations in Japan. As in Korea, there have been an astonishingly large number of adaptations of *Journey to the West* in Japan. The earliest Japanese translation has been described as an "interminable 'relay' as the complete work was collaborated [upon] by several translators, based on different versions of *Journey to the West*."[41] Since the publication of *The Illustrated Complete Version of Journey to the West* (J. *Ehon Saiyū zenden*) in 1883, a reprint, abridgement, or adaptation of the novel has emerged every three to five years right up to the present day, making Sanzō (the Japanese pronunciation of Sanzang) and his disciples household names in Japan.

Since the Edo period (1603–1868), Sanzō has been depicted as an androgynous figure. In the woodblock print illustrations of *A Vernacular Version of Journey to the West* (J. *Tsūzoku saiyūki*) by Tsukioka Yoshitoshi (1839–1892), he appears as a beautiful young man (fig. 10.6). In keeping with *ukiyo-e* painting conventions, good-looking young men are portrayed in soft lines, lending

FIGURE 10.6 Sanzō in Tsukioka Yoshitoshi's woodblock illustrations.

them a feminine beauty that differentiates them from ugly, ordinary, or macho men. Sanzō's delicate face is a stark contrast to the ferocious appearance of his three disciples. His purple cassock indicates his virtue and nobility, as purple was considered a noble color that ordinary people were forbidden to wear in premodern Japan. After Buddhism came to Japan, however, the court allowed exceptionally virtuous monks to wear purple.

Sanzō's transformation into a woman can be traced back to the novel *Women's Journey to the West in the Current Style* (J. *Fūzoku onna saiyūki*). Written by Tamenaga Shunsui (1790–1844) and published in 1828, the novel belongs to a popular genre of the time called *onna-mono* (female plays). Closely linked to the theatrical genre of *kabuki*, which from around 1629 was known for its all-male cast and cross-dressing actors, in *onna-mono* almost all male protagonists are recast or intentionally conceived as females. In addition to *Journey to the West*, other Chinese vernacular novels, including *Romance of the Three Kingdoms* and *The Water Margin*, were adapted into this form of "female presence."[42] In *Women's Journey to the West*, the pilgrimage team is replaced by a group of four women: Mitsuhime, Takako, O-Sago, and O-Ino. The novel depicts their quest to exact noble vengeance for the death of Master Kiyomi. Sanzō's female counterpart, Mitsuhime, is portrayed as a young girl with a distinguished Buddhist background. She grows up in a temple, and at the age of fifteen is entrusted by Priest Trepiṭaka with the grand mission of restoring Master Kiyomi's household.[43]

Various imaginaries of Sanzō appear in modern Japanese film, television, anime, and manga. In the first Japanese film adaptation of *Journey to the West*, *Songoku* (J. *Enoken no songokū*, 1940), for instance, Sanzō is a handsome middle-aged man in Buddhist dress who appears solemn and carries the aura of a teacher and guru. This image was replaced by that of a teenage boy in the 1959 color film *Songoku* (a.k.a. *Monkey Sun*). In this production, Sanzō is played by a young boy with a delicate complexion and closely cropped hair who appears vulnerable in the face of dangerous circumstances. Although the two films were produced by the same company (Toho) and had the same director (Kajirō Yamamoto), there is a discernable change in the image of the monk, presumably reflecting a significant aesthetic change in the presentation of masculinity after World War II.

This androgynous image of Sanzō is on full display in *Monkey* (J. *Saiyūki*), a two-season TV drama that premiered on Nippon TV in 1978. The series not only caused a sensation throughout Japan but also garnered a cult following in New Zealand, Australia, the UK, and South Africa. The actress Masako Natsume (1957–1985) played Sanzō in this drama, setting a precedent for having women play the role. The character's androgyny is highlighted in *Monkey* to the extent that at one point in the story Monkey disguises Sanzō as a beautiful woman to whom the lascivious pilgrim Pigsy (J. Hakkai; Ch. Zhu Bajie) is sexually attracted.

In subsequent TV productions, including the 1993 version of *Saiyuki* on Nippon TV, 1994's *New Monkey* on Nippon TV, and 2006's *Saiyuki* on Fuji

Television, it became almost a convention to assign the role of Sanzō to a female actor. In the 1993 drama, there is even a scene in which Pigsy tries to woo Sanzō and have sex with him, calling Sanzō a "beautiful woman." In addition, the drama introduces a female human character who was Monkey's first love when he was still a human being. Sanzō is a descendant of this character and looks very similar to her. Given this background, Monkey's attachment to Sanzō can be easily interpreted as based on romantic feeling, either toward his first love or Sanzō himself.

Japanese popular culture allows a much more creative and diverse space for interpreting and representing the Buddhist masculinities embodied by Sanzō than does Chinese culture. The bold alterations of the character in Japanese productions have sometimes even irritated Chinese audiences. When *Monkey* (1978) was broadcast on China's CCTV, it drew severe criticism from both the authorities and the public and was suspended after just three episodes.[44] Viewers were angered by what they saw as absurd and arbitrary changes to a masterpiece. In particular, they were unable to accept the Tang Monk being played by Natsume.

There have been approximately seven female images of Sanzō in Japanese anime and manga. Other works imply Sanzō's femininity in various ways. For example, in the ninth Doraemon film (a popular animation series in Japan), *Doraemon: The Record of Nobita's Parallel Visit to the West* (1988), the protagonist Nobita travels back to 645 CE and meets the Monkey King (who turns out to be Nobita himself) and Sanzō. Although Sanzō is male in this production, it is noteworthy that a promotional poster for the film shows Shizuka Minamoto, the beautiful female lead role in the anime, in the role corresponding to Sanzō among the team of pilgrims comprising Nobita and his three friends.

Sanzō's femininity also makes him one of the key characters in Japan's female-oriented BL (Boys' Love) subculture, which typically represents same-sex romances between young boys (sometimes fantasized in women's clothes) in an androgynous way. *Patalliro Saiyuki!* (1982) is a representative example. An adaptation of the *Journey to the West* narrative, this TV animation (produced by Toei Animation) is based on a manga by Mineo Maya, who is known for his sarcastic parody (J. *kuso*) style. The original manga was serialized in several manga magazines, including the famous *Flowers and Dreams* (J. *Hana to yume*), which targets a young female readership.

Sanzō is the lead character in *Patalliro Saiyuki!*, an effeminate, pretty young boy with green eyes and a long golden strand of curly hair covering his right eye. The character is voiced by a female actor, which adds to his feminine beauty. He wears a golden crown and purple cassock during the journey and is frequently molested because of his pretty appearance. For instance, one scene features a fictional arhat named Bango Lohan, who was Sanzō's lover and student in Sanzō's previous life as the Golden Cicada. At one point during the pilgrims' scripture-seeking journey, Gokū (Monkey) leaves Sanzō in anger after being misunderstood. Sanzō is then deceived by Bango Lohan and loses his virginity to him when the arhat claims that he can grant Sanzō the power to control Gokū. After Gokū returns, he laughs at his master and describes him as a credulous *bishōnen* (beautiful boy) who has just been cheated by a playboy.

The fact that this manga was produced by a man invites analysis of the male gaze on BL-style male beauty. Kazumi Nagaike discusses the queerness in the consumption of the homosexual by heterosexual men. He uses the term *fudanshi* ("rotten boys"), a play on the term *fujoshi* ("rotten girls," which refers to female fans of BL), to describe heterosexual male BL readers and even producers. As illustrated by the example of the image of Sanzō in *Patalliro Saiyuki!* and other works, the feminization of this character who is supposed to embody a supreme standard of Buddhist masculinity demonstrates "the existence of the (subconscious) psychological male desire for self-feminization through male readers' identification with those images of seemingly gay men that were originally desired by and for women. This aligns with a temptation felt by many men to negate the socially imposed construction of a strong 'masculine' ego."[45]

In sum, through translation, adaptation, and recreation, Xuanzang has been a widely circulated and popular leitmotif in East Asia for centuries. His image has undergone various transformations in Japanese and Korean popular culture and has been largely associated with male effeminacy or even femininity. In this process, Buddhist gender notions have fueled a diverse range of queer imaginations and representations, which effectively challenge and negotiate with hegemonic masculinities in an Asian context.

* * *

Xuanzang became a popular character in vernacular literature and the visual arts long after his death. His many representations bespeak popular desires and imaginations associated with Buddhist masculinities. Wu Cheng'en's classic novel *Journey to the West* has ingrained in the Chinese mind an image of the Tang Monk as a Confucian scholar who struggles between his desires and Buddhist faith, an image that has continually resonated in modern film and TV adaptations of the novel. The representation of and controversies surrounding the Tang Monk in the 1986 TV drama series reflect the negotiation between the imagination of Chineseness and global hegemonic discourse of masculinity. Despite concerns over the character's effeminacy and various attempts to remasculinize him, the most popular and widely accepted image of the Tang Monk in the Chinese symbolic order remains that of a young scholar characterized by vulnerability and feminine beauty.

The transnational circulation and reproduction of this male image within East Asia have contributed to the rise of a feminine type of aesthetic in male representations in popular culture. Many factors have made the Tang Monk the focal point of this reimagination and feminization. First, the all-male pilgrimage team has become too dull for the modern audience in terms of gender diversity, and hence a female leading role is needed due to commercial concerns. The Tang Monk's personality traits, such as frailty, simple goodness, and garrulousness, are conventionally associated with the feminine and thus made him more womanish than the female demons and monsters in the novel. Second, the transformations of the image in Japanese and Korean popular culture reflect a fluid and ambiguous notion of gender, which defies binary categorization. This deep-rooted cultural trope has been intertwined with imaginations and interpretations of the Buddhist doctrines in East Asia. Lastly, the depiction of Xuanzang (Sanzang/Samjang/Sanzō) as a woman or the allocation of the role to a female actor also shows mockery or parody of Buddhist knowledge and canonized literature in popular culture. In a nutshell, the image of Xuanzang combines masculine and feminine qualities in ways that significantly challenge and enrich our understanding of gender and masculinity in the modern context. Through the lens of this image's transformation from "an eminent patriarch of Chinese Buddhist tradition" to an icon of soft and queer masculinity in East Asia,[46] this study demonstrates how imaginaries of Buddhist manhood interact, negotiate, and are manipulated by hegemonic masculinity, which itself should be understood as a historically changing and multifaceted discourse of normative manhood.[47]

NOTES

1. Geng Song, " 'Little Fresh Meat': The Politics of Sissiness and Sissyphobia in Contemporary China," *Men and Masculinities* 25, no.1 (2022): 68–86.
2. For example, see Kam Louie, *Theorising Chinese Masculinity: Society and Gender in China* (Cambridge: Cambridge University Press, 2002); Geng Song, *The Fragile Scholar: Power and Masculinity in Chinese Culture* (Hong Kong: Hong Kong University Press, 2004); and Martin W. Huang, *Negotiating Masculinities in Late Imperial China* (Honolulu: University of Hawai'i Press, 2006).
3. Geng Song, "Masculinizing *Jianghu* Spaces in the Past and Present: Homosociality, Nationalism, and Chineseness," *Nan Nü: Men, Women, and Gender in China* 21, no. 1 (2019): 107–29.
4. Louie, *Theorising Chinese Masculinity.*
5. See Stephen H. West and Wilt L. Idema, "An Introduction to the World of *The Western Wing*," in *The Moon and the Zither: The Story of the Western Wing*, ed. and trans. Stephen H. West and Wilt L. Idema (Berkeley: University of California Press, 1991), 83.
6. This account comes from the *Old Tang History* (*Jiu Tang shu*). Liu Yinbo, comp., *Xiyou ji yanjiu ziliao* (Shanghai: Shanghai guji chubanshe, 1990), 99.
7. Song, *Fragile Scholar.*
8. *Xiyou ji* (hereafter XYJ), chapter 54.
9. Cai Tieying, comp., *Xiyou ji ziliao huibian* (Beijing: Zhonghua shuju, 2010), 406.
10. In common discourse, the "four masterpieces" also include *Dream of the Red Chamber* (*Honglou meng*), *Water Margin* (*Shuihu zhuan*), and *Romance of the Three Kingdoms* (*Sanguo yanyi*).
11. C. T. Hsia, *The Classic Chinese Novel: A Critical Introduction* (Ithaca, N.Y.: Cornell East Asia Series, [1968] 1996), 160.
12. Zhang Jinchi, *Xiyouji kaolun* (Harbin: Heilongjiang jiaoyu chubanshe, 2003), 96. All quotations from Chinese articles and books are my own translations unless otherwise noted.
13. Song, *Fragile Scholar*, 126.
14. Wu Cheng'en, *Journey to the West*, trans. W. J. F. Jenner (Beijing: Foreign Languages Press, [1982] 2002), 2:408.
15. Hsia, *Classic Chinese Novel*, 126.
16. Song, "Little Fresh Meat," 70.
17. Hsia, *Classic Chinese Novel*, 126.
18. Zhang, *Xiyouji kaolun*, 110.
19. XYJ, chapter 54.
20. Also known as *The Story of How Master Trepiṭaka of the Great Tang Fetched Sūtras* [*Da Tang Sanzang fashi qujing ji*], the book is a colloquial narrative (narrated in prose and punctuated with verse) of Xuanzang's pilgrimage written by an unknown author. Monkey and a prototype of Sandy appear in the book as the pilgrim's companions and guardians, although Pigsy does not appear. See Anthony C. Yu, "Hsi-yu chi," in *The Indiana Companion to Traditional Chinese Literature*, vol. 1, ed. and comp. William H. Nienhauser Jr. (Bloomington: Indiana University Press, 1986), 414.

21. Cai Tieying, *Xiyou ji ziliao huibian*, 84–85.
22. Cai Tieying, 84–85.
23. According to Louie, *Theorising Chinese Masculinity*, both *wen* and *wu* are regarded as masculine qualities in Confucian culture, although there has been a notable tendency to prioritize *wen* over *wu* since the Song dynasty.
24. "Chongbo chao 3000 ci, Xiyou ji shenqing jinisi shijie jilu," People.cn, November 17, 2014, http://culture.people.com.cn/n/2014/1117/c172318-26041340.html.
25. The division of the three actors is as follows: season 1, Wang Yue (episodes 6, 9, and 10), Xu Shaohua (episodes 4, 5, 7, 8, 11, 12, and 14–16), and Chi Chongrui (episodes 13 and 17–25); and season 2, Xu Shaohua and Chi Chongrui.
26. "Buke siyi, Xu Shaohua fuchu, 86 ban Tangseng cengshi sanren banyan yi jiao," Beiqingwang, June 20, 2017, https://read01.com/zh-hk/dQKyLo.html#.X7TZ9eXitPZ.
27. "Tangseng Chi Chongrui yu 'fupo' Chen Lihua: Shi zhenai haishi 530 yi?," *Tengxun xinwen*, October 30, 2020, https://xw.qq.com/cmsid/20201030A0E73X00.
28. "Tangseng Chi Chongrui."
29. "Chi Chongrui geren hunshi you guo jici hunyin diyiren qizi zhaopian, Chi Chongrui de erzi duoda le," Tianya bagua wang, May 14, 2019, http://www.tianya999.com/enta/2019/0514/17801148.html.
30. "Liang 'tangseng' huiying Zhang Jizhong 'xiao bailian' shuo: qing zunzhong yuanzhu," *Shenyang ribao*, September 14, 2007, https://yule.sohu.com/20070914/n252144795.shtml.
31. Benjamin Brose, *Xuanzang: China's Legendary Pilgrim and Translator* (Boulder, Colo.: Shambhala, 2021), 254.
32. The term "Tang Monk team" was first put forward by Alibaba Group's former CEO Jack Ma (Ma Yun) in 2003. According to him, the four-member team is an ideal one with complementary members, and the Tang Monk plays the role of a good "leader" (*lingdao*) "with a clear goal, a strong sense of responsibility, the ability to incite others, and compassion for others." Ma Yun, "Tangseng de tuandui shi zuihao de tuandui," *Qiyejia tiandi* no. 2 (2004): 42–43.
33. See Hongmei Sun, *Transforming Monkey: Adaptation and Representation of a Chinese Epic* (Seattle: University of Washington Press, 2018).
34. *Park Tong-sa Eonhae*, published around 1677 as an updated version of *Park Tong-sa* with annotations, was an authoritative Chinese-language textbook in Chosŏn Korea. The book mentions and cites various versions of *Journey to the West* that presumably existed prior to Wu's novel. See Pan Jianguo, "*Piao tongshi yanjie* jiqi suoyin *Xiyou ji* xintan," *Lingnan Journal of Chinese Studies* 6 (2016): 211–29.
35. Song Jin-ha, *Xiyou ji yu Dongya dazhong wenhua: yi Zhongguo, Hanguo, Riben wei zhongxin* (Nanjing: Fenghuang chubanshe, 2011), 115.
36. See Foong Woei Wan, "A Korean Odyssey Retells *Journey to The West* as a Comedy About Crazy Love." *Straits Times*, January 18, 2018, https://www.straitstimes.com/lifestyle/entertainment/monkey-and-bull-story.
37. For online comments on *A Korean Odyssey* by Chinese audiences, see https://movie.douban.com/subject/27069434/reviews (accessed December 9, 2020).
38. Quoted in Liu, *Xiyou ji yanjiu ziliao*, 600.

39. For an extensive typology of Buddhist attitudes toward gender, see Bernard Faure, *The Power of Denial: Buddhism, Purity, and Gender* (Princeton, N.J.: Princeton University Press, 2003). It should be noted that, instead of a monolithic entity, the term "Buddhism" covers a wide range of "doctrines, ideologies, and practices," which have "relative autonomy and distinct dynamics" (2).
40. See Judith Butler, *Gender Trouble: Feminism and the Subversion of Identity* (London: Routledge, 1990); and Jack Halberstam, *Female Masculinity* (Durham, N.C.: Duke University Press, 1998).
41. Yevheniy Vakhnenko, "Reception of *Journey to the West* in Early Modern Japan" (master's thesis, University of British Columbia, 2017), 11.
42. Vakhnenko, "Reception of *Journey to the West*," 29–35.
43. Vakhnenko, 45–47.
44. See "Nihonjin no 'Saiyūki ai' wa chūgokujin ga menbokunai to kanjiru hodo," Record China, June 11, 2016, https://www.recordchina.co.jp/b141052-s0-c30-d0038.html.
45. Kazumi Nagaike, "Do Heterosexual Men Dream of Homosexual Men? BL *Fudanshi* and Discourse on Male Feminization," in *Boys Love Manga and Beyond: History, Culture and Community in Japan*, ed. Mark McLelland, Kuzumi Nagaike, Katsuhiko Suganuma, and James Welker (Jackson: University Press of Mississippi, 2015), 190–91.
46. Brose, *Xuanzang*, 244.
47. See Raewyn Connell and James W. Messerschmidt, "Hegemonic Masculinity: Rethinking the Concept" *Gender & Society* 19, no. 6 (2005): 829–59.

Additional Primary Sources

Lau, Jeffrey, dir. *A Chinese Odyssey* [Ch. *Dahua xiyou* 大話西遊]. Hong Kong: Xi'an Film Studio and Choi Sing Film Company, 1995.

———. *A Chinese Tall Story*. Hong Kong: Emperor Motion Pictures, 2005.

Park Hong-kyun, Kim Jung-hyun, and Kim Byung-soo, dirs. *A Korean Odyssey* [K. *Hwayugi*]. Seoul: JS Pictures, 2018.

Wu Cheng'en. *Journey to the West*. Translated by W. J. F. Jenner. 4 vols. Beijing: Foreign Languages Press, 2002 [1982].

Bibliography

Aoki Toshi 青木敏, Fukuda Jun 福田純, Ikehiro Kazuo 池広一夫, Kuroda Yoshiyuki 黒田義之, Tanaka Yasutaka 田中康隆, Watanabe Yūsuke 渡邊祐介, and Yamazaki Daisuke 山崎大助, dir. *Monkey* [J. *Saiyūki* 西遊記]. Nippon TV and International Television Films, 1978.

Brose, Benjamin. *Xuanzang: China's Legendary Pilgrim and Translator.* Boulder, Colo.: Shambhala, 2021.

"Buke siyi, Xu Shaohua fuchu, 86 ban Tangseng cengshi sanren banyan yi jiao" 不可思議，徐少華復出 89版唐僧曾是三人扮演一角. Beiqingwang 北青網, June 20, 2017. https://read01.com/zh-hk/dQKyLo.html#.X7TZ9eXitPZ.

Butler, Judith. *Gender Trouble: Feminism and the Subversion of Identity.* London: Routledge, 1990.

Cai Tieying 蔡铁鹰, comp. *Xiyou ji ziliao huibian* 西遊記資料匯編. Beijing: Zhonghua shuju, 2010.

"Chi Chongrui geren hunshi you guo jici hunyin diyiren qizi zhaopian, Chi Chongrui de erzi duoda le" 遲重瑞個人婚史有過幾次婚姻第一任妻子照片，遲重瑞的兒子多大了. Tianya bagua wang 天涯八卦網, May 14, 2019. http://www.tianya999.com/enta/2019/0514/17801148.html.

"Chongbo chao 3000 ci, Xiyou ji shenqing jinisi shijie jilu" 重播超3000次《西遊記》申請吉尼斯世界紀錄. People.cn, November 17, 2014. http://culture.people.com.cn/n/2014/1117/c172318-26041340.html.

Connell, Raewyn, and James W. Messerschmidt. "Hegemonic Masculinity: Rethinking the Concept." *Gender & Society* 19, no. 6 (2005): 829–59.

Ehon Saiyū zenden 繪本西遊全傳. Wu Cheng'en 吳承恩 and Yajima Gogaku 八島五岳. 4 vols. Tokyo: Hōki Tokubē, 1883.

Faure, Bernard. *The Power of Denial: Buddhism, Purity, and Gender.* Princeton, N.J.: Princeton University Press, 2003.

Fly, Superboard [K. *Nalala syupeobodeu*]. KBS, 1990.

Fūzoku onna saiyūki 風俗女西遊記. Tamenaga Shunsui 為永春水. Edo: Eijudō, 1828.

Halberstam, Jack. *Female Masculinity.* Durham, N.C.: Duke University Press, 1998.

Hong-kyun, Park, Kim Jung-hyun, and Kim Byung-soo, dirs. *A Korean Odyssey* [K. *Hwayugi*]. Seoul; JS Pictures, 2018.

Hsia, C. T. *The Classic Chinese Novel: A Critical Introduction.* Ithaca, N.Y.: Cornell East Asia Series, [1968] 1996.

Huang, Martin W. *Negotiating Masculinities in Late Imperial China.* Honolulu: University of Hawai'i Press, 2006.

Huo Jianqi 霍建起, dir. *Da Tang Xuanzang* 大唐玄奘. Beijing; China Film Group Corporation and Eros International, 2016.

Ichikura Haruo 一倉治雄, Monna Katsuo 門奈克雄, and Sugimura Rokurō 杉村六郎, dir. *New Monkey* [J. *Shin Saiyūki* 新西遊記]. Tokyo; Nippon TV, 1994.

Katō Yūsuke 加藤裕将, Narita Gaku 成田岳, and Sawada Kensaku 澤田鎌作, dir. *Saiyūki* 西遊記. Tokyo; Fuji Television, 2006.

Kimata Akiyoshi 木俣堯美 (a.k.a. Izumi Seiji 和泉聖治), dir. *Saiyūki* 西遊記. Tokyo; Nippon TV, 1993.

Lau, Jeffrey, dir. *A Chinese Odyssey* [Ch. *Dahua xiyou* 大話西遊]. Hong Kong: Xi'an Film Studio and Choi Sing Film Company, 1995.

——. *A Chinese Tall Story.* Hong Kong: Emperor Motion Pictures, 2005.

Li Yuan 李源, dir. *Xiyou ji houzhuan* 西遊記後傳 [*After Journey to the West*]. Xi'an: Shaanxi Broadcasting Corporation, 2000.

"Liang 'tangseng' huiying Zhang Jizhong 'xiao bailian' shuo: qing zunzhong yuanzhu" 倆"唐僧"回應張紀中"小白臉"說 請尊重原著. *Shenyang ribao* 沈陽日報, September 14, 2007. https://yule.sohu.com/20070914/n252144795.shtml.
Liu Yinbo 劉蔭柏, comp. *Xiyou ji yanjiu ziliao* 西遊記研究資料. Shanghai: Shanghai guji chubanshe, 1990.
Louie, Kam. *Theorising Chinese Masculinity: Society and Gender in China*. Cambridge: Cambridge University Press, 2002.
Ma Yun 馬雲. "Tangseng de tuandui shi zuihao de tuandui" 唐僧的團隊是最好的團隊. *Qiyejia tiandi* [Entrepreneur World], no. 2 (2004): 42–43.
Maejima Ken'ichi 前島健一, dir. *Patalliro Saiyuki!* パタリロ西遊記. Tokyo: Magic Bus, 2005.
Nagaike, Kazumi. "Do Heterosexual Men Dream of Homosexual Men? BL *Fudanshi* and Discourse on Male Feminization." In *Boys Love Manga and Beyond: History, Culture, and Community in Japan*, edited by Mark McLelland, Kuzumi Nagaike, Katsuhiko Suganuma, and James Welker, 189–209. Jackson: University Press of Mississippi, 2015.
"Nihonjin no 'Saiyūki ai' wa chūgokujin ga menbokunai to kanjiru hodo" 日本人の"西遊記愛"は中国人が面目ないと感じるほど. Record China, June 11, 2016. https://www.recordchina.co.jp/b141052-s0-c30-d0038.html.
Pan Jianguo 潘建國. "*Piao tongshi yanjie* jiqi suoyin *Xiyou ji* xintan 《朴通事諺解》及其所引《西遊記》新探." *Lingnan Journal of Chinese Studies* 6 (2016): 211–29.
Park Hong-kyun, Kim Jung-hyun, and Kim Byung-soo, dir. *A Korean Odyssey* [K. *Hwayugi*]. Seoul; JS Pictures, 2018.
Shibayama Tsutomu 芝山努, dir. *Doraemon: The Record of Nobita's Parallel Visit to the West* [J. *Doraemon: Nobita no parareru saiyūki* ドラエモン：のび太のパラレル西遊記]. Tokyo: Toho, 1988.
Song, Geng. *The Fragile Scholar: Power and Masculinity in Chinese Culture*. Hong Kong: Hong Kong University Press, 2004.
——. " 'Little Fresh Meat': The Politics of Sissiness and Sissyphobia in Contemporary China." *Men and Masculinities* 25, no.1 (2022): 68–86.
——. "Masculinizing *Jianghu* Spaces in the Past and Present: Homosociality, Nationalism, and Chineseness." *Nan Nü: Men, Women, and Gender in China* 21, no. 1 (2019): 107–29.
Song Jin-ha 宋貞和. *Xiyou ji yu Dongya dazhong wenhua: yi Zhongguo, Hanguo, Riben wei zhongxin* 《西游記》與東亞大眾文化——以中國、韓國、日本為中心. Nanjing: Fenghuang chubanshe, 2011.
Sun, Hongmei. *Transforming Monkey: Adaptation and Representation of a Chinese Epic*. Seattle: University of Washington Press, 2018.
"Tangseng Chi Chongrui yu 'fupo' Chen Lihua: Shi zhenai haishi 530 yi?" "唐僧"遲重瑞與"富婆"陳麗華，是真愛還是530億？ *Tengxun xinwen* 騰訊新聞, October 30, 2020. https://xw.qq.com/cmsid/20201030A0E73X00.
Tsūzoku saiyūki 通俗西遊記. Tsukioka Yoshitoshi 月岡芳年 (1839–1892). Japan (place unknown): Fukushimaya Tashichi (Senkindo), ca. 1864–1865.
Vakhnenko, Yevheniy. "Reception of *Journey to the West* in Early Modern Japan." Master's thesis, University of British Columbia, 2017.

Wan, Foong Woei. "A Korean Odyssey Retells *Journey to the West* as a Comedy about Crazy Love." *Straits Times*, January 18, 2018. https://www.straitstimes.com/lifestyle/entertainment/monkey-and-bull-story.

West, Stephen H., and Wilt L. Idema. "An Introduction to the World of *The Western Wing*." In *The Moon and the Zither: The Story of the Western Wing*, edited and translated by Stephen H. West and Wilt L. Idema, 77–153. Berkeley: University of California Press, 1991.

Wu Cheng'en 吳承恩. *Journey to the West* [Ch. *Xiyou ji* 西遊記]. 4 vols. Translated by W. J. F. Jenner. Beijing: Foreign Languages Press, [1982] 2002.

Yamamoto Kajirō 山本嘉次郎, dir. *Songoku* 孫悟空 (a.k.a. *Enoken's Songoku* エノケンの孫悟空). Tokyo: Toho, 1940.

——. *Songoku* 孫悟空 (a.k.a. *Monkey Sun*). Tokyo: Toho, 1959.

Yang Jie 楊潔, dir. *Xiyou ji* 西遊記 [*Journey to the West*]. China Central Television, 1986.

Yu, Anthony C. "Hsi-yu chi." In *The Indiana Companion to Traditional Chinese Literature*, vol. 1, edited and compiled by William H. Nienhauser Jr., 413–18. Bloomington: Indiana University Press, 1986.

Zhang Jianya 張建亞, dir. *Xiyou ji* 西遊記 [*Journey to the West*]. Beijing: Ciwen Media Company, 2011.

Zhang Jinchi 張錦池. *Xiyouji kaolun* 西遊記考論. Harbin: Heilongjiang jiaoyu chubanshe, 2003.

ELEVEN

Real Monks Don't Have *Gṛhastha* Sex

Revisiting Male Celibacy in Classical South Asian Buddhism

AMY PARIS LANGENBERG

BUDDHISM IS FAMOUS for its celibate monks. The self-contained, sexually continent monk, shaven headed and immaculate in his gender-ambiguous robes, is iconic. Buddhist forms of religious professionalism that do not require long-term celibacy—Tibet's noncelibate practitioners, Japan's married priests, and Newar Buddhism's householder monks—are sometimes regarded as baroque exceptions to this ideal. The sexual practices included in Buddhist Tantra have been the subject of debate, confusion, and even judgment; some people have wondered how a tradition for which male celibacy is so definitional could end up embracing a yoga that centers the male heterosexual experience as a path, rather than an obstacle, to enlightenment. Even within the study of the classical Indian tradition, scholars have noted with curiosity depictions of monks, and the Buddha himself, as sexy, hypermasculine, and irresistible to women.[1] They have also pondered in surprise the obsessively detailed, almost pornographic, nature of rulings on sex in Buddhist Vinaya (disciplinary texts).[2]

Although the historically situated nature of all Buddhist traditions is part of the answer to why and how sexuality had been incorporated into elite institutions and practices in certain times and places, here I would like to unbundle and analyze not those examples that seem to diverge from expectations, but rather the expectations themselves.[3] In particular, I would like to reconsider the ideal of male celibacy in the classical Buddhist tradition, through the lens of the Vinaya, asking again: What is the sex that celibate monks are supposed to forgo, exactly? Are any sexual acts or emotions tolerated or overlooked in the Vinaya and why? What sort of masculine person is classical Buddhist celibacy meant to produce? Is there another normative masculinity to which classical Buddhist celibacy is—at least in part—a response?[4]

It may be helpful to pause and consider some of the terms employed here, especially *masculine, masculinity,* and *normative,* as they relate to the theoretical interventions of masculinity studies, an outgrowth of gender studies that explores the socially constructed dimensions and internally diverse nature of masculine identity and performance. Of particular relevance is "hegemonic masculinity": a concept associated with the work of Australian sociologist Raewyn Connell (also cited as R. W. Connell) that is built on the dual foundation of culturally constructed masculinity and Antonio Gramsci's Marxist notion of "hegemony." Connell's understanding centers the importance of normative masculinity for enacting men's dominance over women and implies a hierarchical ordering of superior and inferior masculinities, as well as women's consensual compliance to their subordination. Connell's explication of the idea does not assume that the majority of men actually realize the ideals of any given hegemonic masculinity; hegemonic masculinity is normative, but not statistically normal. According to Connell and coauthor James Messerschmidt, research from the 1980s showed that hegemonic masculinity "embodied the currently most honored way of being a man, it required all other men to position themselves in relation to it, and it ideologically legitimated the global subordination of women to men."[5] However, ongoing sociological and historical research also indicated that hegemonies were challenged, and that "older forms of masculinity might be displaced by new ones."[6]

This chapter maps two competing masculinities in relationship to one another: the classical Buddhist ideal of the male celibate found in Buddhist Vinaya texts and the roughly contemporaneous ideal of the married householder, or *gṛhastha,* found in elite Vedic Hindu religious texts. I make no specific argument about which masculinity—celibate monk or virtuous householder—was hegemonic and which a pretender in early India, nor do I make a detailed historical argument about their respective developments over time.[7] My evidence is primarily literary, and my primary point in making the comparison is to revisit Buddhist male celibacy in its classical form, teasing out dimensions that have not been previously emphasized while clarifying what is at stake in establishing such a norm as hegemonic within Buddhist society. Bringing in Connell's idea of hegemonic masculinity as a framework highlights the way Buddhist male celibacy can function as a method for achieving and maintaining male autonomy, mastery, and power vis-à-vis women, not merely or exclusively as a technique for spiritual mastery of the self. Moreover, understanding classical forms of Buddhist male celibacy to have been in the service of a potentially hegemonic Buddhist masculinity in competition with the non-Buddhist masculine ideal of the virtuous householder provides a background against which a more fundamental insight flashes forward—namely, that the pragmatic disciplining of the male Buddhist ascetic's sexuality found in Vinaya traditions is more a refusal of a certain kind of sex—householder sex—than a utopian attempt to eliminate sex and desire altogether.

"The Gold Standard for Sex"

Tracking the gradations of offense assigned to various sexual behaviors in the Pāli monks' (P. *bhikkhu*; Sk. *bhikṣu*) Vinaya, Janet Gyatso reached the conclusion that "the human female is considered the gold standard for sex," and that penetrative sex in the vagina of a woman constitutes the prototype for sexual behavior that results in defeat or expulsion (P., Sk. *pārājika*) for a Buddhist monk.[8] Penetrative sex that too closely mimics the prototypical heterosexual act proscribed by monastic discipline (i.e., sex to the depth of a sesame seed or deeper in any of three major orifices of animals, spirits, or humans of any gender) also constitutes a defeat. By contrast, masturbation, which, too, is fueled by craving and results in a pleasurable sexual response, is a lesser offense (though still relatively serious). In Buddhist monastic discipline, the halo of the forbidden penetrative heterosexual act is capacious, encompassing behaviors that structurally resemble the heterosexual act and behaviors leading up to it. Behaviors significantly outside of this halo—for instance, those in which a penis does not make contact with an orifice (and semen is not shed)—are deemed less serious departures from the ideal of sexual purity.

As Gyatso compactly notes, "Sex specifically for Buddhist monasticism, which is a specialized matter" is "not necessarily to be equated with the more general message on sex in, say, the *suttas* [Sk. *sūtras*]."[9] I will also bracket the sophisticated psychological analysis of desire and meditative technologies developed to counter lust found in classical South Asian Buddhism, as such concerns are arguably not primary in the Vinaya.[10] I follow Gyatso in treating Vinayas first and foremost as socially functioning documents, concentrating on how they constitute performative scripts for producing a certain normatively male-gendered person and promoting a certain structure for religious community.

I focus here on the social context of classical Buddhist male celibacy as envisioned in Buddhist discipline not because its soteriological dimensions are unimportant. They *are* important, as is clear from the list of Vinaya's ten benefits, which include karmic and spiritual rewards as well as protecting the unity and reputation of the community.[11] However, notwithstanding the innovative work of Janet Gyatso, Bernard Faure, and Gregory Schopen, I am convinced that the bulk of scholarly explanations of Buddhist male celibacy have relied too much on Buddhist soteriology and neglected to examine in detail the thick sociohistorical context of sex and celibacy in ancient South Asian religion.[12] They have also tended to lump male and female celibacy together, which, as I will explore, effaces some illuminating differences.[13] This overprivileging of male Buddhist celibacy's soteriological benefits is at least partially the product of an unexamined methodological lens that invites us to accept as true Orientalist stereotypes of the pure, dispassionate, disembodied Buddhist male celibate. A romanticized image of the Buddhist male celibate leaves us at a loss when the same tradition we assume holds the overcoming of sexual desire to be a central aim and dogma celebrates male elites' sexual charisma, makes room for them as practitioners of sexual yogas, supports their continuing emotional intimacy with their wives after ordination, and sacralizes their seduction of young novices.

According to Gyatso, Vinaya logic hinges on the physical facts of sex acts, not just the mental attitude accompanying them. Her explanation as to why this is so, and why the human female is "the gold standard for sex," centers on the social functionality of Buddhist discipline. She writes:

> The *vinaya* rules are the blueprint for the functioning of a special kind of community, a denatured home for the homeless defined by exceptional commitments to discipline and by renunciation of normal family and social life. Drawing on the ascetic urge that had long been percolating in Indic civilization, Buddhist monasticism circumscribed some activities in order to facilitate others. The

> growth of the meticulous and detailed legal system of the *vinaya* reflects a project by which forbidden activities were defined as precisely as possible so as, in turn, to define precisely who was a member of the community.[14]

Gyatso's functionalist analysis of the rules proscribing sex in the Pāli Vinaya is a starting point for my argument about male celibacy in Buddhist monasticism. In what follows, I build on Gyatso's basic thesis by reconsidering the role of desire and pleasure in determining the seriousness of sex acts, and by drawing on scholarship about Hindu legal traditions (Sk. *dharmaśāstra*) to better understand exactly what form of "family and social life" is renounced through Buddhist male celibacy. In particular, I will argue that the family and social life that is renounced through celibacy is normative—according to a certain historically specific Indic vision of householdership—but not "normal" in the sense of being a human universal of sexual intimacy or somehow belonging to a generic human sexuality. In fact, as I will document, some sexualities well known in the ancient South Asian world, as today, are only moderately regulated in the Vinaya.

As I read them, Vinaya rules upholding the Buddhist male celibate ideal do not represent the naive and simplistic hope that sexuality can be expunged from the monastic mind and body altogether. The collective wisdom represented by the Vinaya literature is humane and psychologically astute in its nuanced depictions of human love and lust. Vinaya lawmakers were also savvy about the ancient South Asian religious landscape in which they hoped their community would survive and thrive. I argue here that the ideal of Buddhist male celibacy as legislated in the Vinaya is not primarily a restrictive norm aimed at eliminating human desire in general. It is better described as a surgical strike on a particular Indic form of reproductive male sexuality, the best representative of which is the *gṛhastha* or twice-born householder.[15]

Distinguishing the Absence of Desire and Legal Celibacy

An understanding of what Cabezón refers to as "the theory that undergirds the law"— that is, the Buddhist soteriology that critiques sensual desire—is detectable in the Vinaya genre of Buddhist writing.[16] When a monk is set upon and raped or fellated by passing village women, for instance, his lack of mental commitment to and enjoyment of the act leads to his exoneration. Similarly, acts that would otherwise be completely innocuous are deemed offenses depending on whether the perpetrator's senses are inflamed or not.[17] I agree with Gyatso, however, that the legal and soteriological dimensions of Buddhist celibacy are distinguishable. In other words, the absence of desire or intention in the mindstream of a practitioner and the legally valid celibacy of a monk are not quite the same thing.

The best illustration of tensions between mental purity and legal celibacy happens to be the most famous Vinaya narrative of all: that of Sudinna, a monk who unwillingly sleeps with his wife at the request of his parents and thereby brings about the promulgation of the first *pārājika* rule ordaining celibacy (i.e., Pārājika I). Several themes are consistent across most or all sectarian versions of the story.[18] First, Sudinna has pure spiritual intentions and is satisfied with his life as a monk when he transgresses against the celibate ideal. In two versions, Sudinna is even forced to fast almost to the death in order to persuade his wealthy parents to finally allow him, their only son and heir, to go forth as a homeless ascetic.[19] After Sudinna lives for a time as a Buddhist mendicant, a famine brings him back to his hometown, where his family connections assure that he will still receive alms. Upon his return, his family attempts to persuade him to return to the various pleasures of householding. He repeatedly refuses and declares himself to be satisfied with his life as a *pravrajita* (one who has gone forth). In the Pāli text, he twice claims to be delighted (*abhirato*) with his life.[20] When his parents ask that he impregnate his wife, thus ensuring the continuity of the family lineage and preventing the family riches from reverting to the state, Sudinna acquiesces. Although he does not seek out sex with his wife, he does, in the end, plant his seed "thrice," according to most versions.[21] The Mūlasarvāstivāda text is anomalous in describing him as full of "lust and attachment" and "burning with sensual desire" when he looks again upon his perfumed and adorned fertile young bride.[22]

In these accounts, Sudinna is depicted as pure minded and devoted to celibacy. He hunger-strikes to gain permission from his unwilling parents to ordain. When he goes forth, he willingly leaves behind a happy life of affection, privilege, and wealth. Even after experiencing the realities of mendicancy and enduring a famine, he is still not tempted by the comforts of home. It is a sense of filial duty rather than simple lust that leads him to impregnate his wife. Why is Sudinna's narrative, which features a chaste rather than a lusty monk, deemed the foundational myth of the celibate ideal in Buddhist Vinaya? One answer could be that it is a pedagogy meant to illustrate why even disciplined Buddhist celibates must be on their guard against their sexuality. I favor a different explanation, which focuses more on the nature of the sex that Pārājika I is attempting to prohibit.

Vinaya Lawyers' Relative Indifference to Same-Sex Female Intimacy

The Sudinna story gives evidence of distinctions between legal celibacy and soteriological desirelessness in classical Indian Buddhism. Perhaps stronger evidence is given, however, by comparing the Vinaya's rulings on heterosexual sex to rulings on female-female relationships that are found in the nuns' (Sk. *bhikṣuṇī*) Vinayas. In brief, female-female intimacy between monastic women is not as strictly regulated as sex involving a penis. Indeed, texts regulating female intimacy provide a useful point of comparison with Vinaya rules for maintaining the male celibate ideal, as they seem to indicate that eliminating certain types of penetrative heterosexual acts are a higher Vinaya priority than stamping out sexual behaviors in the *saṅgha* (monastic community; Sk. *saṃgha*) in general. In the examples given here, I primarily reference the Pāli and Mahāsāṅghika-Lokottaravāda nuns' Vinayas, the two traditions extant in Indic languages.

In general, rules governing sexual behaviors for nuns are found in a different category of offense than the parallel rules for monks. For instance, nonpenetrative physical intimacy between a nun and a man is a *pārājika,* the most severe category of offense, but a *saṅghātiśeṣa,* the second most serious category, in the case of a monk and a woman.[23] Intentional emission of semen (i.e., masturbation to the point of ejaculation) is always a *saṅghātiśeṣa*-level offense for monks. In contrast, the Mahāsāṅghika-Lokottaravāda nuns' Vinaya categorizes masturbation by nuns using devices or water or root vegetables as a "grave offense" (Sk. *sthūlātyaya*) rather than a more serious *saṅghātiśeṣa*-level offense.[24] While passages in the nuns' Vinayas do appear to speak of nuns pleasuring one another, penetrative sex between two women (using fingers or a device such as a dildo or root vegetable) does not appear to count as a *pārājika*. Such an act is mentioned in passing only in two of the sectarian nuns' Vinayas that I know of and never does it fall into the most serious categories of offense.[25] In contrast, the monks' version of Pārājika I forbids penetrative sex in any of the three orifices with all genders, specifically mentioning men, women, intersex (P., Sk. *ubhatovyañjanaka*) and queer (P., Sk. *paṇḍaka*) genders.[26]

The Mahāsāṅghika-Lokottaravāda nuns' Vinaya tradition contains an interesting text that seems to speak to female monastic intimacy, if indirectly. This text from the *saṅghātiśeṣa* section of the Vinaya criticizes two nuns for "spending time together intimately mingled in body" and "mingled in speech."[27] Feeling that the two are guilty of concealing each others' faults, the other nuns criticize their relationship and living arrangement, eventually reporting them to the Buddha. The Buddha rules that two nuns shall not spend time together intimately concealing one another's faults.[28]

The language of "living together intimately" and "mingled in body" in the Sanskrit text is not explicit and direct, but it does suggest female same-sex intimacy, even more so because the Sanskrit words used to connote—if not denote—intimacy (*saṃsṛṣṭā* and *saṁsarga*) appear in the *Kāma sūtra* as terms for sexual intimacy.[29] The same language is used in a range of Vinaya contexts to refer to close relationships with inappropriate people (but not necessarily sexual ones in every case).[30] Another Vinaya narrative in which a young novice nun becomes pregnant from her relationship with a layman employs identical language to refer to an inappropriate sexual relationship.[31] Notably, this text, which is found in the *pācattika* section of the Mahāsāṅghika-Lokottaravāda nuns' Vinaya,[32] includes further commentary, seemingly as an afterthought, specifying that should two nuns live together intimately, spending time delighting in one another, they must be separated.[33] In the texts cited here, what is explicitly named and proscribed is female-female intimacy leading to collusion in concealing faults, not specific sexual acts between women.

In sum, in Buddhist Vinaya traditions the same-sex passions of women are dimly, briefly, and vaguely noted as compared to the extensive cataloging of male sex acts one finds in the monks' Pārājika I, and the similar cataloging of women's sexual acts with men or third-sexed individuals in the nuns' Pārājika I text.[34] They are also more lightly punished in the Vinaya compared to male homosexual or heterosexual sex or, one might say, penetrative sex involving a penis and semen.[35] Given the assumed centrality of the Buddhist critique of desire in all of its forms, and the remarkable amount of detail included in the monks' Pārājika I text, why would female sexuality not involving a penis be so indirectly referenced or lightly regulated in Buddhist disciplinary texts? It may have something to do with what we could characterize, using contemporary terminology, as a marginalization of female queerness in Buddhism combined with ignorance about modalities of female intimacy on the part of male monastic lawyers. Female-female intimacy *was* known, however, in ancient South Asia. For instance, Vātsyāyana's *Kāma sūtra* mentions women's sexual activities with one another in two places. Women of the harem are described as using dildos, bulbs, roots, and fruits to satisfy each other, and there is also mention of girls penetrating one another sexually prior to marriage.[36] A less reductive explanation is that while female-female sexual intimacy is discouraged, it is not the main target of Buddhist celibacy. As I will argue, the real object of Buddhist sexual prohibitions—the sexual behavior that Buddhist male celibacy (the Cadillac of Vinaya norms) is specifically designed to exclude—is the religiously endorsed heterosexuality practiced by the *gṛhastha*, or married "stay-at-home" (as opposed to homeless or medicant Buddhist) man of virtue. The fact that same-sex female intimacy, which does not involve a real penis or semen and does not resemble virtuous householder (*gṛhastha*) sex, is comparably of such little concern for Vinaya lawyers supports this claim.

Gṛhastha Sex

Research on Hindu legal (i.e., dharma) studies has highlighted the historical emergence of the *gṛhastha*, the householder upheld in the Hindu legal tradition as occupying the most important of the four stages of life and the linchpin of Brahmanical society. While the married man as sacrificer was important in earlier Vedic literature (1500–300 BCE), the *gṛhastha* as such did not yet exist. The term *gṛhastha* emerges as the preferred word for householder and as a concept embodying a particular religious ideal of holy householding only with the legal literature (*dharmasūtras* and *dharmaśāstras*; 300–100 BCE). According to Stephanie Jamison and Joel Brereton, the likely origin of the term *gṛhastha* is among the mendicant Buddhist and Jain orders, rather than the Vedic context.[37] For instance, it appears in three Aśokan Rock Edicts (third century BCE), where it refers not to an ordinary layperson, but to a stay-at-home holy person, usually forming an oppositional pair with the *pravrajita* ("gone-forth" ascetic). Though they occupy contrasting categories, *gṛhastha* and *pravrajita* are both religious men pursuing elevated spiritual aims in the Aśokan case. In later post-Aśokan Brahmanic legal literature, the *gṛhastha* appears as a similarly holy, not average or secular, person, one that upholds a well-articulated set of religious duties and is beholden to disciplinary norms, just like the ascetic. As Patrick Olivelle notes, therefore, most ordinary men living in (and after) Aśoka's times would have been householders "without being technically *gṛhasthas*."[38]

In Olivelle's description, authors of Hindu legal texts espoused "a *gṛhastha*-theology propounding the centrality of the married householder engaging in ritual and sexual activities and procreating children."[39] These proponents of Hinduism were, in the centuries before and just after the turn of the Common Era, in some competition with non-Hindu mendicant groups—notably, the Buddhists and Jains, from whom they seem to have appropriated the term *gṛhastha*. A central aim of the dharma corpus was to promote the *gṛhastha* as a stay-at-home counterpart to the wandering ascetic through the ritualization of everyday functions such as eating, excretion, dressing, sleeping, and sex. The *gṛhastha* was beholden to a demanding set of formal ritual obligations, purity laws, dietary restrictions and, importantly, regulations concerning sexuality that are likened to other forms of sexual purity (Sk. *brahmacarya*). Here, Olivelle quotes Yājñavalkya, one of the later (fourth–fifth century CE) authors of legal treatises, to that effect: "A woman's season consists of sixteen nights. During that period he should lie with her on even nights; *thus he remains a true celibate*."[40] Here, we see that sexual purity—or, as Olivelle glosses it, celibacy—is understood in terms of correct and circumscribed sex rather than no sex at all.

According to the dharma authors, the *gṛhastha* is religiously bound to have sex with his wife during her fertile period, or "season" (Sk. *ṛtu*). A woman's season begins with a bath four days following the conclusion of her monthly bleeding and continues for sixteen days total. According to Āpastamba, the earliest of the dharma authors, the *gṛhastha* should not have sex during the day, should only engage in sex wearing a special garment, should not continue to lie with his wife after the sex act is finished, and should bathe promptly after sex.[41] According to two later lawmakers, Manu and Yājñavalkya, a *gṛhastha* is to fulfill his sexual obligation by offering his seed into his wife's womb on the analogy of sacrificial ritual.[42] This ritualized sex is called "the placing of the embryo" (Sk. *garbhādhāna*). Baudhāyana cautions that a *gṛhastha* who fails to have sex with his wife for three years accrues the guilt of abortion. A *gṛhastha* that fails to have sex with his wife during even one fertile period causes his dead ancestors to "lie during that month in her menstrual discharge." This is also true for one who has sex with his wife outside of her season, or one who deposits his semen in a place other than her vagina.[43]

Aśvaghoṣa's (ca. second century CE) play *Of Sundarī and Nanda* (Sk. *Saundarananda*) depicts the passionate love between Nanda (the Buddha's half-brother) and his bride, Sundarī. What follows is a small representative sample of Aśvaghoṣa's depiction:

> The couple relished each other
> Blinded by inebriated lust,
> As if they had become the butt
> Of the god and goddess of love;
> As if they had become the nest
> Of Pleasure and Joy incarnate;
> As if they had become the bowl
> Of Thrill and Content incarnate.[44]

Olivelle states that the type of passionate marriage epitomized by Nanda and Sundarī "is at the very heart of Brahmanical world view: marriage, household life, and the mutual love and faithfulness of husband and wife to each other," and that their love for one another epitomizes "the very ideal of household life and conjugal love of Brahmanical theology."[45] By my reading of this passage, however, Nanda and Sundarī's lovemaking resembles not the ritualized and disciplined sex of the *gṛhastha* with his wife as described by the dharma authors, but something closer to the worldly pleasure-seeking of the "man-about-town" (Sk. *nāgaraka*) and his paramour that is the *Kāma sūtra*'s focus. Though dharma texts do note that the *gṛhastha* should have sex with his wife when she requests it and not just when he initiates, the conjugal life prescribed as normative and desirable by the *brahman* authors of the dharma texts is, by and large, focused on the goal of impregnation, not female pleasure, and appears in moments even to discourage any expression of emotional intimacy, reciprocity, or playfulness. This is why it is hard to entirely agree with Olivelle's statement that *gṛhastha* sex is "diametrically opposed to the ideal of celibate asceticism."[46] It may be opposed in the sense of being "stay-at-home" (*gṛhastha*) rather than "wandering forth" (*pravrajita*), but it resembles asceticism in its attention to discipline, obedience to norms, concern for purity, and ritualization of ordinary life functions, including sex.

As indicated by Aśoka's rock edicts, the concept of the *gṛhastha* as holy householder was acknowledged outside of orthodox *brahman* circles. Recent scholarship on the term shows that *gṛhastha* was used variously outside of *dharmaśāstric* contexts. The classical *Treatise on Statecraft* (Sk. *Arthaśāstra*), which Mark McClish argues "was redacted by an editor congenial to the authority of [Brahman] sacred writ" (i.e., the Triple Veda and dharma treatises), epitomizes the individual duty of the *gṛhastha* as "matrimony with equals of a different lineage, having sex with his wife in her season, worship of the gods, ancestors, and guests, generosity to servants, and eating the remainder."[47] According to McClish's research, the classical Indian work on erotics, the *Kāma sūtra,* also knows the *gṛhastha* but emphasizes the material rather than the ritual dimensions of householding. This is the case even though its author, Vātsyāyana, pays lip service to the Brahmanical ideologies of caste (Sk. *varṇa*) and stations of life (Sk. *āśrama*). Vātsyāyana describes householdership for the man-about-town (the *Kāma sūtra*'s intended audience):

> When his education is complete, a man should become a householder [*gārhasthyam adhigamya*] by means of wealth obtained as a gift, through conquest, through purchase, or wages, or obtained from his family, or both, and he should follow the conduct of a man-about-town. His abode is in the company of good people, whether in a city, or town, or large market-town, or where his livelihood may allow. There he should establish his residence near water, with an orchard, apportioned into areas for different activities, and provided with two bedchambers.[48]

Notably, instead of mentioning the domestic fire or marriage, Vātsyāyana describes an ideal setup for throwing parties. In McClish's words, "For Vātsyāyana, being a *gṛhastha* means having one's own dwelling, an independent social life, and access to sex."[49] McClish notes Vātsyāyana's failure to "fully reconcile the differences between" the man-about-town and the *gṛhastha* models, despite his attempts to align his treatise with Brahmanical social ideologies.[50] As far as sexual practices are concerned, the two models are far apart, indeed.

Real Monks Don't Have *Gṛhastha* Sex

The earliest strata of Pāli *suttas* know a figure called the *gahaṭṭha* (Pāli for *gṛhastha*), who is often contrasted, as in the Aśokan edicts, with the ascetic who wanders forth.[51] However, because these first Pāli references originated several centuries earlier, they are unlikely to be directly engaging the Brahmanic ideal of the holy householder as he comes into view in the dharma literature in the last several centuries BCE. Vinaya references to the *gṛhastha/gahaṭṭha* are generic and, like the Aśokan rock edicts, do the work mainly of pairing him with the *pravrajita*.

The Vinaya (which developed more or less in tandem with the early dharma texts) does reference a type of ritualized sex somewhat similar to the religiously obligatory sex practiced by the *gṛhastha*. The Pāli term *aggadāna* (literally, "foremost gift") is used a number of times when laywomen offer their bodies as charity (P., Sk. *dāna*), whether in response to monks' encouragement or of their own accord. Of course, monks' receptivity to *aggadāna* is considered to be an offense against the discipline.[52] One of the Pāli Vinaya texts in which a monk requests the foremost gift is preceded directly by another small text in which a monk accuses a laywoman of not giving him what she gives her husband—that is, sexual intercourse (P. *methuna*). The juxtaposition of these two texts suggests a parallelism between married sex and *aggadāna*.[53] It is possible that *aggadāna* is a vernacular reference to contemporaneous understandings in *brahman* circles that correct married sex is akin to a religious offering.

Although the Vinaya does not appear to directly mention *gṛhastha* sex, I argue that the Buddhist monastic rule of celibacy targets *brahman gṛhastha* sex for two reasons. First, Sudinna, whose story is the origin tale of Pārājika I, clearly has *gṛhastha* sex with his wife in that he performs his ritual duty as her husband by depositing his semen in her womb during her fertile period. Only the Mūlasarvāstivāda version of this story mentions that any passion or lust is involved, and even then only at the last minute, when Sudinna beholds her anointed with oils and perfumes in her bridal finery. In all other versions, he performs his sexual role purely out of a sense of duty to lineage, parents, and, presumably, his wife (though of course he must have felt something like physical desire to carry out the task three times). In Pārājika I, Sudinna's performance of the prototypical duty of a *gṛhastha* is the very definition of what it is to be "defeated," or no longer a monk.

Second, the sort of sex that is most severely punished in Pārājika I of the monks' Vinaya is penetrative sex involving the monk's penis and a woman's vagina, or anything close enough to that type of sex to spook the Vinaya lawyers. All of the sectarian Vinayas follow the same pattern. For example, the Sarvāstivāda Vinaya states that any fully ordained monk who "perform[s] the act of sexual intercourse with any one, down even to an animal," has committed a *pārājika* offense.[54] The canonical commentary of the Pāli Vinaya further elaborates that intercourse refers to penetration of the male organ into the female organ even to the length of a sesame seed, and even further that all genders, all orifices, and all orders of being are forbidden.[55] Cabezón observes that, in the later Mūlasarvāstivāda commentarial tradition, the feeling of physical contact (distinguishable from intentionality or a mind of desire) is mentioned as an important feature of a sex act leading to defeat.[56] He avers, "Although the breaking of the vow requires that the monk experience pleasure, it does not require orgasm."[57] In any case, the emphasis on penetration and a tight enough fit (so to speak) between the male organ and orifice, resulting in the pleasurable sensation of contact, resembles very closely what is required for reproductively fruitful heterosexual sex.

By taking *gṛhastha* sex as the prototype for Vinaya prohibitions on sex, some of the more eccentric passages for which the Vinaya is so famous start to make sense. For instance, the Pāli Vinaya rules that a monk suffers defeat for inserting his male organ in the female organ of a rotting corpse, but not for collecting the bones of a woman, reconstructing her, and then having sex with her. Similarly, a monk suffers defeat from having sex with the mouth of a decapitated head only if his penis makes contact with sides, palate, and roof of the mouth.[58] Having sex with a plaster figure or wooden doll is a lesser offense in the Pāli Vinaya.[59] Does the lack of fleshiness common to the skeleton, plaster figure, and wooden doll make having sex with them less egregious from the perspective of the Vinaya lawyers? This reading is borne out in a remarkable passage from Buddhaghoṣa's (fl. ca. 370–450 CE) important Vinaya commentary, which analyzes the disciplinary consequences of having sex with corpses in various stages of decay in greater detail. While having sex with a rotting corpse whose female organ is up to fifty percent intact results in defeat, Buddhaghoṣa notes that "if one practices a sexual act on a piece of flesh that is separated from a dead body by a dog, then one becomes guilty of a *dukkaṭa* [wrongdoing]" (a general category of minor bad behaviors).[60] A similar logic holds in the particularly confounding case of the monk who inserts his thumb in the sexual organ of a young girl, who subsequently dies as a result of this abuse. Nonetheless, the monk's transgression is deemed a serious (P. *saṅghādisesa*) offense, but not a "defeat." Again, from a Pārājika I perspective, the sexual behavior of this monk does not involve penetration with his penis and is therefore considered mere sensual touching, making it a somewhat less serious offense despite the fact that he does penetrate her vagina, and despite the harm done to the child.[61] It could be argued that the logic in all of these cases hinges on how closely the monk's experience of sex resembles heterosexual penetrative sex with a woman.

As Gyatso perceptively notes, "partner parity" goes away when the Vinaya legislates actions that potentially lead to but are not themselves penetrative sex.[62] In other words, acts that potentially lead to *gṛhastha* sex, or reproductive heterosexual sex with a woman, are more serious transgressions than acts that might be precursors to other sorts of sex. Caressing a woman with a mind of desire, then, is a more serious transgression than caressing a man, a third-sex individual, or an animal. The Pāli *Vinaya* titrates situations even further. If a monk caresses a woman but is not sure she is a woman or believes her to be a man or a third-sex individual, or an animal, he commits a grave offense. If, however, he caresses a man, even if he believes him to be a woman, he commits only a wrong-doing.[63] In other words, actual physical contact combined with lust for a woman is worse than physical contact with a woman without female-directed lust, which is in turn worse than physical contact with a man, even if a monk desires him as he would a woman. In the legal literature, the physical parameters of sexual behaviors, and more specifically questions about whether they fall within the orbit of *gṛhastha* sex, are of greater consequence than their affective dimensions.

* * *

In summary, heterosexual sex with a woman and anything resembling or leading up to it is of great concern for monastic lawyers. Penetrative sex acts involving a penis, penetration, pleasurable sensation resulting from physical contact, and an impassioned mind are disciplined to the highest degree. Pleasurable physical contact without penetration is disciplined at various levels depending on the gender or species of the partner and the intentionality of the monk. Sexual intimacy between two women, which involves neither a real penis nor pleasure resulting potentially in the ejaculation of semen—nor heterosexual desire as such—is more vaguely referenced and punished less severely.

While we are used to paying attention to the hierarchical distinction made between laypeople and monastics in Buddhist sources, we may have missed the significance of a more subtle distinction between the *gṛhastha* and the *pravrajita* that scholars of classical Hinduism have recently brought to the fore. Given the disagreements and competing claims of Vedic Brahmanical religion, as epitomized in the dharma literature and the epics, and mendicant religions such as Buddhism and Jainism, it would not be surprising if monastic lawyers wished to find some basis for a distinction between the asceticism of the stay-at-home and the asceticism of the wanderer. The stay-at-home ascetic ideal was one that valorized self-mastery and the purification of daily living; the Buddhist *pravrajita* could not claim superiority on those counts. His celibacy, a refusal of exactly the sort of reproductive sex held to be ritually obligatory for the *gṛhastha*, earned him distinction, however. Understanding Pārājika I to script a strategic ritualized rejection of the type of reproductive heterosexual penetrative sex valorized in dharma treatises, not merely or exclusively a generalized disciplining of human sexual desire, makes all the more sense given an Indic Buddhist lifeway that rejects the tawdriness of embodied existence (*saṃsāra*) with all of its womb-based reproductive messiness.[64]

According to the Vinaya tradition, then, a real monk is a man of virtue who doesn't participate in the reproductively oriented, penetrative, sacralized sex of the *gṛhastha*. He never deposits his semen into the womb of a woman. His chaste masculinity, which allows him to retain his seed, is defined in the Vinaya primarily against the disciplined manliness of the Vedic-Hindu stay-at-home ascetic, not against the libertine man-about-town described in the *Kāma sūtra*. The female celibate is a marginal person in this Vinaya social project. Her same-sex (and autoerotic) transgressions seem not seriously to disrupt the structural integrity of discipline as far as monastic lawyers are concerned and therefore need not be extensively cataloged or fiercely policed.

It is certainly the case, as Gyatso suggests, that heterosexual intercourse with a woman threatens Buddhist monastic communities because it could result in the birth of children, although unwanted pregnancies are typically problems assigned to women. Here I argue that it is also problematic because this is the sort of reproductive sex that virtuous householders are required to have. To understand themselves as special religious men distinct and better than *gṛhasthas*, Buddhist monks must clearly differentiate their own form of celibacy from *gṛhastha* celibacy. To put it differently—and taking up again the theoretical language of masculinity studies—the authors of classical Buddhist male celibacy establish a competing masculine hegemony, one that upholds many shared cultural norms, such as purity and ascetic restraint, but establishes dominance over women through segregation and strict hierarchy rather than cooption of their reproductive powers and a messier, closer in, more ongoing maintenance of male superiority.[65]

Providing evidence that Buddhist and Brahmanical celibate ideals—*bhikṣu* and *gṛhastha*—existed as competing variations on early Indic hegemonic masculinity is background to a more pointed insight about Buddhist male celibacy. Here, I argue that male celibacy as scripted in Buddhist disciplinary texts is strategic, fundamentally targeting male participation in reproductive heterosexual sex, not sexual desire in general. It is almost as if the Vinaya lawyers, whose extensive knowledge of human sexuality is well evidenced by the thicket of rules and addendums that is Pārājika I, realized that the broader landscape of human love and lust—queer, fetishistic, autoerotic, fantasy-based, nonreproductive, romantic, postmenopausal, extramarital, nonejaculatory, polyamorous, promiscuous—is simply too vast, too subtle, and too varied to ever be completely contained by the net of Buddhist discipline. As the diverse history of sexual practices and social arrangements in Buddhist societies shows, they were right.

NOTES

1. John Powers, *A Bull of a Man: Images of Masculinity, Sex, and the Body in Indian Buddhism* (Cambridge, Mass.: Harvard University Press, 2009).
2. Janet Gyatso, "Sex," in *Critical Terms for the Study of Buddhism*, ed. Donald S. Lopez Jr. (Chicago: University of Chicago Press, 2005), 276–77; I. B. Horner, ed. and trans. *The Book of the Discipline [Vinaya-piṭaka]* (Bristol: Pali Text Society, [1938–1966]1993–2014), 1:xxi; L. P. N. Perera, "Sexuality in Ancient India: A Study Based on the Pali Vinayapitaka" (PhD diss., University of Kelaniya, Sri Lanka, 1993), 90–93.
3. For a general overview, see Amy Paris Langenberg, "Sex and Sexuality in Buddhism: A Tetralemma," *Religion Compass* 9, no. 9 (2015): 277–86. For further references on sexuality and sexual practices in Buddhism, see Amy Paris Langenberg, "Buddhism and Sexuality," Oxford Bibliographies Online, https://www

.oxfordbibliographies.com/display/document/obo-9780195393521/obo-9780195393521-0244.xml (accessed December 5, 2022).

4. In asking these questions, I am building on—but also contributing a new idea to—work on Buddhist celibate masculinity by José Cabezón, Janet Gyatso, and John Powers.
5. Raewyn Connell and James W. Messerschmidt, "Hegemonic Masculinity: Rethinking the Concept," *Gender & Society* 19, no. 6 (2005): 829–59, 832.
6. Connell and Messerschmidt, "Hegemonic Masculinity," 833.
7. There are multiple Vinaya traditions, each likely regional, and the period of their respective aggregation was likely centuries. The *gṛhastha* ideal was codified in Brahmanical legal texts, which were also multiple, regional, and compiled over centuries. The arguments put forward here are based mostly on internal literary evidence set against a background claim that elite classical Hindu legal texts (*dharmasūtra* and *dharmaśāstra*) and Vinaya are loosely contemporaneous traditions originating in various regions of North India, and that both Buddhists and Vedic Hindus were defining religious ideals of masculinity in terms of householdership during more or less the same span of time.
8. Gyatso, "Sex," 280.
9. Gyatso, 274.
10. Horner, *Book of the Discipline*, 1:ix.
11. These ten are found at the end of the commentary on the first *pārājika* in the Pāli Vinaya. See Horner, *Book of the Discipline*, 1:37–38. For a discussion of the ten benefits of Vinaya, see also José Ignacio Cabezón, *Sexuality in Classical South Asian Buddhism* (Somerville, Mass.: Wisdom, 2017), 199.
12. Perera, "Sexuality in Ancient India," is an exception in his sensitivity to the sociocultural context of Buddhist Vinaya. Cabezón has criticized how Gyatso, Powers, and Faure "create a dichotomy between the moral/ethical/soteriological views of the Vinaya (favored by the Buddhist tradition) and their own social/functionalist/pragmatic interpretations"; he does admit, however, that "the Vinaya *itself* does go to great lengths to explain its role in the Buddhist soteriological project . . . this corpus is not concerned with the theory that undergirds the laws. But that does not mean that such a theory does not exist, that it is not presumed, and that it is not treated elsewhere in Buddhist sources" (*Sexuality*, 198). My bracketing of soteriological concerns does not constitute a theoretical position on interpreting the Vinaya, but is merely a heuristic to facilitate drilling down into the question of what sort of masculine man a celibate Buddhist monk is meant to be.
13. Cabezón is an exception; see 189–93. Derrett also makes useful distinctions between male and female rules. See J. D[uncan] M. Derrett, "Monastic Masturbation in Pāli Buddhist Texts," *Journal of the History of Sexuality* 15, no. 1 (2006): 1–13.
14. Gyatso, "Sex," 287.
15. This is an ideal that comes to be articulated in Brahmanic circles more or less simultaneously to the development of the sectarian Vinayas in ancient South Asia. Different Buddhist sects follow different Vinaya: those of the Theravādins,

Mahāsāṅghikas, Mahāsāṅghika-lokottaravādins, Mahīśāsakas, Dharmaguptakas, Sarvāstivādins, and Mūlasarvāstivādins. Today Theravāda Buddhists follow the Theravāda Vinaya; Mahāyāna Buddhists follow the Dharmagupta Vinaya; and Vajrayāna Buddhists follow the Mūlasarvāstivāda Vinaya. See Klaus Pinte, "Vinaya," Oxford Bibliographies Online, https://www.oxfordbibliographies.com/display/document/obo-9780195393521/obo-9780195393521-0244.xml (accessed December 5, 2022).

16. Cabezón, *Sexuality*, 198.
17. Gyatso, "Sex," 282.
18. All of the sectarian Vinayas contain a version of the Sudinna narrative, and, as Anālayo argues, considering them together allows for a fuller picture of the early communities' approach to sexual restraint. For a translation of the Mahāsāṅghika, Mahīśāsaka, and Mūlasarvāstivāda versions, see Anālayo, "Sudinna (Pār 1)," in *Vinaya Studies* (Taipei: Dharma Drum, 2017). For an English translation of the Dharmaguptaka version and a comparison with the Pāli (Theravāda) version, see P. Pradhan, "The First Pārājika of the Dharmaguptaka-Vinaya and the Pali Suttavibhaṅgha," *Visva-Bharati Annals* 1 (1945): 1–34. For another translation of the Mūlasarvāstivāda version, see Giuliana Martini, "The Story of Sudinna in the Tibetan Translation of the Mūlasarvāstivāda Vinaya," *Journal of Buddhist Ethics* 19 (2012): 439–50. The Pāli text is translated, of course, in Horner, *Book of the Discipline*.
19. Mahīśāsaka and Theravāda sectarian Vinayas. See Anālayo, "Sudinna," 39–46.
20. Vin. iii.17; Vin. iii.18.
21. The *Mahāsāṅghika* version does not mention this. See Anālayo, "Sudinna," 38.
22. Anālayo, 52.
23. *Saṅghātiśeṣa* (in Sanskrit, *saṅghādisesa* in Pāli) is the category of offenses requiring temporary penance.
24. These rules are found in the "miscellanies" (*prakīrṇaka*) section of this nuns' Vinaya. Gustav Roth, ed., *Bhikṣuṇī-Vinaya Including Bhikṣuṇī-Prakīrṇaka and a Summary of the Bhikṣu-Prakīrṇaka of the Ārya-Mahāsāṃghika-lokottaravādin* (Patna: K. P. Jayaswal Research Institute, 1970), 306–11. For an English translation of the Chinese, see Akira Hirakawa, trans., *Monastic Discipline for the Buddhist Nuns: An English Translation of the Chinese Text of the Mahāsāṃghika-Bhikṣuṇī-Vinaya* (Patna: Kashi Prasad Jayaswal Research Institute, 1982), 392–94, 396–98. The Pāli rules can be found at Horner, *Book of the Discipline*, 3:248–51. Vinaya traditions also include rules against nuns being rubbed and massaged by laywomen, nuns, novice nuns, and so forth, except in case of illness (see, e.g., Hirakawa, *Monastic Discipline*, 347–51) or rules about nuns sharing a bed or a coverlet (Horner, *Book of the Discipline*, 3:304; Perera, "Sexuality in Ancient India," 204).
25. Roth, *Bhikṣuṇī-Vinaya*, 77, 304–5; Hirakawa, *Monastic Discipline*, 104; Ann Heirman, *Rules for Nuns According to the Dharmaguptakavinaya* (Delhi: Motilal Banarsidass, 2002), 2:597; Cabezón, *Sexuality*, 329n840.
26. Horner, *Book of the Discipline*, 3:248.
27. Roth, *Bhikṣuṇī-Vinaya*, 155–56.

28. While the Sanskrit text does not actually make it explicit that the two nuns are intimate with one another, the Chinese translation of the same Vinaya does give some more detailed information regarding the nature of their relationship. To be "mingled in body" means to sleep together on a bed, to sit together on a bed, to eat from the same bowl, to put on each other's robes, and to go in and out together. To be "mingled in speech" means to speak with a defiled mind. Hirakawa, *Monastic Discipline*, 176. The Pāli and Dharmaguptaka versions of this rule seemingly displace the emphasis from any suggestion of intimacy to the problem of collusion in other forms of nonvirtuous behavior. Horner, *Book of the Discipline*, 3:207; Heirman, *Rules for Nuns*, 2:365.
29. Both words are from *saṃ sṛj*: to be joined, united, mingled, or confused, come into contact with, meet (as friends or foes, also applied to sexual intercourse). The *Kāma sūtra* uses *saṃsṛṣṭa* at one point specifically with reference to a young girl's intimate relationship with a nun (1.3.14); in other places, *saṃsṛṣṭa* denotes sexual intimacy (1.5.8, 1.5.8, 1.5.16, 2.8.29) or close association that is not necessarily sexual. Horner, *Book of the Discipline*, 3: 207n1). The *Kāma sūtra* uses *saṃsarga* for kissing (2.8.6), oral sex (2.9.26), "close contact with loose women" (5.6.45), sexual intercourse (6.4.32), and associating with a man (6.5.33). See also Wendy Doniger and Sudhir Kakar, trans., *Kamasutra*, by Vātsyāyana (New York: Oxford University Press, 2002), 130. For *Kāma sūtra* references, see Göttingen Register of Electronic Texts in Indian Languages (GRETIL), "Vatsyayana, Kamasutram," accessed July 29, 2019, http://gretil.sub.uni-goettingen.de/gretil/1_sanskr/6_sastra/6_kama/kamasutu.htm.
30. Horner, *Book of the Discipline*, 3:207n1.
31. Roth, *Bhikṣuṇī-Vinaya*, 225–26.
32. This section includes lesser offenses entailing only atonement.
33. Roth, *Bhikṣuṇī-Vinaya*, 225.
34. Derrett also notes that "the *Vinaya* is not specifically interested in sexual relations between women in nunneries ("Monastic Masturbation," 5). Cabezón observes that, "for a nun (a woman), sex is not *real* sex unless it is with a biological male" (*Sexuality*, 329).
35. Cabezón writes, "What makes penetrative sex weightiest is the fact that it represents a devolution of the monk to the life of the phallus—a life devoted to dominance and conquest in the service of phallic pleasure—precisely the life that monks are supposed to have left behind" (331). However, I agree more with Gyatso's position ("Sex," 280) that the issue of sex as reproductive vs. non-reproductive looms large.
36. *Kāma sūtra*, 5.6.2–4; 7.1.20. The text implies that these women are compensating for inadequate male attention, not acting on same-sex sexual preferences.
37. Stephanie W. Jamison, "The Term *Gṛhastha* and the (Pre)history of the Householder," in *Gṛhastha: The Householder in Ancient Indian Religious Culture*, ed. Patrick Olivelle (Oxford: Oxford University Press, 2019), 3–19; Joel P. Brereton, "*Pāṣaṇḍa*: Religious Communities in the Aśokan Inscriptions and Early Literature," in *Gṛhastha: The Householder in Ancient Indian Religious Culture*, ed. Patrick Olivelle (Oxford: Oxford University Press, 2019), 20–57.

38. Patrick Olivelle, "*Gṛhastha, Āśrama*, and the Origin of Dharmaśāstra," in *Gṛhastha: The Householder in Ancient Indian Religious Culture*, ed. Patrick Olivelle (Oxford: Oxford University Press, 2019), 112.
39. Olivelle, "*Gṛhastha*," 110.
40. Olivelle, "*Gṛhastha*," 113 (emphasis added). This idea is also present in epic literature. See Johann Jakob Meyer, *Sexual Life in Ancient India* (New York: Dorset, 1930), 218 for references.
41. 2.1.16–23, text and translation in Patrick Olivelle, ed., *Dharmasūtras: The Law Codes of Āpastamba, Gautama, Baudhāyana, and Vasiṣṭha* (Delhi: Motilal Banarsidass, 2000).
42. *Bṛhadāraṇyaka Upaniṣad* 6.4.3, text and translation in Patrick Olivelle, ed. and trans., *The Early Upaniṣads: Annotated Text and Translation* (New York: Oxford University Press, 1998), *Manusmṛti* 3.46–47, in Patrick Olivelle, ed., *Manu's Code of Law: A Critical Edition and Translation of the Mānava-Dharmaśāstra* (Oxford: Oxford University Press, 2005); Yājñavalkya 1.76, in Olivelle, "*Gṛhastha*."
43. 4.1.17–19, text and translation in Olivelle, *Dharmasūtras*.
44. Patrick Olivelle, "Aśvhaghoṣa's Apologia: Brahmanical Ideology and Female Allure," *Journal of Indian Philosophy* 49 (2019): 257–68, 264.
45. Olivelle, "Aśvaghoṣa's Apologia," 266.
46. Olivelle, 262. Aśvaghoṣa is known to be a Buddhist poet. Since the *Saundrananda* tells the story of Nanda's transformation from sexually besotted, lovesick husband to celibate monk, it makes sense to assume that his relationship with Sundarī would be the foil for monastic discipline and therefore work against my overall argument that monastic celibacy is opposed to *gṛhastha* sex, not sex in general in the Vinaya. In response to this point, I argue that Aśvaghoṣa's play is centered on the soteriological concerns of the *suttas/sūtras* rather than the social/legal concerns of the Vinaya.
47. Mark McClish, "Householders, Holy or Otherwise, in the *Nīti* and *Kāma* Literature," in *Gṛhastha: The Householder in Ancient Indian Religious Culture*, ed. Patrick Olivelle (Oxford: Oxford University Press, 2019), 151, 153. In his editing and arranging of the text on the page, Olivelle does not include what he labels the "rules of sexual intercourse" as a ritual duty of the *gṛhastha*, but rather includes them under the heading "Marriage." He makes these editing choices even though the "rules of sexual intercourse" are included at the start of the chapter listing the *gṛhastha's* other ritual duties. This seems to be consonant with Olivelle's interpretation of *gṛhastha* sex as suffused by conjugal loyalty and felicity rather than a ritual duty consisting in a nonreciprocal sacrificial depositing of the male seed, aimed at reproduction, not intimacy. Olivelle, *Dharmasūtras*, 131.
48. McClish, "Householders," 167.
49. McClish, 168.
50. McClish, 169.
51. Oliver Freiberger, "*Gṛhastha* in the Śramaṇic Discourse: A Lexical Survey of House Residents in Early Pāli Texts," in *Gṛhastha: The Householder in Ancient Indian Religious Culture*, ed. Patrick Olivelle (Oxford: Oxford University Press, 2019), 58–74.
52. The texts in which lay women offer themselves to monks as *aggadāna* are at Vin. iii.39; translation in Horner, *Book of the Discipline*, 1:61.

53. Vin iii.131; Horner, 1:220. In another series of three texts, a monk requests *aggadāna* from laywomen who ask for advice about becoming pregnant, and another who wishes to be better loved by her husband. Vin iii.123; Horner, 1:226–27.
54. W. Pachow, *A Comparative Study of the Prātimokṣa on the Basis of Its Chinese, Tibetan, Sanskrit, and Pāli Versions*, rev. ed. (Delhi: Motilal Banarsidass, [1955] 2000), 71. Compare with Charles S. Prebish, *Buddhist Monastic Discipline: The Sanskrit Prātimokṣa Sūtras of the Mahāsāṃghikas and Mūlasarvāstivādins* (Delhi: Motilal Banarsidass, 1996), 50–51.
55. Vin. iii, 28; Horner, *Book of the Discipline*, 1:47–48.
56. Cabezón, *Sexuality*, 186.
57. Cabezón, 188.
58. The issue of the level of contact between the monk's penis and the mouth of the severed head is specifically elaborated on in Buddhaghosa's Vinaya commentary. Petra Kieffer-Pülz, "Pārājika I and Sanghādisesa I: Hitherto Untranslated Passages from the Vinayapiṭaka of the Theravādins," in *The Book of Discipline (Vinaya-piṭaka)*, ed. I. B. Horner (Bristol: Pali Text Society, 2014), 357n1.
59. Kieffer-Pülz, "Pārājika I," 355–57.
60. P. V. Bapat and A[kira] Hirakawa, trans., *Shan-chien-P'i-P'o-Sha: A Chinese Version by Saṅghabhadra of Samantapāsādikā* (Poona: Bhandarkar Oriental Institute, 1970), 201.
61. Though it does not make things all that much clearer, Buddhaghosa's Vinaya commentary explains that it is the fact that the monk is aroused by physical touching (*kāyasaggarāgena*) that categorizes this act as a saṅgādisesa-level offense. Kieffer-Pülz, "Pārājika I," 354n4.
62. Gyatso, "Sex," 280.
63. Horner, *Book of the Discipline*, 1:204–5.
64. Amy Paris Langenberg, *Birth in Buddhism: The Suffering Fetus and Female Freedom* (Abingdon-on-Thames: Routledge, 2017).
65. Such willingness to make contact with female impurity in order to achieve certain coveted outcomes such as the birth of sons is what Mary Douglas refers to as a "composting" approach to ritual dirt. For a discussion of how Douglas's notion applies to the classical Indic context, see Amy Paris Langenberg, "Buddhist Blood Taboo: Mary Douglas, Female Impurity, and Classical Indian Buddhism," *Journal of the American Academy of Religion* 84, no. 1 (2016): 157–91.

Additional Primary Sources

Bhikkhu Brahmali, trans. *Theravāda Collection on Monastic Law: A Translation of the Pali Vinaya Piṭaka Into English*. SuttaCentral, 2021. https://suttacentral.net/vinaya (accessed December 5, 2022).

Doniger, Wendy, and Sudhir Kakar, trans. *Kamasutra*. By Vātsyāyana. New York: Oxford University Press, 2002.

Hirakawa, Akira, trans. *Monastic Discipline for the Buddhist Nuns: An English Translation of the Chinese Text of the Mahāsāṃghika-Bhikṣuṇī-Vinaya*. Patna: Kashi Prasad Jayaswal Research Institute, 1982.

Kieffer-Pülz, Petra, trans. "Pārājika I and Sanghādisesa I: Hitherto Untranslated Passages from the Vinayapiṭaka of the Theravādins." In *The Book of Discipline (Vinayapiṭaka)*, edited by I. B. Horner, 1:349–72. Bristol: Pali Text Society, 2014.

Olivelle, Patrick, ed. and trans. *Dharmasūtras: The Law Codes of Āpastamba, Gautama, Baudhāyana, and Vasiṣṭha*. Delhi: Motilal Banarsidass, 2000.

——. *The Early Upaniṣads: Annotated Text and Translation*. New York: Oxford University Press, 1998.

——. *Manu's Code of Law: A Critical Edition and Translation of the Mānava-Dharmaśāstra*. Oxford: Oxford University Press, 2005.

Bibliography

Anālayo. "Sudinna (Pār 1)." In *Vinaya Studies*, 35–68. Taipei: Dharma Drum, 2017.

Bapat, P. V., and A[kira] Hirakawa, trans. *Shan-chien-P'i-P'o-Sha: A Chinese Version by Saṅghabhadra of Samantapāsādikā*. Poona: Bhandarkar Oriental Institute, 1970.

Brereton, Joel P. "*Pāṣaṇḍa*: Religious Communities in the Aśokan Inscriptions and Early Literature." In *Gṛhastha: The Householder in Ancient Indian Religious Culture*, edited by Patrick Olivelle, 20–57. Oxford: Oxford University Press, 2019.

Cabezón, José Ignacio. *Sexuality in Classical South Asian Buddhism*. Somerville, Mass.: Wisdom, 2017.

Connell, Raewyn, and James W. Messerschmidt. "Hegemonic Masculinity: Rethinking the Concept." *Gender & Society* 19, no. 6 (2005): 829–59.

Derrett, J. D[uncan] M. "Monastic Masturbation in Pāli Buddhist Texts." *Journal of the History of Sexuality* 15, no. 1 (2006): 1–13.

Doniger, Wendy, and Sudhir Kakar, trans. *Kamasutra*. By Vātsyāyana. New York: Oxford University Press, 2002.

Freiberger, Oliver. "*Gṛhastha* in the Śramaṇic Discourse: A Lexical Survey of House Residents in Early Pāli Texts." In *Gṛhastha: The Householder in Ancient Indian Religious Culture*, edited by Patrick Olivelle, 58–74. Oxford: Oxford University Press, 2019.

Göttingen Register of Electronic Texts in Indian Languages (GRETIL). "Vatsyayana, Kamasutram." Accessed July 29, 2019. http://gretil.sub.uni-goettingen.de/gretil/1_sanskr/6_sastra/6_kama/kamasutu.htm.

Gyatso, Janet. "Sex." In *Critical Terms for the Study of Buddhism*, edited by Donald S. Lopez Jr., 271–90. Chicago: University of Chicago Press, 2005.

Heirman, Ann. *Rules for Nuns According to the Dharmaguptakavinaya*. 3 vols. Delhi: Motilal Banarsidass, 2002.

Hirakawa, Akira, trans. *Monastic Discipline for the Buddhist Nuns: An English Translation of the Chinese Text of the Mahāsāṃghika-Bhikṣuṇī-Vinaya*. Patna: Kashi Prasad Jayaswal Research Institute, 1982.

Horner, I. B., ed. and trans. *The Book of the Discipline (Vinaya-piṭaka).* 6 vols. Bristol: Pali Text Society, [1938–1966] 1993–2014.

Jamison, Stephanie W. "The Term *Gṛhastha* and the (Pre)history of the Householder." In *Gṛhastha: The Householder in Ancient Indian Religious Culture*, edited by Patrick Olivelle, 3–19. Oxford: Oxford University Press, 2019.

Kieffer-Pülz, Petra, trans. "Pārājika I and Saṅghādisesa I: Hitherto Untranslated Passages from the Vinayapiṭaka of the Theravādins." In *The Book of Discipline (Vinaya-piṭaka)*, edited by I. B. Horner, 1:349–72. Bristol: Pali Text Society, 2014.

Langenberg, Amy Paris. *Birth in Buddhism: The Suffering Fetus and Female Freedom.* Abingdon-on-Thames: Routledge, 2017.

——. "Buddhism and Sexuality." Oxford Bibliographies Online, 2019. https://www.google.com/search?client=safari&rls=en&q=doi%3A+10.1093%2FOBO%2F9780195393521-0244&ie=UTF-8&oe=UTF-8 (accessed December 5, 2022).

——. "Buddhist Blood Taboo: Mary Douglas, Female Impurity, and Classical Indian Buddhism," *Journal of the American Academy of Religion* 84, no. 1 (2016): 157–91.

——. "Sex and Sexuality in Buddhism: A Tetralemma." *Religion Compass* 9, no. 9 (2015): 277–86.

Martini, Giuliana. "The Story of Sudinna in the Tibetan Translation of the Mūlasarvāstivāda Vinaya." *Journal of Buddhist Ethics* 19 (2012): 439–50.

McClish, Mark. "Householders, Holy or Otherwise, in the *Nīti* and *Kāma* Literature." In *Gṛhastha: The Householder in Ancient Indian Religious Culture*, edited by Patrick Olivelle, 150–70. Oxford: Oxford University Press, 2019.

Meyer, Johann Jakob. *Sexual Life in Ancient India.* New York: Dorset, 1930.

Olivelle, Patrick. "Aśvhaghoṣa's Apologia: Brahmanical Ideology and Female Allure." *Journal of Indian Philosophy* 49 (2019): 257–68.

——. "*Gṛhastha, Āśrama*, and the Origin of Dharmaśāstra." In *Gṛhastha: The Householder in Ancient Indian Religious Culture*, edited by Patrick Olivelle, 107–23. Oxford: Oxford University Press, 2019.

Olivelle, Patrick, ed. and trans. *Dharmasūtras: The Law Codes of Āpastamba, Gautama, Baudhāyana, and Vasiṣṭha.* Delhi: Motilal Banarsidass, 2000.

——. *The Early Upaniṣads: Annotated Text and Translation.* New York: Oxford University Press, 1998.

——. *Manu's Code of Law: A Critical Edition and Translation of the Mānava-Dharmaśāstra.* Oxford: Oxford University Press, 2005.

Pachow, W. *A Comparative Study of the Prātimokṣa on the Basis of Its Chinese, Tibetan, Sanskrit, and Pāli Versions.* Rev. ed. Delhi: Motilal Banarsidass, [1955] 2000.

Perera, L. P. N. "Sexuality in Ancient India: A Study Based on the Pali Vinayapitaka." PhD diss., University of Kelaniya, Sri Lanka, 1993.

Pinte, Klaus. "Vinaya." Oxford Bibliographies Online, 2010. https://www.oxfordbibliographies.com/view/document/obo-9780195393521/obo-9780195393521-0174.xml (accessed December 5, 2022).

Powers, John. *A Bull of a Man: Images of Masculinity, Sex, and the Body in Indian Buddhism.* Cambridge, Mass.: Harvard University Press, 2009.

Pradhan, P. "The First Pārājika of the Dharmaguptaka-Vinaya and the Pali Sutta-vibhaṅgha." *Visva-Bharati Annals* 1 (1945): 1–34.

Prebish, Charles S. *Buddhist Monastic Discipline: The Sanskrit Prātimokṣa Sūtras of the Mahāsāṃghikas and Mūlasarvāstivādins*. Delhi: Motilal Banarsidass, 1996.

Roth, Gustav, ed. *Bhikṣuṇī-Vinaya Including Bhikṣuṇī-Prakīrṇaka and a Summary of the Bhikṣu-Prakīrṇaka of the Ārya-Mahāsāṃghika-lokottaravādin*. Patna: K. P. Jayaswal Research Institute, 1970.

Appendix
Character Glossary

aikōshin aikokushin 愛校心愛国心
Ban Chao 班超
Bao Tang 保唐
bishōnen 美少年
bushidō 武士道
Chan 禪
Chang Cheh 張徹
Chen Yi 陳禕
Chi Chongrui 遲重瑞
chigo 稚児
Dahui Zonggao 大慧宗杲
daijōbu 大丈夫
Da Tang Da Ci'en Si Sanzang fashi zhuan 大唐大慈恩寺三藏法師傳
Da Tang Sanzang qujing shihua 大唐三藏取經詩話
Da Tang xiyuji 大唐西域記
da zhangfu 大丈夫
Dōgen 道元
Dongshan Liangjie 洞山良价
Engakuji 円覚寺
Enomoto Shūson 榎本秋村
Fang Rufu 房孺復
Fu Jiezi 傅介子

Fushan Fayuan 浮山法遠
fudanshi 腐男子
fujoshi 腐女子
futai 福態
Gantō 巌頭
gōki 剛毅
Guishan Lingyou 潙山靈祐
Guizong 歸宗
Gulin Qingmao 古林清茂
Guyin Yuncong 谷隱蘊聰
Hakuin Ekaku 白隱慧鶴
He Zhu 賀鑄
hossen 法戦
hō no jissenjō 法の実戦場
Huang Haibing 黃海冰
Huang Tingjian 黃庭堅
Huang Xiaoming 黃曉明
huxue 虎穴
Iizuka Iwao 飯塚巌
Imakita Kōsen 今北洪川
jianghu 江湖
Jikyōryō 自疆寮
jin'gu 金箍
Jingshan Faqin 徑山法欽
jin gang 金剛
jojōbu 女丈夫
Juefan Huihong 覺範慧洪
jūjutsu 柔術
kafū 家風
Kaiseiji 海清寺
Kaizenji 海禅寺
Katsumine Daitetsu 勝峰大徹
keisaku 警策
kendō 剣道
kenzen ichinyo 剣禅一如
kōan 公案
Kojirin 居士林

kokutai 国体
Kōsō 黄巣
Kōzen Gokokukai 興禅護国会
Lau Kar Leung 劉家良
Law Kar Ying 羅家英
Li Ao 李翱
Li Xinchuan 李心傳
Li Zunxu 李遵勗
Linji Yixuan 臨濟義玄
Liu Kai 柳開
Mamiya Eijū 間宮英宗
Masako Natsume 夏目雅子
Masumoto Yoshitarō 増本芳太郎
Meiji 明治
Mineo Daikyū 峰尾大休
mō 猛
Mo Ye 鏌鋣
mo le tau 冇厘頭
mōretsu 猛烈
mōzen 猛然
naiyou xiaosheng 奶油小生
Nakahara Shūgaku 中原秀嶽
Nanzenji 南禅寺
nesshin 熱心
Nie Yuan 聶遠
nikutai senren 肉体銑錬
Nitobe Inazō 新渡戸稲造
Nogi Maresuke 乃木希典
Nyoidan 如意団
Okada 岡田
Oni Daitetsu 鬼大徹
onna-mono 女物
Ōta Tetsuzō 太田哲三
Pansi dong 盤絲洞
Rinzai 臨済
Rōhatsu *sesshin* 臘八接心
rōshi 老師

Saiin'an 済蔭庵
Saiindan 済蔭団
Sakagami Shinjō 坂上眞浄
Samjang 三藏
San Te 三德
Sanzang 三藏
sanzen 参禅
Sanzō 三藏
Satō Teiichi 佐藤禎一
seishinteki shūyō 精神的修養
seiza 静坐
Seppō 雪峰
sesshin 接心
Setchō 雪竇
Sha Wujing 沙悟淨
Shaku Sōen 釈宗演
Shaolin 少林
Shimada Hiroshi 島田宏
Shimokawa Yoshitarō 下川芳太郎
shidafu 士大夫
Shiragami Eizō 白上英三
Shitou Xiqian 石頭希遷
Shi Yan Ming 釋延明
shōjin yūmō 精進勇猛
Shuihu zhuan 水滸傳
Shūmon kattōshū 宗門葛藤集
shūyō 修養
shūyōdan 修養団
sōdō 僧堂
Suga Reinosuke 菅禮之助
Su Shi 蘇軾
Sun Wukong 孫悟空
Tamenaga Shunsui 為永春水
Tasaki Masayoshi 田崎仁義
teishō 提唱
tiehan 鐵漢

Tiantong Rujing 天童如淨
Tsuji Sōmei 辻双明
Tsukioka Yoshitoshi 月岡芳年
tsuyoi otoko 強い男
Uhara Yoshitoyo 宇原義豊
ukiyo-e 浮世絵
Wang Yue 汪粵
wen-wu 文武
Wu Cheng'en 吴承恩
Wudang 武當
Wuzhun Shifan 無準師範
xiao bailian 小白臉
xiaosheng 小生
xiao xianrou 小鮮肉
Xiatang Huiyuan 瞎堂慧遠
Xinghua Cunjiang 興化存獎
Xiyou ji 西遊記
Xu Shaohua 徐少華
Xuanzang 玄奘
Yagyū 柳生
Yamada Jirōkichi 山田次朗吉
Yamaoka Tesshū 山岡鉄舟
yang gang 陽剛
Yang Wulang 楊五郎
Yanqi 彥琪
Yaoshan Weiyan 藥山惟嚴
yin-yang 陰陽
Yongjia Xuanjue 永嘉玄覺
Yuanwu Keqin 圜悟克勤
yūmō 勇猛
yūmōshin 勇猛心
Yunju Daoying 雲居道膺
zaju 雜劇
zazen 坐禅
zazenkai 坐禅会
Zen 禅

Zeshō'in 是照院
Zhang Jizhong 張紀中
Zhang Qian 張騫
Zhenzong 真宗
Zhu Bajie 豬八戒
Zhu Xi 朱熹

Contributors

MEGAN BRYSON is Associate Professor of Religious Studies at the University of Tennessee. Her research focuses on gender and ethnicity in Buddhism and Chinese religions. Bryson has published *Goddess on the Frontier: Religion, Ethnicity, and Gender in Southwest China* (Stanford, 2016), and she is completing a monograph about Buddhist transmission along the Southwestern Silk Road.

KEVIN BUCKELEW is Assistant Professor of Religious Studies at Northwestern University. He specializes in the study of Chinese Buddhism and Chinese religion, especially Chan Buddhism and the relationship between Buddhism and Daoism in China. His current book project explores how Chan masters were characterized as living buddhas in Song-dynasty China (960–1279) and what that phenomenon tells us about understandings of authority, masculinity, and freedom in and around Chan Buddhist circles during the period.

STEPHEN C. BERKWITZ is Professor and Head of Religious Studies at Missouri State University. His recent publications include *Buddhist Poetry and Colonialism: Alagiyavanna and the Portuguese in Sri Lanka* (Oxford, 2013) and "Strong Men and Sensual Women in Sinhala Buddhist Poetry," in *Religious Boundaries for Sex, Gender and Corporeality*, ed. Alexandra Cuffel, Ana Echevarria, and Georgios T. Halkias (Routledge, 2019).

MARCUS EVANS is a PhD candidate at McMaster University. He is currently researching religion in contemporary Afro-Asian encounters and is completing his dissertation, "Transcendence in the Afro-Asian World of RZA and the Wu-Tang Clan." At recent meetings of the American Academy of Religion he presented, "*Man with the Iron Fists*: Anti-Racism and Afro-Asian Solidarity in Film" and "East Asian Religious Dimensions of the Wu-Tang Clan: Racial and Religious Transcendence in the Life-Narrative of RZA."

WARD KEELER is Professor of Anthropology at the University of Texas, Austin. His recent publications include *The Traffic in Hierarchy: Masculinity and Its Others in*

Buddhist Burma (University of Hawai'i Press, 2017) and "Shifting Transversals: Trans Women's Move from Spirit Mediumship to Beauty Work in Mandalay," *Ethnos: Journal of Anthropology* 81, no. 5 (2016).

AMY PARIS LANGENBERG is Professor of Religious Studies at Eckerd College. She is currently coauthoring the book *Abuse, Sex, and the Sangha* with Ann Gleig (Yale University Press, forthcoming). Other publications include *Birth in Buddhism: The Suffering Fetus and Female Freedom* (Routledge, 2017) and "On Reading *Vinaya*: Feminist History, Hermeneutics, and Translating the Female Body," *Journal of the American Academy of Religion* 88, no.4 (2020).

REBECCA MENDELSON is Japanese Studies Librarian at the University of Pennsylvania. Her research focuses on the popularization of Japanese Zen as a prelude to the global Zen boom. Currently, she is revising her dissertation, "Fierce Practice, Courageous Spirit, and Spiritual Cultivation: The Rise of Lay Rinzai Zen in Modern Japan," into a book manuscript.

BEE SCHERER is Professor and Chair of Buddhist Studies at Vrije Universiteit Amsterdam. Scherer's publications include "Queering Buddhist Tradition," *Oxford Research Encyclopedia of Religion* (2021) and "Atypical Bodies: Queer-Feminist and Buddhist Perspectives," in *Cultural History of Disability in the Modern Age*, ed. David T. Mitchell and Sarah L. Snyder (Bloomsbury, 2020).

JOSHUA BRALLIER SHELTON is a PhD candidate at Northwestern University. He has completed two master's theses on masculinity in Tibetan Buddhism: "The Siddha Who Tamed Tibet: A Genealogy of Padmasambhava's Tantric Masculinity in Two Early Namthar" at the University of Colorado Boulder and "Murky, Ambiguous, Fluid: Towards a Queer Buddhist Theological Deconstruction of Toxic Masculinity" at Naropa University.

GENG SONG is Associate Professor of Chinese at the University of Hong Kong. His recent publications include *Televising Chineseness: Gender, Nation, and Subjectivity* (University of Michigan Press, 2022), and *Men and Masculinities in Contemporary China* (co-authored with Derek Hird, Brill, 2014).

DESSISLAVA VENDOVA is Postdoctoral Fellow of East Asian Art and Religion at the Graduate Theological Union. Her publications include "Solving the Riddle of the 'Muhammad Nari Stele': A New Look," in *Gandharan Art in Its Buddhist Context* (Oxford: Archaeopress, 2023), and she is currently working on a book tentatively titled "The Great Life Story of the Body of the Buddha: The Life of Buddha Shakyamuni in Early Buddhist Narrative and Art."

NATAWAN WONGCHALARD is Lecturer of English at Chiang Mai University. Her publications include "Heroes and Representations of Masculinity in Thai Action Films," *Manusya Journal of Humanities* 22 (2019) and "Revisiting the *Ramayana* Through the Oppositional Telling of Anand Neelakantan's *Asura: Tale of the Vanquished* (2012)," *Asian Review* 34, no. 1 (2021).

Index

abuse apologetics, 156
Account of Origins, The (*Nidānakathā*), 33, 42*n*3
Account of Parākramabāhu VI (Pärakumbā Sirita), 90–91
Adamek, Wendi, 52
Anālayo, 306*n*18
androcentrism: modern Rinzai masculinity ideals and, 131, 143, 146, 147; RZA's Buddhist masculinity and, 236, 238; Wu-Tang Clan and, 233, 234. *See also* patriarchy
androgyny, 276–277, *277*, 278–79
anti-Muslim sentiment: Burmese masculinities and, 90, 196, 202*n*8; Nydahl and, 156–57
Āpastamba, 297
aphallophobia, 155, 170*n*3
arahants, women as, 21
Ārṣadhara (king of Zahor), 112
Artinger, Brenna, 155
Ascetic Gautama, *34*; characteristics of, 32–33; defined, 26; as "Fasting Buddha," 45–46*n*47; impermanence and, 40; Middle Way and, 35–36, *35*; positive views of, 46*n*56, 47*n*57; postenlightenment fasting and, 46*n*55; transformation of, 36–37, *37*, 38–39; veneration of, 40–41
asceticism: Buddha's enlightenment and, 38, 47*n*62; early Buddhist ambivalence toward, 46*n*56; First Sermon on, 35–36; *gṛhastha* ideal and, 298–299; hegemonic masculinities and, 38, 41; Jainism and, 37–38, 47*n*61; on loss of great man marks, 33; rejection of, 38, 41; Siddhārtha Gautama's practice of, 24, 33, 35, 38, 46*nn*50, 52, 47*n*57. *See also* Ascetic Gautama
Aśoka, 24, 44*n*26, 296–97, 299
Aśvaghoṣa, 28, 298, 308*n*46
Attanagalu's History in Sinhala (*Eḷu Attanagalu Vaṃśaya*), 82
autonomy/detachment: Burmese femininity and, 198–99, 200; Burmese masculinities and, 183, 187, 193, 194, 196, 197, 198

Ban Chao, 53–54, 55, 61, 72*nn*15, 17
barbaric masculinity, 65, 69–70
Basket of Conduct (*Cariyāpiṭaka*), 81
Baudhāyana, 297–98
Benesch, Oleg, 138, 141

Berkwitz, Stephen, 112
Bhallika, 36
Bhikṣu Bala, 29
Bianji, 261
Bimbisāra (king of Rājagṛha), 28–29, *29*
biological sex, 5–6, 14*n*18
Black American experience: counterhegemonic masculinities and, 249–250; Bruce Lee and, 239, 249; martial arts films and, 249, 254*n*54; RZA's Buddhist masculinity and, 238, *240*, 243, 244, 246, 248
Black exploitation genre, 239, 249
Black Keys, 233
BL (Boys' Love) subculture (Japan), 279–80
Blue Cliff Record (*Biyan lu*; *Hekiganroku*), 143–44
Bodhidharma, 65, 244
Bodhisattva Deva, 26, 44*n*31
bodhisattva kings. *See* Sirisaṅghabodhi; Sri Lankan bodhisattva kings
Bodhisattva, pre-enlightenment Buddha as. *See* Renunciant Gautama
bodhisattvas: as *mahāsattas*, 81–82; in Mahāyāna Buddhism, 80, 84, 113; Padmasambhava and, 112–113; in Theravāda Buddhism, 80–81, 96*n*9
body: negative attitudes toward, 23, 79; perfection in, 21, 42*n*4; virtue/morality and, 23–24, 41, 43*n*17, 44*n*19, 78–79. *See also* great man, marks of; physical characteristics
Boucher, Daniel, 24
brahman ideal, 78
Brereton, Joel, 296
Bridges, Tristan, 125*n*44
brotherhood: RZA's Buddhist masculinity and, 238–39, 240–41; Tang Monk image and, 267–68
Brown, Robert, 46*n*55
Brown, Sid, 203*n*22
Bryson, Megan, 65, 93–94, 109, 192
Buckelew, Kevin, 79, 132, 194
Buddhacarita, 13*n*3
Buddhaghosa, 166, 301
buddhahood: exceptions to body characteristics for, 43–44*n*17; hegemonic masculinities and, 21, 42*n*4; marks of great man and, 22–23, 43–44*n*17; patriarchy and, 21, 42*n*3
buddhānusmṛti, 25
Buddha Side, The: Gender, Power, and Buddhist Practice in Vietnam (Soucy), 10
Buddha, the: abandonment of family, 198; ascetic practices of, 24, 33, 35, 38, 46*n*50, 46*nn*50, 52, 47*n*57; as Bhagavat, 21, 42*n*1; body impermanence and, 40, 43*n*10; death of, 39–40; enlightenment of, 22, 23, 38, 47*n*62; hegemonic masculinities and, 21–22; Padmasambhava and, 104; paradoxes within hegemonic masculinity and, 3; as Sarvārthasiddha, 28, 45*n*34; as sexually attractive, 1. *See also* physical characteristics of Buddha
Buddha und die Liebe, Der (Nydahl), 160
Buddhism: collectivism and, 216, 222; global spread of, 6, 8; gratitude and, 229*n*51; *gṛhastha* ideal and, 296, 297; martial arts films and, 250; multiplicity of, 6–7; nonviolence ethos, 215; Tham Luang cave rescue and, 223–24. *See also* Mahāyāna Buddhism; Theravāda Buddhism
Buddhism and gender, theories, 8, 10
Buddhism, Sexuality, and Gender (Cabezón), 9
Buddhist iconography: Buddha's life stages and, 26; Chan manhood ideals and, 61–68; first appearances of, 25–26, 29, *29*, *30*, *31*, 45*n*44; marks of great man and, 22; monasticism and, 45*n*44; regional differences in, 47*n*57; transformative effects of, 24; as worship focus, 26, 62. *See also* Ascetic Gautama; Renunciant Gautama
Buddhist monastic celibacy, 288; *aggadāna* and, 300, 309*n*53;

Confucianism and, 260, 263; female-female intimacy and, 294–96, 306*n*24, 307*nn*28–29, 34; *gṛhastha* ideal and, 289, 290, 292, 296, 300–1, 302, 308*nn*40, 46–47; hegemonic masculinities and, 289–90, 304; legal vs. soteriological dimensions of, 292–94, 305*n*12; modern Rinzai masculinity ideals and, 131, 148*n*13; penetrative sex prohibitions and, 290, 295, 301–2, 307*n*35, 309*nn*58, 61; reproduction and, 301, 303–4, 307*n*35; sociohistorical context and, 291–92, 305*n*12; Sudinna narrative and, 293–94, 300, 306*n*18; in Tibetan Buddhism, 166
budukuru, 90
Bull of a Man: Images of Masculinity, Sex, and the Body in Indian Buddhism (Powers), 9–10, 78
Burmese masculinities, 183–201; anti-Muslim sentiment and, 90, 196, 202*n*8; autonomy/detachment and, 183, 187, 193, 194, 196, 197, 198; consumerism and, 187–88, 195–96; contemporary attitudes, 195–97; vs. femininity, 198–201, 202*n*22; hegemonic masculinities and, 184, 192–95; hierarchy and, 188–89, 193; *hpòun* and, 193, 203*n*14; kingship and, 194; lay masculinity, 185–87, 193, 194–95; lay vs. monastic, 184–85; monasticism and, 184–85, 187–92, 193, 197; solitary meditation and, 185, 191–92, 193–94; spectrum of power and, 192–93, 194
Bushido: The Soul of Japan (Nitobe), 141–42
bushidō, 129–30, 138, 141–42, 150*n*63
Butler, Judith, 5, 10

Cabezón, José, 6, 8, 9, 10, 106, 120, 185, 292, 301, 305*nn*12–13, 307*n*35
cakravartins (universal rulers): hegemonic masculinities and, 41; marks of great man and, 1, 22, 42*n*6, 78
capitalism, 4, 207
Carrigan, Tim, 2–3, 13*n*4
Cave of the Silken Web, The (*Pansi dong*), 265
celibacy. *See* Buddhist monastic celibacy
Cha-Jua, Sundiata Keita, 249, 254*n*54
Chaloemtiarana, Thak, 215
Chan Buddhism: ambivalence about bodily appearance in, 68; kōan practice in, 143, 145; literary culture and, 61, 69, 73*n*40; RZA's Buddhist masculinity and, 236, 237, 239–40, 242–48, *243*; societal power of, 51–52, 57, 68; transgression and, 64, 68, 70; women in, 52–53. *See also* Chan manhood ideals; *Man with the Iron Fists* films
Chang Cheh, 236, 237
Chang, Sophia, 244–45
Chan manhood ideals (*da zhangfu*), 5, 53; barbaric masculinity and, 65, 69–70; Chan societal power and, 51, 57, 68; enlightenment and, 59; exemplar imitation and, 53–54, 72*nn*15, 17; hegemonic masculinities and, 60–61, 68; marks of great man and, 54, 72*n*17; modern Rinzai masculinity ideals and, 132; Neo-Confucian ambivalence about, 64–65, 70; origins of, 5, 51–52; portraiture and, 61–68; Sri Lankan bodhisattva kings and, 79; superiority of Chan masters and, 56–60, 72*nn*27–28, 73*nn*35, 37; transgression and, 70; *wen-wu* paradigm and, 60–61; women and, 52–53
Chanthawong, Ekkapol (Coach Ek), 218, 223–25, *225*
Charming Cadavers (Wilson), 9
Chen Lihua, 267
Chi Chongrui, 265, *266*, 267, 269–70
chigo, 7, 14*n*21
"China" (Johnson), 250, 254*n*55
Chinese Boxer, The, 247

Chinese masculinities: Confucianism and, 260; *naiyou xiaosheng* ("young scholar as soft as cream"), 266; *wen-wu* dyad and, 60–61, 260, 264–65, 283*n*23; *xiao xianrou* (little fresh meat), 259, 263, 267. *See also* Chan manhood ideals; Tang Monk image
Chinese Odyssey, A (*Dahua xiyou*) (Lau), 268
Chinese Tall Story, A (Lau), 268–269, *269*
Chogyam Trungpa, 156, 158, 160–61, 166–67
Chow, Stephen, 268
cinematic mythic models of masculinity, 234, 236–40; androcentrism and, 236; Black American experience and, 238; Oriental Monk figure in, 239–40, 244, 252*n*34; virtual nature of, 235, 251*n*10
cisheteropatriarchy, 155, 156
civil and martial masculinities. *See wen-wu* (*bun-bu*) dyad
Collection of Long Discourses (*Dīgha nikāya*), 166
Collection of Stories of the Six Perfections (*Liudujijing*), 33
colonialism/imperialism: hegemonic masculinities and, 4; modern Rinzai masculinity ideals and, 136, 137, 139, 141, 142
Commentary on the Great Perfection of Wisdom (*Mahāprajñāpāramitopadeśa*; *Dazhidu lun*) (Nāgārjuna), 43*n*8
Confucianism: Buddhist monastic celibacy and, 260, 263; Tang Monk image and, 262–63, 264, 274, 283*n*23. *See also* Neo-Confucianism
Connell, Raewyn, 2–3, 4, 8, 10, 13*n*4, 60, 94, 107–8, 109, 110, 123*nn*12–13, 16, 130, 146, 156, 192, 226, 235, 289, 290
Copper Island Biography of Padmasambhava (*sLob dpon padma 'byung gnas kyi rnam thar zang gling ma*) (Nyangrel Nyima Öser), 103–4, 111–12, 113–14, 115, 116, 121, 122*n*1
Crenshaw, Kimberlé, 15*n*23
Crest-Gem of Poetry (*Kavsiḷumiṇa*) (Parākramabāhu II), 88–89
critical studies of men and masculinity (CSMM), 107
Crown of Poetry (*Kāvyaśēkhara*), 90
Crown Prince Siddhārtha, 26, 32–33

Dagpo Kagyu tradition, 163, 166
Dahui Zonggao, 64–65, 73*n*52, 132
Dalai Lama, Fourteenth, 160, 166
Dalton, Jacob, 108–9
Daoism, 236, 237, 239
Da Tang Da Ci'en Si Sanzang fashi zhuan (Huili), 261, 262
da zhangfu (great man). *See* Chan manhood ideals
Deeds of the Buddha (*Buddhacarita*) (Aśvaghoṣa), 28
Dehejia, Vidya, 24
Derrett, J. D. M., 305*n*13, 307*n*34
Desser, David, 236
detachment. *See* autonomy
Devadatta, 42–43*n*7
Dhammapāla, 81
Dharmadhatu, 158, 166–67
dharmalogical processes, 22–23, 43*n*9
dhyāna, 36
Diamond Way, 154–55, 156–70; gender stereotypes and, 161–62, 169; heteromachismo in, 161–63, 168, 169; Nydahl background, 158–59; queer people and, 164–68; religious categorization of, 158, 159; sexual ethics in, 159–61, 169, 172*n*26
divine king figure, 92
Dōgen, 64
Doney, Lewis, 122*n*2
Dongshan Liangjie, 55
Doraemon: The Record of Nobita's Parallel Visit to the West, 279
Douglas, Mary, 309*n*65
dülwa (*'dul ba*), 108, 113
Dzongsar Khyentse Rinpoche, 156

8 Diagram Pole Fighter, The (Lau and Liu), 238, 246
eḷu dialect, 88
Engakuji, 129, 131, 133, 134, 136, 139, 140, 147*n*1
enlightenment: of Buddha, 22, 23, 38, 47*n*62; Chan manhood ideals and, 59; high-adrenaline sports and, 162; RZA's Buddhist masculinity and, 246
Enomoto Shūson, 133–34
Entangling Vines (*Shūmon kattōshū*), 145
Entrance to the Way of Awakening (*Bodhicaryāvatāra*), 80
Evans, Marcus, 53

Fang Rufu, 58
Fasting Buddha. *See* Ascetic Gautama
Faure, Bernard, 9, 291, 305*n*12
femininity. *See* gender roles; women
First Meditation, 36
First Sermon, 33, 35–36, *35*, 46*n*52
Five Percent Nation of Gods and Earths, 234
Flower Ornament Sūtra (*Huayan jing*), 56–57
Flowers and Dreams (*Hana to yume*), 279
Fly, Superboard, 273–74, *273*
Foucault, Michel, 5, 10
Foulk, Griffith, 62
fraternity, 216
Freiberger, Oliver, 46*n*56
Fu Jiezi, 54, 72*n*15
Fully Enlightened Buddha, 26
Fushan Fayuan, 59

Galpoṭa Slab-Inscription, 97*n*32
Gampopa, 163, 166
Ganden Potrang, 121
Gautama, Siddhārtha. *See* Buddha, the
Geary, Patrick, 111
gender fluidity. *See* sex/gender fluidity
gender roles: in Burmese society, 198–201; Diamond Way and, 161–62, 169; RZA's Buddhist masculinity and, 236, 241, 253*n*37. *See also* androcentrism; patriarchy; women
gender theory, 110
Ghost Dog (Jarmusch), 248
Ginsberg, Allen, 164
Gleig, Ann, 155
Gramsci, Antonio, 2, 108, 289
Grant, Beata, 52
gratitude, 222–23, 224, 229*n*51
Great Chronicle (*Mahāvaṃsa*), 81–82, 96*n*13
great man, marks of: attempts to fake, 42–43*n*7; Buddha and, 1, 13*n*3, 21, 22, 23, 26, 42*n*5, 78; buddhahood and, 22–23, 43–44*n*17; *cakravartins* and, 1, 22, 42*n*6, 78; Chan manhood ideals and, 54, 72*n*17; development of, 22–23, 41, 43*nn*8–9; loss of, 33; perfections and, 13*n*2; Renunciant Gautama and, 32. *See also* physical characteristics
Great Story (*Mahāvastu*), 32, 33
Great Tang Records on the Western Regions (*Da Tang xiyu ji*), 261
gṛhastha (householder ideal), 290; asceticism and, 298–99; Aśvaghoṣa on, 308*n*46, 398–99; circumscribed sex and, 297, 308*n*40; *Kāma sūtra* on, 299–300; origins of, 289, 296–97, 305–6*nn*7, 15; penetrative sex prohibitions and, 301; reproduction and, 292, 297–98, 302, 303–4, 308*n*47; Sudinna narrative and, 300
Gulin Qingmao, 65, 68
Gunawardana, Leslie, 84–85
Guyin Yuncong, 57–58
Gyatso, Janet, 290–92, 293, 302, 303, 305*n*12, 307*n*35

hagiography, 111
Hakuin Ekaku, 132
Halperin, Mark, 59–60, 73*nn*35, 37
Hanuman ideal, 206, 211–16, *213*, *214*, 218–19, 226, 227*n*26, 228*n*34
Hartung, Caty, 159, 167
Heart of a Young Man, The (Vajiravudh), 209

hegemonic masculinities, 1, 2–3, 13*nn*3–4; aphallophobia and, 155, 170*n*3; asceticism and, 38, 41; Black alternatives to, 249–50; Buddha and, 21–22; buddhahood and, 21, 42*n*4; Buddhist ambivalence toward, 22; Buddhist monastic celibacy and, 289–90, 304; Burmese masculinities and, 184, 192–95; Chan manhood ideals and, 60–61, 68; contemporary effeminate stereotypes and, 101; contradiction and, 70; gendered adaptability and, 125*n*44; global capitalism and, 207; homophobia and, 164; inaccessibility of, 20; institutional power and, 109–10; intersectionality and, 3–4, 8; modern Rinzai masculinity ideals and, 130, 146; normalization of, 7; Padmasambhava and, 115–18, 119, 125*n*44; paradoxes within, 3; patriarchy and, 2, 13*n*4, 125*n*44; perfect body and, 21, 42*n*4; postcolonial critique and, 123*n*16; reproduction and, 107, 123*n*12; Sri Lankan bodhisattva kings and, 93–94; Thailand, 206–8; Tham Luang cave rescue and, 206, 217–18; transnational Tibetan Buddhism and, 156; violence and, 107–8, 109, 111, 123*n*13. *See also specific masculinities*
Heo Young-man, 273–74
heteromachismo, 161–63, 168
heteropatriarchy, 155, 156
He Zhu, 54
Hinduism, 211, 216; *gṛhastha* ideal and, 289, 296
Hinsch, Bret, 68
hip-hop, 250
Hirshberg, Daniel, 122*n*2
historical Buddha. *See* Buddha, the
History of the Hatthavanagalla Monastery (*Hatthavanagalla-vihāra-vaṃsa*), 82
homosexuality: Diamond Way and, 164–68; female-female intimacy, 294–96, 306*n*24, 307*nn*28–29, 34–36
Hong Jung-eun, 274, *275*
Hong Mi-ran, 274, *275*
honor, 185
Hopkins, Jeffrey, 167
Hori, Victor, 150*n*68
hpòun, 193, 203*n*14
Hsia, C. T., 262
Hsieh, Ding-hwa, 52
Huang Haibing, 270, *271*
Huang Tingjian, 54
Huang Xiaoming, 272
Huili, 261, 262

Iida Tōin, 148–49*n*29, 151*n*75
Iizuka Iwao, 131, 138
Illustrated Complete Version of Journey to the West, The (*Ehon Saiyū zenden*), 276
Imakita Kōsen, 140
imperialism. *See* colonialism/imperialism
individuality, 4
Indonesia, 201
Indra, 28, 39, 44*n*37
Indrabodhi, 112
Inoue Tetsujirō, 150*n*63
Inquiry of Ugra (*Ugraparipṛcchā*), 80
interbeing, 222, 224–25
intersectionality, 3–4, 8, 15*n*23
Iwamura, Jane Naomi, 251*n*10, 252*n*34

Jainism, 37–38, 47*n*61, 297
Jamison, Stephanie, 296
Jarmusch, Jim, 248
Jātaka stories, 42*n*3, 80–81, 82, 88–89
Jeennoon, Phachalin, 213–14
Jeru the Damaja, 250
Jētavanārāma Slab-Inscription, 84, 86
Jewel Ornament of Liberation (*Thar rgyan*) (Gampopa), 166
jin gang, 237
Jingde-era Record of the Transmission of the Lamp (*Jingde chuandeng lu*), 56
Jingshan Faqin, 58, 59–60
Johnson, Charles, 250, 254*n*55
Journey to the West television series (1986), 265–68, *266*, 272, 283*n*25
Journey to the West television series (Zhang Jizhong, 2011), 269–71, *271*

Journey to the West (*Xiyou ji*) (Wu Cheng'en), 3, 4, 259, 261–65, 274–75, 282*n*10
Juefan Huihong, 62–63, 70
jūjutsu, 140, 150n54

kabuki, 278
Kaizenji, 135, 140
Kalu Rinpoche, 160–61, 165
Kāma sūtra, 295, 296, 298, 299–300, 307*n*29
Karlin, Jason, 130
karma: asceticism and, 33, 46*n*50; marks of great man and, 22–23, 43*n*9; monasticism and, 68; rebirth and, 23–24
Karma Kagyu school, 159, 160, 161, 163. *See also* Diamond Way
Karmapa, Sixteenth, 164, 165
Katsumine Daitetsu, 132–33, 134
Kawanami, Hiroko, 200
Keeler, Ward, 10, 22, 211
Kelley, Robin D. G., 252*n*28
kendō, 129–30, 137–41, 142, 149*n*47
Keyes, Charles, 8–9, 10
khwam-katanyu (gratitude), 222–23, 224
kingship: Burmese masculinities and, 194; *cakravartins*, 22, 41, 42*n*6, 78; Hanuman ideal and, 212. *See also* Sirisaṅghabodhi; Sri Lankan bodhisattva kings
Kinugawa Kenji, 73*n*52
Kitiarsa, Pattana, 210
kōan practice, 132, 137, 142–46, 149*n*38, 150*nn*67–68, 151*n*75
Korean culture, Tang Monk image in, 273–76, *273*, *275*
Korean Odyssey, A (*Hwayugi*), 274–76, *275*
Kōzen Gokokukai, 133, 134
Krondorfer, Björn, 123*n*7
kṣatriya ideal, 78
Kunan, Saman, 217–18, 219, 221–22, 224
Kusa (Sri Lankan king), 88–89

Lacanian theory, 155, 170*n*3
Laqueur, Thomas, 5
Lau, Jeffrey, 268–69, *269*
Lau Kar Leung, 236, 237, 238, 239, 244
Law Kar Ying, 268
Laws of Nārada, 5–6
Lay Zen (*Koji Zen*) (Shimokawa Yoshitarō), 148*n*29
Lee, Bruce, 239, 249, 252*n*28
Lee, John, 2–3, 13*n*4
Lee Seung-gi, 274
Leggett, Trevor, 149*n*44
Levering, Miriam, 9, 52, 132
Li Ao, 60, 73*n*35
Linji Yixuan, 63–65, *66*, *67*, 69, 70, 73*n*52
Liu, Gordon, 237, 238, 240, 244, 246
Liu Kai, 70
Li Xinchuan, 59–60
Li Yuan, 270
Li Zunxu, 57–59, 72*nn*27–28
Lohanchun, Pak, 224, *225*
Lotus of Compassion (*Karuṇāpuṇḍarīka*), 47*n*57
Louie, Kam, 60, 130, 283*n*23
luk phu chai, 211, 224

Ma, Jack (Ma Yun), 283*n*32
"Macho Buddhism" (Scherer), 154–55, 157
Mahājanaka (bodhisattva king), 81
Mahākāla, 65
Mahākāśyapa, 58
mahākāvya genre, 89
mahāpuruṣa, 5, 52
mahāsattas (Great Beings), 81–82
mahāsiddhas, 159, 160
Mahāyāna Buddhism, 80, 84, 113, 145
Mahinda IV (Sri Lankan king), 86
Makley, Charlene, 10
Mamiya Eijū, 132
Mandārava, 112
manga, 279–80
Man with the Iron Fists films (RZA), 6, 233; Black American experience and, 240, *240*; brotherhood in, 240–41; cinematic mythic models of masculinity and, 237; gender polarity in, 253*n*37. *See also* RZA's Buddhist masculinity

Manu, 297
Māra, 24–25, 37, 44*n*26
martial masculinity: Burmese kingship and, 194; Tang Monk image and, 270; Thailand, 209, 214–15, 216. *See also* Chan manhood ideals; modern Rinzai masculinity ideals
masculinities: androcentrism as defining, 234; Buddhist studies scholarship on, 105–6; civil and martial (*wen-wu* dyad), 60–61, 130, 147*n*4, 260, 264–65, 283*n*23; classical Chinese literary tradition and, 236–37; contemporary effeminate stereotypes and, 3, 101; counterhegemonic, 249–50; hip-hop and, 250; interpersonal origins of, 110; modern Chinese *xiao xianrou* trend, 259; multiplicity of, 5–6, 109, 123*n*16, 192, 235; *siddha* archetype, 111–12; toxic, 155–56
Masculinities (Connell), 8
Masumoto Yoshitarō, 135
Matteini, Michele, 62
Maya, Mineo, 279
Mazu Daoyi, 72*n*27
McClish, Mark, 299
mchod yon (patron-priest relationship), 121
meditation: Ascetic Gautama and, 36, 38; Burmese monasticism and, 189–90; Burmese solitary ideal, 185, 191–92, 193–94; Diamond Way and, 163; modern Rinzai practice and, 131, 134–35, 137, 142–43, 149*n*47, 150*n*67; tantra and, 161
Mendelson, Rebecca, 53, 276
Message of the Goose (*Haṃsasandēśaya*), 90
Messerschmidt, James, 130, 146, 235, 236, 289
Middle Way masculinity, 22, 35–36, 37, *37*, 38, 41
Minamoto, Shizuka, 279
Mineo Daikyū, 137, 148*n*29
mō, 133
modern Rinzai masculinity ideals, 129–47; androcentrism and, 131, 143, 146, 147; *bushidō* and, 129–30, 138, 141–42, 150*n*63; dharma combat (*hossen*) and, 138, 149*n*44; hegemonic masculinities and, 130, 146; Japanese imperialism and, 136, 137, 139, 141, 142; *kendō* and, 129–30, 137–41, 142, 149*n*47; kōan practice and, 132, 137, 142–146, 149*n*38, 150*nn*67–68, 151*n*75; lay practice and, 131, 139, 144; life and death and, 137; monasticism and, 131, 148*n*13; nation-building and, 129, 130, 131, 134, 138, 140, 141; rigorous practice and, 134–35, 137, 148*nn*23, 25; self-cultivation (*shūyō*) practices and, 129, 130, 132–33, 136; Shimokawa Yoshitarō on, 135–37, 144–46, 148–49*nn*29, 33; *wen-wu* dyad and, 130, 147*n*4; women and, 131, 132
monasticism: Buddhist iconography and, 45*n*44; Burmese masculinities and, 184–85, 187–92, 193, 197; Chan manhood ideals and, 55, 62, 68; gratitude and, 222–23; hierarchy in, 188–89; late-life entrance into, 188, 191–92, 198; literati competition with, 73*n*37; modern Rinzai masculinity ideals and, 131, 148*n*13; sex/gender fluidity and, 8–9, 260, 261; *siddhas* and, 124–25*n*30; Thai masculinities and, 8–9, 15*n*24, 207, 210, 211, 222–23; Tham Luang cave rescue and, 223, 224, *225*, 229*n*55; women and, 199–201, 203*n*22, 294–96, 306*n*24. *See also* Buddhist monastic celibacy
Monkey (*Saiyūki*) (1978), 278, 279
Monkey (Waley), 262
mōretsu, 133, 135, 137
Morgenthaler, Fritz, 164
Mrozik, Susanne, 9, 23, 78–79
Mr. Son (Heo), 273–74
Mūlasarvāstivāda vinaya, 42*n*7
Myanmar, 201–2*n*2. *See also* Burmese masculinities

Nagaike, Kazumi, 280
Nāgaviṣṇu, 112
naiyou xiaosheng ("young scholar as soft as cream"), 266
Nakahara Nantenbō, 148*n*29, 151*n*75
Nakahara Shūgaku, 135, 140
nak leng (thug) ideal, 210, 215
namtar, 110, 112. *See also Copper Island Biography of Padmasambhava; Testament of Padmasambhava*
Nanda, 43*n*7, 298
Nanyue Huairang, 72*n*27
Nanzenji, 133
Nārāyaṇa, 47*n*62
Naresuan (legendary king of Thailand), 209
Nash, Manning, 203*n*14
Natsume, Masako, 278, 279
Nattier, Jan, 158
Neo-Confucianism, 64–65, 70
neoliberalism, 155
Ne Win, 196
New Journey to the West, 273
New Monkey, 278
Nhat Hanh, Thich, 222
Nie Yuan, 270, *271*
Niśśaṅkamalla (Sri Lankan king), 86, 97*n*32
Nitobe Inazō, 141–42
Nogi Maresuke, 136, 146
Norbu Öden (Tibetan king), 108
normative masculinity. *See* hegemonic masculinities; *specific masculinities*
nuns: Burmese femininity and, 199–201, 203*n*22; sexual intimacy among, 294–96, 306*n*24
Nyangrel Nyima Öser, 103–4, 111–12, 113–14, 115, 122*n*1
Nydahl, Hannah, 159, 162, 167
Nydahl, Lama Ole, 154; anti-Muslim sentiment and, 156–57; background of, 158–59; high-adrenaline sports and, 162; on homosexuality, 164–68; sexual promiscuity of, 159–60, 167. *See also* Diamond Way
Nyingma school of Buddhism, 103, 104, 111
Nyoidan, 134–35, 140
Of Sundarī and Nanda (Saundarananda) (Aśvaghoṣa), 298
Oguri Sōtan, *67*
Oh Yeon-seo, 274
Ōishi Masami, 149*n*29
Olivelle, Patrick, 297, 298, 308*n*47
Ongiri, Amy, 239
onna-mono, 277–78
Orgyen Lingpa, 103, 104, 111–12, 113–14, 115
Orientalism, 3, 8
Oriental Monk figure, 239–40, 244, 252*n*34
Oruvaḷa Sannasa, 86–87
Osottanakorn, Narongsak, 217, 219–20, *219,* 228*n*45
Ōta Tetsuzō, 135
Ozaki Yukio, 141

Padmasambhava: adaptability and, 117–19, 125*n*44; bodhisattvas and, 112–13; early texts on, 122*n*1; five sciences and, 115, 118, 125*n*36; hegemonic masculinities and, 115–18, 119, 125*n*44; institutional power and, 109–10; interactions with female characters, 124*n*20; life story of, 104–5; major biographies of, 103–4, 122*n*2; Nyingma school and, 103, 104, 111; scholarship on, 105; taming activities, 104–5, 106, 113–15, 119; tantra and, 80, 104, 105, 106–7, 108, 109, 111, 119–20; Tibetan landscape as feminine and, 105, 115; violence and, 108, 109, 113–14; Yarlha Shampo and, 114, 125*n*32
Pāli canon, 44*n*25
paṇḍaka, 5, 7
Parākramabāhu II (Sri Lankan king), 88–89
Parākramabāhu VI (Sri Lankan king), 86–87, 90–92, 94
pāramīs (*pāramitās*) (perfections), 24, 80–81, 82
parinirvāṇa, 39–40
parivāra, 215–16

Park Tong-sa Eonhae, 273, 283*n*34
Pascoe, C. J., 125*n*44
Patalliro Saiyuki!, 279, 280
Patriarchs' Hall Collection (*Zutang ji*), 54
patriarchy: aphallophobia and, 155; buddhahood and, 21, 42*n*3; gendered adaptability and, 125*n*44; hegemonic masculinities and, 2, 13*n*4, 125*n*44; masculinity as normative and, 106, 123*n*7; transnational Tibetan Buddhism and, 155, 156. *See also* androcentrism
Paul, Diana, 9
perfections (*pāramīs*; *pāramitās*), 13*n*2, 24, 80–81, 82
physical characteristics: Sri Lankan bodhisattva kings and, 89, 91, 94–95. *See also* great man, marks of; physical characteristics of Buddha
physical characteristics of Buddha: *brahman* ideal and, 78; *kṣatriya* ideal and, 78; *mahāpuruṣa* epithet and, 5, 52; marks of great man, 1, 13*n*3, 21, 22, 23, 26, 42*n*5, 78; transformations compared to flower, 38–40; transformative effects of, 24–25, 41, 43–44*nn*17, 25
Pollock, Sheldon, 87
postcolonial critique, 123*n*16
Powers, John, 6, 9–10, 23, 24, 52, 78, 185, 305*n*12
praśasti literature, 83, 85–86
Price, Zachary, 250
primary and secondary sex characteristics, 6, 14*n*18
Protass, Jason, 73*n*40

queerness: BL (Boys' Love) subculture and, 280; Diamond Way and, 164–68
queer theory, 169–70
Quintman, Andrew, 111

Racharin, Satira, 216
Rama I (king of Thailand), 212, 214, 218, 227*n*22
Ramakien, 206, 212, 213–15, 216, 227*n*22
Rāmāyaṇa, 211–12, 214
Recluse Gautama, 26, 28–29, *29*, *30*, 32–33
"Recommendation for Quiet Sitting, A" (Suzuki), 133
Record of Linji (*Linji lu*), 63, 64, 69
Red Thread, The: Buddhist Approaches to Sexuality (Faure), 9
Reeser, Todd, 95
Remembering the Lotus-Born (Hirshberg), 122*n*2
Renunciant Gautama, 26–29, *27*, *30*, *31*, 32, 45*nn*35, 41, 44–45, 79
reproduction: Buddhist monastic celibacy and, 301, 303–4, 307*n*35; *gṛhastha* ideal and, 292, 297–98, 302, 303–4, 308*n*47; hegemonic masculinities and, 107, 123*n*12
Reynolds, Frank E., 212
Rhi, Juhyung, 47*n*57
Ricoeur, Paul, 159
Riding the Tiger (Nydahl), 164
Rinzai Zen. *See* modern Rinzai masculinity ideals
Romance of the Three Kingdoms, 278
RZA (Ruler Zig-Zag-Zig Allah), 6; Chan Buddhism and, 243–46; Wu-Tang Clan founding and, 251*n*1. *See also* RZA's Buddhist masculinity
RZA's Buddhist masculinity, 6, 233–51; androcentrism and, 236, 238; Black American experience and, 238, *240*, 243, 244, 246, 248; brotherhood and, 238–39, 240–41; Chan Buddhism and, 236, 237, 239–40, 242–48; cinematic mythic models and, 236–40, 251, 251*n*10; counterhegemonic masculinities and, 249–50; gender roles and, 236, 241, 253*n*37; hardness and, 246–47, *248*, *253n47*; Bruce Lee and, 239, 252*n*28; qi training and, 246–47, *247*; virtual nature of, 235, 251*n*10

Saiin'an (Kojirin), 139
Saiindan, 140–41
Saiyuki (2006), 278–79
Sakagami Shinjō, 135

sakdina system (Thailand), 206–7
Śākyamuni Buddha. *See* Buddha, the
sak yant, 215, 228*n*34
sallekhanā, 38
Samuels, Jeffrey, 80
samurai, 141. *See also bushidō*
Śāntarakṣita, 104, 107, 112, 113, 119
Sari (Nara-period Japanese nun), 5
Sarvārthasiddha, 28, 45*n*34
Satō Teiichi, 136, 137
Scalena, Adam, 208
Schaeffer, Kurtis, 111
Schalow, Paul Gordon, 9
Scherer, Bee, 5
Schopen, Gregory, 291
Scott, Joan, 111
Segal, Lynne, 70
self-cultivation (*shūyō*) practices, 129, 130, 132–33, 136
self-sacrifice, 82–84. *See also* Sri Lankan bodhisattva kings
Sequel to Journey to the West, A (*Xiyou ji houzhuan*) (2000), 270, *271*
sesshin, 134–35, 148*n*23
Setchō (Xuedou Chongxian), 144
sex/gender fluidity: Diamond Way and, 167, 169; matrix and, 6; monasticism and, 8–9, 260, 261; Padmasambhava and, 118; Tang Monk image and, 276, 284*n*39; translation issues and, 5
Sexton, Patricia, 218
Sexuality in Classical South Asian Buddhism (Cabezón), 10, 185
sexual promiscuity: Burmese lay masculinity and, 186; Nydahl, 159–60, 167
Shahar, Meir, 237
Shaku Sōen, 133
Shamar Rinpoche, 159
Shambhala, 156, 158
Shaolin tradition: Bodhidharma and, 244; RZA's Buddhist masculinity and, 236, 237–38, 239, 243–44; Wu-Tang Clan and, 233
Sharf, Robert, 62, 145
Shelton, Joshua Brallier, 79, 80
Shimada Hiroshi, 134, 140
Shimokawa Yoshitarō, 135–37, 144–46, 148–49*nn*29, 33
Shiragami Eizō, 140–41
Shiragami Ikkuken, 150*n*57
Shitou Xiqian, 54
Shi Yan Ming, 243–44
Shunpo Sōki, *67*
siddhas, 111–12, 124*n*26. *See also* tantra
Sirisaṅghabodhi (bodhisattva king), 81–84, 96*n*13
Sitagu Sayadaw, 187–88, 190, 202*nn*8, 10
Socially Engaged Buddhism, 169
Sogyal Rinpoche, 156, 160–61
Song Jin-ha, 273
Songoku (*Enoken no songokū*), 278
Song of Realizing the Way (*Zhengdao ge*) (Yongjia Xuanjue), 56–57, 62
Soucy, Alexander, 10
Sri Lankan bodhisattva kings, 83–95; Chan manhood ideals and, 79; as embodiments of gods, 89, 92; in eulogistic inscriptions, 85–88; hegemonic masculinities and, 93–94; identity limitations, 84–85, 86, 87, 97*n*32; physical characteristics of, 89, 91, 94–95; *praśasti* literature and, 83, 85–86, 87, 88; scholarly inattention to, 84; in Sinhala court poetry, 88–93; Sirisaṅghabodhi as paradigm for, 83–84; virtue/morality and, 89, 91–92
Stanton, Richard, 217
Story of Aśoka (*Aśokāvadāna*), 24–25
Story with Poems of How Trepiṭaka of the Great Tang Fetched Sūtras, The (*Da Tang Sanzang qujing shihua*), 264, 282*n*20
Strong, John, 13*n*2
subordinated masculinities, 13*n*14. *See also* Tang Monk image
Suga Reinosuke, 140
Suh, Sharon, 248
Sujātā, 37
Su Shi, 54
Sutasoma (bodhisattva king), 81

Sūtra on the Origin of the [Buddha's] Practice (*Xiuxing benqijing*), 38–39
Su Zhe, 73*n*35
Suzuki, D. T., 132, 133
sword of Mo Ye, 57, 72*n*25

Tambiah, Stanley, 195
Tamenaga Shunsui, 277–78
Tang Monk image, 259; androgyny and, 276–77, *277*, 278–79; brotherhood and, 267–68; comedy and, 268; Confucianism and, 262–63, 264–65, 274, 283*n*23; Japanese versions of, 276–80; *Journey to the West* novel and, 3, 4, 259, 261–65, 274–75, 282*n*10; *Journey to the West* television series (1986) and, 265–68, *266*, 272, 283*n*25; Korean versions of, 273–76, *273*, *275*; management and, 272, 283*n*32; masculine purity discourse and, 263–64, 267; origins of, 260–61; queerness and, 280; remasculinization of, 269–72, *271*; scholar-beauty romance genre and, 261; sex/gender fluidity and, 276, 284*n*39; transnational interest in, 282–83; Nicholas Tse and, 268–69, *269*; *xiao xianrou* (little fresh meat) discourse and, 263, 267
tantra: abuse and, 156; barbaric masculinity and, 65; Diamond Way and, 160, 167–68; gender roles and, 161–62; homosexuality and, 167–68; Padmasambhava and, 80, 104, 105, 106–7, 108, 109, 111, 119–20; queer theory and, 169–70; violence and, 108–9, 124–25*n*30
Tasaki Masayoshi, 135, 140
Tasker, Yvonne, 247
Teo, Stephen, 236–37
Testament of Padmasambhava (*Padma bka' thang yig*) (Orgyen Lingpa), 103, 104, 111–12, 113–114, 115, 116, 117–18, 121
Testimony of Ba (*dBa' bzhed*), 122*n*1
Thailand: female monasticism, 199. *See also* Thai masculinities; Tham Luang cave rescue
Thai masculinities: gratitude and, 222–23, 224, 229*n*51; Hanuman ideal and, 206, 211–16, *213*, *214*, 218–19, 226, 227*n*26, 228*n*34; monasticism and, 8–9, 15*n*24, 207, 210, 211, 222–23; *nak leng* (thug), 210, 215; *sakdina* system and, 206–7; Thai boxing and, 210–11, 213; Western influences and, 227*n*10; Wild Tiger Corps and, 208–9, 216. *See also* Tham Luang cave rescue
Tham Luang cave rescue (2018), 216–26; Hanuman ideal and, 218, 219–22, *219*, *221*, 226; hegemonic masculinities and, 206, 217–18; interbeing and, 222, 224–25; monasticism and, 223, 224, *225*, 229*n*55
Theravāda Buddhism: bodhisattvas in, 80–81, 96*n*9; collectivism and, 223; nuns in, 199, 203*n*22; origins of, 96*n*5; Thai masculinities and, 207, 210–11, 215
36th Chamber of Shaolin, The (Lau), 237–39, 244, 252*n*21
Tiantong Rujing, 64
Tibetan Buddhism: globalized, 155–56, 158, 165, 166; guru devotion tradition in, 162–63; homophobia in, 165–66. *See also* Diamond Way; Padmasambhava
Tokyo Higher Commercial School, 134, 135, 148*n*21
toxic masculinity, 155–56
Traffic in Hierarchy: Masculinity and Its Others in Buddhist Burma (Keeler), 10
translation issues, 4–5
Trapuṣa, 36
Treasury of Abhidharma (*Abhidharmakośa*) (Vasubandhu), 160, 166
Treatise on Statecraft (*Arthaśāstra*), 299
Tri Songdétsen (Tibetan emperor), 104, 105, 108, 112, 113, 115–17
Tse, Nicholas, 268–69, *269*
Tsuji Sōmei, 138, 149*n*44
Tsukioka Yoshitoshi, 276–77, *277*

Uhara Yoshitoyo, 140
ukiyo-e, 276–77

universal rulers. *See cakravartins*
Upagupta, 24–25, 43–44*n*17
Upaka, 46*n*52
ūṛnā, 33
uṣṇīṣa, 33

Vail, Peter, 210, 215
Vajiralongkorn (Rama X) (king of Thailand), 216, 220
Vajiravudh (Rama VI) (king of Thailand), 208–9, 212–13, 216, 227*n*10
Various Matters in the Vinaya of the Mūlasarvāstivādins (*Mūlasarvāstivāda-vinaya-kṣudrakavastu*; *Genben shuo yiqie youbu pinaiye zashi*), 39
Vasubandhu, 160, 166
Vātsyāyana, 299–300
Vendova, Dessislava, 79
Vernacular Version of Journey to the West, A (*Tsūzoku saiyūki*) (Tsukioka Yoshitoshi), 276–77, *277*
Vessantara (bodhisattva king), 81
Vijayabāhu I (Sri Lankan king), 86
Vinaya: Burmese monasticism and, 189, 200; multiple versions of, 305–6*nn*7, 15; sociohistorical context of, 291–92, 305*n*12; ten benefits of, 291, 305*n*11. *See also* Buddhist monastic celibacy; monasticism
violence: hegemonic masculinities and, 107–8, 109, 111, 123*n*13; kōan practice and, 143–44; Padmasambhava and, 108, 109, 113–14; RZA's Buddhist masculinity and, 241, 242–43; tantra and, 108–9, 124–25*n*30; Thai *nak leng* (thug) ideal and, 215. *See also* martial masculinity
Violence of Liberation, The: Gender and Tibetan Buddhist Revival in Post-Mao China (Makley), 10
Virtual Sangha, 168
virtue/morality: body and, 23–24, 41, 43*n*17, 44*n*19, 78–79; Sri Lankan bodhisattva kings and, 89, 91–92
Virtuous Bodies (Mrozik), 9
Visalo, Phra Paisal, 222
Volanthen, John, 217

Waley, Arthur, 262
Wallis, Roy, 158
Wang Danyi, 276
Wang Yue, 265–66, *266*
warrior ideal. *See* martial masculinity
Water Margin, The (*Shuihu zhuan*), 237, 278
wen-wu (*bun-bu*) dyad, 60–61, 130, 147*n*4, 260, 264–65, 283*n*23
Whitaker, Jarrod, 4–5
white supremacy, 3
Wild Tiger Corps (Sue Pa), 208–9, 216
Wilkins, Fan Che, 250
Wilson, Liz, 9
women: as *arahants*, 21; Burmese Buddhism and, 187; *bushidō* and, 141–42, 150*n*65; in Chan Buddhism, 52–53; *da zhangfu* concept and, 52–53; in imperial Japan, 150*n*65; lay Rinzai practice and, 131, 132; in *Man with the Iron Fists* films, 241; in martial arts films, 236; monasticism and, 199–201, 203*n*22, 294–96, 306*n*24; Tang Monk image and, 274–76, 277–78, 279; Vinaya and, 305*n*13. *See also* androcentrism; gender roles; patriarchy
Women in Buddhism: Images of the Feminine in Mahāyāna Tradition (Paul), 9
Women's Journey to the West in the Current Style (*Fūzoku onna saiyūki*) (Tamenaga Shunsui), 277–78
World War II, 139, 140–41
Wu Cheng'en, 259. *See also Journey to the West*
Wudang tradition, 233, 236, 239, 243–44
Wu, Daniel, 234
Wu-Tang Clan, 6, 233, 234, 251*n*1. *See also* RZA's Buddhist masculinity
Wuzhun Shifan, 64
Wyatt, Don J., 69–70

xiao xianrou (little fresh meat), 259, 263, 267
Xiatang Huiyuan, 64
Xuanzang, 40, 260–61. *See also* Tang Monk image
Xuanzang (film) (2016), 272
Xu Shaohua, 265, 266–67, *266*

Yājñavalkya, 297
Yamada Jirōkichi, 140
Yamada Shōji, 138
Yamaoka Tesshū, 139–40, 141
Yanagida Seizan, 69
yang gang, 236–37
Yang Jie, 266
Yanqi, 57
Yaoshan Weiyan, 54, 55, 60, 73*n*35
Yarlha Shampo, 114, 125*n*32
Yip, Man-Fung, 236
Yoginī tantras, 161–62
Yongjia Xuanjue, 56–57, 62–63, 70
Yuanwu Keqin, 59
Yunju Daoying, 54–55

Zen. *See* modern Rinzai masculinity ideals
Zendō, 129
Zeshō'in, 137
Zhang Jianya, 269
Zhang Jinchi, 262, 263–64
Zhang Jizhong, 269–71, *271*
Zhang Qian, 54, 72*n*15
Zhu Xi, 64–65, 70
Zwilling, Leonard, 9

GPSR Authorized Representative: Easy Access System Europe, Mustamäe tee 50, 10621 Tallinn, Estonia, gpsr.requests@easproject.com

www.ingramcontent.com/pod-product-compliance
Lightning Source LLC
Chambersburg PA
CBHW022029290426
44109CB00014B/802